Storytelling

STORYTELLING
Process and Practice

NORMA J. LIVO
SANDRA A. RIETZ

Foreword by
LAURA SIMMS

LIBRARIES UNLIMITED, INC.
Littleton, Colorado
1986

Copyright © 1986 Norma J. Livo and Sandra A. Rietz
All Rights Reserved
Printed in the United States of America

LIBRARIES UNLIMITED, INC.
P.O. Box 263
Littleton, Colorado 80160-0263

Library of Congress Cataloging-in-Publication Data

Livo, Norma J., 1929-
  Storytelling : process and practice.

  Includes bibliographies and index.
  1. Story telling. I. Rietz, Sandra A. II. Title.
LB1042.L55   1986   372.6′4   85-23681
ISBN 0-87287-443-5

This book is lovingly dedicated to the next storytellers:

Dru, whose hands are in this book;

Jody and Todd, who are already telling stories;

Davin and Emily, who are part of a story;

Lauren, Kim, Eric, Robert, Steve, Denise and Niki, who all have stories of their own....

Contents

Foreword

Norma Livo and Sandie Rietz have gathered the threads of vital information on oral tradition and their own lifetime of experience as storytellers to make a book about the art of the storyteller. The entire book is sung through with a sense of generosity, excitement, and humility. It is generous because, as they remind us so often, a story is not alive unless it is given away . . . retold anew . . . or taken off the static page and reinvigorated by spoken words, shared imaginations, and the rhythm of life. The book offers us a means of learning how to give a story away. It is imbued with excitement for two reasons: because the genuine art of the storyteller almost vanished with the dissolution of traditional cultures; and because Norma and Sandie are participating in the thrilling act of perpetuating the essence of orality in a technological, multicultural society that needs stories in order to survive. Lastly, it is a book softly spun with humility since it is an impossible task to write a book about an art form that is virtually more like life than life itself, and whose history is timeless.

In a traditional culture there is not usually a method, or "how to" course for storytellers. There are, however, discipline, study, and practice: Over a long period of time, the student absorbs the wisdom, knowledge, and lore of a culture, or of one family's history. And talent and understanding are severely tested by the experience of performance. There can be a great deal of refining and critique from elders, teachers, and storytellers—for one is carrying the seeds of truth and history that are both actual and mythological. In many cases the storyteller is the library of an entire community. If a storyteller dies without passing on their stories, a treasure can be lost that is unretrievable . . . the heart of a culture, its teachings, and its memory disappear forever.

Vi Hilbert, a Native American elder of the Skagit Peoples from Seattle, Washington, had a dear relative "Aunt" Susie Sampson. Every day Aunt Susie recounted to herself the stories she knew, so they would not be forgotten. Fortunately, in her later years they were recorded by Leon Metcalf. Since the Lushootseed language is an oral, rather than a written language, it is almost impossible for anyone to translate . . . impossible for anyone not of the culture and language. The words imply far more than their content and sound. Vi Hilbert relearned her childhood language and devoted her life to translating these stories and her people's language. But, even that was not sufficient. For should the stories be captured on the page and not told they would lose their intention and rich value. Thus, Vi herself became a storyteller. She also trained young people, Indian and non-Indian, to tell these stories.

The process of becoming a storyteller was and is for Vi's students a rigorous and intense task. They learn a new language in the most profound sense: The students learn everything from the intricacies of Lushootseed grammar to basket weaving and undertake the demanding practice of memorization and improvisation in English and Lushootseed.

Not all of us have the good fortune to study with a traditional teacher. Not all of us have the storehouse of experience which Norma Livo and Sandie Rietz garnered growing up in "oral" households. Yet, we all have our personal experiences and our dreams and we have access to books in which narrative texts have been preserved. These seeds of story hold in their brittle skin wisdom, humor, and knowledge that when spoken-between-people can come to life.

This book is much needed. Over a period of seventeen years, through a series of auspicious incidents and accidents, I became a storyteller. During this time I have had to learn how to articulate and explain what I do. For most people do not know what storytelling is. The authors offer us information about the profound way in which storying occurs. They offer us hints about bringing a story to life in performance, they affirm the importance of storytelling. By its very nature, this book informs us in order to inspire further investigation, experimentation, and study. It is happily not a "how to" book. Rather, it is an abundant feast.

Years ago, Laurens Van Der Post wrote about a Bushman man from South Africa who wanted to die when he was in jail because he could no longer hear the stories of his people. Stories are his people's most precious possession, he wrote, for they are the hieroglyphics of the soul. They have the capacity to give meaning and refreshment to our lives. Recently, in a New York elementary school a fourth-grade girl revealed to me her fear that "if there were no more stories, there would be no world. Because stories made the world." Norma Livo and Sandie Rietz recognize and respond to the fact that it is our delightful responsibility in today's world to keep storytelling alive.

Laura Simms

Preface

When we decided to write a storytelling book, we encountered a major problem. How in *writing* do you demonstrate and teach an act that is oral and that takes its definition from the shapes and behavior of oral language? A book is not a storytelling. A story written down is not a storytelling. A story-telling cannot be put into a book — it cannot be captured by the conventions of a written language. A storytelling book is a contradiction. The oral literature is *oral*.

When we *tell* a story, the audience is right there. The circumstances that will influence the shaping and building of the story during the telling are right there. The audience becomes a part of the telling. How can the moment of the "storying" — with audience, story, and storyteller directly and immediately engaged — be written down without losing the essence of the oral story? A storytelling cannot be encoded into print.

The storyteller is produced by an oral dynamic. Traditionally, the story-teller did not read to learn either the stories or how to tell them. Storytellers always learned their art orally, by listening to and telling stories, sometimes by participating in the formal oral training provided by a culture for its story-tellers. The stories themselves are best preserved and maintained, paradoxi-cally, by giving them away orally rather than by writing them down in order to "save" them.

Transcribed (written) oral stories are flat, shadowy things which lack the life, color, and form that are inherent in the oral telling. A written language can neither encode the telling of a story nor save the conventions governing the practice of an oral literature. People who treasure an oral literature write it down only when they think it is threatened with extinction. They otherwise protect oral literature from the loss of integrity that comes with transcription. While students of a given oral literature may record the stories in order to study them, preservation lies in the oral telling. Storytellers, by telling the stories, give them away, and in giving them away, preserve them.

The oral literature is the original literature, existing before written language and having its own rules for practice and preservation which did not (could not) include written language. Yet, today, many of these oral mechanisms for teaching storytellers and keeping the stories alive in human memory are, themselves, lost. The stories have been written down. We don't remember what they sounded like or looked like. We don't remember how to tell them or what to do, either in the role of teller or in that of audience. We often find the stories pressed between the covers of a book, like last summer's rose petals. How do we restore (restory) them?

The current interest in and concurrent revival of the art of storytelling include an understanding of the relationship between oral language/telling and the integrity of the oral story and the view of storytelling as a distinctive art form. The "new" storyteller has discovered what cultures have known for generations — that an oral literature recoded into a written language is not an extension of the written literature, but a lost dimension of human experience and creativity and a forgotten application of oral language. Individuals who revive the stories and storytelling by learning to tell stories by nontraditional means are revivalist storytellers. Some revivalist tellers learn orally, but without the strict rules for training and memory development provided in the cultural context of a fully operational oral literature. Some revivalist tellers learn from print, or from some combination of print experience and oral language experience with stories and storytelling. The revivalist storyteller is one who reinvents a process and reinvests the transcribed oral story with its oral language definition. A written text about storytelling is an important tool for any storyteller who must revive stories and storytelling without the aid of traditional training, hence the decision to produce this book. However, we recognize the contradiction involved in using one language process in order to explain the operations of another.

We are both traditionalist storytellers in that we both have grown from storytelling and performance backgrounds. We are students of storytelling to the extent that we have stepped aside from the act of storytelling to examine process and product. And we are revivalist storytellers in as much as we use print and other nontraditional media to find material, to recast material into oral language, to teach others to tell, and to expand upon our own skills.

The survival of storytelling, today, depends largely upon nontraditional approaches to the training of storytellers and to the saving of the corpus of the human oral literature within the repertoires of individual tellers. The genuinely traditional storyteller, chosen and trained orally within the constraints of the oral literature of a culture, is a rare creature, especially in post-technological societies. Some combination of revivalist strategies for practice and for preservation of an oral literature mark the development of most current storytellers. Through revivalist activity, we are reinvesting a literature, redefining it, repossessing it. The methods that we use, the ideas that we borrow, the cross-cultural practices and traditional habits that we learn and adapt may one day constitute a set of new traditions for practice and preservation. By incorporating old into new, the oral literature, using today's revivalist storyteller as a tool, is finding its own way to live on in a new age and without the traditional supports of tribe and closely knit cultural community.

We learned to tell stories from parents, grandparents, aunts and uncles, brothers and sisters, and from traditions of performance in both families: workshopping, square and round dancing, playing singing games and dances, playing folk instruments, swapping stories and lies, and remembering a generation of involvement in vaudeville. As children we listened, watched, and participated, learning to do by doing. We were welcomed as competent performers into adult levels of performance when we were not yet adults. We entered into storytelling and related activity convinced that we were adults (people) among adults (people) doing adult (people) things. When the adults played for their own adult reasons, we were in the play. We were not "children" separated from adult entertainments, nor were the stories and other performance activities concocted exclusively for our entertainment while the adults chose some other form of play for themselves.

We are grateful to our own families — parents, grandparents, aunts and uncles, brothers and sisters: David Jackson, Mae Kline Jackson, Rube Jackson, Mary Kline, Howard Jackson, Maxine Jackson, David Jackson, Jr., David Jackson III, Lavina McKissick, and Helen Jackson O'Neil; Maria Fischer Ninstil, Charles Ninstil, Charles Rietz, Adelaide Rietz, Edwin Schmidt, Helene Rietz Schmidt, Elsie Rietz Bernier, Anne M. Ninstil Rietz, Bert E. Rietz, Richard R. Rietz — for giving the stories, songs, games and dances to us; and to husbands George O. I. Livo and Dennis L. Weems for providing continued support, encouragement and example. The first and most important gift was a parental attitude which did not segregate the children to special "childlike" activity. We were people, and we did people things with other people. Our age was not viewed as a limitation. We learned that stories and storytelling are not simple inventions for children, but profound experiences for everyone. The second gift was the conviction that readiness was ours to determine. When we were ready — and we thought ourselves so when we were very small — we performed along with the others. Our performances, no matter how constructed and executed, were accepted as whole things. We learned competence because we saw a vision of that competence reflected in the attitudes and responses of others. The third gift was a view of risk taking that encouraged experimentation and that demonstrated the nature of risk in performance. We learned to manage risk taking and to make the judgments which accompany it in the process of making stories, singing songs, dancing dances, and playing games and musical instruments. We also learned that what we did was valuable, or we would not have risked to perform it. The fourth gift was the "how to" that we learned through demonstration and opportunity to practice, and the fifth was the content: the stories, songs, games and dances themselves. We thank those who gave these things to us by giving them away in turn. Our gratitude is in the stories and in the telling.

In the capacity of storyteller, we give to people an oral literature which belongs to them. We do not own the stories, nor the processes by which we make them. We transmit these in order to save them. Through the act of story-telling, we give to others the storyteller's unrestricted vision of community as people and the invitation to join in the story in any manner for which the participant is ready. We identify the value of the oral literature by taking risks in order to tell it. We risk the performance for the sake of preservation. And in the performance, we give the stories—process and practice. We give away what was given to us. We can keep it only by handing it on.

1

Storying Our Lives
The Talking Literature

That is really the reason God made human beings—because He loves to listen to stories.

(traditional Hasidic story)

What is the function of "story" and "storying"?

What is the function of storytelling?

What is the function of the storyteller?

What roles do "story," "storying," and storytelling play in our lives?

Why is the practice of the oral literature so important today?

A story, a story.
Let it come.
Let it go.

"Story" is a mystery that has the power to reach within each of us, to command emotion, to compel involvement, and to transport us into timelessness. "Story" is a structural abstraction perhaps built into human memory, a way of thinking, a primary organizer of information and ideas, the soul of a culture, and the mythic and metaphoric consciousness of a people. It is a prehistoric and historic thread of human awareness, a way in which we can know, remember, and understand.

Somewhere beyond the Red Sea,
Beyond the Blue Forest,
Beyond the Glass Mountain,
And beyond the Straw Town,
Where they sift water and pour sand. . . .

. . . there was once a very worthy king . . .

THE HAUGHTY PRINCESS*

There was once a very worthy king, whose daughter was the greatest beauty that could be seen far or near, but she was as proud as Lucifer, and no king or prince would she agree to marry. Her father was tired out at last, and invited every king and prince, and duke, and earl that he knew or didn't know to come to his court to give her one trial more. They all came, and next day after breakfast they stood in a row in the lawn, and the princess walked along in the front of them to make her choice. One was fat, and says she, "I won't have you, Beer-barrel!" One was tall and thin, and to him she said, "I won't have you, Ramrod!" To a white-faced man she said, "I won't have you, Pale Death;" and to a red-cheeked man she said, "I won't have you, Cockscomb!" She stopped a little before the last of all for he was a fine man in face and form. She wanted to find some defect in him, but he had nothing remarkable but a ring of brown curling hair under his chin. She admired him a little, and then carried it off with, "I won't have you, Whiskers!"

So all went away, and the king was so vexed, he said to her, "Now to punish your *impedence*, I'll give you to the first

---

*This version of "The Haughty Princess" by Patrick Kennedy was originally printed in *Fireside Stories of Ireland*.

beggarman or singing *sthronshuch* that calls;" and, as sure as the hearthmoney, a fellow all over rags, and hair that came to his shoulders, and a bushy red beard all over his face, came next morning, and began to sing before the parlour window.

When the song was over, the hall-door was opened, the singer asked in, the priest brought, and the princess married to Beardy. She roared and she bawled, but her father didn't mind her. "There," says he to the bridegroom, "is five guineas for you. Take your wife out of my sight, and never let me lay eyes on you or her again."

Off he led her, and dismal enough she was. The only thing that gave her relief was the tones of her husband's voice and his genteel manners. "Whose wood is this?" said she, as they were going through one. "It belongs to the king you called Whiskers yesterday." He gave her the same answer about meadows and cornfields and at last a fine city. "Ah, what a fool I was!" said she to herself. "He was a fine man, and I might have him for a husband." At last they were coming up to a poor cabin. "Why are you bringing me here?" says the poor lady. "This was my house," said he, "and now it's yours." She began to cry, but she was tired and hungry, and she went in with him.

Ovoch! there was neither a table laid out, nor a fire burning, and she was obliged to help her husband to light it, and boil their dinner, and clean up the place after; and next day he made her put on a stuff gown and a cotton handkerchief. When she had her house readied up, and no business to keep her employed, he brought home *sallies* (willows), peeled them, and showed her how to make baskets. But the hard twigs bruised her delicate fingers, and she began to cry. Well, then he asked her to mend their clothes, but the needle drew blood from her fingers, and she cried again. He couldn't bear to see her tears, so he bought a creel of eathenware, and sent her to the market to sell them. This was the hardest trial of all, but she looked so handsome and sorrowful, and had such a nice air about her, that all her pans, and jugs, and plates, and dishes were gone before noon, and the only mark of her old pride she showed was a slap she gave a buckeen across the face when he *axed* her to go in an' take share of a quart.

Well, her husband was so glad, he sent her with another creel the next day; but faith! her luck was after deserting her. A drunken huntsman came up riding, and his beast got in among her ware, and made *brishe* of every mother's son of 'em. She went home cryin', and her husband wasn't at all pleased. "I see," said he, "you're not fit for business. Come along, I'll get you a kitchenmaid's place in the palace. I know the cook."

So the poor thing was obliged to stifle her pride once more. She was kept busy, and the footman and the butler would be very impudent about looking for a kiss, but she let a screech out of her the first attempt was made, and the cook gave the fellow such a lambasting with the besom that he made no second offer. She went home to her husband every night, and she carried broken victuals wrapped in papers in her side pockets.

A week after she got service there was great bustle in the kitchen. The king was going to be married, but no one knew who the bride was to be. Well, in the evening the cook filled the princess's pockets with cold meat and puddings, and says she, "Before you go, let us have a look at the great doings in the big parlour." So they came near the door to get a peep, and who should come out but the king himself, as handsome as you please, and no other but King Whiskers himself. "Your handsome helper must pay for her peeping," said he to the cook, "and dance a jig with me." Whether she would or no, he held her hand and brought her into the palour. The fiddlers struck up, and away went *him* with *her*. But they hadn't danced two steps when the meat and the *puddens* flew out of her pockets. Every one roared out, and she flew to the door, crying piteously. But she was soon caught by the king, and taken into the back parlour. "Don't you know me, my darling?" said he. "I'm both King Whiskers, your husband the ballad-singer, and the drunken huntsman. Your father knew me well enough when he gave you to me, and all was to drive your pride out of you." Well, she didn't know how she was with fright, and shame, and joy. Love was uppermost anyhow, for she laid her head on her husband's breast and cried like a child. The maids-of-honour soon had her away and dressed her as fine as hands and pins could do it; and there were her mother and father, too; and while the company were wondering what end of the handsome girl and the king, he and his queen, who they didn't know in her fine clothes, and the other king and queen, came in, and such rejoicings and fine doings as there was, none of us will ever see, anyway.

"Story" is a universal mirror that shows us the "truth" about ourselves — who and why we are. When we look into this mirror, we see daily routine and mundane circumstance transformed into something profound. "Story" takes the ordinary and binds it into all of human existence, revealing the significance of the trivial. Through "story" we can transcend the experience of daily living and know our selves as more enduring than the little occurrences that mark our individual existences. Inside "story" we can accept pain, find justice, and experience exaltation. Inside "story" we can recognize and understand our own motivations, because we are the people in the stories. When we enter into "story" we find the story inside ourselves. "Story" defines humanity.

THE FUNCTION OF STORY AND STORYING

"Story" is its own reality. It is a configuration in memory that is quite independent of the specific details of any given event. We all recognize "story" and are easily able to distinguish between something told that is "storied" and something that is not. "Story" is a way of knowing and remembering information — a shape or pattern into which information can be arranged. It serves a very basic purpose; it restructures experiences for the purpose of "saving" them. And it is an ancient, perhaps natural order of mind — primordial, having grown along with the development of human memory and of language itself. "Story" is a way of organizing language. Even very young children recognize "story" and can shape language and ideas into its forms (Sutton-Smith 1981).

"Story" is a concept that has organizational and archetypal dimensions. Although individual stories have somewhat different patterns or shapes specific to their content, each is a subpattern or subshape of the overall structure that we recognize as "story." "Story" is regenerative, the master structure from which all stories derive. All stories conform to the rules that govern story structure or they would not be stories. Storied information is a content, the details of a given circumstance, that have been reconfigured to fit the conceptual requirements of "story" — made into the shape of a story. By imposing the concept of "story" onto a circumstance or happening, greater coherence and sensibility are achieved within the event itself, and otherwise isolated and disconnected scraps of human experience are bound up into something whole and meaningful.

"Storying" is an act. It is what we do to information when we transform it into a story — we story events. Reconfiguration of the memory of an event into the shape of "story" helps us to better remember the event, even though "story" may change the memory by imposing its own shape upon it. Storied events are somehow bigger than themselves, because they have been invested with the greater truth of "story." Storying is a vehicle for transcending time, for binding people together with the future, the past, and one another, for extending commonality of experience, for ordering events to make existence more sensible and meaningful. Storying brings a higher level of comprehensibility to the things we do. When we story, we join with others emotionally and intellectually, and we generate a sense of "rightness' and belonging (Hillman 1975). Our private lives become part of a greater collective experience, and we make important personal discoveries.

Because storying imparts an additional rationality and a special truth to storied information, the truth of "story" itself, we often begin a story with a story opening. The opening reminds audiences of the special truth of "story" and helps make the transition from daily to story reality. Story openings place the audience in the proper "story" frame of reference, in "story" time.

Storyteller: I'm going to tell a story.

Audience: Right!

Storyteller: It's a lie.

Audience: Right!

Storyteller: But not everything in it is false.

Audience: Right!

    (Sudanese ritual opening)

Storyteller: Under the Earth I go.
                On the oak leaf I stand.
                I ride on the filly
                That was never foaled,
                And I carry the dead in my hand.

    (Celtic ritual opening)

Storying is a game we play with events and reality. The game releases us from the obligations of the moment and transports us into a place seemingly untouched by time, a different universe governed by universal truths. In that "other" place, we can enter into storying in fun, to play, without consequence to our selves, but also with the promise of insight and understanding.

The ability to put self, personal experiences, and personal information into "story" may be critical to psychological well-being (Hillman 1975, 1979). "Story" is a frame of reference for our lives, and storying makes our lives important. "Destoried" adults are people who have lost the ability to story their experiences—to see themselves in a more universal perspective and to invest their doings with a greater sensibility and coherence. Such individuals require "restorying" in order to bring their sense of self, place, and time into better balance (Hillman 1975, 1979). The "more attuned and experienced is the imaginative side of personality, the less threatening the irrational, the less necessity for repression, and, therefore, the less pathology acted out in literal, daily events" (Hillman 1979). Imagination must be restored/restoried to "a primary place in the consciousness in each of us. 'Story' is a way in which the soul finds itself in life" (Hillman 1979, 43-45). We desire stories and the greater organization of our lives which they represent (Bettelheim 1976).

Storying is a measure of humankind and a way of "embracing the household of humanity" (Benjamin 1968, 203). It is as natural as breathing. It is a restructuring of language and ideas into something bigger and more universal. People make and crave stories. By showing us who we are, stories liberate us from the otherwise meaninglessness of daily toil. Storying is a means by which we can recognize significance in our lives.

THE FUNCTION OF STORYTELLING

"Story" is a mental program or structure, a way of organizing and understanding something. "Story" might very well be an invention of the human mind, which we impose upon events or information to create logic and sensibility. "Story" might not be outside the body, but inside it, an artifact of thinking. Storied information, which is "slotted" or reconfigured into story shape, is more easily remembered and can be told to others in a conventionally arranged manner.

Perhaps because of the organization of the human brain, we tend to see "story" all around us and are inclined to story memory as a natural act. ("Story" is in everything, because we put it/see it/expect it there.) And we have invented a variety of ways to tell others our stories: theater, song, written literature, recitation, and oral literature. The vehicle for the oral literature is storytelling. While other forms of story delivery "tell" stories in the generic sense of the word, story*telling* remains a distinct and unique method for making stories available to others.

WHAT STORYTELLING IS

Storytelling is an art form. A recent publication, *The Oxford Companion to Children's Literature* (Carpenter and Prichard 1984), defines storytelling as "a term used to describe the oral telling of stories to groups of children in libraries and other institutions." The National Association for the Preservation and Perpetuation of Storytelling (NAPPS) provides a much broader and richer definition: "Storytelling is an art form through which a storyteller projects mental and emotional images to an audience using the spoken word, including sign language and gestures, carefully matching story content with audience needs and environment. The story sources reflect all literatures and cultures, fiction and nonfiction, for educational, recreational, historic, folkloric, entertainment and therapeutic purposes" (*Yarnspinner*, 8). Nowhere in this last definition is there any mention of age of audience, setting, or reading aloud. Storytelling is an oral art form whose practice provides a means of preserving and transmitting images, ideas, motivations, and emotions that are universal across human communities.

Storytelling is a unique and distinct way of storying; it has a historic, ritual, rule-governed, patterned integrity that sets it apart from other forms of making stories. It is the primary vehicle for the maintenance and exercise of the oral literature, which, in turn, has its origins in oral language use, play, and invention and, as we said above, in the need to remember events and ideas over time. The oral literature can only be preserved through oral language transmission. The practice of the oral literature is storytelling.

Storytelling is an ancient form. Although its evolution cannot be precisely documented, the telling of stories is an old practice, so old, in fact, that it seems almost as natural as using oral language. Human beings may very well have told stories almost as soon as they had language or signals with which to tell them. Children do (Sutton-Smith 1981).

Storytelling is a sophisticated practice. Although many people today view the oral literature as something for children and for that reason disdain it (a sad reflection of our patronizing attitude toward children, their needs, and interests), storytelling practice and the stories told are the sophisticated inventions of adult populations. Storytelling was and is a means of publicizing, remembering, and confirming a culture's history and cosmic consciousness. That children attend to stories is a mark of their humanity, not a measure of some imagined intellectual limitation. A literature fashioned in the shapes of the oral language will be accessible to those who speak the language. A written literature will only be accessible to those who can read it. Perhaps because a child's introduction to the oral literature is immediate, while incursions into written literature must await the development of reading ability, adults think that oral stories and storytellings are for children. Storytelling and oral stories are for everyone. Watch as adults become taken in by a told story and see if this is not so. To restrict storytellings to groups of children on the grounds that both are "simple" denies the intelligence and sophistication of both. Age is not relevant to the practice of storytelling. The telling of stories is something that *people* do. It is human.

Storytelling is a ritualized, patterned act. A storyteller takes the part of a mediator between a people and its literature. Just as stories have structure, the storytelling must also conform to rules governing its shape. It must be conducted in a manner that is in concert with the oral literature traditions of the culture. Openings, closings, types of audience/teller interactions, degree of formality, use of artifacts and ritual devices are sometimes prescribed. Observation of the rules by audience and teller allows the story to come forward. The audience and teller together use the rules of the telling itself as a framework in which to construct the story, in which each knows his or her part, and in which each can exercise his or her expectations and predictions for "story" and stories. A storytelling is an organized, controlled, rule-governed storying of information, using the story shapes of the oral literature, the people, and the medium of the live storyteller.

Storytelling is an immediate experience. It is situation dependent, or context embedded. That is, the exact circumstances of each storytelling are different, characterized as they are by the nature of the setting, time of day, composition of the audience, immediate needs or concerns of the audience, agenda of the program, and a host of other factors. Since a story emerges as an on-the-spot construction, storytelling is a *process* for making stories. The absolute shape of a specific story told on a specific day cannot be predicted or controlled by the storyteller. Although the storyteller works within the framework of story content and structure and must observe the rules of the telling, the audience owns the story. What happens in any given storying will depend upon the situation of the telling—the integrated context in which the telling takes place. A story is not a recitation that must take the same shape with each repetition. The situation-dependent story, though it may be essentially the same story with each telling, will never be told in precisely the same manner twice. With each telling the story is new, even for the audience for whom it is familiar.

Storytelling is a negotiation. Making or encoding the oral story during the storytelling is the shared task of both audience and storyteller. Unlike the physically separated and different tasks of the writer and the reader of the printed story (Smith 1982), audience and teller negotiate a story into being in a highly dynamic interactive process. The teller may know specific story content that is not known to the audience, but all participants in the telling have a role to play in bringing a story into reality. All hold in common a "cluster of intentions and expectations, constraints and guidelines" (Smith 1982, 172) that direct the telling and help to shape the story. These guidelines are specific to the nature of storytelling ritual, the expected and predicted aspects of story structure and content, the general sense of "rightness" in the culture, and the mutual understanding of "play." In the storytelling, participants know what to do; they know why they do it, and they know what they intend to accomplish.

In this process of negotiation between teller and audience, the teller conducts or mediates but does not perform in a theatrical sense. (The difference is related more to teller/audience intimacy and shared task than to actual teller behavior during telling.) Storytelling is not a spectator sport. The audience actively builds the story and is in the story with the teller. The role of the teller, then, is to give over ownership of the story to the audience and to allow the audience to encode the story using the teller as the medium.

Because the storyteller delivers the story in keeping with audience expectations for the nature of oral discourse, audience participation is facilitated. Storytelling ritual, play, and story shape are governed by convention. The teller is constrained to limit his or her behavior and story reconstructions to those conventions that will, in turn, make the story sensible and that will allow the audience to participate in story making using those features the audience knows and identifies as "story." In particular, a story has a discourse structure that conforms to the literary specifications of the culture in which it originated. The teller makes the story concrete by organizing language and paralinguistic elements in accord with these structural conventions. In a sense, the teller stories by fitting information into previously invented and ordered "slots" (Downing and Leong 1982) that the audience recognizes as a familiar story pattern. (See chapter 2.) Because such patterns of slots are mutually understood, the audience can predict and control story shape during telling and participate directly in story construction. As the teller tells, the audience becomes involved in slotting information into known patterns of organization.

There are five principal types of participation: ritual, coactive, bantering, predictive, and eye contact.

Ritual participation involves the audience in formal chanting, singing, movement, noisemaking, and language repetition play and/or invention. Such within-telling activity is a matter of convention for given stories. It is expected, and a part of the play. The slots in such stories are learned as givens for audience participation. Everyone knows what to do. The doing together within the framework of the story confirms community and reinforces belonging. Cumulative stories such as "The Fat Cat" (Kent 1971), "The Old Woman and Her Pig" (Rockwell 1975), "Titty Mouse and Tatty Mouse" (Wiggin 1954), "The Gingerbread Man" (Rockwell 1970), "Tatty Mae and Catty Mae" (Martin 1970), and "Too Much Noise" (McGovern 1967) allow the audience to build the story through the use of given language forms in given story structure.

Coactive participation, usually a spontaneous and encouraged inter- action, draws the audience into movement, song, and language making as the teller reconstructs the story. This type of audience activity is not precisely defined by story convention; audience chanting, singing, etc. is not in general a specified and required ritual as it is with ritual participation stories. But spontaneous audience chanting, singing, clapping, moving, and repeating along with the teller confirm the notion of told "story" as a negotiated product. Audiences *expect* to help with the telling. They *expect* that they will interact overtly and "own" the story themselves. Far from feeling upstaged at such moments, or deciding that the coactive audience is out of control, the teller should take audience coactivity during telling as a positive measure of the degree to which he or she has been able to successfully tell the audience into the story.

Audience/storyteller banter, also usually quite spontaneous, most often occurs in less formal tellings. Liar's contests and tall tale tellings invite dialogue between teller and audience. Bantering is a rather sophisticated activity, in that it pulls the teller away from the story line and allows him or her to make editorial remarks without slipping out of the role of teller. Bantering also provides the audience with immediate control over story direction and shape. The best circumstances for bantering occur when the audience knows the story and the banter can constitute play with elements of the story and circumstances of the telling. Though banter may lead the story around—the teller must be flexible, quick-witted, and very much in control of the story as an abstraction—participants generally follow the conventional story forms. The intent is to play with the story and its content, not to meander the story out of its own identity. A bantered story is a genuine negotiation in which audience and teller create a once-in-a-lifetime piece of oral literature while respecting one another's roles. (On one memorable occasion, the audience deliberately and perversely bantered a twenty-minute story into a one-hour affair without violating overall story structure. The product, in this case, was a very sophisticated extension of a story that was well known to the audience— else it could not have happened. The play was calculated but joyful, and the teller was flexible enough to follow audience lead without losing the story. As often happens with the bantered story, many discoveries were made, and now-famous one-liners were invented. Today the story is both longer and funnier than it was before that telling.)

Predictive participation is more covert than the other types of audience participation described. However, it is just as active and just as much governed by audience sense of ownership of "story." Individual listeners "induce a mental structure" on storied content during the telling (Smith 1982, 64). Because the audience comes to the telling with a sense of "story" and an understanding of story schemata and archetypal content — a mental paradigm — the audience is as much in control of "story" and storying as is the teller. While the teller supplies specific story content and detail, the audience makes "motivational, psychological, physical causation and enactment inferences" (Downing and Leong 1982, 220) to organize the story during telling. Listeners, they go on to say, reconfigure story relations by "linking people, time, place, things and general context of given events" (220), and they create an "event chain" (220) of logical relationships. The interactive nature of this process is a dynamic that exists between teller, listener, and story and that results in as many private story negotiations and reconstructions as there are listeners in the audience.

Eye contact during telling helps to maintain the immediacy and intimacy of the oral literature experience. Eye contact is, in large measure, the constant reminder of the situation dependency of the telling of a story. Sometimes, the story is "given" to the listener through "convergence of gaze" (Smith 1982, 81). The audience can control the teller and the shape of the story by looking and by eye movement. The sensitive teller is both aware of the power of this interaction and able to use it to learn how to improve his or her tellings. The teller who avoids eye contact violates the understood shared context of the telling and denies the audience its ownership in the story-making process.

Through such negotiating activities as ritual participation, coactivity, bantering, prediction, and eye contact, the audience is able to make the story along with the storyteller, and, by doing so, claims its rightful ownership of the literature.

Storytelling is an entertainment. Since the audience builds the story along with the teller, the audience is an immediate part of the storytelling. Unlike spectators during certain other types of entertainment, the storytelling audience entertains itself by entering directly into a spontaneous play controlled by the rules for negotiation. Stories are, of course, instructive. Despite some of the conventions of formal education that presume that learning should be hard and painful, real learning is easy and fun (Smith 1982). Learning is highly entertaining, especially when the learner is in control of the process. Storytelling is also a problem-solving activity. Problem solving is very motivating and entertaining in storytelling, since the storying itself defines both process and problem and specifies the nature of the solution. Finally, since the stories are mirrors that reflect our passions and inclinations through the employment of archetypes and humor, we are entertained by laughing and crying over our own circumstances. Unlike other forms of entertainment, in which the audience is regaled by some "other," outside-of-self activity, in the storytelling the audience itself — as a collective representation of the human condition—is the object of the play. And, within the safety of the boundaries of the storytelling game, learning about ourselves by making ourselves the object of the play is an experience that brings great delight and inner satisfaction.

Storytelling is a game. A storytelling is bound by rules that govern the behavior of the story, the storying, the storyteller, and the audience immediately before, during, and immediately following a telling. The rules that control the story itself are those specifying story structure and language (see chapter 2). These rules also meet the expectations of the audience for the manner in which stories should work. Scollon and Scollon (1979) describe the patterns of four that structure the stories of Northern Athabaskan cultures. They document cases in which listeners from one language community (of some twenty-four Athabaskan language communities) understood stories that were told in another Athabaskan tongue completely unintelligible to them, because the two language communities shared an identical expectation for story structure. They write, "It is as if by understanding everything but the words, one has understood most of the story." Scollon and Scollon (1979, 1) also demonstrate that story translations (i.e., from Chipewayan to English) require attention to pattern as well as to words. While the Chipewayan version of a given story required patterned sets of two and four, the English translation transformed the story to patterns of three, a customary arrangement in English-language stories. Hopi cosmology is based on fours (Waters 1963), and many Hopi stories reflect this organization (Mullett 1982). A storyteller who violates a story by redefining its structure has broken the rules.

Furthermore, the storying, or the construction of the story, is also, as we said, governed by the rules of story structure. The audience and teller slot story content into the organizational framework of the story. In addition, both teller and audience must honor the rules for negotiation.

The storyteller is obliged to conduct the game, to provide for audience entry into it. The storytelling is initiated by ritual (liturgy or protocol) that announces a shift of realities—from this time to the "other" or "story" time, from today's truth to "story" truth. The participants "cross over" into the place where the stories happen and where they are personally safe from both story and real-life consequences. Many traditional storytellers lead the audience into the game by "calling them over." Using conventions not unlike game-signaling calls such as "Olley olley oxenfree!" the storyteller must enter game space and time first, then "pull" the audience in. To do this, the teller assumes the role of "other." The teller is no longer himself or herself, but the timeless one or the ancient one—the one of the stories. Then the teller calls the audience, or pulls them into the game. One call-response ritual opening for storytellings actually names the phenomenon of crossing over, and the audience asks the teller to pull them in.

Storyteller:	Let's tell another story.
	Let's be off!
Audience:	Pull away!
Storyteller:	Let's be off!
Audience:	Pull away!

(Origin unknown)

Other call-response openings (Pellowski 1977; Wolkstein 1978) signal audience readiness to play and mark the initiation of the collective consciousness of the circumstances of the telling, or the shift into the realm of game.

| Storyteller: | Cric! |
| Audience: | Crac! |

(West Indies)

| Storyteller: | Hello . . . |
| Audience: | Hellooooooooooo . . . |

(West Africa)

| Storyteller: | A story, a story. |
| Audience: | Let it come. Let it go. |

(West Africa)

Nonresponse openings may be added following the initial interchange between audience and teller to further establish the nature of story reality.

Storyteller:	We do not really mean . . .
	We do not really mean . . .
	That what we say is true.

(Asanti)

Still other opening rituals are intended to begin the story itself, identifying the story as a game.

| Storyteller: | Once there was, and once there was not . . . |

Formal closings, which signal the end of ritual play, pull the audience back into real time, releasing them into daily routine and its normal consequences. Some ritual closings end an individual story.

Storyteller: Leaves are green for a little while.
                 Then they fade to yellow,
                 Fall to earth and wither,
                 And become dust.

(Anglo-Saxon)

Some end the storytelling itself.

Storyteller: And now, you can have your supper,
                 And say your prayers,
                 And go to bed.
                 Morning is wiser than evening.

(Russia)

The storytelling is a place where rules different from those of daily circumstance prevail. The telling is a game. The storyteller, using ritual devices that are themselves rule governed, conducts the audience members into and out of the game, binding them into story reality, then letting them go. The safety of game, which we all know is a part of rule-governed play, is in place throughout a storytelling, enforced by the presence of the storyteller and the general knowledge that the teller is the special person, the "other" one, the one who controls the stories. Game awareness is further reinforced by the shared knowledge that the stories are mysteries existing in a place that cannot be reached by ordinary means.

WHAT STORYTELLING DOES

Storytelling brings people together for a shared purpose. An oral literature is the collective creation of a people. It re-presents and recreates their shared cosmology or model for the manner in which the universe works. When people gather to listen to stories, they enter into a form of cultural communion using the oral literature as a vehicle and the storyteller as a medium. Through the "rites of telling" and the structure and content of its literature, a people, as we said, reaffirms their belonging as a community and reconfirms their understanding of "rightness" and "truth." People who gather together to hear oral stories are revealed to themselves through the archetype of story itself and the archetypes within a given story.

Storytelling keeps us "safe" from the "consequences." Because the archetypal content of stories constitutes such a powerful set of images or statements about what it means to be human, because strange and impossible things happen in stories, and because the consequences to story characters for misbehaviors can be so severe, audiences need to understand the limitations of story truth. The storytelling, which is a framework or structure in which stories are told, is designed to keep audiences safe from both real-time and "story"-time consequences by making the storying experience into a game. The game rules allow us to experience what the characters experience, but only vicariously. We can learn from the literature without having to suffer the "real" consequences, either inside the story or in our own real lives. Inasmuch as the stories reflect us, they are true. But we also understand that "story" time and "story" place are mystical, mythical creations of the storytelling. Therefore, the stories are also game frameworks that, while they are not false, have their own truth or reality in a place apart from daily circumstance. We need not be afraid for ourselves because of what happens in the stories, yet we can learn how to "be" if we listen for that reality that can be brought back from the story into our own lives.

Storytelling uses the oral language. Oral stories are encoded in oral language. Although initially that may sound redundant, understanding the process of such encoding is at the heart of storytelling. Oral language has its own special conventions, devices, and effects. It is different from written language and is poorly, if at all, encoded in written language. Oral stories make noises, assume postures, and voice effects; they move, bend, and breathe. The oral story is soft and malleable. It yields to the pleasures and needs of its audience. Its language is not the precise and unchanging form of the written story, created by a single author, but the evolving, flowing language of the community.

Written language cannot encode the linguistic forms and paralinguistic elements of the oral story. The oral language is the special medium for preservation and transmission of the oral literature. An oral story cannot be preserved in print. Paradoxically, it can only be saved through the seeming impermanence of the oral language. To survive at all, the oral literature must be practiced. It is the oral aspect of the oral story that enriches the literary experience, contributing images and emotions that escape the devices of written language and making the stories accessible to everyone.

Storytelling remembers cultural archetypes. An archetype is a model, prototype, or pattern for the construction or recognition of other like things. Archetypal patterns are, in the Jungian definition, subconscious images, ideas, or patterns of thought universally present in memory in all individuals within a culture and, presumably, inherited from the ancestors of the race. Characters within stories, thematic content of stories, common patterns of story structure, and even "story" itself are archetypal. We story information because the pattern for "story" as a way of knowing and organizing lies deep within the psyche (Hillman 1975). Likewise, we recognize certain story characters and themes as universal because they are already known to us in subconscious memory. We understand that story content is not to be literally interpreted, but that the story is to be appreciated in terms of its own universal reality. (Storytelling openings remind audiences that the story is its own truth.) Because of its archetypal nature, there is a more profound and "real" truth in "story" than in the common reality of daily experience.

Jungian psychologist James Hillman (1975), to whom we have referred several times already, explores the archetypal nature of "story" and of character and thematic aspects of story content. He suggests that "story" itself is archetypal—a primary organizer of memory. "Story," the primary archetype, presents secondary archetypes in the forms of motifs, characters or personalities, behaviors or habits, relationships, needs, experiences, and events. Each is discussed below.

MacDonald's (1982) motif catalog includes such categories as test stories, wise man and fool stories, deception stories, chance and fate stories, and reward and punishment stories. The Appalachian story "The Two Old Women's Bet" (Chase 1948) contains both fool and deception motifs—two women deceive their husbands, who are entirely gullible. "Salt" (Zemach 1965) presents the "lucky accident" type of chance and fate motif, here involving Ivan the Fool, the youngest brother, who manages to make his fortune by selling a cargo of salt. The motif introduces a recognizable and universal circumstance. Motifs are generally cross cultural.

The youngest sister or brother (representing innocence, humility, honesty, and good), the fool (illogic and fate), the old woman/man (death), the mistreated child or stepchild, the uncaring parent or stepparent, the witch or stepmother-witch (evil), and fearsome beast are characters recognized for their universal traits. We do not know them as individuals, but as representations or collective embodiments. "Cinderella" includes several common archetypal characters. Cinderella herself is both the youngest and the mistreated stepchild. Jack, of "The Jack Tales" (Chase 1943) is a youngest brother. Witches abound in stories: "Rapunzel," "Snow White," "Hansel and Gretel," "Sleeping Beauty" are familiar ones. Each archetypal character is "known," perhaps, because the potential to display at least some of the traits of each archetype is present in us all. Some of the archetypal characters are frightening or disturbing. They make us uncomfortable because they are a reality within and around us.

Archetypal behavior is, in part, associated with archetypal character. We expect the youngest child to respond kindly to animals or hungry people, even at his or her own expense, and even when the (usually two) older siblings will not. We do not expect the youngest to want riches or power. We expect the fool to use silly logic or to make stupid bargains. We expect the trickster to cheat or fabricate, and we also expect that the punishment will fit the crime. As with archetypal character, we recognize within ourselves the capacities for such universal behavior and can identify such behavior when we meet it, even in daily life. Character behavior is also patterned and highly predictable. The characters do not act to serve idiosyncratic, personal ends, but to reveal us to ourselves.

Several archetypal relationships can be identified in "Hansel and Gretel": father/children, stepmother/children, witch/children. In "Sleeping Beauty" we find a married relationship, as well as jealous parent and jealous parent (witch)/children connections (see MacDonald 1982). Some of the promised and perceived relationships between people in the real world may be born of archetypal expectations. The relationships between the characters, experiences, and events within the story are also designed to show the universality of our own circumstances and behavior.

Archetypal needs are basic human needs or requirements—love, security, understanding, acceptance, success, community and companionship, happiness, knowledge. In many stories, the character seeks to fill one or more of these basic needs. Finding love or security or success, then, becomes the quest, and the events of the story lead to the solution of the character's original problem—satisfaction of an identified requirement. The need for success is a particularly interesting motif. Not only do stories tell of individuals looking for success, but they define success itself. Generally, success is not wealth, power, beauty, and possessions; it is often portrayed as generosity, honesty, and humility. Success is not things, but attitudes; not what one can accumulate, but what one can give away. Success stories, unlike many in the real world, suggest that those who do not desire wealth and power, etc., shall achieve it. "The Jack Tales" (Chase 1943) and "Salt" (Zemach 1965) clearly illustrate the paradox.

Abandonment, fear of being devoured, devouring, torture, inability to do a required task, getting lost, fear of being abused and abuse, and meeting a beast/witch/devil are some of the darker experiences included in stories. Happier experiences have to do with story justice, an archetype in its own right. Generosity, humility, and kindness are rewarded. Greed is punished. The abused and mistreated triumph. All is finally set to rights, but not without a necessary amount of pain and sacrifice or some frightening moments. What constitutes the "right," sensible, correct ending is culture specific. The Bollinger Series (1952, 32: 5-7) notes that the western European sense of justice is notably absent from many African stories—the good wife dies at the hands of the bad wife and is not resurrected. However, the archetypal shape of justice within the stories is correct for the culture.

Archetypal story features recall truths embedded deep in memory. Some archetypes are pleasant reflections, and others can be quite distressing. None are likely to be found intact outside of "story." Yet all are recognizable, at least as potentials, in the life and habits of the individual. Archetypes represent a remarkable level of awareness: a culture's consciousness of its own being, a people's collective understanding of humanness and individual self-awareness.

Archetypes are, moreover, tools that can be used, through storying, to expand and extend human knowing and human awareness. Story archetypes mirror many aspects of the human condition, and audiences "reflect" stories by participating in them during a storytelling. We find ourselves within the archetypes presented. We are "in" the story; we become the story, in a sense, and its truth lives in us during the telling.

Storytelling remembers the shapes of stories. The told story is reconstructed from a set or sets of in-memory maps for story structure, or story grammar. The storyteller knows specific story content and the shape of the story into which that content is to be fitted. The act of storying that happens during the storytelling reconstructs the grammar of the story from the abstract memory of the storyteller. The teller reiterates story grammars with each story he or she tells, reminding us of the manner in which we organize and remember information by storying it. We learn story shapes and we learn to story by participating in storytelling activity. Storytelling aids in the development of memory suprastructures.

Storytelling constructs "cosmic consciousness." The perceived shape of the cosmos is reiterated in the patterns of "story" within a culture. Story patterns confirm the cultural definition of order. The story pattern that satisfies the listener's expectations (sets of two, three, or four) is understood to be correct and sensible. Story coherence is a function of story structure, which, in turn, is a reconstruction of a world view. The storytelling is the game through which we can learn and confirm our understanding of the organization of the universe.

Storytelling preserves the oral literature by changing it. Unlike many other methods or forms for making stories, storytelling provides for the maintenance of its literature by offering a natural vehicle for its evolution. Because the literature is owned by a people instead of individuals, and because the circumstances of the storytelling affect the shape of the story, the people in the audience work on their stories through the act of telling. Once again, the storyteller is best characterized as a medium through which a people can exercise the option to reshape and refine the literature and to make its structure and content consistent with a changing world view. The oral tradition is founded upon collective ownership of its literary contents and upon the paradox of preservation through change. It operates on the principle of consistency through flexibility. It is responsive to the needs of the people who own it. While other forms of literature/storying are more rigid — new stories may be added to the overall body of the literature, but once admitted are not to be altered — oral stories themselves are reconstructed with each telling through negotiation.

MISPERCEPTIONS OF STORYTELLING

Many misperceptions of storytelling exist. The term suggests stereotypical images of librarians reading and showing picture books, teachers and groups of very small children, flannel boards, theatrical productions, stand-up narrations of memorized (written) text, recitations, Polaroid cameras ("the nation's storyteller"), the creation of written text — poems, books, stories — and, finally, something that grown-up people don't do.

Stories can be made in many ways. Paintings can tell stories. Dance, sculpture, a variety of forms of music, plays, movies, TV, and mime all provide a means for presenting storied information. Although these forms can tell stories, none of them is story*telling*.

The discriminating features of story*telling* have to do with the relation-ship between the story, the teller, and the audience during the telling. The story is a negotiated oral language production that is shaped by the immediate circumstances of the telling and that belongs to the audience. The told story is not a fixed, final form repeated identically at each telling, nor is it the private creation and possession of one author. Because of the nature of story ownership and the manner in which audiences interact during a telling, story-telling is not theater or a play put on for others by a few. Because the told story is an oral encoding of an oral literature, storytelling is neither story reading nor the recitation of written literature. Because the story is the focus of storyteller-audience interaction (the audience sees the story, not the person of the teller), storytelling is not to be found in the manipulation of props or scenery. Because the structure of the oral story is unique, complex, and highly evolved, storytelling and the stories in the oral literature bear no resemblance to those in basal readers. Basal-reader story reading or recitation is no substitute for the telling of the oral literature. Finally, because the oral literature is an ancient form whose content, structure, and history have integrities of their own, storytelling is not a subskill within a reading program. Information can be organized in and out of human memory in many ways and transmitted through a variety of media, but only story*telling* is storytelling.

Storytelling is a literary activity, an art form in its own right, a form of entertainment, and the vehicle for the practice and preservation of a literature. It is an ancient and precious legacy. Its apparent ephemerality, that it must be preserved through the short-lived forms of an immediate transmission—oral language—is its great strength and accounts for its general accessibility to people of all ages and across cultures. It is the vehicle for encoding and remembering who we are, why we are and what we are supposed to do about it. Storytelling belongs to us all.

THE FUNCTION OF THE STORYTELLER

The storyteller is a chosen one: a transmitter of a history and/or a morality, a preserver of cultural memory, a repository of information, a walking library, a cultural and literary resource. In many cultures in which the oral literature is (or was) the primary literature (it always is the original literature), storytellers were chosen and trained by a variety of methods. Regardless of the means by which a storyteller becomes one or learns the art, the storyteller is, in many respects, the tool and servant of the culture and the property of the literature. The storyteller is the agent for the transmission and preservation of the oral literature and, very often, the trainer of the next generation of storytellers. Even in cultures with written literatures, the story-teller is the primary encoder of the oral literature. (Written language does not encode the shapes of the oral story.) The storyteller is charged with the job of remembering the contents and structures of the stories that contain our system of beliefs and remind us of the right order of things.

The storyteller is the "other."

> Under the Earth I go.
> On the oak leaf I stand.
> I ride on the filly
> That was never foaled,
> And I carry the dead in my hand.
>
> (Celtic ritual opening)

The Celtic ritual opening defines the idea of *storyteller*: someone who can enter into another reality and who promises to negotiate between the audience and that other reality—to tell the audience into another place and time. The teller operates the mutually understood ritual that releases both teller and audience from the confines of common routine and expectation. He or she initiates the play that brings story reality into being through the experience of storying, or story reconstruction. During the telling, the teller stories information *with* rather than *for* an audience in a manner consistent with the mythic and metaphoric consciousness of the audience and with the cultural origins of the story itself.

In order to perform this function, the storyteller cannot act as an individual personality. The individual person who is also the storyteller relinquishes control while the telling is in progress. The storyteller is the other, the ancient one, the game initiator and player, the one who keeps the stories, the one who can take us safely from one time, place, and reality to another and back again. The storyteller must be greater than a single individual, and invested with special capabilities. (The reference to capabilities has to do with the cosmic and mystical dimensions of the literature and not with the talent of any given teller.) The storyteller "calls us over," then "calls us back." A person empowered to do this must be somewhat transcendent. The storyteller is all storytellers, and the storyteller is also the embodiment of the literature.

At the same time that the storyteller must act as "other," he or she also lends very tangible dimensions of his or her real-life personality to the making of the story. This apparent contradiction can be resolved by considering that the literature "borrows" the entire entity of the storyteller during a storytelling: voice, mannerisms, sense of humor, all. As we said, the audience does not "see" the teller during a storytelling. The audience "sees" the story. The teller is a transmitter, a means to an end. The storyteller's individual person in invisible, but his or her personality may help to shape the story.

The storyteller is a problem solver. Every aspect of storytelling, from finding stories to tell to the actual delivery, involves problem solving. The teller is confronted with the constraints of his or her own personality and the kinds of stories it can support; with his or her own literary background and expectations for story structure, which will limit the kinds of stories he or she can tell effectively; with his or her own overall capability to encode the oral story using language and paralinguistic effects; with the nature and composition of a given audience or with the requirements of a specific story-telling program. The storyteller must also contend with problems related to time: story length or program length and audience tolerance, preparation time, and problems related directly to the shape of the story.

Perhaps the most interesting act of problem solving in which the storyteller engages is the act of story encoding—the storying itself. The teller must integrate elements of language, paralanguage, story structure and content, and negotiation with the audience to make the story. Fortunately, these integrative processes are primarily subconscious. Conscious attention to such devices in the story comes before the telling. Too much conscious attention during telling could result in a tangled tongue.

The storyteller is a living library. The storyteller is the mythic, meta-phoric, and literary memory of a culture. He or she is the repository of a literature and, in this capacity, belongs to the culture, to the people, and to a different dimension of time than that which encompasses the lifetime of the individual. While an individual storyteller may come and go, "the storyteller" ("the other") remains. Should a given storyteller fail to pass the information on to the next teller, the stories and all they encode would be irretrievably lost. Therefore, many cultures have devised elaborate techniques for choosing and training storytellers in order to keep the stories from being extinguished—techniques involving a redundancy of storytellers and a redundancy of information.

Today's storyteller, who must often go to written resources to find material, expands the immediate library of the oral literature with each oral story he or she takes out of print and encodes into oral language. The current concept of *library* seems not to include the storyteller as a permanent part of its holdings. Although storytellings happen in libraries, the library only inventories such things as books, records, films, microfilm, microfiche, and the like. It does not include the body of the oral literature among its collections. Perhaps, along with their high-tech additions, modern libraries might consider acquiring a live storyteller.

WHAT THE STORYTELLER DOES

The storyteller selects, prepares, and delivers stories. Although these three activities are listed separately and treated as distinctly different operations in subsequent chapters, they tend to be integrated in practice. From beginning to end, the telling of a story is a whole that cannot be broken into discrete bits and pieces and then reassembled mechanistically. Although there must be a beginning with a story—the storyteller must find the story—and although some preparation can precede the first telling, selection, preparation, and delivery tend to be simultaneous.

After the teller chooses a story and attends to the preliminary aspects of encoding, the story must be told before an audience. [The act of story negotiation will further influence story preparation and selection.] A storyteller and a story always have a dynamic relationship. The teller is always discovering nuances and depths to stories, even years after initial selection. A storyteller may also "unselect" a story years after telling it for the first time. The audience and the negotiating process influence the continued interaction between the storyteller and a given story. A story is never fully developed, never fully known, never absolutely perfect.

The storyteller conducts the game. The storyteller is the living representative of the rules for "story," storying, and storytelling. The teller brings the rules to the audience and operates them. Without the teller, the audience cannot play. Someone must assume the identity of the other, for only the other can manipulate a set of rules intended to transcend time and space. One might argue that if the storyteller is sick, someone in the audience can take over. But that is precisely the point—the someone from the audience must become the storyteller. There can be no game without the storyteller.

The storyteller works toward "easy" and "natural" technique. The teller works the story in cooperation with the audience, employing a carefully balanced combination of tension and ease. The tension is not terror, panic, fear, or nerves, but a controlled level of psychological energy that the teller draws from the excitement of the experience of telling, the readiness of the audience, and his or her awareness of the requirements of the task. The ease is a controlled level of relaxation adopted by the teller during the telling that allows him or her to "play" with the story and to have fun with the telling. Experienced tellers make telling look easy. They will confess, however, that telling becomes harder and harder as they become more aware of story requirements and tasks and as they discover the sometimes profound and awesome depths of the stories they tell.

Natural is not easily defined. Certainly it does not mean *automatic*, for a telling is situation dependent. The teller must always be alert to the specific requirements of a given telling. But the teller can become so familiar with and friendly with a story that he or she "knows" what is "right" with regard to specific interpretations during telling. The teller makes the story look, feel, and sound perfectly natural while maintaining his or her own level of deliberate control. *Natural*, then, is not looseness or letting go, but the condition in which teller and story's capabilities and requirements have been integrated to best suit both. They meet during the telling and become a single entity.

Remembering that the storyteller is the other and not himself or herself during telling can help to maintain an easy, natural teller attitude. The teller does not need to be self-conscious during the telling, since the "self" is not telling the story. "Storyteller," the archetypal repository of cultural cosmologies, is doing the telling. Ritual telling routines and ritual play are designed to clarify the separation between "storyteller" and the individual personality of the teller. These conventional devices allow the teller as individual to step aside and the teller as other to operate. Beginning storytellers must learn to make and sustain the shift from self to other for telling. Initially, they must consciously trust the power of the ritual to protect them. The audience is not there to watch a potentially silly or embarrassing performance, but to enter into the ritual with the teller. The teller can undo the ritual aspect of a telling by retaining "self" during telling and by expressing self-consciousness and embarrassment through self-aware employment of props, movement, language, and paralinguistic effects. When the teller abandons the role of other for the self-conscious demeanor of self, the audience will also become embarrassed and uncomfortable.

Naturalness requires practice. Ultimately, practice must be taken before the audience, since each interpretive element a storyteller introduces into a story is a hypothesis that can only be tested before others who also know "story" and story conventions. Teller and story come together in a trial-and-error process for each new telling. And with each new telling both teller and story engage in a mutual problem-solving exercise. The teller learns stories and how to tell stories by telling them. The teller develops a sense of story convention by attending storytellings. And the teller makes a story his or her own only through repeated tellings, through trial and error, through teller/audience/story negotiation, and through gradual discovery of hidden story requirements and nuances.

For every story in the teller's repertoire, there must be a beginning. There must be selection, preparation, and countless actual deliveries before audiences. The moment of readiness for the first telling can only be determined by the teller. However, the teller should not expect the story to be perfect at that moment. Story and teller grow together as a result of repeated live tellings in which audiences help the teller assess and develop technique, style, and the use of interpretive elements. Living oral stories are always changing and growing in keeping with the needs of audiences and the abilities and literary insights of tellers. The relationship between teller and story is a vital and dynamic one in which the story never becomes old, static, or frozen. The story can always be renegotiated, can expand, and can contribute to the development of the teller's capacity. Teller and story mature together, becoming intimate friends and sharing secrets. Time must be allowed for such evolutions.

The storyteller holds the mirror. The storyteller places the story before the audience. Because the story is organized in structures that we know are "right" and sensible, and because the story contains archetypal characters, situations, etc., that we have invented, we can see ourselves and our universe in the mirror. However, the images projected in the mirror are larger-than-life reconstructions of ourselves, more universal representations. The effect of storying is to lend a universal truth to common circumstance. The mirror of the story shows us to ourselves against the images of a larger cosmology. By recognizing ourselves in this larger dimension, we can proceed on a daily basis with a clearer understanding of who we are. Such recognition brings release and renewal. The more we come to know who we are through "story," storying, and storytelling, the more we can be liberated from the limitations of our selves, and, at the same time, the more we can comfortably be what we are.

THE PLACE OF STORYTELLING TODAY

Numerous sociologists and biologists have commented on the human condition in the posttechnological age to the effect that we are operating a space-age technology, trying to keep all its rather frightening applications under control, with mental and social processes that have advanced only a little beyond the cave. While this may seem a somewhat extreme position, most of us would agree that, along with the advances the sciences have provided, we need a concomitant development of an understanding of purpose and a redefinition of morality.

The human animal has not changed to such a degree that the archetypes presented in the oral literature are no longer applicable. Today, perhaps more than ever, we need to see ourselves in a cosmological sense. The stories, with motifs and archetypes shared across cultures, religions, and language groups; "story" itself as a form of organization recognized by all people; the act of storying and storytelling as universally understood operations—these things that belong to the practice and preservation of the oral literature are buried deep in the human psyche (Bettelheim 1976; Hillman 1975). They are ancient, transcending more recently developed human differences and the technological changes that loom so large.

Oral stories and storytellings are intimations of something very old, something that has its roots in the origins of language and human culture. In the act of storying, we are all one community. In storytelling, and in the hands of a competent storyteller, we discover that community and one another. This is our literary heritage—our inheritance. We have no less need of it today than we ever have had. The oral literature is a human invention, a legacy, whose purpose it is to bind us together in recognition of our universal commonalities at a profoundly rich level of humanness. When we find ourselves together in the stories, we discover that we are not different; we are remarkably alike. In the context of the storytelling, we are obliged to acknowledge our shared humanity. As W. R. S. Ralston (1873) expressed it, "One touch of storytelling may, in some instances, make the whole world kin."

REFERENCES

Benjamin, Walter. 1968. *Illuminations*. New York: Harcourt Brace Jovanovich.

Bettelheim, Bruno. 1976. *The Uses of Enchantment: The Meaning and Importance of Fairy Tales*. New York: Alfred A. Knopf.

Bollinger Foundation. 1952. *African Folktales and Sculpture*. New York: Pantheon Books.

Carpenter, Humphrey, and Mari Prichard. 1984. *The Oxford Companion to Children's Literature*. New York: Oxford University Press.

Chase, Richard. 1943. *The Jack Tales*. Boston: Houghton Mifflin.

Downing, John, and Che Kan Leong. 1982. *Psychology of Reading*. New York: Macmillan.

Harrell, John, and Mary Harrell. 1977. *A Storyteller's Treasury*. Berkeley, Calif.: Box 9006.

Hillman, James. 1975. *Loose Ends*. Dallas, Tex.: Spring Publications.

———. 1979. "A Note on 'Story.' " *Parabola*. Vol. 4, No. 4 (November): 43-45.

Kent, Jack. 1971. *The Fat Cat: A Danish Folktale*. New York: Parents Magazine Press.

Martin, Bill, Jr. 1970. *Tatty Mae and Catty Mae*. Bill Martin's Instant Readers. New York: Holt, Rinehart & Winston.

MacDonald, Margaret Read. 1982. *The Storyteller's Sourcebook: A Subject, Title and Motif Index to Folklore Collections for Children*. Detroit, Mich.: Neal-Schuman in association with Gale.

McGovern, Ann. 1967. *Too Much Noise*. Boston: Houghton Mifflin.

Mullett, George C. 1982. *Spider Woman Stories*. Tucson, Ariz.: University of Arizona Press.

Pellowski, Anne. 1977. *The World of Storytelling*. New York: R. R. Bowker.

Ralston, W. R. S. 1873. *Russian Folktales*. London: Smith, Elder.

Rockwell, Anne. 1975. *The Three Bears and Fifteen Other Stories*. New York: Crowell.

Rockwell, Anne. 1979. *The Old Woman and Her Pig and Ten Other Stories*. New York: Crowell.

Scollon, Ron, and Suzanne Scollon. 1979. "Cooking It Up and Boiling It Down: Abstracts in Athabaskan Children's Story Retelling." Alaskan Native Language Center.

Smith, Frank. 1982. *Understanding Reading: A Psycholinguistic Analysis of Reading and Learning to Read*. New York: Holt, Rinehart & Winston.

Sutton-Smith, Brian. 1981. *The Folkstories of Children*. Philadelphia, Pa.: University of Pennsylvania Press.

Waters, Frank. 1963. *The Way of Hopi*. New York: Ballantine Press.

Wiggin, Kate. 1954. *Tales of Laughter: A Third Fairy Book*. Garden City, N.Y.: Doubleday.

Wolkstein, Diane. 1978. *The Magic Orange Tree*. New York: Alfred A. Knopf.

Yarnspinner. 1980. Vol. 5, No. 4 (October). Jonesborough, Tenn.: National Association for the Preservation and Perpetuation of Storytelling.

Zemach, Harve. 1965. *Salt*. New York: Follett.

2

Developing Story Memory
Story Structure and Convention

We do not really mean . . .
We do not really mean . . .
That what we say is true.
(Asanti ritual opening)

What is story structure?

How can story structure help the storyteller to
remember and tell stories?

How does a storyteller "map" a story?

Which types of story structures or grammars can the
storyteller expect to find in oral stories?

Which stories are organized around these structural
types?

Which other patterns in stories will aid storyteller
memory?

"Story" reorganizes experience into a shape different from that of its original occurrence. In that sense, perhaps, our recounting of events in storied form is not quite the "truth." On the other hand, story itself is a truth, and storied information is invested with a new dimension of reality through the act of storying. By storying, we reconfigure information from one kind of structure to another, one kind of truth to another. And we *do* really mean—the intent is implicit in the Asanti opening—that what we say is true.

Stories have structure. They are orderly; they conform to grammatical conventions or rules that we recognize as "story" structure, much as sentences conform to rules that we recognize as conventional sentence structure. "Sense of story," like "sentence sense," is an individual's in-memory map, or program, for story shapes and behaviors (i.e., story grammar) and is very likely acquired during language learning as a part of oral language development. Like sentence grammar, story grammar can be thought of as generative (Meyer and Rice 1984)—a set of abstractions for pattern from which stories never before told can be formed, presented, and recognized as stories. The listener learns story structure rules—the suprastructures of stories—as organizing frameworks for story content, and, eventually, recognizes these as regular, conventional, and predictable patterns for the arrangement of information. Even very young children acquire and have knowledge of, and therefore expectations for, story grammar (Kintsch 1977; Mandler 1978; Stein and Glenn 1979; Sutton-Smith 1981).

Story structure is not an accidental or idle invention, but the profound product of a culture's evolved perceptions of the way the universe works. Story patterns or grammars are sophisticated devices for organizing and remembering information. The storyteller remembers story content (internal detail) by learning the story pattern. The telling of a given story is "driven" by structural memory. Pattern is the skeleton upon which the teller expands, develops, and tailors the story.

Storytellers may not be fully aware of their employment of these implicit, internal sets of story grammar rules during telling, but they are most certainly using them, probably to perform two very necessary functions. First, story structure allows the teller to organize and "slot" any given content into a shape that lends sensibility and coherence to that content. The structure is the matrix or framework into which the content is embedded. Second, story structure provides the teller with his or her primary memory device for story content. The specific content of any given story is most likely stored in memory in relation to the sensibility and coherence lent it by story structure, and story structure itself becomes "a strategy for retrieval of information contained in the story" (Meyer and Rice 1984, 340). Without knowledge of story structure (conscious or otherwise), neither audience nor teller would realize the special interrelationships of ideas and events as they are organized within "story," and neither would be able to remember and reiterate information and happenings with the ease provided by "story" as memory device.

DISCOURSE STRUCTURE

Discourse structure is a language suprastructure (grammar) existing at the paragraph, chapter, section, book, or "story" level, into which specific content is embedded. Discourse structure orders, organizes, interrelates, and lends internal coherence to groups of ideas. It is the structure (organization of text) beyond sentence structure that brings collective sensibility or logic to the ideas we present. Many forms of text structure are conventional — rule-governed and expected shapes into which, by mutual agreement, people organize information. These common shapes — the paragraph, for instance — can be described structurally and operationally without reference to any specific content. (We could construct a paragraph about hiking or trains or cake decorating. The organizing construct or framework would still be the paragraph, regardless of the subject.) These "top-level" shapes are used to carry content and may very well be represented in memory, in the form of abstract rules, each in its own right, exclusive of any given body of content. Such conventional discourse structures may, then, influence both the representation of a given content and the structuring of that content in memory, since a specific content must adopt the shape of such a larger grammatical form (i.e., "story") when slotted into it.

"Story," even though it is oral, is a kind of text or discourse structure. The uniqueness of "story" as a structural convention, as a memory activity, may, in fact, derive from the oral nature of "story" and storying. A written story, while it obeys written conventions, does not need to adhere to a strict and precise application of specific oral discourse structure rules. The text can take on some rather unconventional shapes, because through print human memory can be extended beyond the immediate limitations of the mind. But the oral story depends for its very existence upon the reliability of human memory. Perhaps the highly structured, exacting conventions of (oral) "story" were evolved in order to prevent stories and their respective contents from being forgotten and lost. Downing and Leong (1982) write, "The more a story conforms to an ideal structure, the better it will be recalled" (235). The sets of structures that constitute recognizable oral stories, and "story" itself as an abstract, rule-governed representation, are very regular and very idealized.

"Story" integrity and recognizability are, in fact, a matter of structure — the manner in which a given story binds information together into some sort of coherent whole. A random collection of bits of information not organized into a conventional story shape is denied story status. Generally, discourse lacking a clear-cut and cause/effect-related beginning, middle, and end is not recognized as a story. Text that fails to present a setting plus an episode (problem to be solved plus events leading to problem solution) or series of episodes (Rumelhart 1975) is not considered a story. Treatments of information that are recognized as stories utilize special "knowledge structures" or memory programs already present in the minds of storytellers and audiences, developed as a result of repeated exposures to told stories. The in-memory conventions of "story" are never formally taught; they are learned cognitive structures—sets of rules from which people can generate and understand stories (Smith 1982).

STORY STRUCTURE

Numerous attempts have been made to examine and describe the conventions, structures, and habits of "story" and of the oral literature. Two general approaches to describing the behavior of stories exist. The earliest, historically, is essentially taxonomic. MacDonald (1982) divides stories into motif, title, theme, subject, ethnic, geographic, and even archetypal categories. Propp (1958) organizes stories by characters, character type, and includes some mention of structure. Most collections of oral stories in print also present limited taxonomies. One can locate collections of stories grouped by topic, character type, ethnic origin, etc. Taxonomic descriptions of "story" are related to content, not to structure. These descriptions are useful to the teller for the purposes of locating and selecting stories, especially for construction of specialty programs, but they do not help the teller remember the story for retelling, except, perhaps, in the most generalized fashion. The taxonomies only make reference to elements of story content in the absence of story structure.

A more recent view of "story" considers the grammaticality of stories, which, exclusive of their respective contents, are seen to follow predictable, rule-governed sequences (Meyer and Rice 1984). Stories have "top level structures," grammars, or "overall organizing principles" that "can be described independently of any given content," according to Meyer and Rice (1984, 327), in much the same manner as a sentence can be described in terms of its internal functions (agent, action, object) without the need to use specific words (The dog chewed the bone). Story-grammar approaches to story description, then, present patterns, sets of rules that, when used to slot story content, result in a story utilizing conventional forms (Mandler and Johnson 1977; Kintsch 1977; Rumelhart 1975). All the descriptions below attempt to provide a formula for "story" in general and present models into which any specific story shape can be fitted and mapped. In the examples that follow, S stands for story, and E for episode.

1. S = a series of "causally connected parts"

2. S = setting + event structure

    (Mandler and Johnson 1977)

3. S = setting + episode(s)

    E = problem + event(s) leading to problem solution.

    (Rumelhart 1975)

4. S = setting category + episode system (of single or embedded or chained episodes)

episode system = initiating event + action + direct consequence (of action). (The episode system is a "higher order category" incorporating the entire story with the exception of the setting category.)

(Stein and Glenn 1979)

Any of these given formulas for "story" can be used to map a specific story. Figure 2.1 shows Rumelhart's (1975) formula for describing a hypothetical story structure. Rumelhart's story grammar, like other story grammars, identifies "story" as a specific type of discourse structure, accounts for the presence and interrelationship of those elements that give "story" its overall

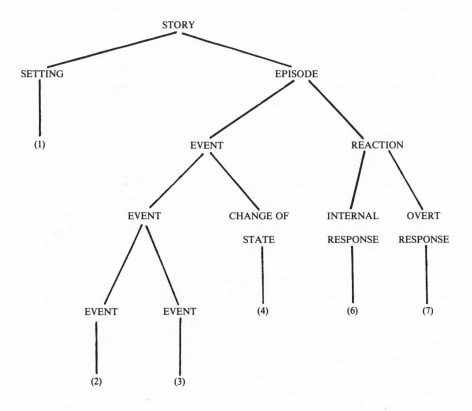

Fig. 2.1.

structural identity and integrity, and describes "story" convention. Story grammars such as this one map the major slot arrangements that make "story" a strategy for memory organization, for retention of specific content in memory, and for information retrieval during storytelling. Story grammars, as we said, can be viewed as generative—that is, from a given set of rules for story in memory, the storyteller can generate any number of stories by reconstructing the story pattern and fitting the story content into it. The audience uses its knowledge of story structure to identify ideas and relationships between ideas, to predict and presuppose logic, significance, order, cause/effect, and general coherence during telling.

RECOGNIZING STORY STRUCTURE

Overall, a story *is* a story because it employs a recognizable set of general conventions or features that give it its identity as "story." However, each story is a different arrangement of the elements of story structure. Each story has its own special grammar, derived from application of the general conventions (rules) of "story," and each story operates somewhat differently from all others with regard to the orderings of settings, episodes, events, actions, responses, problems, solutions, and resolutions. A specific story is recognizable and distinct, because it embeds story content and manipulates story rules in keeping with its own special formula. The teller must recognize both the generalizable aspects of a given story structure and the special structural effects that make a story unique.

Though many storytellers may not be aware of the story maps designed by story grammarians (tellers as a group are usually not inclined to examine story grammars), they would certainly recognize and accept as givens the conventions described in the grammatical formulas. After all, a story is a story because it has a certain kind of shape and does, within limits, some predictable things. The general conventions of story, then, constitute a primary level of organization and memory for the storyteller. It is the special, specific employment and organization of these conventions, one story at a time, at which the memory task for the teller begins.

Whether or not the storyteller is fully aware of the structure of a given story, he or she depends significantly upon that structure in remembering and reconstructing story events and details during telling. Developed ability to consciously evaluate story pattern or structure will greatly aid teller memory for stories, since the teller can use structure awareness to map story content. Lack of awareness of and attention to the exact structure of a given story can even lead to violation of the shape of the story during telling, because an individual tends to slot information in keeping with his or her own internalized rules for story structure. If these are different from the prescribed shape of a specific story, the teller is likely to *re*structure the story using his or her own rules (Smith 1982).

Practiced storytellers do not memorize stories word for word or sentence by sentence. They learn the particular structural idiosyncracies of a story (plus required ritual language, necessary specific dialogue, and other important special effects) and then use their own natural style and language to *rebuild* the story by a process of orderly slotting of story content (including minute detail) into the structure of the story. (If teller narration sounds memorized, it is probably the result of practice and the gradual development of additional story-specific rules used during story reconstruction at each retelling.) For instance, the teller knows that his or her story begins with an introduction to a setting and a cluster of short events contained in the setting category, followed by the development of a set of problematic circumstances for the main character or characters. The first task in story rebuilding during telling, then, is to fit specific story detail into the setting and problem development slots in the story structure—to "tell" that information. Since establishing setting and problem is required conventional storying behavior, both teller and audience now expect an event or series of events, or episodes contained in events, leading to the solution of the problem. The teller learns the event arrangement—how many, in what order, character activities and responses in each, internal cause/effect relationships between—and then reconstructs the body of the story by fitting appropriate story detail, character talk, ritual language, and meaningful paralinguistic effects into the events in the order in which the events occur. The last event in the sequence usually solves the problem. Finally, the teller "tells" the information that fits into the resolution, conclusion, and "moral of the tale" slots, if these are present in the story. The teller's in-memory story map might look like this:

1. **Introduction to setting/characters: Events in setting category— development of problem**

    The development of the problem might, itself, involve the telling of a minor series of events. If so, the in-memory map would slot these.

    a. Problem establishing event 1

    b. Problem establishing event 2

    c. etc.

2. **Problem**

    Clarification/statement/description of the problem

3. **Event sequence**

    In the event sequence, the character or characters undertake a series of actions designed to solve the problem. Sometimes, these activities lead directly to problem solution in a straight, linear fashion. A direct, linear problem solution might map as follows:

   a.   Event 1—Leads logically to next event

   b.   Event 2—Leads logically to next event

   c.   Event 3—Leads logically to next event

   d.   etc.

   e.   Event second to last—Leads logically to last event, or problem solution

Alternative event sequence

Some event sequences could better be described as "embedded" rather than direct and linear. That is, the character(s) attempt(s) to solve the original problem, only to create more problems. Often these additional problems are cumulative—problem 1 creates problem 2, which creates problem 3, which creates problem 4. Then problem 4 solves problem 3, which solves problem 2, which solves problem 1.

a.   Event 1—Attempt to solve problem 1 instead causes problem 2

  b.   Event 2—Attempt to solve problem 2 instead causes problem 3

    c.   Event 3—Attempt to solve problem 3 instead causes problem 4

    d.   Event 4— Solution of problem 4 allows return to problem 3

  e.   Event 5—Solution of problem 3 allows return to problem 2

f.   Event 6—Solution of problem 2 allows return to problem 1 and leads logically to slot 4—problem solution

The evolution of problems in such an event sequence can be remembered as cause/effect relationships between events. Each new problem is embedded in its predecessor, since it is the effect of the preceding action, and it must be solved, *before* the preceding problem can be addressed. In a sense, embedded problem sequences "wind up" like a clock spring as characters get into more and more difficulty, then "unwind" as characters systematically undo their complicated circumstances. The event items a through f above would be considered episodes if each had internal events of its own leading to causes and solutions, each of its own respective problem.

4.   **Resolution (problem solution)**

The last event is sometimes organized differently than its predecessors. It may contain a slightly different content or a different arrangement of content, and therefore might be considered to be a special slot.

5. **Conclusion**

The conclusion slot provides the teller with the structure for the "therefore" or "so what" aspects of the story.

6. **Moral**

Some stories add a formal, ritual instruction to story conclusion.

Story-specific content is slotted into the story map in memory. Storyteller memory for a given story, then, incorporates aspects of structure and content, and, perhaps, a formula for integrating the two during telling. The following outline illustrates such integration, with the rudiments of content slotted into a basic story structure framework.

THE WIDE-MOUTHED FROG*

Introduction to setting/characters: Events in setting category — development of problem

Wide-mouthed frog lives with wife along riverbank. (Details about home, surroundings, etc., are given here.) Wife about to have babies — what to feed them? Husband agrees to find out, and sets off from home on a quest for an answer to the question.

Problem

How to find out what to feed wide-mouthed frog babies.

Event sequence

Event 1 — Frog meets mouse.

Frog says, "Hello! I'm a wide-mouthed frog. What do you feed your babies?"

Mouse answers, "Grain, cheese. Steal it."

Frog responds, "That's probably not a good thing to feed to wide-mouth frog babies. Thank you."

Frog hops on.

Event 2 — Frog meets snake.

Repeat entire event for snake.

Substitute snake answer: "Raw eggs. Steal 'em."

---

*Origin of this version unknown.

Event 3 — Frog meets owl.

> Repeat entire event for owl.
>
> Substitute owl answer: "Live mice. Swallow 'em whole. Spit out the bones."

Event 4 — Frog meets lion.

> Repeat entire event for lion.
>
> Substitute lion answer: "Red raw meat. Chew it all down."

Event 5 — Frog meets dragon.

> Insert description of dragon and dragon activity (roasting marshmallows on a stick using own breath, pulling them off gooey, eating them, teeth sticking together, etc.)
>
> Frog calls up to dragon.
>
> Dragon answers down to frog, "I feed my babies wide-mouthed frogs."
>
> (Embedded problem — If the dragon discovers that the frog has a wide mouth, the frog might be fed to the dragon's babies.)

Resolution (Problem solution)

Alternative 1 — Dragon catches (and eats) frog.

Alternative 2 — Frog narrows mouth to avoid detection.

In this version of the story, the frog does not solve his original problem — what to feed his own babies. Only the embedded problem is solved. Young audiences often fail to get the joke. They don't like to see the frog get eaten. An effective storyteller can create quite an endearing character in the frog and have children chanting and coacting along with the frog throughout the story. Children also fail to understand the significance of the narrowing of the frog's mouth at the end of the story. They are waiting for the conventional ending in which the frog finds out what to feed his children and goes home to report to his wife. Since this does not happen, children often suggest alternative endings for the story in which the frog gets his answer and goes home — an interesting example of children's expectations for story convention.

Conclusion

Teller's choice — either alternative given above.

> If alternative 1, dragon ceremoniously chews and swallows frog. (Some dragons have been known to burp. Others wouldn't dream of it. These last types of dragons tend to use linen

napkins. The teller never knows exactly which sort of
dragon will turn up in a given telling until the end of the
story.)

If alternative 2, frog's mouth narrows slowly, dramatically, obviously.
This activity is accompanied by a rolling of the eyes and,
perhaps, a froggy expletive. Given the shape of the
mouth during this exercise, some of the better known
froggy expletives cannot be articulated. The best one,
here, is *Ooooooooohhhhhhhhhh*, along with an appropriate pitch pattern.

Given a chance, children in an audience will provide still other
alternatives.

Moral

None given in this case. Young members of the audience can and will
supply one, or several, if consulted.

This story map could also include additional specific language that the teller
had invented; pitch, stress, and juncture employment; movement; characterization, voice; and other paralinguistic features. It is important for the
storyteller to understand that his or her memory for the specific content and
performance aspects of any given story is very probably built into, or slotted
into, the memory for story structure. Story structure in memory "frames" and
orders memories for story content. During a telling, story structure provides
the bones upon which the meat of the story is hung.

Storytelling, when viewed in this manner, is a problem-solving activity in
which the teller must transform abstract memories for story grammar,
language, paralanguage, and story content into an integrated, whole, concrete,
palpable surface product—the oral story. During the transformation from
abstract in-memory rules for the story to the story that is seen and heard, the
teller is faced with the task of integrating many pieces of the story. This
integration is essentially a *building* process. And, as with the building of
anything, the teller gets better at building the story product with each repeated
telling. We learn to solve a problem by solving it; we learn to tell a story by
telling it.

Unless the storyteller begins work on a new story with some in-memory
information about it (structure, content, language, etc.), he or she will not be
able to tell it at all. Each subsequent retelling is a possibility—a hypothesis.
What the teller is doing, in a way, is trying out a particular integration of the
memories for the story while producing the concrete story product. Each
retelling is a different integration of the same information in memory, a
slightly different speculation regarding how the in-memory abstractions
should be fitted together and in what concrete forms they should appear. Each

retelling is a different solution to the same problem: "How should this story work?" Each telling will help the teller answer that question, as will audience response to teller experimentation and interpretation. Each solution to the problem will lend regularity to the overall shape of the story and grace and control to the telling. The teller will "own" the story only after many tellings, many hypotheses, many attempts to solve the problem.

The structure of the story is the bedrock memory around which the teller can experiment with the integration of story content, language, and paralinguistic elements. Each retelling or rebuilding of the same story will result in a totally new and different product, one that has never before been heard. But story structure will remain constant. When the teller chooses to develop a story for telling, then, the articulation of structure in memory—the bones—comes first.

MAPPING STORY STRUCTURE

When the storyteller learns a story, he or she maps it in memory. The story map contains aspects of event sequence structure, number sets, overall top-level structure, participation opportunities, and specific story content. During the telling, all of these elements are integrated to produce the concrete product—the told story.

Some storytellers map stories "naturally." They do not require the use of physical aids, but simply recognize and remember story shape and content after a reading or a telling. The experienced teller, and one who has had extensive exposure to the oral literature, will recognize a variety of story shapes readily, because experience has contributed to the development of many story structure maps in memory. Other storytellers might require some sort of memory aid.

Some tellers take notes. However, notes that do not reflect some of the structural peculiarities of the story are often of little help.

Some tellers make outlines. If outlining is a viable means of making a memory map for a teller, the outline that takes the shape of overall conventional "story" is probably the best approach. The outlines provided in this chapter might serve as examples, or the teller might want to use those of Rumelhart (1975) or other story grammarians. Such outlines usually order and organize story episodes and events and otherwise conform to the shape of the story. Forcing a story into the shape of a fixed outline form is usually not as helpful and can even distort the shape of the story.

The teller can map a story by clumping both events and content according to the number pattern of the story. If a story is set in groups of three, the teller can jot notes that integrate story content and number pattern in the groups of three specified in the story.

The teller might draw an "octopus outline" or a "semantic web." In both cases, the teller can choose to map either event structure or number pattern or both. (See fig. 2.2).

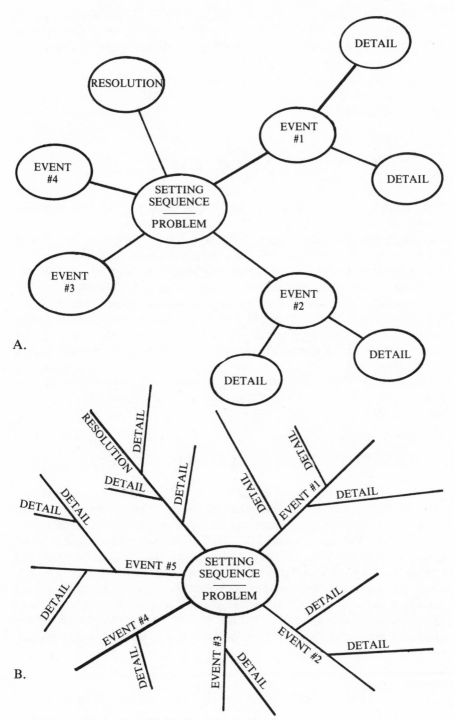

Fig. 2.2. A: "Semantic web"; B: "Octopus outline."

Any story outline can be extended by the addition of side notes indicating where and which type of participation will take place during telling, where various paralinguistic effects can be employed, and where chanting and ritual language can be used to good effect. (See chapter 3.)

The teller might also want to employ alternative and more traditional memory devices, many of which can be and should be used along with the telling. (See chapter 3.)

STORY STRUCTURE TYPES

Within the general pattern for "story" (see general maps of conventional story grammars above), the oral literature presents regular, rule-governed, recognizable "subpatterns" or "suborganization categories" for the slotting and remembering of information. Teller recognition of these patterns should not be considered a nonessential academic exercise. Structure knowledge is one's insurance against panic forgetting—a very basic dimension of survival. Knowing story pattern is the beginning and continued foundation for further development of story memory, technique, and control. Structure memory can and does save the teller from "blanking out" information (story content) during telling. A storyteller remembers more than one kind of structure for each story. He or she learns episode/event sequences, number patterns, and participation types. When the storyteller examines a new story and prepares to tell it, he or she should look for these different dimensions of organization within a story. Each story more than likely employs aspects of all of these simultaneously.

EPISODE/EVENT SEQUENCES

One very effective means of building story memory is to examine the shape of the event sequence—the arrangement of actions in the story. Event sequences in oral stories have evolved into general patterns or conventional configurations that seem, with some minor differences, to be in use in many cultures. Identification of the type or category of event sequence pattern will simplify memory work by clarifying the nature of the task of content slotting.

Event sequence patterns are conventional forms that appear again and again in many stories. They are substructures within "story" that lend more specific aspects of organization to information. Teller recognition of this pattern in a given story is an immeasurable aid in story development and delivery.

The Cumulative Sequence Type

The cumulative story can be described generally as a setting category plus an episode system containing a problem and a series of events leading to problem solution. Problem solution in the cumulative story is accomplished through the use of a specialized event series or sequence that is additive. It is perhaps the most conventional, strictly governed, ritualized formula for story structure in the oral literature.

The cumulative story often requires more memorization of specific content and language than other story types and allows for the greatest extent of very controlled, ritualized audience interaction. Such stories offer the audience the delights of language play and, often, the opportunity to engage in collective chanting, singing, and repetition of story parts. Because the cumulative type of story is so rule bound and prescriptive, it is highly predictable. Audiences can "tell" cumulative stories along with the storyteller, because audiences already know the story rules and can predict story sequence.

While stories and storytellings are understood to be games, stories built upon cumulative patterns are games within games, the cumulative exercise itself being a play embedded within the larger game of "story." The cumulative game is a "winding up," or a collecting and adding together of items, experiences, and people. In some cumulative stories, the added elements "unwind" rapidly at the end, signaling problem solution. The play of winding up and unwinding in the cumulative story is often more important than plot action. Many cumulative stories have little real action at all; the story simply winds up or collects a series of items and then unwinds them. Action in stories like "The Fat Cat" (Kent 1971), "The Tabby Who Was Such a Glutton" (Asbjornsen and Moe 1960), "Fourteen Hundred Cowries" (Fuja 1971), "La Hormiguita" (Hayes 1982), and "The Old Woman and Her Pig" (Johnson et al. 1977) amounts primarily to that necessary to wind and unwind a listing of items. Some cumulative stories do combine some plot action with cumulative play; for example, "The Three Goats" (Literature Committee 1950), "The Silly Goose War" (Johnson et al. 1977), and "Wali Dad the Simple-Hearted" (Lang 1949).

Not all cumulative stories are identical structurally. In order to help the teller distinguish the critical features of the different types of cumulative patterns, cumulatives can be divided into four subcategories, each being a different specific type or formula. While the categories are not absolutely discrete, and some cumulative stories might overlap or simply not fit at all, these four primary distinctions should help the teller recognize, organize, and learn many common cumulative-type stories.

Type A Cumulative—Winding Only

Stories that class in this first cumulative category are those that wind up only. They make a list of items but do not repeat that list as each new item is added. They also do not unwind the list to signal story end. The familiar story "The Fisherman and His Wife" (Johnson et al. 1977) which, incidentally, appears in many cultures and contains a much-used motif, is an example of a winding, nonrepetitive list structure. The list does not unwind at the end of the story.

THE FISHERMAN AND HIS WIFE

1. Fisherman catches magical fish.

2. Fish persuades fisherman to release it.

3. Fisherman tells wife story to justify coming home empty-handed.

4. Wife insists he return to demand that the fish grant a wish.

Cumulative sequence begins.

Wife makes six such requests for wishes. The fish grants each wish. The cumulative (collective) effect is in the additive nature of the wishes granted.

     a.   Hovel to cottage

     b.   Cottage to castle

     c.   Castle to king

     d.   King to emperor

     e.   Emperor to pope

     f.   Pope to God

5. Fish refuses to grant last wish.

6. Fisherman and wife are returned to living in their original hovel. The result of the last wish is pope to hovel rather than pope to God, making the cumulative form cyclic.

Some ritual chanting is included with each new wish. Action remains essentially identical, with some minor changes, i.e., the color and motion of the sea from one wish to the next.

"The Fisherman and His Wife" also illustrates a common secondary feature of many cumulative stories—circularity. The last element to be added to the list brings the characters back to the circumstances they were experiencing at the start of the tale. The event sequence describes a cycle.

The teller might develop a structure outline to aid memory. For the type A cumulative, such an outline might look like this:

THE SEVENTH FATHER OF THE HOUSE*

Setting — Big, beautiful farm, characterized as castle

Problem — Tired traveler desires lodging for night.

Event sequence — Traveler approaches seven men in sequence, each older than his predecessor. Each in the sequence is the father of the one before. The traveler must obtain permission to stay from the eldest. Each event in the sequence is essentially the same, with a few substitutions to describe location and physical appearance of each older "father" of the house.

Traveler approaches "father" (physical description is given here).

Repeat language

Traveler: Good evening, father. Can you put me up for the night?

Father: I'm not the father of the house. Go to [location] and talk to my father.

Traveler goes to the location named. There he finds and approaches the next father.

Seven such events occur in sequence.

1. Father (adult) — Old; gray hair and beard
   Location — Outside, chopping wood

2. Father (youth) — Even older
   Location — On knees in front of hearth, blowing on fire

3. Father (child) — Much older; shivering, shaking, teeth chattering
   Location — Sitting at table in parlor, like a child, reading a book

4. Father (toddler) — Trying to smoke a pipe, hands shaking, huddled up
   Location — Sitting on settle

5. Father (infant) — Old, old man, no sign of life, but big pair of eyes
   Location — Lying in bed

---

*In Asbjornsen and Moe 1960.

6. Father (newborn) — Ancient old man, no bigger than a baby, shriveled up
    Location — Lying in cradle

7. Father (fetus) — Little ash-white form with likeness of human face
    Location — In horn hanging on wall

Resolution — Last father gives permission. Problem solved.

Conclusion — Traveler is well fed and given a comfortable place to sleep.

This story is not cyclic — the last event does not bring the characters back to their beginning circumstances. On the other hand, it is a story about a life cycle. As the traveler speaks to each older father in the sequence, the description of each subsequent father reverses the aging process, the chosen metaphor providing the image of a younger and younger person. The paradox the story presents through the use of both (direct) forward and (implicit) reverse cumulative has to do with the relativity of youth and age. The "oldest" father is both oldest and youngest. The "youngest" father is both youngest and oldest. Younger audiences can enjoy the language play in the story and participate in chanting the ritual greetings, questions, and answers. More mature audiences can appreciate the double cumulative play — young to old and old to young — and the message thus delivered regarding the life cycle. "The Seventh Father of the House" is a fine example of a cumulative-type story that employs a simple (cumulative) structural formula to make a profound statement and that uses the device of cumulative play to create levels of recognition and enjoyment for audiences of varied levels of maturity. It provides something for everyone.

Other type A cumulative stories include:

"The Lad Who Made the Princess Say 'You're a Liar' " (Asbjornsen and Moe 1960)

"Taper Tom, Who Made the Princess Laugh" (ibid.)

"The Ram and the Pig Who Went into the Woods to Live by Themselves" (ibid.)

"The Hare Who Had Been Married" (ibid.)

"Hans in Luck" (*New Wonder World* 1951)

"Prudent Hans" (ibid.)

"Clever Else" (ibid.)

"Wali Dad the Simple-Hearted" (Lang 1949)

"The Great Bear" (Jablow and Withers 1969)

"The Separation of God from Man" (Bollinger 1964)

"One Trick Too Many" (Ginsburg 1973)

"Usha, the Mouse Maiden" (Gobhai 1969)

"Stone Soup" (Brown 1947)

"How Soko Brought Debt to Ashanti" (Courlander and Herzog 1947)

"The Tinker and the Ghost" (Johnson et al. 1977)

"The Husband Who Was to Mind the House" (ibid.)

"Wee Robin's Christmas Day" (Literature Committee 1950)

"Squintums" (ibid.)

"Epaminondas" (Merriam, 1968)

Type B Cumulative—Winding and Unwinding

The difference between cumulative types A and B lies in the endings of the stories. While the type A story often describes a circle and does not include a relisting of all the accumulated items in the sequence, the type B story unwinds the added events by repeating or naming each in either forward or reverse order in the last event. "The Cow-Tail Switch" (Courlander and Herzog 1947), "The Silly Goose War" (Johnson et al. 1977), and "Master of All Masters" (ibid.) illustrate the type. Many type B cumulative stories are not cyclic; the unwinding at the end of the story, rather than the completion of a circle, signals the end. The type B cumulative, like the type A, does not include repetitive exercises during the listing of items in the event sequence. The cumulative effect is achieved through a piling up of items or incidences that, in the end, will have some collective impact. Sample outlines for the three type B cumulative stories mentioned here follow.

THE COW-TAIL SWITCH*

Setting—Liberian rainforest, hill overlooking Cavally River, Kundi village

Events in setting category 1 (a short series of events, narrated without elaboration to set stage for problem)

1. Ogaloussa, father of six sons, goes hunting.
2. Fails to return.

---

*In Courlander and Herzog 1947.

3. Eventually family and village forget about him.

4. Puli, a seventh son, is born to Ogaloussa's wife.

5. Puli learns to talk.

6. Puli asks, "Where is my father?"

7. Ogaloussa's older sons search for and find Ogaloussa.

Problem 1—Ogaloussa is dead. Sons must use their special powers to restore him.

Event sequence 1

1. First son puts bones together.

2. Second son covers bones with sinews and flesh.

3. Third son puts blood into body.

4. Fourth son puts breath into body.

5. Fifth son puts power of movement into body.

6. Sixth son gives power of speech to body.

Resolution 1—Through sons' cumulative effort, Ogaloussa is restored to life.

Conclusion 1—Ogaloussa and sons go home.

Events in setting category 2

1. Ogaloussa, wife, family, and village celebrate.

2. Observation of ritual and ceremony.

3. Making of the cow-tail switch.

4. Ogaloussa's use of same.

5. People covet same.

6. Ogaloussa says he will give switch to son who did most to restore him to life and bring him home.

7. Argument ensues.

Problem 2—There are seven sons (including Puli), but only one switch. Which son most deserves to have it?

Event sequence 2—Sons argue. Each asserts his claims to switch.

Repeat language

First son says, "It was I who gave him bones. I deserve it most!"

Repeat for all sons except Puli, substituting number of son and what was given for each.

1. First son
2. Second son
3. Third son
4. Fourth son
5. Fifth son
6. Sixth son

Resolution 2—Ogaloussa gives switch to Puli.

Conclusion 2—If Puli had not asked about his father, no one would have remembered him and searched for him.

Moral—A man is not really dead until he is forgotten.

"The Cow-Tail Switch" is built around two problems. The solution to the first problem is described using the winding-up cumulative device. Each of the sons contributes to the restoration of their father. The additive effect of their separate powers brings Ogaloussa back to life. The solution to the second problem involves the employment of the unwinding device. In order to determine which son will receive the gift of the switch, the separate powers of each of the six sons must be examined in isolation, hence the repeat of all six, resulting in the unwinding. The audience understands the unwinding especially as it contrasts with the winding. Not one of the powers of the six sons alone was sufficient to restore Ogaloussa. The accumulation was necessary. The unwinding reminds us that the whole is greater than the sum of its parts.

The two problems in the story are bound together logically in part through the employment of the cumulative devices of winding and unwinding. Even though the two problems are quite different, each is resolved by cumulative organization of story content (problem 1 winds and problem 2 unwinds the same information). "Anansi the Spider" (McDermott 1972), a very similar story, also uses the combination of winding and unwinding devices to lend coherence to a two-problem story.

THE SILLY GOOSE WAR*

Setting—Man has wife as silly as a goose.

Events in setting category
1. Man finds large pot of money.
2. Tells wife.
3. Wife tells baron.
4. Baron summons man, demands the pot of money.

Problem—How to undo what is done and convince the baron that there never was a pot of money.

Event sequence (winding, but with different actions in each event)
1. Man invents Silly Goose War. Prepares his wife to conduct the war. Pretends to save wife.
2. On way to see baron, man tosses bagel over wife's head—wife concludes it is raining bagels.
3. Come upon dog howling inside barn. Man insists it is devil torturing baron.
4. Arrive at baron's.
5. Baron demands pot of money.

Resolution (unwinding)
1. Man denies existence of money.
2. Wife questioned.
3. She claims that money was found:
   a. A week before Silly Goose War.
   b. Which was on the night it rained bagels.
   c. Which was when she and husband heard devil torturing baron in the barn.
4. Baron drives man and wife from house.

Conclusion—Man is able to keep money for himself.

In "The Silly Goose War," the cumulative is used to solve one problem. The winding is the sequence of events or actions undertaken by the main

---

*In Johnson et al. 1977.

character to solve his problem. The unwinding is the solution to the problem. During the winding, each addition to the cumulative is handled as a single story event. The unwinding presents all three items in the cumulative within the framework of a single event.

MASTER OF ALL MASTERS*

Setting: Events in setting category

1. Girl goes to fair to hire out as servant.
2. Old gentleman engages her.
3. Takes her home.
4. Teaches her household terminology.

Winding begins.

Each item with "What would you call [item]?"

Girl answers using two possible common names.

Gentleman provides his peculiar name.

Repeat language

Gentleman: What would you call [item]?

Girl: [Name], or [name], or whatever you please, sir.

Gentleman: No, you must call this [name].

a. Item: The master
   She: Master or mister
   He: Master of all masters

b. Item: Bed
   She: Bed or couch
   He: Barnacle

c. Item: Pantaloons
   She: Breeches or trousers
   He: Squibs and crackers

d. Item: Cat
   She: Cat or kit
   He: White-faced simminy

---

*In Johnson et al. 1977.

e. Item: Fire
   She: Fire or flame
   He: Hot cockalorum

f. Item: Water
   She: Water or wet
   He: Pondalorum

g. Item: House
   She: House or cottage
   He: High topper mountain

Problem—House catches on fire. Girl must warn her master.

Event sequence (unwinding)—Girl says, "Master of all masters, get out of your barnacle and put on your squibs and crackers, for white-faced simminy has got a spark of hot cockalorum on her tail, and, unless you get some pondalorum, high topper mountain will be all hot cockalorum."

Resolution—none

Conclusion—none

"Master of All Masters" uses nonsense language play as well as winding and unwinding to make a game of the cumulative device. It is told quickly, precisely, and contains little action. Since the problem is, in effect, a punch line with no resolution, the winding occurs in the setting category. The unwinding merely describes the problem. We never do discover whether or not the master and servant can use such nonsense language to keep the house from burning down. But, then, the outcome is of little concern, since the game played in the story is the point of the tale. We feel no need to resolve the problem.

Other type B cumulative stories include:

"The Princess Who Always Had to Have the Last Word" (Asbjornsen and Moe 1960)

"Good Day, Fellow!" "Axe Handle!" (ibid.)

"The Ash Lad and the Good Helpers" (ibid.)

"Gudbrand of the Hillside" (ibid.)

"Happy-Go-Lucky" (Wiesner 1972)

"Dauntless Little John" (Calvino 1980)

"The Little Girl Sold with the Pears" (ibid.)

"The Land Where One Never Dies" (ibid.)

"The Feathered Ogre" (ibid.)

"How Thunder Makes the Lightning" (Jablow and Withers 1969)

"How Spider Obtained the Sky God's Stories" (Bollinger 1964)

"If Someone Does Good to You, You Should Do Good in Return" (ibid.)

"The Brementown Musicians" (Johnson et al. 1977)

"The Ram and the Pig Who Went into the Woods" (ibid.)

"The Flying Ship" (Literature Committee 1950)

"The Tree That Flew" (Belting 1953)

Type C Cumulative — Repetitive-Winding and Unwinding

The third type of cumulative formula adds the device of repetition to the additive (winding) part of the story. "The Tabby Who Was Such a Glutton" (Asbjornsen and Moe 1960), "The Fat Cat" (Kent 1971), and "The Cat and the Parrot" (Johnson et al. 1977) — all the same story — are good examples of the repetitive-winding and unwinding type pattern.

THE TABBY WHO WAS SUCH A GLUTTON*

Setting — Man on farm with large, gluttonous tabby.

Problem — Man can no longer afford to feed cat. Decides to drop her into river with rope around her neck.

Event sequence — In each event, the cat eats someone or something else. Each event is identical, but for the substitution of the new item to be eaten and the lengthening list of items to be repeated.

Repeat language

Tabby:	Good day to you, [name of new person].
Person:	Good day to you, tabby. Have you had any food today?
Tabby:	Oh, I've eaten a little today, but I'm almost fasting. I've only had [cumulative list — new item added with each new event], and hey-hey if I don't take you, too!
Narrator:	And then she went and gobbled [name of new person] up.

---

*In Asbjornsen and Moe 1960.

1. Tabby eats a bowl of porridge and a little trough of drippings, escapes by jumping out window, finds old man in barn threshing.

2. **Repetitive Winding** begins.

     Tabby: Good day to you, man of the house.

     Man: Good day to you, tabby. Have you had any food today?

     Tabby: Oh, I've eaten a little today, but I'm almost fasting. I've only had a bowl of porridge and a little trough of drippings, and hey-hey if I don't take you, too.

     Narrator: And then she went and gobbled the man up. (Tabby goes to cowshed—finds old woman milking.)

3. Repeat to eat old woman.

4. Repeat to eat bell cow.
    (Goes to home pasture.)

5. Repeat for man chopping branches.
    (Goes to rock pile.)

6. Repeat for stoat.
    (Goes to hazel bush.)

7. Repeat for squirrel.
    (Goes to edge of woods.)

8. Repeat for fox.

9. Repeat for hare.

10. Repeat for wolf.

11. Repeat for bear cub.

12. Repeat for she-bear.

13. Repeat for he-bear.

14. Repeat for bridal procession.

15. Repeat for funeral procession.

16. Repeat for moon.

17. Repeat for sun.

18. Repeat for billy goat. **Final winding**—"Oh, I've had a little, but I'm almost fasting," said the tabby. "I've only had a bowl of porridge, a little trough of drippings, and the man of the house, and the woman in the cowshed, and the bell cow in the stall, and the branch-chopper in the home pasture, and the stoat in the rockpile, and the squirrel in the bush, and Slypaws the Fox, and Hoppity Hare, and Glutton

Greylegs, and Frisky Bear, and Snappish She-Bear, and Bruin Fine Fellow, and the bridal procession on the road, and the funeral procession by the church, and the moon in the sky, and the sun in the heavens, and hey-hey if I don't take you, too."

Goat: You'll have to fight me first.

Resolution (unwinding)

1. Goat butts tabby off bridge and into river.

2. Tabby bursts open.

3. All items eaten come out in forward order (i.e., the bowl of porridge first).

Conclusion—none

The focus of the story is on the game of additive repetition. The object for the audience is to be able to keep up with the teller by holding the increasingly long list in memory and by joining in on the repeat with each new event.

The repetitive-winding and unwinding type of pattern extends language and memory play directly to the audience through repetitious and ritual language, action, chanting, and memory building. The cumulative effect is direct and tangible with each new event, rather than implicit as in cumulative types A and B. With each repetition, the audience confirms the growing collection of items by active chanting of a longer and longer list. The conventional ending is the unwinding, usually also the solution to the problem. Some repetitive-winding and unwinding stories do tell a circular tale in which the main character returns to his or her original state of being at story end. The hungry cat stories are all cyclic.

Such stories are games embedded in story frames as much as they are a chronologically sequenced series of events. The more general conventions of "story" (setting, problem, conclusion) seem often to be employed primarily as devices for setting up the game. The joy and challenge for the audience is in the collective, mutual play more than in predicting direction of action and plot. Outcome in the repetitive-winding and unwinding cumulative story is highly predictable, precisely because the structural formula is so restrictive. The game is the repetitive winding as much or more than it is the story.

Audience participation in the repetitive-winding and unwinding story is often almost total. The audience, in effect, tells the story along with the teller. The chanting of repetitive-winding lists provides a play situation in which everyone can win—by learning the sequence. There are no penalties for not getting the whole list in the first encounter with the story. Audiences often ask for a story again, initially for list memorization, later to confirm their control of the cumulative and to play with its linguistic and paralinguistic elements.

Other type C cumulative stories include:

"Fourteen Hundred Cowries" (Fuja 1971)

"La Hormiguita" (The Little Ant) (Hayes 1982)

"The Old Woman and Her Pig" (Johnson et al. 1977)

Type D Cumulative — Repetitive- Winding, Non-unwinding

The last type of cumulative uses the repetitive device during winding but does not unwind at the end of the story. Like the type A pattern, this formula finishes the story with the full list in the last repetition and often completes a cycle. "The Three Goats" (Literature Committee 1950) ends with all elements in the list added together but not unwound. "The Pancake" (Johnson et al. 1977) works in the same manner and is cyclic.

THE PANCAKE*

Setting: Events in setting category

1. Woman bakes a pancake for her seven children.

2. Each begs a taste

   Repeat language (contains short, cumulative, repetitive-winding sequence)

First bairn:	Oh, give me a bit of the pancake, mother dear; I am so hungry.
Second bairn:	Oh, darling mother . . .
Third bairn:	Oh, darling, good mother . . .
Fourth bairn:	Oh, darling, good, nice mother . . .
Fifth bairn:	Oh, darling, pretty, good, nice mother . . .
Sixth bairn:	Oh, darling, pretty, good, nice, clever . . .
Seventh bairn:	Oh, darling, pretty, good, nice, clever, sweet . . .

3. Woman promises each a bit of pancake.

4. Pancake overhears, becomes afraid.

5. Pancake jumps from pan, runs (rolls) away.

Problem — For the woman and her children, to retrieve the pancake.

For the pancake, to escape certain demise.

---

*In Johnson et al. 1977.

Event sequence

1. Woman, children, and her husband give chase.

2. They yell, "Whoa, stop!" but the pancake is too fast for them.

3. **Repetitive winding** begins.

   a. Pancake rolls until it meets a man.

Man:	Good day, pancake.
Pancake:	God bless you, Manny Panny.
Man:	Dear pancake, don't roll so fast; stop a little and let me eat you.
Pancake:	When I have given the slip to Goody Poody, and the Goodman, and seven squalling children, I may well slip through your fingers. Pancake rolls on and on until it meets a hen (Henny Penny).

   b. Repeat for Henny Penny. Add Manny Panny to cumulative list. Recite entire list in forward order.

   c. Repeat for Cocky Locky. Add Henny Penny.

   d. Repeat for Ducky Lucky. Add Cocky Locky.

   e. Repeat for Goosey Poosey. Add Ducky Lucky.

   f. Repeat for Gander Pander. Add Goosey Poosey.

   g. Repeat for Piggy Wiggy, to "God bless you, Piggy Wiggy." Then pancake rolls on rapidly.

4. Piggy Wiggy calls after pancake, offers to travel along to insure pancake's safety.

5. They enter a wood and come to a stream, which the pancake cannot cross.

6. Pig offers to swim pancake across.

Resolution—Pig swims pancake to center of stream, eats pancake. (In some versions, pig tells pancake to climb on his back, then begins swimming. When in water, tells pancake to climb to his head, as water is getting deeper; then to snout; then flips pancake into his mouth.)

Conclusion

Narrator:	. . . and the poor pancake could go no further. Why—this story can go no further either.

Like the type C cumulative, story action in type D is often limited. The game is the repetitive-winding play, the chanting, the high degree of story shape predictability, and audience control over the story through ritual interaction. The great sense of satisfaction audiences often experience from participation in the repetitive-winding type of cumulative story grows out of their ownership of the story and the collective, community ritual the story provides.

Other type D cumulative stories include:

"The Pot of Marjoram" (Calvino 1980)

"Master Rabbit and the Berries" (Bollinger 1964)

"Talk" (Courlander and Herzog 1947)

"The Ferryman" (Hardendorf 1968)

"Why Mosquitoes Buzz in People's Ears" (Aardema 1975)

"The Three Goats" (Literature Committee 1950)

Cumulatives Combined with Other Structures

Some stories employ the cumulative device embedded within a more complicated pattern that also utilizes other structural formulas. "The Tinker and the Ghost" (Johnson et al. 1977) contains a type A cumulative (winding only) pattern embedded in a larger and quite different, chronological story structure.

THE TINKER AND THE GHOST*

Setting: Events in setting category

1. Esteban, a tinker, listens to goodwives' story about haunted castle (castle and what befalls those who go there are described).

2. Learns of reward offered by castle owner for staying all night in castle on All Hallows Eve.

3. Accepts dare to stay in castle on that night.

4. Lists his requirements — food, etc.

5. Wives bring him supplies.

Problem — To last the night.

---

*In Johnson et al. 1977.

Event sequence

1. Esteban goes to castle, moves supplies in, builds a fire, gets comfortable, begins to fry bacon and drink wine.

2. **Cumulative sequence** begins.

   a. Thin voice begins to wail, "Oh me! Oh me! Oh me!"
   Voice and Esteban talk. Esteban continues to cook. Voice cries, "Look out below! I'm falling!" Man's leg falls onto hearth with thump.

   b. Esteban continues to cook and eat. Voice again, dialogue and description. Second leg falls.

   c. Same—trunk falls.

   d. Same—two arms fall.

   e. Same—head falls.

   f. Body assembles itself.

   For each new event in the cumulative, the teller must learn a somewhat new dialogue and remember changes in voice, new items that Esteban is eating and cooking, and articles of clothing on the various falling body parts. The only cumulative structure is the falling of and assembling of the body itself.

3. Esteban and ghost talk. Ghost explains that Esteban is first man to stay beyond the falling of the limbs.

4. Ghost explains his predicament.

5. Ghost asks Esteban to help free him, save his soul, and allow him to enter heaven.

6. Esteban and ghost go out to courtyard and there dig for three bags of money.

7. Esteban follows ghost's instructions—removes ghost's clothing.

Resolution—Ghost disappears; Esteban spends peaceful night in castle. Villagers find Esteban eating next morning. He shows them evidence (clothing) of ghost's disappearance, loads moneybags on donkey, and walks away.

Conclusion—Esteban collects 1,000 gold *reales* in reward from the lord of the castle; gives copper coins in first moneybag to church, silver coins in second to the poor, and keeps the gold coins in the third along with the 1,000 *reales*. He lives in idleness and great contentment for many years.

Most of the events leading to problem solution in "The Tinker and the Ghost" are arranged in a noncumulative, nonrepetitive simple chronology. The language, both descriptive and dialogue, is different in each event. The cumulative device is used within the chronology to build the body of the ghost; it does not constitute the whole of the event sequence. Such a story makes use of two types of story structure. Here, the teller learns a chronology, then remembers a cumulative sequence embedded within it.

We might safely assume that the cumulative device is a very old, early form of discourse structure, invented in response to a natural need to remember lists or chains of happenings or items. The cumulative device itself is not a story, but something contained within "story." The added elements of setting, problem, resolution, and conclusion are a "story frame" into which the cumulative is set. Cumulative stories, then, are highly conventionalized formulas or patterns for saving related, additive sequences of information in memory. They are mostly memorized lists, chains, or strings of similar "bits," fixed for memory within the formal structure of repeated language, chanting, and play, then "framed" within "story" to provide a more global sensibility and shared reference.

The repetitive-winding cumulative types (C and D), in which teller and participants add and chant back all elements within a lengthening sequence, are rehearsal procedures that many of us use to memorize any sequence of related information. The conventional form that we now call cumulative may have evolved from such deliberate, intentional memory-making activity, becoming a literary institution (in the structural sense) designed to aid memorization when written language did not exist.

The primitive beginnings of "story" and play with elements within "story" may be somehow associated with necessary, early list making and deliberate rehearsals of information to insure the retention of information in memory and to provide for information retrieval. Even more primitive cumulative forms can be overheard in the language play and crib talk of very young children (Cazden 1975). Perhaps the cumulative form is a reflection of a developmental stage of human brain organization. Cumulative orderings of information would, then, be expected, predictable, and "sensible." "Story" embedded cumulative orderings would seem to be a natural evolution, with the cumulative device – probably the older form – finding a useful place within the newer structure or organizational framework of "story."

Such a hypothesis might account for the widespread use of and general recognition of cumulative stories. Stories that employ cumulative devices have a special appeal for audiences of all ages and cultures. We all "know" these stories, somehow. Even very young children, who have not yet realized "story," will recognize, participate in, and delight in the cumulative play within stories.

Evidence suggests that cumulative structure is very old, is a memory device that is in widespread use, and most likely preceded the evolution of "story" itself. When we tell or participate in cumulative stories, we experience and play with something organizational that is ancient, and that may be a common feature of "mind."

The Event-Repeat Sequence Type

Like cumulative stories, stories patterned on repeated events operate according to a strict set of rules. They are also highly conventionalized and therefore very predictable. Like other types of stories, event-repeat stories employ the required qualifying features of "story" — setting, problem, sequence of events, resolution, and conclusion. Within the sequence of events, however, this type of story organization requires the use of only one event, told again and again, which contains essentially the same language and internal structure in each repeat.

Most event-repeat stories contain more action (plot) than the cumulative types, though the repetitive nature of story organization still provides for a significant degree of audience participation and play. Some such stories prescribe the number of times the event must be repeated before the problem is resolved. The teller must be especially sensitive to audience tolerance and interest when telling an event-repeat story in which the number of repeats is not a given. Audiences understand, from personal experience, that some problems are best solved by sheer persistence — that a problem may have one viable solution, but that impact on the problem can only be achieved by deliberate reiteration of that single action. They don't, however, always have to hear twenty-five repeats of the same event during a telling to fully appreciate the significance of the action.

Two common types of event-repeat configurations are identifiable in familiar stories. In both, the same action is repeated over and over to arrive at the problem's solution. And both use the event itself as a slot into which to fit story content — here action. The less complicated no-substitution event-repeat story makes no changes or substitutions within the event but simply employs the same collection of linguistic and paralinguistic features in each new repeat. In the substitution type of event-repeat story, some degree of content change is inserted into slots within the event itself, but the overall shape of the event is not disturbed.

The No-Substitution Event Repeat

Simple no-substitution event-repeat stories maintain the strictest adherence to form during the sequence of events. The exact language (both narration and dialogue), sounds, motions, and other paralinguistic effects remain identical from one repeat of the event to the next. The teller's task involves learning the single event, learning how to accommodate entry into the sequence of event repetitions from the event or events in which the problem is established, learning how to exit the repetitious sequence for problem solution, and determining how many event repeats are necessary to carry the story. (This last consideration is not left to teller discretion in stories in which the event-repeat number is prescribed. If event-repeat numbers are to be set by the teller, audience attention and tolerance become an important factor.)

"The Hedgehog and the Hare" (Grimm and Grimm 1969) is a strict event-repeat type of story in which a hedgehog and his wife together manage to win a race against a hare by exhausting him with repeat performances of the same effective strategy. Story narration develops the action or strategy fully only a few times (the number is left to the teller's discretion); the audience is then informed that the two hedgehogs repeated the same action seventy-seven times more before winning the race. The audience has the opportunity to play with the repetition in the several complete event narrations provided by the teller but is spared the intolerable exercise of suffering through seventy-seven more fully expanded event repeats.

"The Gunniwolf" (Harper 1967) is similar. A girl must escape from a wolf. She solves her problem by acting out a sequence of identical escape/run/get caught/fool the wolf/escape events. For the sake of maintaining audience interest and willing participation, the repeated event is best given expanded narration three to four times between the establishment and solution of the problem. Audience understanding that the girl probably has to run away from the wolf more than four times is implicit.

THE HEDGEHOG AND THE HARE*

Setting: Events in setting category

1. Hedgehog meets hare; they exchange greetings.

2. Hare makes rude comments about hedgehog's legs.

3. Hedgehog boasts of his running capacities despite legs.

4. Hare disputes hedgehog's claims, and a wager is made.

5. Time and place for a race is set.

Problem—Hedgehog must beat the hare in a race or lose both self-respect and the wagered prize.

Event sequence

1. Hedgehog returns home to explain problem and his solution to his wife. (Before cooperating, she has some pointed comments to make regarding her husband's behavior.)

2. Wife removes apron, both go to site for race, a furrowed field.

3. Wife hides in furrow at one end of field; hedgehog stands in same furrow at other end.

---

*In Grimm and Grimm 1969.

4. Hare arrives, stands in furrow adjacent to hedgehog.

5. Hare and hedgehog agree to race down the two furrows to opposite end of the field.

Event repeat begins.

    a. Race begins.

    b. Hare actually runs the distance; hedgehog merely ducks down.

    c. Just as hare arrives at distant end of furrow, wife stands up— shouts, "I'm here already!"

    d. Hare is stunned—dialogue ensues.

    e. Hare and hedgehog's wife agree to run the race again, up the furrow.

Event repeat—Hare arrives at hedgehog's furrow end.

Event repeat—Hare arrives at wife's furrow end.

6. Narration—Hare runs seventy-seven times more.

Resolution—Hare is exhausted; hedgehog wins wager.

Conclusion—Hedgehog and wife go home to enjoy fruits of their efforts.

Moral (sometimes implicit)—Wit is often more important than physical size, shape, or strength, and careless boasting sometimes brings misfortune.

THE GUNNIWOLF*

Setting: Events in setting category

1. Girl setting off to pick flowers in meadow is warned by mother to stay away from woods. (Description of meadow and woods is included.)

    a. Mother describes wolf and danger of being eaten.

    b. Mother tells girl that if ever confronted by wolf, she is to stand still and say "I no move!"

    c. Girl promises obedience, goes to pick flowers, sings as she picks.

    d. Description of flower picking; audience participation in action and accompanying song.

---

*In Harper 1967.

2. Event 1 repeated with addition:
    e. Girl forgets warning, picks flowers deep into woods.
    f. Girl becomes lost in woods.
3. Wolf also in woods; smells girl, runs to her.

Problem — Girl is confronted by wolf and in danger. How to escape?

Event sequence

Event repeat begins.

1. Girl remembers mother's directions and stands still.
2. Wolf asks girl why she does not move.
3. Girl gives "I no move!" response.
4. Wolf asks girl to sing her song again.
5. Girl sings; wolf falls asleep.
6. Girl sees wolf asleep, runs away.
7. Wolf realizes girl has escaped; gives chase.
8. Wolf confronts girl.
9. Girl remembers mother's directions and stands still.

Event repeat (number of times left to teller's discretion)

Final (escape) event — extend chase portion of event.

Resolution — Girl outruns wolf; arrives home safely.

Conclusion — Teller discretion.

The Substitution-Type Event Repeat

The substitution type of event-repeat story also achieves problem solution by sheer weight of activity. The character or characters succeed as a direct result of doggedly consistent responses to the problem. However, the repeated event in the substitution-type story itself contains prescribed slots into which a slightly different content is substituted with each repeated event. In "The Wide-Mouthed Frog," the event is repeated five times. With each repeat, the name of an animal and the answer to the frog's question is changed. In "The Three Billy Goats Gruff" (Asbjornsen and Moe 1960) the event is repeated three times. Slots within the event that take substitutions are those naming the size of the goat and the goat's responses to the troll. "The Five Chinese

Brothers" (Bishop 1938) presents its event four times. Substitution slots allow for changing the prescribed mode of execution, the number of the brother returning to be executed, and the reason for his subsequent survival.

The substitution type of event repeat still qualifies as an event-repeat type because the single repeated event remains structurally the same from one repeat to the next, because the single event acts as a miniframe (within "story") into which specific information can be slotted, and because the information slotted (substituted) from one event repeat to the next is of the same category (e.g., the first slot in the repeated event in "The Wide-Mouthed Frog" always takes the name of an animal). Memory development for this type of story structure involves learning the shape of the event, learning the slots into which substitutions are made within the event, learning the categories of information prescribed for each substitution slot, and, finally, learning the specific information substituted for each new event repeat. The teller also learns precisely how many event repeats are given in the story. Usually the substitution type of story structure does not leave the number of event repeats to the discretion of the teller.

THE HUNGRY SPIDER AND TURTLE*

Episode 1

Setting: Events in setting category 1

1. Turtle, out walking, meets spider.

2. Spider invites turtle to lunch.

3. Spider loads table with food.

4. Spider invites turtle to eat, but then notices turtle's dirty feet.

Problem 1 — Turtle must go down the path and across the road to the stream to wash his feet before eating. While turtle washes his feet (he is very slow) spider eats part of the lunch.

Event sequence 1

Event repeat begins.

1. Turtle and spider sit down to eat.

2. Both shake out napkins, pick up silver, etc.

3. Spider notices turtle's feet.

---

*In Courlander and Herzog 1947.

Repeat language

> Spider: Turtle, look at your feet! They are dirty! It's a rule
>   in my house that we eat with clean feet!
>
> (Turtle looks at his feet.)
>
> Turtle: They are dirty. I will have to go wash them.

4. Turtle lumbers out door, down path, over road to stream, washes his feet, then returns.

5. When turtle returns, spider has eaten fully one-quarter of the food that had been on the table.

6. Turtle replaces napkin, picks up silver, prepares to begin eating.

7. Spider notices turtle's feet.

Repeat event three times more.

Substitutions

Slot 3, each repeat — Turtle's response to spider's insistence that he wash his feet becomes increasingly frustrated and irritated. His voice becomes louder: "But I *did* wash my feet!"

Slot 3 — Add narration — turtle lays down silver, places napkin on table.

Slot 3, each repeat — Substitute "Well, but they are still dirty. I will go wash them again" for "They are dirty. I will have to go wash them."

Slot 5, first repeat — Spider has eaten one-half of all of the food.

> second repeat — three-fourths of food
>
> third repeat — all of food

End event repeat.

Resolution 1 — Spider has tricked turtle.

Conclusion 1 — Turtle thanks spider for hospitality and promises to return the favor.

Episode 2

Setting: Events in setting category 2

1. Spider, out walking, meets turtle.

2. Turtle invites spider to lunch.

3. Turtle lives at bottom of a pond.

Problem 2 — Spider must get to bottom of pond to eat, but he is too light. The surface tension of the water prevents him from breaking the surface and swimming down to turtle's table.

Event sequence 2

Event repeat begins.

1. Spider can see food on turtle's table, and he is very hungry.
2. Spider climbs onto rock, leaps into water.
3. He is too light. He cannot break surface of water.
4. Spider runs around on water's surface watching turtle eat.
5. Turtle eats fully one-quarter of the food on the table.

Repeat event three times more.

Substitutions

Slot 5, first repeat — Turtle eats one-half of the food on the table.

second repeat — three-fourths

third repeat — all

Slot 2, third repeat — Spider fills his pockets with rocks.

Slot 3, third repeat — Now spider is heavy enough to sink to the bottom of the pond.

Slot 4, third repeat — Spider sits at table, shakes out napkin, picks up silver, prepares to eat. Turtle says, "It is a rule in my house, Spider, that we take our coats off to eat at the table." Spider takes off coat; is now weightless and pops to surface.

Slot 5, third repeat — Turtle eats all remaining food.

Resolution 2 — Turtle has tricked spider.

Conclusion 2 — Turtle finishes eating, swims to surface, and informs spider that he was delighted to have had the opportunity to return the favor. Justice is served.

Moral (at teller's discretion) — Turnabout is fair play.

The teller will notice the embedded nature of the story. Two episodes bring the interplay of trickery and justice full circle. The first episode concludes with an injustice, and audiences generally expect resolution of such injustice. Hence they are ready for the second episode. Without it, the story would not make sense. Each episode is a repeat of the other, with specific changes and substitutions within, and with the roles of the two characters reversed. The event repeats are embedded in the event sequences within the episodes. Though both episodes are framed by whole-story structure, a larger framework exists to bind the episodes into a coherent whole. The first conclusion poses the larger, implicit problem having to do with justice. The second conclusion satisfies audience expectation for retribution and resolution in the face of foul play.

THE BEETLE'S HAIRPIECE*

Setting: Events in setting category

1. Beetle scavenges food on outskirts of Hopi village of Oriabi.
2. Is caught by village children.
3. Suffers their taunts and jokes concerning his baldness.
4. Escapes and returns home in shame.

Problem—Beetle thinks that to be accepted by people in village, and to respect himself, he must have hair.

Event sequence

1. Beetle finds deer hide in forest.
2. Brings hide home, removes hair from hide.

Event repeat begins.

3. a. Beetle fixes deer hair to self with sticky gum from a tree.
    b. Goes to Oriabi.
    c. Children recognize beetle, realize what he has done.
    d. Children taunt and make jokes.
    e. Children strip sticky gum from beetle's back and chew it.
    f. Beetle returns home in shame.

Substitutions

First repeat
    Slot 3a — White sap from cactus
    Slot 3b — Same as original event, and sap dries and cracks in
             sun

*In Courlander 1970.

Slots 3c-3d — Same as original event

Slot 3e — Omit

Slot 3f — Same as original event

Second repeat

Slot 3a — Beetle finds coyote hide and pine tar. Fixes coyote hair to self with tar. (He wishes to go to the dance at Oriabi.)

Slot 3b — Attaches hairs night before dance. Goes to sleep. Night cold hardens tar. Beetle is stuck to ground.

Slot 3c — Beetle cannot get up in morning to go to Oriabi, because he is glued to the ground with pine tar.

Slot 3d — Beetle can hear singing and dancing, but is immobilized.

Slot 3e — Afternoon sun softens tar, frees beetle.

Slot 3f — Beetle is shamed by his foolishness.

Resolution — Beetle decides that he is better off without hair.

Conclusion — Beetle cleans himself, climbs to top of his house, and declares that beetles were meant to be bald.

Narrator: "And ever since then, that is the way it has been."

"The Beetle's Hairpiece" requires substantial substitution of content from one event to the next. The last event, in particular, takes many additional changes, since it is the event from which the resolution emerges. Still, each of the three events presents the same attempt at problem solution. The beetle does not solve his problem as a result of persistence, however. The audience is aware from the beginning of the tale that he must rethink his basic assumptions. Some attempts to solve a problem, if they are ineffective approaches, cannot help no matter how many times they are repeated. This story uses the event-repeat device to remind us that we must sometimes examine and change the problem-solving strategy itself.

MOLLY WHUPPIE*

Setting: Events in setting category

1. Poor family cannot feed children.

2. Parents abandon three youngest (girls) in woods.

3. Youngest and cleverest of three is Molly Whuppie.

Problem—Girls must survive. They are homeless, cold, and hungry.

Event sequence

Episode 1 (chronological, leading into repeated sequence)

Setting 1

1. Girls travel.

2. At dusk, come to house.

3. Beg woman of house to let them in, feed them.

4. She does so, but protests—her husband is a giant. If he finds them, he will eat them.

5. While they are eating, he comes home.

6. Woman protects girls, but giant insists they stay the night.

7. Puts them to bed with his three daughters.

8. Ties straw ropes around their necks.

9. Puts gold chains around his daughters' necks.

Problem 1—Giant intends to harm Molly and her sisters.

Event sequence 1

1. Molly suspects a trick—stays awake.

2. Switches the straw ropes and chains.

3. Giant kills own daughters.

Resolution 1—Molly and sisters escape to king's house.

Event repeat begins.

Episode 2

1. Molly tells king about adventure with giant.

2. King asks Molly to return, to steal giant's sword. Promises to marry his eldest son to her eldest sister if she succeeds.

---

*In Johnson et al. 1977.

Problem 2—Molly must get back into giant's house, take sword, and escape.

Event sequence 2

1. Molly returns, hides under giant's bed.
2. Takes sword; it rattles and wakes giant.
3. Giant chases Molly.

Resolution 2

1. Molly escapes.
2. Molly gives sword to king.

Conclusion 2—Molly's eldest sister is married to king's eldest son.

Episode 3

Setting 3—Same as setting 2; substitute purse for sword, second sister and second king's son.

Problem 3—Same as problem 2; substitute purse for sword.

Event sequence 3

1. Same as event sequence 2.
2. Same as event sequence 2; substitute purse.
3. Same as event sequence 2.

Resolution 3—Same as resolution 2; substitute purse.

Conclusion 3—Same as conclusion 2; substitute second sister and second king's son.

Episode 4

Setting 4—Same as setting 2; substitute ring, Molly and youngest king's son.

Problem 4—Same as problem 2; substitute ring.

Event sequence 4

1. Same as event sequence 2.
2. Same as event sequence 2; substitute ring.
3. Giant catches Molly.

Event repeat ends.

Episode 5 (chronological, leading to problem resolution)

Setting 5—Same as setting 2.

Problem 5—Molly must escape from giant.

Event sequence 5

1. Giant asks Molly what she would do with him if their circumstances were reversed.
2. She answers that she would put him in sack with dog, cat, scissors, needle, and thread and hang him on wall, then go into woods, get stick, and beat sack.
3. Giant takes suggestion.
4. Molly tricks wife into exchanging places.
5. Wife climbs into sack.
6. Giant returns, beats wife in sack.
7. Discovers mistake, chases Molly.

Resolution 5—Molly escapes, gives ring to king.

Conclusion 5—Molly marries king's youngest son.

Resolution (implicit)—Molly's cleverness earns her a permanent home.

Conclusion (implicit)—Molly and her sisters live with king and his sons.

"Molly Whuppie" embeds smaller stories within the overall, top-level structure of the larger story. The general problem that Molly and her sisters confront is solved only after she has faced five internal problems. She solves each of these problems within a storylike episode, three of which (2, 3, and 4) are substitution-type event-repeat devices. The teller can remember the larger story easily by cataloging the five episodes within: episode 1 sets Molly up for the three stealing episodes, and episode 5 is the chronology that releases Molly from the stealing sequence. All five episodes require teller mapping of event structure, recall of substitutions, and memorization of some ritual language.

Both types of event-repeat stories (no-substitution and substitution-type patterns) are highly conventionalized, ritualized story shapes. Audiences can participate actively by chanting or saying the repeated events with the teller. Once familiar with the substitutions in a given story, the audience can also do substitution-type stories aloud. Both patterns very likely represent old strategies for memory-making and information retrieval, and both reiterate a common approach to problem solving—persistence. Johnson et al. (1977) sometimes include some substitution-type event-repeat stories within the cumulative category, presumably because a series of repeats of the same activity to solve a problem does have a cumulative effect. In "The Five Chinese Brothers" (Bishop 1938), for instance, the villagers eventually abandon their attempts at execution; the brothers exhaust the villagers' repertoire of methods. But such collective or cumulative effects in event-repeat stories seem to have more to do with content than with structure. From the point of view of the teller, whose immediate problem is to remember the story for telling, learning a single event to repeat and/or into which to slot specified substitutions is a memory-building approach to telling that makes the substitution-type event-repeat structure designation seem more practical.

Event-repeat sequences of both types seem to reflect common life experiences set into "story" framework. The repetitious nature of the event sequence illustrates a sometimes useful strategy for problem solving: persistence of activity—wearing down the opposition. Sometimes a problem can be solved by making slight adjustments (substitutions) in the strategy from attempt to attempt without changing the essential nature of the approach.

Audiences participate in problem solution directly in stories of these two types, both through chanting and talking along with the teller during repeated sequences and by assessing the usefulness of the repeated activity in the solving of the problem. Some event-repeat stories make a deliberate joke of the persistent use of the one strategy when problem solution obviously requires a shift in approach. Through participation, audiences learn to assess problem situations and to match appropriate approaches for problem solving to a variety of troubling circumstances.

Other event-repeat stories of both types include:

"The Bluebird and the Coyote" (Brown 1979)

"Why Coyote Stopped Imitating His Friends" (ibid.)

"The Fisherman" (Courlander 1962)

"The King's Drum" (ibid.)

"Little Gold Star" (Hayes 1982)

"The Blacksmith in the Moon" (Jablow and Withers 1969)

"The Wrestling Contest between the Cat and the Tortoise" (Fuja 1971)

"The Parson and the Sexton" (Asbjornsen and Moe 1960)

"Little Freddie and His Fiddle" (ibid.)

"Squire Per" (ibid.)

"The Smart Man and the Fool" (Bollinger 1964)

"The Caterpillar and the Wild Animals" (ibid.)

"How It Came About That Children Were First Whipped" (ibid.)

"The Beautiful Girl Who Had No Teeth" (ibid.)

"The Flying Shoes" (Jameson 1973)

"Vasilissa the Fair Cinderella" (Johnson et al. 1977)

"Coyote and the Crying Song" (Courlander 1970)

"The Sun Callers" (ibid.)

"Coyote's Needle" (ibid.)

"The Lad Who Went to the North Wind" (Johnson et al. 1977)

"The Tongue-Cut Sparrow" (ibid.)

"From Tiger to Anansi" (ibid.)

"The Three Little Pigs" (Literature Committee 1950)

"The Travels of a Fox" (ibid.)

"The Straw Ox" (ibid.)

The Chronicle Pattern

The simple chronicle-type story utilizes neither the repetitious nor the cumulative devices of the previously described categories. Such a story, instead, consists of a series of nonrepetitious, noncumulative events, each structurally different from the others, and each relating one step in a logical sequence of chronological cause-and-effect activity leading to problem solution. As with other structure types, "story" frames the event sequence, providing extended meaning and coherence for the event list through employment of the conventions of setting, problem, resolution, and conclusion.

The chronicle story meets audience expectations for coherence and continuity primarily through the employment of logic in the relationships between and ordering of events in the sequence. Sensibility in the story is achieved by relating the events in a reasonable, explicable order and by demonstrating the clear relationships between each event in the sequence. Logic and order are the governing conventions, rather than repetition or accumulation.

The chronology can be viewed as a type of historical reporting—a series of happenings that occur in a given order for good reasons slotted into "story" frame. The general structure of the event sequence might be characterized as a series of empty slots, none of which has the same internal structure as any of the others. The events in the series of events can be fitted into the slots in sequence. Each event is told using language and paralinguistic effects that are different from all other events in the sequence. The addition of other story conventions (setting, problem, resolution, conclusion) contributes a larger perspective, reason, and sensibility to the simple narration of a string of cause-and-effect-related events and provides specific purpose and motivation for character activity.

Problem solution is achieved as a result of the logic and sensible ordering of the events or actions taken by the character or characters, of the nature of the actions undertaken, and of the relationships between them. In the most rudimentary of such chronicles, the story is built about a single problem and presents no internal complications or additional problems to be resolved before the major problem can be addressed. The character extricates himself or herself from a single dilemma by acting out a logical, step-by-step series of actions focused on the same problem. Character problem-solving activity might be insightful and deliberate or bumbling and lucky, but it is always linear and direct, reflecting a series of events in time. "The Fate of the Turtle" (Lang 1949), a story that appears in the oral literatures of many cultures, is a good example of a simple chronicle of events directed to the solution of a single problem.

THE FATE OF THE TURTLE*

Setting: Events in setting cagegory

1. Wild ducks and turtle live together in pond.
2. They become good friends.
3. One year, rains do not come.
4. Pond begins to dry up.
5. Ducks resolve to fly away to find water.
6. They go to bid farewell to turtle.
7. Turtle begs ducks not to leave him to die.

Problem — How to transport turtle away from drying pond.

Event sequence

1. Ducks withdraw to consult.
2. They develop a plan.
3. They return to tell turtle of their decision.
   a. They will transport turtle.
   b. They will carry a stick between them.
   c. Turtle must hold fast to stick with mouth.
   d. Turtle must remain still and hang on tightly throughout.
   e. Especially, turtle must not try to talk.
4. Turtle eagerly promises absolute obedience.
5. Ducks and turtle start out, turtle clinging to stick with mouth.
6. They fly over mountains, rivers, lakes, fields, towns.
7. Turtle is very brave and has faith in his friends.

---

*In Lang 1949.

8. People on ground see turtle flying and exclaim about the wonder of a flying turtle.

9. Turtle becomes arrogant—thinks of himself as flying under his own power.

10. Turtle thinks people envy him his ability to fly.

11. Turtle, in a prideful moment, opens mouth to speak to people.

Resolution—Turtle falls to earth and is broken to pieces.

Conclusion—Ducks decide that swift death afforded by fall is at least a better one than that which turtle would have suffered if he had stayed at pond.

Moral (implicit or stated, depending upon story version)—Arrogance and pride can lead to the open mouth and free tongue, which can, in turn, result in one's downfall.

Some stories present more complicated chronologies, in which an initial problem may lead to collection of subproblems ("Why Tortoises Are Sacrificed," Fuja 1971), in which two or more chronologies covering the same time period are narrated in succession, or in which two or more chronologies are related in the order in which they occurred in the story ("The Monkey and the Crocodile," Johnson et al. 1977). In all such stories, the principal internal structure is the simple chronicle of events set in a larger story frame. Teller memory for more complicated arrangements in which more than one chronology is related can be aided by identification of the problem or problems to be solved in the story and the organization of event sequences within the larger, top-level story structure.

Other chronicle stories include:

"Dinewan the Emu and Goomble-Gibbon the Turkey" (Johnson et al. 1977)

"Mr. Crow Takes a Wife" (ibid.)

"The Singing Tortoise" (Courlander and Herzog 1947)

"The Messenger to Naftam" (ibid.)

"Guinea Fowl and Rabbit Get Justice" (ibid.)

"The Monkey and the Crocodile" (Johnson et al. 1977)

"Rapunzel" (ibid.)

"The King O' the Cats" (ibid.)

"The Princess of the Rice Fields" (Kimishima 1970)

"The Legend of the Orange Princess" (Gobhai 1971)

"Concerning the Leopard and the Hedgehog" (Fuja 1971)

"The Sad Story of the Tadpole" (ibid.)

"Oni and the Great Bird" (ibid.)

"The Twins" (ibid.)

"The Elephant and the Cock" (ibid.)

"The Wise Dog" (ibid.)

"The Wooden Spoon and the Whip" (ibid.)

"The Man Who Paddled to the Moon's House" (Jablow and Withers 1969)

"Why the Sun and the Moon Live in the Sky" (ibid.)

"The Foolish Father-in-Law" (ibid.)

"The Ship with Three Decks" (Calvino 1980)

"Those Stubborn Souls, the Biellese" (ibid.)

"How Rabbit Brought Fire to the People" (Brown 1979)

"How Rabbit Fooled Wolf" (ibid.)

"The Fast Men" (Courlander 1962)

"The Donkeys Ask for Justice" (ibid.)

"The Lion's Share" (ibid.)

"The Tree That Walked" (Belting 1953)

The Embedded-Story Pattern

Some stories act as frames for whole stories. For instance, "The Liar's Contest" (Courlander and Prempeh 1957) is a story with one problem to solve, within which four smaller stories are told. The following story map illustrates the manner in which the four internal stories are embedded into the primary story. Though the map lacks mention of specific content, it indicates locations and relationships of the embedded stories inside the top-level or primary structure. The event sequence contains a series of whole stories, each of which has its own internal story structure. Each embedded story makes use of a recognizable structural device. Embedded stories 1, 2, and 3 are chronicle types. Embedded story 4 is somewhat cumulative.

Setting

Problem

Event sequence

       Story 1

     Transitional event

       Story 2

     Transitional event

       Story 3

     Transitional event

       Story 4

Resolution

Conclusion

Moral

THE LIAR'S CONTEST*

Setting: Events in setting category

1. Fly, moth, and mosquito are hunting; they come upon Anansi the Spider.

2. They attack Anansi with the intent of killing and eating him.

3. They are not, together, strong enough to subdue Anansi, nor is he, alone, strong enough to beat them.

4. After a long struggle, all four are exhausted, but no one is victorious.

5. Anansi asks why they attack him. They reply that they are hungry, are hunting, and that all living things must eat — that they intend to eat him.

6. Anansi suggests that, since they could not subdue him, they surely cannot eat him. And why should he not eat them?

---

*In Courlander and Prempeh 1957.

7. Because, they reply, he could not subdue them.

8. Then, suggests Anansi, a lying contest will determine who will eat whom.

9. The fly, moth, and mosquito agree.

10. Anansi outlines the terms of the contest. Each will tell an outrageous story. If Anansi concludes that the stories of the fly, moth, and mosquito are not true, they may eat him. If they conclude that Anansi's story is not true, he may eat them.

Problem—To tell a story (lie) that is so outrageous that the listeners will cry falsehood, thus determining who will eat whom.

Event sequence

Story 1: the moth's story—One time, four days before I was born, my father was clearing new ground with his bush knife. But he cut his foot and had to go to bed. So I got up, finished clearing the ground, plowed, planted and tended the seed, harvested the crop, and, four days later, when I was born, my father was already a rich man.

Transitional event: Anansi's response—Anansi thinks about the story while the fly, moth, and mosquito await his answer. He says, finally, "How true, how true." Since they did not expect such an answer—they expected him to say "That is a lie!"—they are forced to go on.

Story 2: the mosquito's story—One time, I had been hunting. I had killed and eaten an elephant and was lying in a clearing, playing with the elephant's ear, when a leopard came walking by. Since I was no longer hungry, I decided to play with the leopard. I chased him, caught him, grabbed him by the neck, shoved my fist down his throat, grabbed his tail from the inside, and pulled him inside out. The leopard had just eaten a sheep. Now the sheep was on the outside. and the leopard was on the inside. The sheep thanked me and grazed off into the grass.

Repeat transitional event.

Story 3: the fly's story—One time, when I was out hunting, I sighted an antelope. I raised my gun, took aim, and shot at the antelope. Then I ran forward, caught the antelope by the neck, killed it, and skinned and quartered it, and then my bullet came flying by. I caught the bullet and replaced it in my gun. Because I was very hungry and wished to eat my catch alone, I climbed a tree with the meat, built a fire, cooked the meat, and ate it all. When I was finished, I was so fat that I could not climb down from the tree. Do you know that I had to go home to my village, get a rope, come back, and tie it to a limb of the tree to let myself down?

Repeat transitional event. And then it is Anansi's turn.

Story 4: Anansi's story—One time I was walking through the forest when I came upon a coconut lying in the path. I picked up the coconut and called to anyone who could hear, "I have just found a coconut. If no one claims it, then it is mine." No one claimed it. I took it home, planted, watered, and tended it, and it grew. At last, it was a mature coconut tree with coconuts of its own. When the coconuts were ripe, I climbed the tree and cut down three of them. Then I cut each coconut open with my bush knife. When I cut open the first coconut, a fly came out. When I cut open the second, a moth came out. When I cut open the third, a mosquito came out. Because the coconut belonged to me, the tree that grew from the coconut belonged to me. And because the tree belonged to me, the coconuts that grew on the tree belonged to me. And because the coconuts that grew on the tree belonged to me, the contents of the coconuts belonged to me. So, the fly, the moth, and the mosquito belonged to me. Because they belonged to me, I could do with them whatever I pleased. And I pleased to eat them. However, when I tried to eat them, they ran away. I have been looking for them ever since. And here they are—my fly, my moth, and my mosquito.

Resolution

1. Fly, moth, and mosquito are struck dumb.
2. They would like to say "How true," but cannot without admitting to being Anansi's property—in which case he would eat them.
3. They cannot say "That is a lie!" because they would then lose the contest, and Anansi would eat them.
4. They say nothing, but run off into the forest.

Conclusion—To this day, when spiders go hunting, they hunt for flies, moths, and mosquitos. And when they catch them, they eat them, because flies, moths, and mosquitos belong to spiders, and because the spider won the liar's contest.

"The Silent Princess" (Lang 1949) contains three embedded stories. Both "The Numskull and the Rabbit" (Johnson et al. 1977) and "The Parrot" (Calvino 1980) contain one embedded story apiece.

THE SILENT PRINCESS

Setting

Problem

Event sequence

1. Episode
2. Episode
3. Episode
4. Episode
5. Episode
   Embedded story
6. Event
7. Episode
   Embedded story
8. Event
9. Episode
   Embedded story
10. Event

Resolution

Conclusion

"The Numskull and the Rabbit" and "The Parrot" illustrate two ways in which a story can be embedded within a larger story frame. In "Numskull," the embedded story is inserted and narrated as an intact piece. In "Parrot," the embedded story is broken into eight sections that are narrated in alternation with the telling of the larger story.

THE NUMSKULL AND THE RABBIT

Setting

Problem

Event sequence

1. Event
2. Event
3. Event
4. Event
5. **Embedded story**
6. Event

7. Event
8. Event

Resolution

Conclusion

THE PARROT

Setting

Problem

Event sequence
1. Event
2. **Embedded story** — Episode 1
3. Event
4. **Embedded story** — Episode 2
5. Event
6. **Embedded story** — Episode 3
7. Event
8. **Embedded story** — Episode 4
9. Event
10. **Embedded story** — Episode 5
11. Event
12. **Embedded story** — Episode 6
13. Event
14. **Embedded story** — Episode 7
15. Event
16. **Embedded story** — Episode 8
17. Event
18. Event

Resolution

Conclusion

All of the embedded-story examples slot the embeddings into the primary or top-level story frame in a different manner. When the teller learns a story that contains embedded stories, he or she is remembering an arrangement or structure as well as a content. Even if the storyteller chooses not to make maps requiring the conscious effort and structure awareness of those given here, he or she must nevertheless construct a memory for the ordering of pieces.

Generally, embedded stories within larger or primary stories are part of the solution to the primary story problem. The act of telling the story or stories within the main story frame lends sensibility and coherence to the primary story and gets the character out of trouble. Epic oral literature is a form of top-level structure that binds together and orders long sequences of structurally singular but content-related stories, e.g., "Gilgamesh: Man's First Story" (Bryson 1966) or "He Who Saw Everything: The Epic of Gilgamesh" (Reagles 1966). In "Arabian Nights" (Lang 1951), a larger and rather thin story frame or top-level structure provides the glue for a vast collection of stories, not all of which are sequential or content related. The Eddas of the Norse mythology (Colum 1920 and Crossley-Holland 1980) and the Germanic hero sagas (Picard 1958) are story series in which the individual stories are told in sequence, embedded within the larger structure of a culture's mythical history. In such epic sequences, each embedded story has its own story structure that must be learned for telling just as the teller might learn a story that is not embedded in a larger structure. In addition, the teller must learn the story frame into which the stories are slotted and the arrangement of the stories within the larger structure.

Pattern-type Combinations

Many stories are suprastructures that frame more than one of the patterns or devices described in the previous categories. "The Feathered Ogre" (Calvino 1980) uses a chronicle of events, an event-repeat sequence, and a type B cumulative winding and unwinding device within a story frame that has only one problem. "Coyote and the Rolling Rock" and "Crow and Hawk" (Brown 1979) and "Frog's Wives Make a Ndiba Pudding" (Courlander 1962) combine a chronology with substitution-type event repeats. "The Little Girl Sold with the Pears" (Calvino 1980) uses both a chronology and a type B cumulative.

Stories that employ more than one pattern are more complex than those that accomplish problem solution using only one pattern. They are more difficult to remember, since their content is slotted using more than one structural convention, and they are more difficult to tell. They are also more likely to be confusing to young and less experienced audiences, because problem solution is often not accomplished in a simple, direct, linear fashion. Especially with these types of stories, storyteller memory depends upon structure knowledge. For tellers who do not become familiar with the patterns governing the shape of a story, memory failure is common and occurs in a proportion related to story length and structural complexity. The teller should be able to identify the various structural devices in operation in the more complex story and use his or her knowledge of these to keep the story content under control during telling.

Number Patterns

In addition to the conventions governing organization of information into event patterns, stories often are set into patterns of "sacred" numbers. Three is perhaps the most common number providing organization for story content in the stories of many European cultures. Story content is arranged in sets of three, with threes embedded in threes or in multiples of three. For example, three brothers go off together to find their fortunes. Each is confronted by three problems, undergoes three trials, meets three princesses, must choose from among three alternatives, finds three objects, is given three magic items, has three chances to achieve a goal, meets a witch on a stove with three legs. The content of the narration, and even story detail, is fixed in sets of three. Story structure is also arranged in threes, regardless of the type of event pattern in use. For instance, an event is repeated three times, or three substitutions are used in the event, or there are three problems in the story, or three major episodes. Ritual language can also be controlled by the magic number, with phrases or chanted elements requiring three repetitions.

"Ivan Bull" (Hamlyn 1975) is typical. Three boys grow three times as fast as ordinary people, then find three horses and go to seek their (three) fortunes. They meet and vanquish three dragons who are the husbands of three maidens. The first dragon has three heads, the second six, and the third nine. The boys cut the heads from the dragons in sets of three. Three also is the dominant number in "The Artful Soldier and the Czar's Three Daughters" (Hamlyn 1975). The three daughters of the czar disappear, one by one, on their seventeenth birthdays. Three men — two generals and a common soldier — offer to find the girls. The girls are held captive in three castles by dragons with three, six, and nine heads respectively. The soldier cuts the heads off the dragons in sets of three. He pulls on a rope three times to get assistance from the generals. When the generals doublecross the soldier, he uses three magic eggs to prove that he saved the princesses. The story is divided into threes structurally as well. The events in the setting category describe the three disappearances. The event sequence contains three episodes, each of which has three events embedded within it. (Each of the three events is a substitution-type event-repeat pattern.) In "The Brides of the Bear" (Hamlyn 1975), three sisters go off in turn to become (unwilling) brides of the bear. Each girl is warned not to open the third cupboard. (The first two do, of course, and are killed by the bear.) The third girl saves her sisters, then returns home herself. The story contains three episodes, each of which has three embedded substitution-type repeated events.

Some familiar stories are organized in sets of seven and twelve. "Hans in Luck," "Prudent Hans" and "The Fisherman and His Wife" (*New Wonder World*, 1951) are patterned on sevens. "The Fisherman and His Wife" is a cumulative with seven items in the winding list. "The Great Bear" (Jablow and Withers 1979), "The Seventh Father of the House" (Asbjornsen and Moe 1960), "The Separation of God from Man" and "Master Rabbit and the

Berries" (Bollinger 1964), "The Cow-Tail Switch" and "Talk" (Courlander and Herzog 1949), "The Cat and the Parrot" (Johnson 1977) and "The Flying Ship" (Literature Committee 1950) are all cumulative stories in which the cumulative list, winding and unwinding, contains seven items.

"The Twelve Mikitas" (Hamlyn 1975) is organized in twelves, nines, and threes. A merchant has a trade that extends over nine czardoms, nine mountains, and nine seas. He also has three sons who have three dreams. The youngest, Mikita, refuses to tell his dream to his father and therefore is sold three times. He eventually must rescue his last owner, the czar. In his adventures, he gains eleven brothers who look exactly like him (the twelve Mikitas), who meet and marry twelve princesses.

Although stories set in fives and nines are more rare in European cultures, they can be found. "One Trick Too Many" (Ginsburg 1973) contains sets of fives, as does "The Beautiful Girl and the Fish" (Fuja 1971). "The Ram and the Pig Who Went into the Woods" (Johnson et al. 1977), a Scandanavian version of "The Brementown Musicians," is a cumulative also patterned on the number five. "The Fat Cat" (Kent 1971) and "La Hormiguita" (Hayes 1982) are both cumulative repetitive-winding and unwinding stories in which the number of items in each cumulative list is nine.

Many Native American stories are constructed in twos and fours or multiples of fours, the number having a magical/mythical and spiritual significance. "The Rooster" and "The Mockingbird and the Maiden" (Brown 1979) and "The Beetle's Hairpiece," "Coyote and the Crying Song," and "The Sun Callers" (Courlander 1970) are Hopi tales patterned on the number four. "How the Buffalo Were Released on Earth" (Apache/Comanche), "How Rabbit Fooled Wolf" (Creek), "Skunk Outwits Coyote" (Comanche), "The Bluebird and the Coyote" (Pima), and "Crow and Hawk" (Cochiti) (Brown 1979) are stories patterned on the number four.

African tales are also often constructed in fours. "The Fisherman" (Liberian) and "The Lion's Share" (Somalian) (Courlander 1962); "From Tiger to Anansi" (Ashanti) (Johnson et al. 1977); "Kassa the Strong One" (West African) and "The Hungry Spider and Turtle" (Ashanti) (Courlander and Herzog 1947); "How the World Got Wisdom" (West African) (Arkhurst 1964); and "Why Tortoises Are Sacrificed" (Yoruba) and "Kin Kin the Cat" (Yoruba) (Fuja 1971) are all four patterned.

The number pattern of a story is an integral part of its top-level or discourse structure. Quite often the structure types described in the preceding section are limited by a number pattern. For instance, a cumulative story based upon the number seven will contain seven items in the cumulative list. A story with embedded stories based upon threes and multiples of three will have episodes, events, characters, language chanting, problems, and settings in groups of three. The overall story structure is not lost, but only further specified by the number pattern of a story.

As with event sequence structure types, number patterns aid teller memory. They organize information within overall story structure and help the teller to remember "how many" by providing a finite number of slots into which information can be fitted.

The numbers upon which stories are constructed are significant to the culture to which the stories belong. They often have religious meaning and are a reflection of the manner in which a people has organized its perceptions of the physical and spiritual worlds. The "correctness" of a given number is learned within the larger frame of reference of the culture. The stories teach the number as an aspect of "truth" within the culture, reiterate what the culture "knows," and develop the individual's expectations for sensibility. Each individual who tells stories comes to the telling experience with a predisposition for one or more such numbers. Stories set in those familiar numbers will be the easiest to remember and tell, not because the stories themselves are intrinsically easier, but because the teller already has expectations for that aspect of story organization.

When storytellers, especially beginners, select stories, they might consider working with tales that are based on the familiar number or numbers. Most probably the teller will make such selections unconsciously, because stories based upon the "right" number will make more sense. An inexperienced teller who selects a foreign story based upon an unfamiliar number might very well distort the story during telling by reorganizing it to fit a more familiar number. Such distortions are destructive of story integrity and cultural intent. As a storyteller becomes more experienced and hears and reads many stories, he or she will develop a sense of the use of other numbers. Then he or she can provide honest renditions of stories with less familiar number patterns.

Participation Types

Story organization and language determine the manner in which audiences can interact with the story and the teller during telling. (See chapter 3.) The nature of audience participation in any given story is a part of story structure. Ritual participation is usually associated with singing and chanting and with repetitive language within the story. The more conventional (therefore the more predictable) the story structure, the more likely that the audience will be able to tell and chant along with the teller. Much ritual participation is possible with the cumulative stories. Some ritual participation can occur with event-repeat stories. Coactive participation is most likely with stories whose structures and contents are not quite as strictly governed as cumulatives, and whose sequences are not as predictable. Bantering is a type of participation that is encouraged and allowed by the teller. However, highly conventionalized stories such as the cumulative and event-repeat types are less likely to lend themselves to bantering simply because the audience is involved with ritual chanting or singing. Bantering is more likely to occur with stories that are less predictable, and in which prescribed audience behavior is less structured. Predictive and eye-contact participation are givens for all stories.

When selecting and developing stories, the storyteller must consider the types of participation that a given story might allow and then work with the story to make the best use of its capacities. Participation gives the story to the audience; it brings the audience into the story. Each type of story structure will allow and disallow specific types of audience participation.

CONCLUSION

A teller cannot tell a story effectively without having some sense of the structural elements that govern the story and into which specific story content is slotted. The structure memory, containing aspects of event sequencing, number patterning, and participation opportunities, is the foundation for control of the story and for the development of and slotting of special effects invented by the teller to make the story come alive. The only alternative to story development using story structure is word-for-word memorization,. a method that often leads to flat recitations rather than inter-active negotiations.

Pattern awareness is the mark of the culturally sensitive and honest storyteller. A story is configured in a particular manner because it reconstructs a people's perceptions. A people expects that its stories will behave in a prescribed way. While a storyteller might adjust story content to better meet the needs of a certain audience or to better accommodate his or her abilities, restructuring the story itself is a serious violation of and denial of the originating culture's view of "truth" and "universe." Pattern violation, whether undertaken to make a story conform to the story structures of one's own culture or to make a story carry a moral for which it was not designed, causes confusion. Such rearrangements of story organization present inconsistencies in cause and effect that disrupt the audience's ability to predict and interfere with listener expectations. A single storyteller cannot make a story "better" by changing its structure and pattern, which represent generations of evolution within a specific cultural context.

Storyteller expectations for story grammar and other aspects of patterning will significantly influence story shape and the organization of content within story. Individuals will retell or restructure information to fit their own sense of "right" and "true," adding or removing pieces to achieve "sensibility" (Smith 1982; Scollon and Scollon 1979). To avoid infusing discontinuity and incoherence into oral stories, the storyteller might learn to recognize the shapes of stories and deliberately prepare for story delivery with conscious knowledge of the structural and patterned restrictions of the material. Knowledge of story structures will also enable the storyteller to conduct a more spontaneous and easy negotiation with the audience and will open the game of telling to a variety of types of interactive play. The teller who does not need to concentrate on producing a word-for-word recitation is able to have fun.

REFERENCES

Aardema, Verna. 1975. *Why Mosquitoes Buzz in People's Ears*. New York: Dial Press.

Arkhurst, Joyce Cooper. 1964. *The Adventures of Spider*. Boston: Little, Brown.

Asbjornsen, Peter Christian, and Jorgen Moe. 1960. *Norwegian Folk Tales*. New York: Viking Press.

Belting, Natalia. 1953. *Three Apples Fell from Heaven*. New York: Bobbs-Merrill.

Bishop, Claire H. 1938. *The Five Chinese Brothers*. New York: Coward-McCann.

Bollinger Foundation, Inc. 1964. *African Folktales and Sculpture*. New York: Pantheon Books.

Brown, Dee. 1979. *Tepee Tales of the American Indian*. Holt, Rinehart & Winston.

Brown, Marcia. 1947. *Stone Soup: An Old Tale*. New York: Scribner.

Bryson, Bernarda. 1966. *Gilgamesh: Man's First Story*. New York: Holt, Rinehart & Winston.

Calvino, Italo. 1980. *Italian Folktales*. New York: Pantheon Books.

Cazden, Courtney B. 1975. "Play with Language and Metalinguistic Awareness: One Dimension of Language Experience." In Charlotte B. Winsor, ed., *Dimensions of Language Experience*. New York: Agathon Press.

Colum, Padraic. 1920. *The Children of Odin*. New York: Macmillan.

Courlander, Harold. 1973. *Tales of Yoruba Gods and Heroes*. Greenwich, Conn.: Fawcett Books.

_____. 1970. *People of the Short Blue Corn: Tales and Legends of the Hopi Indians*. New York: Harcourt Brace Jovanovich.

_____. 1962. *The King's Drum and Other African Stories*. New York: Harcourt, Brace and World.

Courlander, Harold, and George Herzog. 1947. *The Cow-Tail Switch and Other West African Stories*. New York: Holt, Rinehart & Winston.

Courlander, Harold, and Albert Kofi Prempeh. 1957. *The Hat-Shaking Dance and Other Tales from the Gold Coast*. New York: Harcourt, Brace and World.

Crossley-Holland, Kevin. 1980. *The Norse Myths*. New York: Pantheon Books.

Downing, John, and Che Kan Leong. 1982. *Psychology of Reading*. New York: Macmillan.

Feagles, Anita. 1966. *He Who Saw Everything: The Epic of Gilgamesh*. Glenview, Ill.: Scott, Foresman.

Fredrickson, C. H. 1977. "Semantic Processing Units in Understanding Text." In R. O. Freedle, ed., *Discourse Production and Comprehension*. Norwood, N.J.: Ablex.

Fuja, Abayomi. 1971. *Fourteen Hundred Cowries and Other African Tales*. New York: Lothrop, Lee and Shepard.

Ginsburg, Mirra. 1973. *One Trick Too Many—Fox Stories from Russia*. New York: Dial Press.

Gobhai, Mehlli. 1971. *The Legend of the Orange Princess*. New York: Holiday House.

_____. 1969. *The Mouse Maiden*. New York: Hawthorne Books.

Grimm, Jacob, and Wilhelm Grimm. 1969. *The Hedgehog and the Hare*. Cleveland, Ohio: World Publishers.

The Hamlyn Publishing Group, Ltd. 1975. *Russian Fairy Tales*. London: Hamlyn.

Hardendorff, Jean. 1968. *The Frog's Saddle and Other Tales*. Philadelphia, Pa.: Lippincott.

Harper, Wilhelmina. 1967. *The Gunniwolf*. New York: Dutton.

Hayes, Joe, 1983. *Native American Folk Tales*. Santa Fe, N. Mex.: Mariposa.

_____. 1982. *The Day It Snowed Tortillas*. Santa Fe, N. Mex.: Mariposa.

Jablow, Alta, and Carl Withers. 1969. *The Man in the Moon: Sky Tales from Many Lands*. New York: Holt, Rinehart & Winston.

Jameson, Cynthia. 1973. *The Flying Shoes*. New York: Parents Magazine Press.

Johnson, Edna, Evelyn R. Sickels, Francis Clarke Sayers, and Carolyn Horovitz. 1977. *Anthology of Children's Literature*. Boston: Houghton Mifflin.

Kent, Jack. 1971. *The Fat Cat: A Danish Folktale*. New York: Parents Magazine Press.

Kimishima, Hisako. 1970. *The Princess of the Rice Fields*. New York: Walker/Weatherhill.

Kintsch, W. 1977. "On Comprehending Stories." In M. A. Just and P. A. Carpenter, eds., *Cognitive Processes in Comprehension*. Hillsdale, N.J.: Erlbaum.

Lang, Andrew. 1951. *Arabian Nights*. New York: Longmans, Green and Co.

_____. 1949. *The Olive Fairy Book*. New York: Longmans, Green and Co.

The Literature Committee of the International Kindergarten Union. 1950. *Told under the Green Umbrella*. New York: Macmillan.

MacDonald, Margaret Read. 1982. *The Storyteller's Sourcebook: A Subject, Title and Motif Index to Folklore Collections for Children*. Detroit, Mich.: Neal-Shuman.

Mandler, J. M. 1978. "A Code in the Node: The Use of a Story Schema in Retrieval," *Discourse Processes* 1.

Mandler, J. M., and M. S. Johnson. 1977. "Remembrance of Things Parsed: Story Structure and Recall," *Cognitive Psychology* 9.

McDermott, Gerald. 1972. *Anansi the Spider: A Tale from the Ashanti*. New York: Holt, Rinehart & Winston.

Merriam, Eve. 1968. *Epaminondas*. New York: Follett.

Meyer, Bonnie J. F., and G. Elizabeth Rice. 1984. "The Structure of Text." In P. David Pearson, ed., *Handbook of Reading Research*. London: Longman.

The New Wonder World: A Library of Knowledge, Vol. 5. 1951. Chicago, Ill.: Shuman.

Picard, Barbara L. 1958. *German Hero-Sagas and Folktales*. New York: Walck.

Propp, V. 1958. *Morphology of the Folktale*. Bloomington, Ind.: Indiana Research Center in Anthropology, Folklore and Linguistics.

Rumelhart, D. E. 1975. "Notes on a Schema for Stories." In D. G. Bobrow and A. M. Collins, eds., *Representing and Understanding*. New York: Academic Press.

Scollon, Ron, and Suzanne Scollon. 1979. "Cooking It Up and Boiling It Down: Abstracts in Athabaskan Children's Story Retelling," Alaskan Native Language Center.

Smith, Frank. 1982. *Understanding Reading: A Psycholinguistic Analysis of Reading and Learning to Read*. New York: Holt, Rinehart & Winston.

Stein, N. L., and C. G. Glenn. 1979. "An Analysis of Story Comprehension in Elementary School Children." In R. O. Freedle, ed., *New Directions in Discourse Processing*. Norwood, N.J.: Ablex.

Sutton-Smith, Brian. 1981. *The Folkstories of Children*. Philadelphia: University of Pennsylvania Press.

Wiesner, William. 1972. *Happy-Go-Lucky*. New York: Seabury Press.

3

Preparing, Developing, and Delivering Stories

A story.
A story.

Let it come.
Let it go.

(African ritual opening)

Of what aspects of story and storying should a
storyteller be aware?

How does a storyteller prepare a story?

How does a storyteller remember a story?

How does a storyteller bring an audience "into" a
story?

Which elements of oral language are important in
storytelling?

Which paralinguistic elements can help make the oral
story effective?

How can a storyteller develop (author) stories?

What does a storyteller need to know about story
delivery?

The effective storyteller is a transparent medium and negotiator for the construction of the story, not an actor using the story to support a personal performance. The teller gives back to the people a literature they created, not one that he or she invented. For that reason, the personal characteristics and abilities of the storyteller become a part of the story. The teller tells himself or herself into story reality, then ceases to be a personality separate from it. The audience sees and hears the story, not the teller, during the storytelling.

References to opacity and transparency are common ones in language and literature and can be usefully applied to storytelling. *Opaque*, in the context of storyteller and storytelling, is intended to mean something that is visible, that can be seen — an object of which the user or viewer is consciously aware. The story, not the storyteller, should be opaque. *Transparent* refers to something necessary to the working of a process but something that is not "seen" — a vehicle or tool that transmits the opaque object. Although the storyteller is not invisible during a storytelling, he or she is also not the focus of the telling. The audience is able to "look through" the good storyteller to see the story. The storyteller is like a pane of glass. We look through the glass to see the thing behind it (Downing 1982, p. 108). The glass itself is visible (opaque, an object) only when it is not working properly, when it is uneven, dirty, or cracked. The language applications from which the terms *opaque* and *transparent* are borrowed characterize language as a vehicle or tool for carrying meaning. The language user does not look at the language itself, but at the meaning. Language is transparent. We look "through it" to meaning. Meaning is opaque (Cazden 1975).

Because story structure and storied content together are a form of cultural memory — a way of preserving and reconstructing cultural knowledge — the effective storyteller is one who can allow the story to reflect its own truth. The story is a mirror consisting of expected structural conventions and content archetypes in which members of the audience can recognize themselves and confirm the rightness of their cultural frame of reference. The storyteller holds the mirror. The story is also a construction negotiated by audience and teller together, using what the audience and the storyteller already know about how stories work and how the culture organizes the universe. The storyteller conducts the negotiation within the context of the ritual storytelling. The story and the circumstances of the telling own and manipulate the storyteller.

Paradoxically, a story is most powerful in the hands of a storyteller who also owns and manipulates the story. Such a storyteller is aware of all of the aspects of the telling process and knows about and can control the structural, linguistic, and paralinguistic dimensions of the story. By learning to operate the story, and by making the story his or her own, the storyteller is better able to allow the story to find its own way in the telling. The storyteller who has not come to a sufficient degree of conscious intimacy, ease, and comfort with the story through story preparation and development often has difficulty allowing the story its own unselfconscious and separate existence. A story that is independent of the self-aware machinations of teller personality will be opaque.

The storyteller prepares and develops the story by building a set of expectations for his or her own behavior and story and audience behavior during telling. The teller learns to control the rules of storying the same way a child acquires his or her first language—through experience and practice, trial and error. The teller will "access" storying capabilities as subconscious patterns in memory by watching other storytellers, by listening to told stories, and by entering into the dynamics of storyteller/story/audience interactions. Learning to handle a story in its oral form is a subtle acquisition of ability, more inductive than the formal types of instruction to which most of us are accustomed. The teller might expect to have control of some of the conventions of the oral tradition before he or she consciously recognizes and "knows about" them.

Getting ready to tell a story is a part of the problem-solving process of storytelling, which begins with story finding and ends with delivery. Despite what is "known" about storytelling or what can be said about the singular problematic aspects of telling stories, learning to tell a story is a trial-and-error operation. Whether the story is new to the teller or an old, familiar, comfortable friend, the essence of storytelling resides in the process of story reconstruction, which must be done on site, with an audience, and under a specific set of circumstances.

Although the storyteller might know the story as an abstraction before the actual moment of telling, the circumstances of the storytelling itself are a testing ground for the various linguistic and paralinguistic shapes the teller has developed for story delivery. The storyteller invents the concrete forms the story will take—character voice, movement, noise, and sound effects—and sets these before the audience as a series of propositions. Character A has a low voice, character B a sinister slouch, character C a pursed mouth and a perpetually whiney tone. The audience finds these propositions acceptable and credible according to its own literary readiness and its cultural and literary experiences and expectations. Experienced tellers learn to tailor some aspects of the shapes of their stories to better meet the known expectations of different types of audiences. Thus a storyteller might have more than one way of presenting parts of a story, a given character, or bits of narration. The abstract story in teller memory is not fixed and frozen, but rather a series of possibilities that can be reconstructed as mixtures or "sets" of alternative shapes.

A storyteller might begin by examining some of the rudimentary and preliminary problems inherent in telling: problems related to story finding and selection, compatibility between teller and story, story memory, story preparation and delivery, play and ritual initiation, and audience negotiation. The storyteller must first find stories that seem to be good candidates for telling and then make specific selections from these in keeping with his or her abilities, interests, and particular program needs.

DEVELOPING AWARENESS

A preliminary step in learning the self-control needed to allow the story to take over is the development of teller self-awareness. Identifying one's own habits in story choice, use of language and paralinguistic effects, development of characters, balance of narration with acting out and character talk, and use of noise and body interpretation can help the storyteller make decisions during story preparation that will strengthen the story during delivery.

AWARENESS OF TYPES OF STORIES CHOSEN

Many storytellers begin telling with a small collection of very similar stories. Even more experienced tellers may be drawn to a limited number of story types. The compulsion to select and tell only certain kinds of stories most probably derives from teller experience with, expectation for, and familiarity with the oral literature. Some tellers seem to tell mostly tall tales or expanded lies. Others tell anecdotal accounts and family histories. Still others find that their strengths as tellers are best utilized with animal tales, or tales having origin motifs, or stories about princesses that must be rescued, tricksters that make trouble, or dangerous trials that must be undergone. Still other tellers confine their tellings to stories of particular ethnic or geographic origins. Whatever the motivation, storytellers often restrict their repertoires to stories that have many similar properties, whether in social, cultural, thematic, character, structure, or participation type, or in geographic setting. Even beginning tellers, while experimenting with many different kinds of stories, will show signs of such preferences in their developing repertoires.

The natural attraction of a storyteller to types or categories of stories often reveals some dimensions of teller expectation and capability. Stories that are chosen "naturally," by allowing the teller's own sense of "rightness" and "fit" to prevail during selection, will usually be strong stories for that storyteller. "Natural" story selection is a good way to begin the development of a repertoire. Naturally selected stories are not as difficult to prepare, since the teller already "knows" them and likes them.

If a storyteller examines the stories in his or her working collection to find patterns, similarities, and story groups, he or she will have a more conscious set of guidelines with which to go about finding new stories. If the teller seems to be attracted to "fool" and "foolishness" stories, more of the same type can be located easily in a motif listing (MacDonald 1982). He or she could also use that knowledge to expand his or her repertoire with conscious deliberation. For instance, a storyteller who has learned to tell a substantial number of coyote stories might want to explore raven, crow, fox, Anansi (the spider), and Loki (Norse mythology) tales. These will not violate the teller's preferences or expectations, since the teller would seem to be interested in trickster tales as a generic group. A teller who tells stories of Italian origin might find that he or she is equally attracted to other cultures' versions of a favorite. Tellers of stories of Italian origin might be curious about "The Tabby Who Was Such a Glutton" (Asbjornsen and Moe 1960), the Norse version of "The Parrot" (Calvino 1980), or "The Fat Cat" (Kent 1971), the Danish equivalent.

AWARENESS OF USE OF
CONVENTIONS OF ORAL LANGUAGE

After gaining a minimum amount of experience working in front of an audience, a storyteller should be in sufficient control of one or two stories that he or she can begin to pay attention during telling to the way he or she uses language. A story contains certain images and ideas that must be expressed. How is the teller using the conventions of oral language—breathing, pausing, pitch and invention of special pitch contours, stress, juncture, drawn-out vowels, staccato articulation of consonant sounds—to carry the story? "Fe fi fo fum" can be said in many ways, none of which can be adequately encoded in a written story without the addition of notation. How the teller says "Now, you be careful how you step in them pies" or "And he scraped all them leetle froggie legs off'n the flat surface of that ice" is important to story strength and credibility. As the teller develops the story through preparation and telling, he or she will settle upon the most effective ways to render various aspects of the language of the story.

Even after a story has become a familiar friend, one still finds changes to make in the oral language encoding of the story that further enhance story reality. Conscious attention to the oral language shapes of the story and experimentation with different interpretations of the same language will improve both the story and teller control of the story and will extend teller capability for employment of oral language conventions in general.

AWARENESS OF USE OF
PARALINGUISTIC EFFECTS

Noise, movement, body language, and facial expression are part of the oral story. They are conventions of the oral literature that cannot be encoded directly into print. They can only be "told about" in narration. In the oral story, however, the storyteller has the option of recoding these written narrations as actual noise, movement, body language, or facial expression. Wind blows through bare tree branches, rattling them, helping to establish mood and tone. Water splashes against a stone wall, rocks rumble, feet thump on the ground, teeth crunch bones, a character whistles. Shapes—a bloated, puffed-up frog; a table overloaded with food—are important story ingredients. Noises, movements, and shapes provide setting and depth, convincing the listener that he or she is in the story environment. Additional effects — the posture of a character, perhaps — are implicit rather than narrated and can also be conveyed physically. The storyteller must study the story to "see" and "hear" these special effects and must make deliberate, critical decisions regarding which effects are appropriate, where to put them, and how they will be done. Paralinguistic elements are a natural part of the anatomy of the oral story and constitute one means by which the able storyteller can tell the audience into story reality. These effects are also negotiable elements within the story, parts that audiences often delight in inventing and doing along with the teller.

Storytellers differ significantly in the manner in which and degree to which they make use of paralinguistic effects, even in the same story. For that reason, a single story will be different with each new teller who renders it. Although paralinguistic effects can be overdone, the proper and optimum employment of such effects depends to a large extent on the teller's personality and capabilities. Provided that the paralinguistic interpretations are not inappropriate to the mood and tone of the story, a storyteller can "pull off" whatever devices he or she can control convincingly, with ease and comfort, and without obvious self-consciousness or embarrassment. The best effects are those that fall within range of the natural behavior of the storyteller. By being himself or herself, the storyteller will avoid awkward, clumsy, affected, and/or unnatural interpretations.

Some level of awareness of one's own paralinguistic behavior during a telling, and a studied knowing about the effects that work best, will help in the assessment and preparation of new material. A teller can then consciously decide, for instance, to encode a character's physical appearance with the body or to use language, instead, to describe the character's actions.

The preparation of paralinguistic devices to encode oral material should be both a natural and a deliberate effort. Some aspects of the oral story simply beg for nonlanguage interpretation. The storyteller should, however, approach the use of paralinguistic devices with a measure of commonsense caution. The strongest and most convincing tellings use noises, motions, and expressions that feel "right" and comfortable. Effects that are awkward and that violate the natural personality and habit of the teller should be avoided. In the effective telling, the storyteller disappears into the story; all of his or her behavior is a part of the fabric of the tale. What the teller does becomes story reality, not teller reality. Therefore, paralinguistic activity that is unnatural for the teller will also be unnatural for the story and will make the teller more visible as a personality separate from story reality.

AWARENESS OF BALANCES BETWEEN NARRATION AND CHARACTER TALK AND ACTIVITY

The storyteller is narrator, characters, actions, noises, motions, and other shapes within the story. The storyteller becomes narrator as he or she becomes an observer within the story, an omniscient presence that can look on and tell *about* the people and events in the tale. A storyteller can choose to narrate a story in its entirety. The telling would then consist wholly of descriptions of people, places, actions, talk, noise, and movement. Many in-print versions of oral stories are essentially long narrations with some character monologue and dialogue. The encoding limitations of written language make narration of special oral language and paralinguistic effects necessary. The storyteller can examine the written story to identify those parts of the story that would be more effective if "done" rather than narrated. For instance, in "The Gunniwolf" (Harper 1967) the girl and the wolf stand side by side. The written version of the story must narrate their proximity to one another. The storyteller can suggest their locations by stepping slightly to the left when the girl talks, slightly to the right when the wolf talks. The audience does not need a narration to see where the two are standing.

In addition to the use of quotations, the written story also narrates character talk. A prince and princess have a conversation, coyote asks locust what kind of song he is singing, the youngest brother agrees to share his bread and water with an old man. In all cases, the narrator might simply suggest that the conversations occurred and indicate the content of each, without the audience's knowing what the characters actually said. Or the storyteller can substitute the conversations themselves for the narrations. How much character talk to balance against narration is often a decision the storyteller must make. Character talk should be included when, in the teller's assessment, it will strengthen the overall effect and credibility of the story.

In order to make good use of dialogue and monologue within the context of the story, the storyteller must be able to control interpretation of character personality and voice. The teller should know and do what he or she is capable of doing. If the teller is uncomfortable with a direct presentation of the character, or cannot control the character's language and other personal habits, narrating "around" the character's talk and activity might be more convincing to the audience than a clumsy nonnarrative treatment. Using dialect, if that is appropriate, is acceptable if, once again, the teller can do it properly. A character's language done in the teller's own dialect is more believable than a poorly rendered accent.

Story characters do not share the safety and omniscience of the narrator/teller. They do not "know" the story; they live in the story events for the first time with each telling, experiencing the same happenings and learning the same lessons. Each character "sees" the unfolding of story events from his or her individual and particular point of view. No two story characters are likely to "see" the same story or experience the same sequence of events. No story character knows what omnicient narrator, teller, and audience know. No story character can predict story outcome or evaluate his or her actions in light of the action of the entire story. A story is often, therefore, told from more than one point of view. Some story events are subject to narrator comment, extra-story evaluation, and editorializing. Some story events "happen" through character talk and action.

Each character within a story is living his or her own reality. Each character experiences that reality emotionally, and each has a different set of reactions. Characters may or may not share an emotional perspective. The emotional disposition of each character may or may not also reflect the mood and tone of the story itself. The story is a fabric of many emotions. A properly understood character is one for whom the storyteller knows emotional disposition.

Teller ability to represent characters directly through movement, posturing, and character language will expand with experience. At any time in a teller's own development, he or she needs to pay attention to the capabilities of the moment and strive to work within those limitations. Effects that the storyteller obviously cannot handle, even if intended to make the story more real, will only result in making the teller more visible and separate from the story.

AWARENESS OF RITUAL LANGUAGE

Even if a story has specified ritual language, the storyteller must decide how that language will be encoded into the oral story. Ritual language can be sung, chanted, clapped, danced, or just narrated. The audience can be invited to participate, or the storyteller might decide to do the language without audience help. If the audience is to participate, ritual language may require cuing and teaching in order that the language is done as the storyteller intends and that the audience "comes in" properly. Ritual language is an experience. The storyteller designs that experience during story preparation.

The appropriate interpretation of ritual language in the oral story depends largely upon the inclinations, capabilities, and ease of the teller. Ritual language can be chanted or sung or danced, provided that such treatment is appropriate to the story and is within the scope of the teller's abilities. Once again, the shape of the story is governed by teller capacity. During story preparation, the teller must ask himself or herself what special ritual language experiences are provided in the story and, then, how he or she might treat them comfortably and convincingly without appearing to be clumsy or out of control.

AWARENESS OF STORY MOOD AND TONE

Overall story mood, like narrator point of view, is omniscient. The story itself presents a feeling that is larger than the individual dispositions of the characters. The story is, in a sense, a character, in that it has a mood and tone of its own. Internal emotions of characters can sometimes contradict the mood and tone of the story. The effective storyteller can separate overall story mood and tone from the more limited feelings and reactions of the characters within. The richness of the oral story is built upon the contrast and interplay of internal character emotion set against the continuity of omniscient story mood and tone.

AWARENESS OF AUDIENCE INTERACTION

Audiences are usually ready to become directly and physically involved in a story. They seem to understand that a storytelling is not a spectator experience. The more mature and experienced the audience, the more ready listeners are to "jump in" spontaneously. Uninvited interactions, and even planned and cued interactions, can surprise a storyteller and cause a momentary lapse of memory. In the most controlled of situations, audiences can do some very unpredictable things. The storyteller must remain in control of the telling, even when confronted with the most unusual audience activity.

The teller should know his or her own comfort zone with regard to audience interaction and plan, at least, for no more involvement than can be handled. The teller can control most audience interaction by designing the nature of that interplay during story preparation. Ritual language interaction can be calculated. Coactive interaction can be either encouraged or discouraged by the way the teller chooses to present parts of a story. Surprise interactions and bantering should be kept within the context of story and storytelling. A teller who stops a story in order to deal with someone or something in an audience, or who encourages responses that he or she cannot manage effectively, will lose control of the storytelling.

Audiences who are truly in the story are most likely to respond overtly during the telling. They mean to be helpful, not disruptive. A storyteller must be able to incorporate spontaneous audience interjections into the context of the telling. The involved audience, least of all, wishes the teller to become disconnected from the story.

A storytelling should not appear to be a struggle. The storyteller should not be visible (opaque), or a distinct, separate-from-the-story personality. Tellers who are not aware of their own capabilities, and who attempt effects that are either inappropriate to the story or beyond their capacities, can look clumsy. A teller who is obviously nervous, uncomfortable, or out of control will convey those same feelings and incapacities to the audience. Limited experience and ability are not barriers to effective telling, provided that the teller uses his or her capabilities well, remains confident and positive, and provides the audience with a sense that all is under control.

The storyteller's best stories and the best effects will emerge as the teller builds and practices a repertoire. A teller should recognize these strengths. Sometimes a teller will borrow stories and elements of style from other tellers. But even these will refine and change, adapting to fit the personality and inclination of the borrower. Styles, stories, and capabilities grow with exposure and experience. A teller can make the best use of his or her degree of development by being aware of strengths and capabilities and by making deliberate applications of that consciousness during story choice, preparation, and delivery.

However talented a particular storyteller or convincing a specific telling, there is no "right" way to tell a story. The characterizations, movements, language, noise, and other paralinguistic effects that are comfortable for one teller might be awkward for another. Facial expressions that make the story more visible when done by one storyteller may only make another teller's version less so. While storytellers do admire one another's styles and inventions and borrow ideas for adaptation to their own habits, wholesale borrowing of unchanged material and style from another teller is often unsuccessful. Some storytellers are quiet, some very loud. Some tend to soften a story; some make the same story boisterous and noisy. Some are very serious. Some tend to insert funny, spontaneous editorials during narration. Some prefer to narrate almost an entire tale. Others would tell the same story with very little narration. One approach is no more proper than another, provided that the sensibility of the story is not violated through interpretation.

The story must emerge as its own reality, unencumbered by technical difficulties that focus audience attention on teller instead of story. Introduction of effects that are unwieldy, because they are incompatible with the teller's personality and style, are likely to lose their credibility as story elements. Application of effects that fit within the teller's capacities will confirm the storyteller's ease with the story. Audiences are more readily told into stories with which the storyteller is obviously comfortable and which employ devices that the teller can command.

STORY PREPARATION

The shape of the oral story is different from that of the written story. The live telling demonstrates the auditory, kinesthetic, and visual dimensions of the oral literature that cannot be reproduced in print. If the storyteller is gathering material from oral sources, the teller still has to evaluate the effectiveness of the oral dimensions of the story as handled by another teller to decide whether to use them, change them, or omit them. If the teller is searching for stories in the printed oral literature, the problem of making a good oral story is more difficult. The storyteller has to reinvest the story with the appropriate oral language conventions that do not appear in print. The teller will be evaluating the story for the potential employment of special oral effects: movement, noise, voice, characterization, body language and expression, breathing, phrasing, juncturing, intoning. Decisions about where, when, and how to employ these conventions of the oral story, which ones are appropriate to the story, and which are within the range of teller abilities are a part of story preparation. Memory work, practice, and considerations about potential audiences also are story preparation activities.

BUILDING MEMORY CAPACITY

Memory capacity for stories can be extended by reading and listening to stories. Storytellers do not memorize stories. Story memory is similar to language memory. It is a subconscious network of abstract rules that hold and describe the operation of stories and from which stories can be generated. That memory includes operations for the production of story structures, language, archetypes, paralinguistic effects, and storied content. Story rules have recursive properties. A story can be created again and again from rules or constructs in memory. These rules constitute a set of expectations for story behavior from which the storyteller can predict the manner in which stories should work. The storyteller will be able to remember those stories that behave as he or she predicts and expects. The teller can extend capacity to remember stories by first expanding his or her expectations for story behavior. Deliberate and conscious attention to story rules is not necessary to build rules in memory. All the teller need do is become familiar with many different kinds of stories.

Conscious effort to extend memory capacity might best be concentrated on finding groups of stories that fit specific criteria. For instance, the teller might try to find as many stories as he or she can that are cumulative (winding and unwinding), that are set in patterns of three, that are about quests or betrayal or foolishness, that are about frogs or dragons or foxes, that are of West African origin, that are all versions of "Rumplestiltskin" or "Epaminondas." The storyteller is looking for categories or like groups of stories. His or her expectations for one type of structure or one type of character or one ethnic origin can be used to extend memory by finding other stories that also fit those categories.

BUILDING STRUCTURE MEMORY

Though much of story preparation and development may not be deliberately conscious and studied, teller recognition of story structure is an important part of remembering the story. "Story" itself is a paradigm, a model, a way of organizing and understanding information. Story structures are grammatical forms—generic patterns—that can be used to story information. Each general pattern is a configuration of slots (see chapter 2) into which content can be fitted in order to make the whole that we recognize as a story. Storying information requires the fitting of a given body of otherwise unstructured content into one or a combination of these conventional story grammars. Information that has been slotted into a story grammar (storied) is understood in terms greater than the simple facts of its content, because it has assumed the top-level organization of a meaningful pattern ("story") that is larger than itself.

Story patterns are conventional configurations that a storyteller can recognize by type and remember as abstractions. These patterns provide the teller with primary memory for a story—its overall shape and the way in which its content is to be ordered. Initial contact with a new story will often provide the storyteller with a rudimentary sense of story pattern. Story content and language can be remembered by associating them with dimensions of the pattern, by remembering how story content and language are slotted within the larger story configuration (see chapter 2). For instance, the cumulative pattern that binds and orders story content and language in "The Little Ant" (Hayes 1982) determines sequential, interactive, and cause-and-effect relationships. Such relationships in any story are a function of the structure of the story. Introduction of characters, character activity, character interactions, and problem-solving behavior are all, likewise, bound within story structure.

When a storyteller learns a story, he or she maps it in memory. The story map contains aspects of event sequence structure, number sets, overall top-level structure, participation opportunities, and specific story content. During the telling, all these elements are integrated to produce the concrete product—the told story.

As we said in chapter 2, some tellers map stories "naturally." They do not require the use of artifacts, but simply recognize and remember story shape and content after a reading or a telling. The experienced teller, and one with extensive exposure to the oral literature, will recognize a variety of story shapes readily. Experience with stories contributes significantly to the capacity for development of story structure maps in memory. Many tellers also use physical aids to help develop story memory.

Note-taking can help a teller remember basic structural shape and key content items. A set of notes that reflects story organization, important content and detail, and repeated language can be most useful. The storyteller can fill in the remainder of the story with his or her own language. Notes that do not cue the teller to story structure and to necessary aspects of content and language will be of little help.

Outlining is a good technique, since it usually reveals story structure and slots content simultaneously. A general outline form that follows conventional "story" shape (setting, problem, event structure, resolution, conclusion, moral) should suffice for most stories. Structural differences between stories will most likely occur inside these major "story" features. The storyteller will want to include specific and necessary language and references to important content in the outline. The outline will also provide a convenient place for the addition of notations regarding the use of special effects in the story. (See chapter 2.)

A number-pattern outline can be a workable way to remember a story. Threes within threes within threes can be drawn as a picture or "tree" diagram, with notations added.

Semantic mapping or webbing is another technique for marking the organization of a story. (See chapter 2.)

Artifacts and props that are used with the story during telling often become memory devices. The storyteller remembers the story in sections or clumps, the content of each being associated with the showing or using of some piece of material. A set of pictures designed to go with a story can be a good organizational tool. The teller learns and remembers the story structure and content pertaining to each picture in the sequence and then tells from picture to picture.

Side notation for special linguistic and paralinguistic effects can be scribbled onto any outline or on-paper map. These notes might look somewhat like stage directions, written in a code sensible only to the storyteller.

Traditional artifacts and memory devices can also help the teller to remember. Many of these are historic and preceded the invention of written language. The storyteller invested memory of specific stories and of repertoire in such devices. Some of these accompany the tellings of given stories. Other traditional materials (hats, knotted cords) remind the teller of stories to tell. Still others are pieces of stuff saved by a tribal historian and used to help the historian remember and recite tribal history. One teacher/storyteller used a fishing net, draped in a storytelling area, with objects and artifacts caught up in it. Each object represented a story.

ADDING AUDIENCE PARTICIPATION

One of the special conventions of the oral story that differentiates it from the written literature is the immediate, in-context, situation-embedded nature of the experience. The story is created right in front of its consumers; there is no displacement. (Displacement exists between author and reader of written text, since the reader interacts with the text *after*, not during, its creation.) And the consumers, the individuals in the audience, have a substantial effect on the making of the story. They help to shape it through direct and indirect participation in its telling. The storyteller controls the participation by determining the type and extent of interactions that he or she will introduce into the telling. Even stories that contain ritual interactions as givens are subject to storyteller control. If and how a given interaction will be conducted is a dimension of story negotiation that is designed by the storyteller. How and when the audience will be cued and/or taught their interactive role is also for the teller to determine. The teller chooses the terms for interaction during story preparation, then makes these clear to the audience by providing in-context cues during the telling.

Including Ritual Participation

Many stories use devices such as chants or songs that invite audience involvement. In "Petie Pete versus the Witch Bea-Witch" (Calvino 1980) the witch chants,

> Petie Pete, pass me a pear
> With your little paw!
> I mean it, don't guffaw,
> My mouth waters, I swear, I swear!

In "The Dead Man's Arm" (Calvino 1980) a "chorus of voices" sings:

> Many, many have we slain,
> You will be the next to wane!
> Many, many have we slain,
> You will be the next to wane!
>
> Three of our brothers you slew,
> Now we're coming after you!
> Three of our brothers you slew,
> Now we're coming after you!
>
> Six of our brothers you slew,
> Now we're coming after you!
> Six of our brothers you slew,
> Now we're coming after you!

In the original ritual telling of these and other stories containing similar types of conversation in verse, audiences may have sung or chanted with the storyteller. The printed story leaves little or no clue as to how that language was rendered orally. When he or she prepares the story, the storyteller is obliged to determine the method by which such verses will be handled. The verses can be sung, and if so, the teller may have to invent a tune as well. If the verses are chanted, clapping, arm swinging, head nodding, or some other motion might accompany the chant. The storyteller also has the option of doing the verses alone. If the audience is to be involved in the ritual during the telling, the storyteller will have to teach the routine to the audience, either before or during the telling. Once again, the teller is left with a critical decision. Teaching the routine before the telling will delay the story. Teaching the routine in the middle of the telling will interrupt the story. The audience can be drawn in on *some* oral language play without teaching if the teller simply does the routine and then issues the invitation by saying, "Do that part with me again." The repeat of the routine both teaches the language and informs the audience as to their part in the play.

Repetitious language (e.g., the cumulative list), is another story device that invites audience participation. If the teller does not actually teach and cue the audience for the repetition in such stories, many audiences will begin to mouth the repetition without express invitation. It is the story, then, that invites, cues, and teaches. The storyteller might be more in control of the story if he or she determined the manner in which the language was to be done and set the audience up. By deciding to bring the audience into the repetitions rather than doing a solo, the teller can maintain control over the story. A story such as "The Fat Cat" (Kent 1971) provides a good example of repetitious language (a cumulative list) that all but asks an audience for interaction.

Cat: I ate the minister with his walking stick.

I ate the little old lady with the pink parasol.

I ate the seven girls dancing.

I ate the five birds in a flock.

I ate Sko-linkenlot.

I ate Sko-hottentot.

I ate the pot.

I ate the stew.

I ate the little old lady, too.

Still other stories suggest opportunities for interaction even though verses or repetitious language do not appear in the story. "Anansi the Spider" (McDermott 1972) is such a story. The audience can be invited to chant the names and descriptions of Anansi's six sons at the several points in the story at which these are listed. "The Three Goats" (Literature Committee 1950) contains good possibilities for the invention of ritual participation, though the story does not specifically contain it. Likewise, some of the stories in the collection *One Trick Too Many* (Ginsburg 1973) will lend themselves to ritual participation, though the printed stories contain none. In the title story, younger audiences in particular gladly take the part of the fox to chant storyteller-invented language.

"The fox begged to be let in and given a place to sleep" turns into:

> "Oh, please let me in!
> I've been traveling all day.
> My back is tired and my feet are tired and my head is tired.
> I won't take up much room.
> I'll just curl up in a corner by the door."

Such an insertion approaches story development in that the teller adds language to replace a brief narration of the fox's monologue. The immediate pleading of the character rather than narrator explication is better for the oral story. At the same time, it does not violate the content of the original narration. Motions, a natural evolution, accompany the character talk. The members of the audience must be taught the begging routine before the telling, but need no instruction for the motions.

For all types of ritual participation, the storyteller begins by examining the story to locate either the ritual or repetitious language or aspects of the narration that will lend themselves to effective participation. The teller then develops the participation to suit the story, the intended audience, and his or her own capabilities. He or she also designs a teaching, introduction, or cuing method for the audience. Both the participation and the instruction should be easy and natural; they should feel "right" in story and storytelling context and not disrupt the flow of the telling.

Including Coactive Participation

Even though coactive participation is spontaneous, not taught or cued by the storyteller, the teller can plan for coactive interaction during a story preparation. Assessment of a story will reveal those parts of the narration or other story devices most likely to elicit coactivity. Repetitious narrative within the story, character voices, a character who says the same thing over and over again, facial expressions, motions, and hand signals can all compel an audience that is in the story to begin to coact along with the teller. In "The Hungry Spider and Turtle" (Courlander and Herzog 1947), members of the audience often feel compelled to mouth Turtle's talk, or to make hand-washing motions along with the teller, since turtle is soooo sloooow and soooooo seeeriooouuuus. In "Speckled Eggs" coactivity is invited in the form of animal noises and a counting routine:

> "When she got up the next morning, she laid another egg.
> Now she had [insert number—e.g., nine] speckled eggs.
> And did she tell anybody?
> *Noooo! She kept her mouth shut!*"

The audience, without cuing or instruction, yells the number of eggs and the last line. As the list-making progresses, some members of the audience will do the whole routine. Even the most reluctant and/or self-conscious of listeners, once truly bound by the story, will become caught up in coactive interaction. The teller can both be ready for possible coactivity and plan for it by inventing routines — voices, characterizations, counting sequences — that invite it.

Including Bantering Participation

By its very nature, bantering is spontaneous and comes in an unpredictable shape. Bantering is direct, out-loud audience expression of private thoughts that are triggered by the story during telling. The storyteller cannot predict when and what will occur if the audience is allowed or encouraged to banter. Sometimes the members of the audience who do blurt out surprise even themselves. One very common kind of preliminary outburst, which quite often opens the way for more, is "Oh, no!" The teller might indicate a willingness to banter, then, by replying, in story context, directly to the member of the audience who spoke, "Oh, Yes!"

True bantering is a form of editorializing in which the audience listens critically to the story and makes out-loud comments about characters or story content during the telling. The teller who is not comfortable with such interaction can easily discourage it by not responding to it when it occurs. The audience will take a cue from a teller who simply ignores the outburst and continues with the story as if nothing had been said. The teller who responds to bantering by stopping the telling and asking the individual not to interrupt will make the audience very uncomfortable indeed, since bantering is the province of the audience. The teller who is ready and waiting for such fun needs only to respond to one individual with an in-story-context reply that has an editorial content of its own, and the way will be opened for everyone.

The teller who wishes to banter must first be in good control of the story. The audience will depend upon the teller to bring the bantering back to the story line. (The wit involved in integrating unpredictable bantering with the story taxes the teller but, if done well, delights the audience.) Next, the teller must feel comfortable with the audience and with the circumstances of the storytelling. Quite often a teller will decide during preparation of the story whether or not to encourage and allow bantering. The storyteller can plan to signal his or her willingness to banter. The covert message the teller sends to the audience is the measure of his or her comfort and control. Most audiences will refrain from bantering with a nervous, tense, or frightened teller. Audiences do understand the disruptive nature of invasive editorializing. A relaxed audience, in the hands of a relaxed and competent teller, feels a certain ownership and control of the story that sometimes leads to spontaneous blurtings. A teller who responds by bantering back even once has issued the universal invitation. Prolonged eye contact (beyond that which is socially acceptable) can bring on audience bantering. The long look is an invitation. Finally, the storyteller who asks questions of the audience during the telling or who makes his or her own editorial comments, as if the narrator was bantering with the story, is asking for it.

Eye Contact

When preparing the story, the teller might identify specific incidences of character activity, narration, movement, or noise making that also would be enhanced by prolonged eye contact with the audience. Body language rules specify durations of eye contact that do and do not require additional social interaction, usually language. If the teller violates the rules for no-reply contact by looking too long at a single individual, that individual may feel obliged to say something. The moments in the story for extended eye contact and the consequent unspoken invitation for response should be chosen carefully by the teller. Bantering from the audience is a probable result.

Questioning

Deliberate in-story-context questioning of an audience is also a direct invitation for audience reply. "So, what do you think of that?" or "Would you have done that?" or "Was that a smart thing to do?" are open-ended questions that will get immediate answers, especially from younger audiences. (Older, more mature—and more suspicious—audiences might regard such questions as rhetorical and ignore them.) Younger listeners are also more egocentric; their responses often drift out of story context to settle upon some unrelated personal memory.

Teller: Would you have gone down the rope into the well?

Child: We went to Florida once, and we went to this place, and there was a ride where a boat went into a dark cave, and . . .

This kind of audience response is not bantering, since it is not editorial or directly related to the story. Such responses, in fact, interrupt the telling of one story with the telling of another and can cause the storyteller to lose control of the storytelling.

Direct questions that ask for audience opinion can sometimes sound patronizing, particularly if the storyteller really doesn't want to hear an answer. A better, more subtle way to ask the question might be to make a personal statement: "I don't think I would have done that"; "He had better be careful now!" Storyteller editorials like these invite audience reply without sounding quite so patronizing or inviting long, rambling, unrelated discourse.

If a discontinuous and potentially disruptive response happens, it should be stopped politely and promptly. One way to stop it is to ignore it and talk over it. If the individual has managed to gain everyone's attention, the well-intentioned anecdote will have to be interrupted. Disciplinary remarks such as "But that's not in the story," or "We don't want to hear your story now" are also disruptive, outside story context, and potentially damaging to the relationship between teller, story, and audience. A quick in-story-context reply is more effective: "The well probably did look a lot like the cave that you saw in Florida. It was very, very dark, and. . . . "

Immediate storyteller intervention is especially important in school or like settings in which the child audience is subject to the disciplinary action of the adult(s) in charge. The adult who stops the interruption before the teller can control it inside the context of the story effectively ends story reality for everyone, takes control of the story away from the teller, jeopardizes the credibility of the teller, and then leaves the teller to make repairs while finishing the story. The spontaneous blurting cannot be predicted, but incidences can be limited by reduction of the use of open-ended, rhetorical questions that suggest an invitation that the teller may not really intend. An up-raised hand may be the sign that an eager listener is waiting to tell a tangential story of his or her own. The storyteller who calls upon the up-raised hand does so at his or her own peril.

Asking closed questions is a more effective way to invite an audience into direct participation. In "The Fat Cat" (Kent 1971) an old woman makes a stew. Even very young audiences restrict their responses to story context when asked what she put into the stew. This type of interaction limits the audience to the construction of the stew and helps to get the story told. Both turtle and spider put food on the table in "The Hungry Spider and Turtle" (Courlander and Herzog 1947). The audience can suggest food items to be put on the table. The storyteller can find many opportunities in stories for such limited and specific audience invention and contribution. Controlled audience bantering is a good learning experience for younger audiences who are beginners at the negotiation process and who do not yet understand the editorial and story specific forms of interaction.

The storyteller can also ask the audience questions that solicit predictions. A question such as, "And how do you suppose he managed to kill the dragon?" will keep responses closer to story line. The teller must be prepared, however, to allow many members of the audience to have a say. This will delay the story and, for younger individuals, perhaps become more important than the story. Very young children may forget the story entirely. The teller will have to devise a smooth means of bringing the audience back into the story after a predicting episode.

Editorializing

Editorializing is the most mature form of bantering. The storyteller usually is obliged to signal willingness to banter by making editorial comments first. Members of the audience may then understand that the teller has opened the story to that type of negotiation. In "Speckled Eggs," the snake warms himself on a rock every morning in order to wake up. The teller can make editorial comment, perhaps to the effect that the snake is generally cranky until he has done this, and that some people use coffee instead. One teller has added a number of delightful one-line editorials to "The Foolish Frog" (Seeger 1961), including a quick "And it was regular grass-roots movement" after the grass swishes up inside the corner store. This kind of humorous side commentary is an invitation for the audience to "come in."

Though bantering, once begun, requires quick wit and a good degree of control of story and storytelling, it is never intended to disrupt the telling or undo teller control. Even the most outrageous editorializings are done with the understanding that bantering is a form of mutual negotiation of the story. Deliberately disruptive interjections are harassment, not bantering. The teller can control bantering, either by disallowing it altogether or by carefully selecting the type of bantering to be done and the manner in which it will be initiated. Some degree of assessment during story preparation will identify opportunities for more structured question-and-answer experiences. Editorializing is often as spontaneous for the teller as it is for the audience, and it cannot be planned. However, successful one-liners that pop up as surprises during a telling can be assessed and used again.

Conclusion

Audiences participate in the making of a story during telling through eye contact, prediction of story structure and content, and slotting of content. These types of participation are givens and can only be manipulated by the teller through story choice, nature of eye contact, and methods of delivery. The teller cannot really control these dimensions of audience interaction. But the storyteller can control participation through the choices of and development of ritual language, planned coactivity, and bantering during story preparation. By examining the story for possible development of direct, active participation of these types, the storyteller can bring an audience into a story when and in the manner in which he or she chooses and for activity that he or she can manage effectively.

ENCODING THE STORY IN ORAL LANGUAGE

Written and oral languages represent ideas and concepts using different shapes or conventions. Oral language has features that written language either cannot encode—such as breathing—or that it encodes poorly—intonation patterns (pitch, stress, and juncture), phrasing, and quality of voice. Oral language is a sound encoding that uses different parts of the body than does written language, and that may even access a different kind of memory during language production. The oral story is an entirely different phenomenon when it is told than when it is encountered in print, even if the teller faithfully reproduces the printed story word for word.

To make an oral story, especially if working from a printed source, the teller must make many decisions related to employing the conventions of the oral language.

Intonation

Pitch, stress, and juncture are linguistic elements that "fit over" sentences and that can cause dramatic changes in meaning depending on how they are employed. The placement of stress has an influence on meaning that is more than subtle.

/
JOHN kicked the ball.   (Meaning: John kicked it, and not someone else.)

         /
John KICKED the ball.   (Meaning: He didn't do something else to it.)

                 /
John kicked THE ball.   (Meaning: He kicked THIS one, not that one.)

                   /
John kicked the BALL.   (Meaning: He kicked the ball, not something else.)

Pitch contours also have an important effect on the meaning conveyed by a sentence. The meaning of the following sentence changes substantially with the changes in contour. (Read aloud, following the drawn contours, to get the effect.)

John kicked the ball.   (Meaning: You're kidding—he really did? Him? Who would believe it?)

John kicked the ball.   (Meaning: Yes, he did. Really! Would I kid you?)

John kicked the ball.   (Meaning: Statement of fact.)

Juncture refers to breaks in the steady flow of speech. When people talk, they do not stop at the end of each word. The discrete spacings to mark beginnings and endings of words are a convention of written more than of oral language. The spaces between words in print do not represent like spaces in oral language. The oral version of "John kicked the ball" contains no internal junctures. It would sound like this: "Johnkickedtheball." Try reading the following sentences aloud. Juncture only when spaces between words are given in the print.

Thatevening thePrincessagainrefused everyinvitation.

Thatevening thePrincess again refusedeveryinvitation.

Thatevening thePrincess againrefused everyinvitation.

Thatevening thePrincess again refused everyinvitation.

Thatevening thePrincess againrefused every invitation.

One obtains a different effect with each change in juncture pattern.

Intonation is only poorly (sometimes not at all) encoded into print. The storyteller should seriously plan for the effects and meanings that different intonation patterns will create. Without some attention to intonation, a storyteller could invent a meaning that he or she did not really intend.

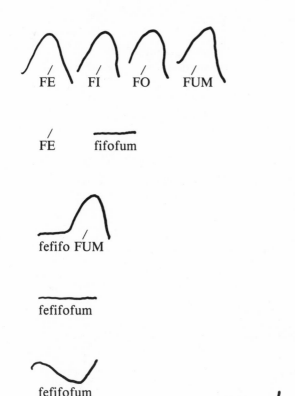

What self-respecting giant would say, "fefifofum"?

Articulation

Written language encodes (*re*presents) the sounds of the oral language imprecisely at best, if it encodes them at all. It does not encode the articulations by which language sounds are produced. The storyteller must decide how to articulate every word of the oral story. This is not, however, an insurmountable volume of work, since simply making the story oral will provide the articulations. But the teller might want to experiment with a variety of sound shapes to find the best way to say a word or phrase. Vowels can be shortened or lengthened. (This is a temporal reference and has nothing to do with phonics.)

To whom do you wish to speak?

Tooooo whooooom dooo youuuuu wish toooooo speak?

Consonants can be softened or lengthened.

> "Ssssssooooooo," said snake. "Sssssssooooome
> peoplllllllllle havvvvvvve nnnnnnnnnnoooo
> ssssssensssse."

Consonants can also be done in staccato effect.

> I saiD, geT ouT!

Additional effects can be achieved by changing the shape of the mouth or the position of the tongue to say a sentence. Say the following sentence.

> (With mouth as wide open as possible)
>
> Hi! I'm wide-mouthed frog!

> (With lips pursed together in a tight O)
>
> Hi! I'm a wide-mouthed frog!

The first articulation is a wide-mouthed frog. The second is an imposter.

> Close the nose and say,
>
> Hi! I'm a wide-mouthed frog with a
> cold in my nose.

Speak through the nose by allowing the breath to escape through the nose while talking.

> Hi! I'm a wide-mouthed frog, and
> I talk through my nose. It's related
> to amphibian anatomy, and I can't
> help it.

Some fortunate people can do Donald Duck—a fine articulatory trick. Articulation decisions are necessary for some parts of a story. Characters talk differently from one another and from the narrator. Changes in articulation of sound will help to establish distinctions between characters. And while narration is likely to require fewer special articulatory effects, imagery in narrated parts of the story is much improved with the use of some deliberately designed articulations.

Dialect

Dialect differences heard in the surface structure of the language have their origins in the system of rules in memory that governs language production and language form. Some dialect differences occur in the sound system of the language, in articulation. These differences are usually referred to as "accents." Other differences can have to do with meanings of words or phrases, word structures, sentence structures, intonations, and inflections.

If the teller intends to use a dialect other than his or her own in a story, usually for character talk, he or she must use it correctly. Since dialect is associated with oral language and is usually poorly encoded in print, the storyteller should listen to the dialect to be used in order to develop an ear for it. Developing dialect from written cues in a story generally does not work. Unless the dialect is a familiar one, and one that the teller has learned to control naturally, through experience with it, it will probably require a substantial amount of practice.

The choice to include dialect in a story is essentially the storyteller's. Dialect can be very effective if it is done convincingly. The teller who has chosen to tell a given story that could use dialect effects but who has not mastered the dialect would do a better job of storytelling without it. An audience will enjoy the story more without a poorly done dialect. Badly rendered dialect makes the teller too visible. It limits teller control of the story and detracts from character credibility. A storyteller's own real abilities should serve as the measuring stick for what should and should not be attempted. The linguistic aspects of the story must be under teller control. When the teller has truly mastered the sounds and shapes of the dialect, it may be added to the story.

A not-so-trivial side note on the concern for dialect in the story has to do with telling regional and/or cultural stories. In many countries, geographic regions with identifiable cultural differences exist. Many of these regions have story traditions of their own, with locally revered casts of characters. Both stories and the characters who populate them "belong" to the people in the region. Storytellers are usually careful, when telling regional stories, to restrict their telling to tales from their own region or from regions with which they are familiar. People are generous, usually, with the latitude they extend to a storyteller. However, many audiences freeze up when a teller who obviously lacks the credentials (lived there, born there, go there often, somehow more than incidentally associated) tells a local story. No matter the quality of the telling, the teller somehow violates unspoken, unwritten rights of ownership. Dialect, of course, is one focus of this warning. It would be best, if the teller is not from New Mexico, has never lived there, and does not "speak the language" in a cultural sense, for him or her to avoid telling local stories and, especially, to avoid trying to use local dialect. Vermonters would not appreciate a Texan telling them Vermont stories. Montanans don't want to hear Charlie Russell or Whoop-up Trail stories from a storyteller from Florida; they want to hear whoppers and benders about the Caloosahatchee River or Lake Okeechobee. Missouri mosquitoes are better, somehow, when told about by a Missourian, even if the telling is done in Duluth, though Minnesotans could regale us all with anecdotes concerning their acquaintanceship with mosquitoes. The differences between people are fewer than the human motivations that we share. The teller will receive a more genuine reception if he or she tells stories from his or her own region and tells them well. We would all rather hear about another culture and another region from someone who knows that culture and region. We are hungry for such news, and we like to have regional differences exposed on the surface while connections, commonness, and cross-cultural, interregional community are confirmed in the deeper meanings of the story.

Tense

"Story" and storying are exercises in "time binding." A story has its own time. It must be told in such a way that the audience is taken into that time. The act of storying brings the audience into "story" time. It is not intended to bring the story into audience present time. Storytelling is a ritual designed, in part, to release the audience from the binding of their own present and allow them to enter into "story" time. ("Story" time is not the present tense of our own time in which we tell stories. It is the time in the story to which we all must go if we wish to see the story play itself out.) The shapes of story language help to bind the audience into story time. Practiced storytellers, whose storytellings are "tight," are either very aware of the language forms they employ during a telling, or they have developed an uncanny sense for fitting the right forms to the right story.

Stories are generally told in a formal past tense. Most of the ritual openings make reference to another time and place, the "other" reality in which the story happens. This other reality is usually characterized as being past—in a long ago beyond measuring. The teller violates both the promise of the ritual opening ("once upon a time") and the requirement of story formality by telling in the present tense. In addition, the present tense is too closely associated with daily reality and the teller's own personality and can strip the story of its timelessness. The storyteller must make a conscious effort to monitor for the use of tense. Beginning tellers at times slip inadvertently from past-tense forms ("she said"), to present ("she says"), and from present to the vernacular ("she goes"). A nervous teller is a candidate for such transgressions. Tense shifting is one mark of the unpracticed storyteller and signals lack of control of story and language. Audiences often react to such shifts with visible nervous movement and discomfiture; the reality of the story is threatened.

A storyteller can learn to control for tense by listening to tapes of his or her live tellings and by finding a friend willing to monitor a telling for tense employment. Practice, experience, and a developing awareness of one's language habits constitute the only long-lasting solution for control of verb forms during a story delivery.

(Some stories and some circumstances within stories do require the use of the present tense. Selected stories—perhaps local yarns and one-liners—may be framed in the present tense for deliberate effect. Selected character talk within a story may also be in the present tense, since, for the character, in-story experiences are present-tense occurrences. The storyteller is obliged to be aware of such monologues or dialogues, as these are often embedded in a story told in the past tense. The teller must switch from the one form to the other as these are required. A character who sometimes talks in the present does not give the storyteller license to shift the entire story to the present tense.)

Finally, the teller should refrain from using currently fashionable expressions in the story. "That old man really bugged him, so he didn't give the man any of his food or wine. Later, when he sat down to eat, he found only stones where his food had been, and that really bummed him out, you know?" Though the storyteller does create much of the actual language of the story, by slotting content into structure, the story does have a general linguistic shape of its own. Most stories do not contain the sidewalk lingo of the day and are only cheapened by its use.

Linguistic Garbage

Most forms of storytelling make a more formal use of language than does everyday conversation. Even though the storyteller must be ready to invent language for slotting into story structure, rather than presenting memorized text, the oral language in use during story delivery is generally more carefully monitored than the forms of common talk. (Exceptions do exist—some tall tales, liar's contest materials, character language within the story.)

The delivery of the oral literature—a storying—is not the place for linguistic mazes. A linguistic maze is a meaningless utterance that finds its way into spoken discourse when the speaker has either forgotten what he or she intended to say (content) or has momentarily lost control of the language itself (form). In both cases, the meaningful integration of language and content is interrupted, but the tongue goes right on, producing the likes of *ummmmm*; *ahhhhhhh*; *well then*; *y'know*; *OK, and thennnnnnn*; *and sooooooo*. Mazes are individual habits used by speakers to close over breaks in the continuous flow of language production. Most people use mazes at regular intervals as they speak.

While mazes are common in daily talk and often serve social purposes as well, they can be very distracting. Their presence suggests to a listener that the speaker is not well informed and/or not in control of ideas and language. The use of mazes in the told story usually identifies the immature, nervous, or unprepared storyteller. The lack of fluency during story delivery evidenced by the presence of mazes contributes to the effect of a story that is out of control.

One way the storyteller prepares a story, then, is to work at elimination of mazing. The teller can develop an awareness of his or her use of mazes by listening for them, taping live tellings, and finding a friend to identify them. (Practice sessions that do not take place before other people tend to produce more mazes, as do early attempts at telling a new story, and cannot be taken as typical of a storyteller's mazing habits.) Most mazing behavior is limited to a few favorite utterances: *umm*; *err*; or *aahhh*. The onset of a maze is often an identifiable moment; it is the linguistic equivalent of the moment before a sneeze and gives a warning that a glitch in language flow is about to occur. A storyteller can learn to recognize this signal and stop mazes before they happen. Because mazes do play a role in language production by providing the speaker with "catch-up" time during which content (ideas) and language forms are reintegrated, they must be replaced with something that will do the same job without causing the same degree of distraction. Silence—a thoughtful pause accompanied by eye contact with the audience—and/or stretching out the nearest vowel—"and he saaaiiiiid"—will serve the same psychological purpose during language production as an *um* or an *ah*. Once the teller is more confident and more practiced, the need to maze will diminish.

Unfortunately, storytelling is a risk-taking enterprise, which puts the teller in a maze-producing situation. Mazing accompanies nervousness, worry, distraction, and experimentation with new material. Practice and experience in front of audiences are the only remedies.

The story should also be clean of all false starting. A false start is an aborted attempt to get something said—a try that stops short of completion. Either the storyteller changes his or her mind about story content or decides that another language form would be more useful. "Then the soldier march. . . . Then the soldier marched . . . the king's soldier marched. . . . He went into. . . . He marched into the gold . . . the golden room, and. . . ." While this example is extreme, it does illustrate the problems with story control, language fluency, continuity of thought, and audience distraction that are both the cause and effect of false starting.

False starting is usually cured with practice and familiarity with the story. The more a teller tells, the fewer the false starts in the story during the telling.

Mazing and false starting happen frequently when a teller is nervous, fearful, and not in complete control of story language, structure, or content. Keeping storying language "clean," that is, free of mazes and false starts, and maintaining a level of formality appropriate to the delivery of a literature requires practice and some degree of awareness of and monitoring of language during telling. As a storyteller becomes more familiar with the language habits of oral stories, he or she will develop a sense (a set of internalized rules) for the language of stories and will be able to set "story" apart from informal conversation through the deliberate selection of language forms. Effective control of the language of the oral literature will help to maintain story opacity, to protect story reality as a place and time apart from that of daily circumstance, and to identify the storyteller as other rather than as self.

USING PARALINGUISTIC ELEMENTS

The oral story is infused with many effects that are not language but that are done in concert with it to enhance a narrative: noisemaking, body language, movement, shape making, characterization, and voice. Whether the storyteller is working from oral or printed material, story preparation will require deliberate decision making with regard to the employment of paralinguistic effects. Some effects will happen "naturally," both during practice and as surprises when the teller is before an audience.

Paralinguistic elements are dimensions of teller behavior during telling that are not governed by language rules (phonology, semantics, and syntax). These elements are used in conjunction with language during story delivery and add extra depth to story imagery as well as specificity of meaning to the language of the story. Just as the language of the story would be flat without the effective employment of intonation (pitch, stress, and juncture), the story itself would appear lifeless without the addition of paralinguistic elements.

The use of paralinguistic elements in the story is often intimately bound up with the personality and capability of the individual teller. Shaping the story with the body, movement during telling, posturing, assuming character voice, and inserting noises are necessary teller behaviors, but two different tellers will not uncommonly apply different paralinguistic shapes to the same story. The story is a different entity in the hands of each different teller.

As the storyteller is developing his or her capacity to carry the story paralinguistically as well as linguistically, he or she should become more aware of the paralinguistic elements present in the deliveries of stories at live tellings. Critical watching of and listening to other tellers will help the storyteller develop expectations for the paralinguistics of the told story, even if he or she does not choose to do what another teller did during telling. Paralinguistic elements are used in a conventional manner in the oral story; they are an intrinsic part of story content and form a dimension of the definition of (oral) "story." Aside from developing a repertoire of specific paralinguistic elements for use in his or her own stories, the teller must also cultivate a sense of oral story paralinguistics.

Movement and Shaping

The story is a collection of images that flow in sequence, one into the other. While language lends shape to the image by describing and telling, the body moves to make and/or shape the image, adding visual description. The personality of a character can sometimes be portrayed more convincingly through movement than through oral narrative. The weight of an object, light or heavy, and, perhaps, a character's surprise at the discovery of that weight, is an excellent opportunity for the employment of the body. Hands and arms, as well as other body parts, can be used to draw visual pictures. A tall tree, a round pot, a skinny dog, a long nose are elements of story content that beg for physical demonstration. Carrots need to be chopped, potatoes need to be dropped into soup, clothing of special concern to the story (e.g., velvet or silk) needs to be shown. Thorns can be touched and drawn away from to demonstrate their sharpness. Frogs hop, squirrels scamper up trees, cats yawn. All of these images can be made using the body.

How much movement is too much? What constitutes too little? Since storytelling is not theater, the teller is not acting out the story per se. He or she is allowing selected parts of the story to become physical by the careful and controlled use of the body. Putting a specific limit on teller movement during telling might unnecessarily restrict experimentation with movement and shaping. However, the teller must use good judgment. He or she cannot demonstrate every story image and therefore should choose the most important images, those that will benefit the most from such interpretation, that would be flat without movement, or that simply beg for activity. A sense of what to interpret through movement and what to leave to narration alone can be learned from attending storytellings and from using one's own understanding of visual sensibility and credibility.

While "too much" movement and shaping cannot be defined specifically, the teller should try to keep movement within the range of teller and audience comfort and use movement to complement aspects of the story. Movement that distracts the audience from the story itself, or that becomes more salient than the story, is probably overdone. Movement that interrupts comfortable telling or that prevents a smooth transition from one part of the story to the next is also probably overdone. Although an extreme case, the example of the teller who rolled with great energy across the floor to show the third little pig making his escape from the wolf might suffice for an illustration of "too much." In this case the audience became so thoroughly amused by the rolling that it lost its concentration. The teller transitioned into the roll from a standing position—an awkward endeavor—and emerged from it dizzy and disconnected from the story line. The entire effort was overly conspicuous and required more contortion than the image was worth; the movement itself became more of an item than the meaning intended. A simple rolling of hands and forearms would have sufficed. Perhaps the teller can evaluate degrees of movement in terms of diminishing returns. What is the least amount of clear and credible movement necessary to carry the image, beyond which no appreciable amount of further image development is possible?

Too little movement can be as distracting as too much. Again, "too little" is hard to identify in terms of specific behaviors. The teller should not be fearful of movement during telling to the extent that he or she delivers the story with the physical flexibility of a fencepost. Stories do move; without appropriate movement, the story loses a part of its special definition. The teller should choose aspects of the story for movement, then be natural, comfortable, and fluent. Tight, nervous, underdone attempts at movement signal teller fear and discomfort to the audience. If the teller intends to show the shape of an egg, for instance, then he or she should do the shape with full, round, easy, relaxed motions. The resulting shape should be a whole egg, with the rounded end and the pointed end, girth and length clarified. A movement that is worth doing is worth the length of time and the physical extension necessary to do it properly, so that the audience can see and react to it, perhaps coact with it. Rushing a movement out of fear or tension is less effective than skipping the movement altogether. Once again, an extreme case can provide an illustration: The teller used his hands to shape items in the story but sat on his hands at all other times; his hands were yanked out for quick, unintelligible flutters, then reinserted between chair and bottom. The overall effect was of nervous, tense lack of control. The audience soon shared the teller's case of the jitters.

To find some happy middle ground between over-executed and under-executed movement during telling, the storyteller might consider that the space immediately around his or her body belongs to the story and is in the story. The teller might use a single arm's length as a radius to mark the minimum space within which full, relaxed movement can occur without danger of extending movement to unnatural proportions. Walking, arm extensions, bowing, and other torso and leg movements do not generally look overblown if they are kept within that space. Half-hearted, weak attempts at movement that do not begin to use the space that belongs to the story look unnatural. Convincing movement within a story makes good use of the space owned by the story during telling, filling it comfortably but not abusing its boundaries.

Convergence of Gaze

The storyteller must use story content to determine those moments in the story that are especially appropriate for prolonged eye contact with the audience. Perhaps a character is making an important statement that has implications for later developments in the story, or is involved in some perfectly foolish activity, or is thinking about what another character has just said. All of these situations might call for the character to look directly at the audience. The teller might also want to look directly at members of the audience when narrating parts of the story that involve specific audience interaction or that suggest special collusion or understanding between the teller as narrator and the audience—for example, when teller and audience share a significant point of information that the story character does not yet know but will eventually discover, and that has predictable consequences.

Usually, moments of eye contact evolve as a natural part of character and narration development. The teller should guard against avoiding eye contact: telling to the floor, to people's foreheads, or to the back wall. Some conscious determination of the use of eye contact that is specific to story content can help to avoid this difficulty. The story belongs to the audience, after all. The teller uses eye contact to assure the audience of that ownership and to bring the audience into the story.

Character Posturing

Characters within "story" are not "us"; they are themselves. Characters live their in-story experiences afresh with each retelling of the story. The audience and teller experience a shared omniscience that the characters do not enjoy. Character in-story behavior is, therefore, a genuine first time every time response to an immediate circumstance. Where appropriate, the storyteller can make effective use of his or her body to project the full image of character-within-situation, by taking on the physical demeanor of the character at that moment in "story" time. The look on the face, set of the shoulders, angle of the body, and positioning of the legs, arms, and hands will all help to clarify character in-story experience and character reaction to it.

While such limited posturing can be utilized to produce positive and convincing effects, the teller must remember that he or she is not involved in a theatrical production. The teller does not act out the character as if involved in an on-stage performance, but uses the body to suggest the character. Experiences at live tellings will help the teller develop a sense of within-story characterization. Development of stories for telling can include some experimentation with aspects of characterization. Often the character will emerge naturally as teller and story become more friendly and familiar. Characters also sometimes grow in front of the audience and in cooperation with the audience. Such occurrences are surprises and confirm the existence of "story" as a separate being that lives in and through the teller.

Character Voice

Story characters do not talk like us any more than they act like us. Characters have voices of their own. Their voices reveal their feelings and reactions within the story and provide clues to their personalities and motivations. For instance, in "Happy Go Lucky" (Wiesner 1972) the wife and husband can be developed quite nicely through the appropriate use of voice. He is proving a point and playing a game for his part of the conversation. He must be clever yet convincingly innocent, since he is working on a hidden agenda. She must be believing, trusting, and happy with his decisions. Neither of these two talk in the same manner—pitch, stress, general body language, phrasing, and facial expression are all different. They are two different people having two different in-story experiences. Each is obliged to react to his or her own perceptions in his or her own voice. Neither of these is, in turn, the voice of the story narrator. The narrator has another voice altogether—the voice of one who has seen this happen before and knows the outcome.

Choosing and developing character voice require that the teller maintain a delicate balance between letting something natural happen and using his or her ability to critically assess a character in order to give the character the proper and convincing personality. The teller should not be fearful of using a collection of voices to help carry a story. Such voices can be used as an extension of story imagery. Once again, however, the teller is not acting in a theater production. Character voices, therefore, should not be overdone, but rather used selectively at moments in which they become the best vehicle for the development of story content.

Character voices should also be the genuine and believable extension of each respective character and should be consistent. Practice and story familiarity will help to define character voice and establish a good degree of regularity. Dialect, while it is not an inappropriate dimension for character development, should be used only when the teller can handle it convincingly. Inappropriate or poorly done dialect can be more of a hindrance than a help to the establishing of overall story credibility.

Noise

Stories make noises. The storyteller has the option of making some of the noises within the story, using voice and body, or using language to describe the noises, or both. A teller should be selective about which noises to actually make, and careful about the contortions used to make them. Calculated simulation of noise can strengthen a telling. The teller might choose to involve the audience in noise making, especially if the in-story noises are consistent, repetitive, and predictable. In "The Fat Cat" (Kent 1971), the stew bubbles and boils in a most enjoyable way. Young audiences like to make that noise. In "The Frogs and the Norther" (Chase 1971), both old man and frogs whistle. The tellings in which the teller incorporates whistling into the narrative are much more effective and pleasing to the audience than those in which he or she simply says that whistling happened. In "The Foolish Frog" (Seeger 1961)—a very noisy story—selected sounds are much better made than told about: chickens clucking, cows mooing, grass swishing, brooks bubbling, and a frog plopping.

The teller might consider, in the development of story noise, trying out and including those noises that will contribute naturally to story imagery and progression and that are especially important to story content. The teller might also examine a story for possible audience interactions through the consistent and predictable use of noise making.

Mood and Tone

Both mood and tone are intrinsic to the effective use of paralinguistic elements. Story mood and tone can be conveyed through movement, eye contact, both narrator and character posturing and voice, rate of telling, and control of breathing, as well as through straightforward narration. Simply telling the audience that the mood is one of fear, or that the tone is one of alarm, will not convince, if characters and other paralinguistic aspects of the delivery do not confirm it. The storyteller, then, can use knowledge of mood and tone established in the story and necessary for story sensibility to help in the development of credible paralinguistic elements and for the evaluation of specific story circumstances, characters, or images that require paralinguistic interpretation.

Rate/Speed

The rate at which parts of the story are narrated, or at which various characters are allowed to speak, is an important part of the expression of mood, tone, and character interaction with circumstance. A slow, easy pace, the appropriate rate for the description of the hippopotamus wallowing in the mud in "Speckled Eggs," might be inappropriate for describing the pancake's flight in "The Pancake" (Johnson et al. 1977) or the frustration of Mmoatia when she meets the gum baby in "A Story, A Story" (Haley 1970). Allowing oneself to feel and experience the story from within can help the teller to develop a sense of rate within story. Rate will vary according to story circumstance. The story itself will dictate its needs. The sensitive teller will consider that specific story segments require different treatments with regard to rate and will develop the story such that rate contributes to the overall credibility of the story.

Breathing

Stories breathe. Certainly, stories are alive in the hands of teller and audience during telling, but how many tellers have considered the literal breathing of the story through the patterns of aspiration of the teller? The story inhales and exhales with the teller; it owns the teller's voluntary and involuntary movements. The use of breath with language—huffing and puffing, controlled diaphragmatic release of a steady stream of air, a deep sigh, the sharp intake of breath, and holding the breath are all a part of the story.

Breathing is so natural an act that making it conscious might confuse. Since the teller already has language, he or she has control of the integration of language and breathing to achieve the various purposes for which language is used. The best way to begin, then, might be to allow characters and narrator to speak naturally and to examine the linguistic and other motivations of narrator and characters within the story. How would the character say this or that? Aspiration or breathing should follow along with general sensibility, presuming that the teller is not fearful of allowing the character to speak naturally. Some special effects can be created using breathing and can be added to the story to extend story imagery and credibility. The Foolish Frog puffs himself up, then explodes. In "Speckled Eggs," the hen cries, choked breath included; the snake hisses and sucks his breath in slowly. The teller can identify those specific story elements that require special treatment through the use of breath and add these to the otherwise natural patterns of breathing and language use of characters and narrator.

Props

Props can sometimes enhance the telling of a specific story and/or encourage or specify audience interaction. While tellers vary in their inclinations regarding the use of props, and some view props as inappropriate altogether, a few considerations are in order. The story is still the most important part of the telling. The story has an individual integrity; it owns all of its conventions and internal devices. It likewise owns its props. Since the teller should consider the props as belonging to the story, props that become so overpowering a presence that the audience is enticed away from the story are inappropriate for storytelling.

Inappropriate props can include materials so unwieldy that the storyteller cannot keep them under control, props that attract more attention as single items than the story itself, props that do not integrate well with the story, and those that are detrimental to the progress of the telling. Props should become a transparent part of the telling and contribute to the opacity of the story. Props that cannot be manipulated with ease or that are individually spectacular tend to become opaque themselves and, therefore, less useful for the purposes of telling the story. The teller might use traditional props, and various musical instruments as guides to how much prop is just right and how much is too much (Feller-Bauer 1977; Pellowski 1977).

The teller might also want to consider the use of props only for selected stories and work to develop a repertoire that includes stories told with and stories told without props. Experience dictates that the teller should be able to tell a given story without props, even if he or she is accustomed to using props with the story. Practiced tellers often claim that they grow away from prop use with experience and that they learn to depend increasingly on other paralinguistic elements to carry a story as they develop their confidence and capabilities. They also discover that props, even for the same story, are more effective with some types of audiences than others, and they abandon props under certain telling circumstances.

Once the storyteller has committed a story to props, the props should be used with ease. They should not be clutched and/or used to keep the hands busy.

Conclusion

The collective, integrated use of paralinguistic elements during telling is a choreography that becomes natural with repeated tellings and that is often "right" subconsciously more than calculated consciously. The teller should be aware, however, that the oral story does depend upon the paralinguistic behavior of the teller for part of its definition, and that stories should be developed with some conscious attention to the deliberate application of paralinguistic effects.

DEVELOPING MEMORY FOR STORY LANGUAGE

Remembering Linguistic Elements

Repetitious Language

Repetitious language within the story must be committed to memory. Often such language is a prescribed and expected part of ritual participation for the audience and a dimension of the audience's sense of "story." Repetitious language is one vehicle by which a story is negotiated. Conformity to the convention of repetitious language in a given story should not be violated.

Character Monologue/Dialogue

If the exact shape of character talk is critical to story flow and outcome, such language must be committed to memory. For instance, in "The Gunniwolf" (Harper 1967) the mother's warning to her daughter early in the story must be worded somewhat specifically. If not, the later dialogue between the wolf and the girl is without precedent and the wolf's language (which also must be done specifically) seems out of context. Without language specificity, the story loses sensibility, and cause-and-effect relationships disappear. Character portrayal and personality can also be illustrated by the use of specific language forms. In such cases, character talk and language style must be learned.

Cues

Some language within given stories must be said in a precise shape because it contains cues to later story developments. If the language is paraphrased or left out altogether, the audience loses a cue from which to make critical predictions and is often later confronted with an event, or character behavior or language, for which there seems to be no motivation. In one type of "quest motif" story, the protagonist is instructed to guard something—a cue that turns out to be critical to subsequent story action. Without the early admonition to "Watch the _____," later story events become incoherent and illogical. The storyteller is often gently reprimanded by an audience when he or she omits such cues during a telling. Such an omission will become apparent later in the story and very likely force the teller to invent a flashback episode to pick up the missing piece.

General Narrative

Most story language need not—indeed, should not—be memorized. The written shape of the story (presuming that the teller is beginning with printed text) is not the negotiated, situation-specific, context-embedded shape that the story will take during telling. The oral story is not a recitation. The concrete shape assumed by the story during telling will occur only once. The story itself is saved in teller memory as an abstraction that is not invested with specific words and phrases. The teller who memorizes a story word for word jeopardizes the telling by making the story into a linguistically frozen or rigid package, by denying the audience its prerogatives with regard to negotiation, and by risking a memory slip that could result in failure to deliver the story altogether. (The memorized story is delivered as a recitation; it is not a storytelling.) With the exception of language forms that must be delivered as givens, flexibility and the ability to say it more than one way are measures of a good storyteller. Because each new telling of a story is a reinvention in which abstract patterns must be rendered into specific language forms, the teller resolves the problem of storying a given body of information with every delivery.

Mapping Paralinguistic Elements

All storytellers make in-memory maps of their stories before telling them. Since these maps are abstract, we can only guess at their shapes. They are probably somewhat different from teller to teller. The on-paper or otherwise physical maps or outlines that tellers make for story preparation are certainly variant. Many storytellers make some use of artifacts or devices to remember a story. But because of our orientation to print, a substantial number of tellers resort to some form of written notation. Part of a story map is structural, containing slotted content. Maps also contain ritualized elements, necessary quotations for precision of language when that is required, and, perhaps, notes regarding the use of special language and nonlanguage effects. The following story is given in more detail and with more carefully arranged notation than the usual scribbles of most tellers. It is intended to illustrate the paralinguistic dimensions of decision making during story preparation.

SPECKLED EGGS*

Setting

One time, and it was a very long time

ago, when the world was newer and people

were more humble, there were many more

chickens than there are today—and they

lived more independently, too. There were

red chickens, and there were blue chickens.

There were green chickens and purple

chickens. There were brown and white,   —audience invention—
direct question: "what kinds
of chickens were there?"

puce and chartreuse chickens. There were

organdy chickens, satin chickens and

burlap chickens, canvas and denim chick-

ens. There were lace, plaid, striped, and

polka-dotted chickens. And, there were—

but only a few—ˈspeckledˈchickens.   pause

---

*Developed by Sandra A. Rietz.

Now, all of those chickens laid eggs,

no differently than today. And it would

stand to reason that:

pause-eye contact —
cue audience to chant

The RED chickens laid RED EGGS!

And the BLUE chickens laid BLUE

EGGS!

And the GREEN chickens laid GREEN

EGGS!

And the PURPLE chickens laid PURPLE

EGGS!

And the BROWN chickens laid BROWN

audience chant

EGGS!

And the WHITE chickens laid WHITE

EGGS!

And the PUCE chickens laid PUCE

EGGS!

And the CHARTREUSE chickens laid

CHARTREUSE EGGS!

And the ORGANDY chickens laid

ORGANDY EGGS!

And the SATIN chickens laid SATIN

EGGS!

And the BÚRLAP chickens laid BÚRLAP

ÉGGS!

And the CÁNVAS chickens laid CÁNVAS

ÉGGS!

And the DÉNIM chickens laid DÉNIM

ÉGGS!

And the LÁCE chickens laid LÁCE   audience chant

ÉGGS!

And the PLÁID chickens laid PLÁID

ÉGGS!

And the STRÍPED chickens laid STRÍPED

ÉGGS!

And the PÓLKA-DOTTED chickens laid

PÓLKA-DÓTTED EGGS!

And the SPÉCKLED chickens laid

SPÉCKLED ÉGGS!

The speckled chickens laid just as

many eggs as the others, but, somehow,   somewhat sadly—
                                                 this is so sad
there néver were as many speckled

chickens.

This story is a documentary about why

there were so few speckled chickens—an

unfortunate circumstance, indeed — and

how that unfortunate circumstance was

remedied. And, for the more astute lis-

teners, a message having to do with

⸺ pause and eye contact

virtuous behavior, as well.

One of the few speckled chickens in

the world in those times was a speckled

hen. She had built a nest in the grass, a

slipshod piece of carpentry. But it was rela-

tively well concealed under the overhanging

branches of a low-growing bottle brush

tree.

Events in setting category

Event repeat begins.

1. Every morning, when this speck-

   led hen awoke, she laid an

   egg. And because she was a

   SPECKLED chicken, it was a

   SPECKLED EGG! (We should

⸺ pause

action, movement, noise, and shaping — Hen lays the egg — this is strenuous work — and add appropriate cackles while laying — she holds egg up afterward and/or cradles it

⸺ pause and eye contact

   expect that it would be! She

   wasn't plaid or denim, after all.)

2. And every morning, after laying

   the egg, she climbed out of her   *strut about moderately—*
                                                chickenlike

   nest and strutted about a bit,

   clucking and crowing (such as

   hens can), "I LAID AN ÉGG! I

   LAID AN ÉGG! I LAID A

   SPÉCK-ÉK, A SPÉCK-ÉK, A   *loud and proud*

   SPÉCK-ÉK-ÉK-ÉK-ÉK-ÉK-ÉK-

   ÉK-ÉK-ÉCKLED ÉGG!
                                                pause—blink—head move-
                                                ments—chickenlike

3. Then, as she did every morning,   *moderate, strut/walk chick-*
                                                enlike—head, face and eye
   she set off down the path to tell   *movements good here*

   everybody all about it: "I laid an

   égg! I laid an égg! I laid a speck-   *as before—with movement*

   ék-ék-ék-ék-ék-ék-ék-ék-éckled

   égg!"

Substitutions begin.

                                                              pause
4. The first person she came to was

   Hippopotamus. He was out in the

   muddiest part of the swamp, wal-

   lowing about. (He did this every

   morning. It was a form of

meditation.) He wallowed ⌐quite⌐   _____ pause

vigorously—like this ⁓ . . .   Teach/cue audience—this is
coactive participation.
Make wallowing/schlup-
ping muddy noises—like
suction. Hippopotamus

a. When he saw Hen he called   lifts one leg at a time out
of the mud—use hands/
arms to simulate leg lift-
out, "Good morning, Hen!   ing to accompany sucking
noises.

And how are you this morn-

ing?"   in voice—facial expression
to characterize, if desired

b. Hen was very proud, of

course, and she answered, "I

am well. And it is a fine   in voice—chickenlike

morning. I laid an egg! I laid

an egg! I laid a speck-ek-ek-

ek-ek-ek-ek-ek-ek-eckled egg!"   as before—with movement

c. "Well, Hen," said Hippopota-

mus, and not without compas-

sion, "I'm very pleased for   _____ pause

you. That ⌐is⌐an⌐achievement⌐   in voice—
expression
of ⌐worth, I'm sure."   _____ pause

d. And Hen strutted off down

the path clucking and mutter-   moderate movement—
Hen walks off as before

ing to herself, but none too

softly, "I laid an egg! I laid an   Hen—as before

/   / / /
egg! I laid a speck-ek-ek-ek-

/ / / / /   /
ek-ek-ek-ek-ek-eckled egg!"

5. The next person she came to was ⌐——————— pause

Elephant. Elephant was standing

belly-deep in the river, taking a

morning bath. It was a daily activ-

ity for Elephant, and, so he said,

fortified him for the events of the

day. He bathed by sucking up

water in his trunk, then spraying

it over his back, like this . . .

teach/cue audience to coactive participation — use arm and hand as a trunk — suck water up with hand in front of body to an appropriate noise — a wet, sloppy, wonderful noise — lift arm overhead and blow water out over back and shoulders to an equally satisfying spraying sound

a. [Repeat 4a.] ——————

as with Hippopotamus — voice and expression for Elephant's character

b. [Repeat 4b.]————————————— as before

c. Elephant answered, in a

kindly manner, "I'm very

happy for you, Hen. This is   voice

indeed pleasant news."

d. [Repeat 4d.] ————————————— as before

6. The next person she came to was ⌐——————— pause

Giraffe. Giraffe, like all giraffes,
——————————— pause
/   ⌐ / | /
had a very long neck. His head

was breakfasting in the trees while

the rest of his body waited around

down below. He chewed up the

leaves like this . . .

Teach/cue audience to co-
active participation. Extend
arm overhead—use hand to
simulate Giraffe's mouth—
chew leaves with appropriate masticating sound—the
mushier the better.

a. [Repeat 4a.] ———————————— as before

b. [Repeat 4b.] ———————————— as before

c. Giraffe answered fondly,

    because he was genuinely fond

    of Hen, "Well! And good

    news, too! My best wishes to

    you and the chick-to-be."

voice and characterization

d. [Repeat 4d.] ——————————— as before

7. The next person she came to was

    Snake. Snake was curled on top of

    a rock, sunning himself. For

    Snake, sunning was what he had

    to do in order to start the day.

    (Some of us have coffee.)

a. [Repeat 4a.] ——————————— as before

b. [Repeat 4b.] ——————————— as before

c. Snake answered ssssssooolis-

sssssitoussssssly, "Why, Henn-

nnnnn. Thissssss isssss news-

sssss of sssome ssssignificans-

ssssse. I am pleassssssed that

you passssssed on the inforrr-

rmmmmmaaaassshhhhhun-

nnn."

begin audience hissing

teach/cue audience to
breathe and hiss—slowly—
sinister and ugly—to suggest
that the snake is dangerous
and not to be trusted—

audience continues hissing
as teller does snake voice
and characterization

d. [Repeat 4d.] —————————— as before

e. Then Snake uncoiled himself

from around his sunning rock

and slithered off into the

brush.

Substitutions end.

8.   Hen walked until noontime, then

returned home to her nest to have

lunch and sit on her egg. When

she arrived at the nest, she peered

into it, only to find that the egg

was gone. And she wailed and

assume an "oh misery me"
expression here—chicken-
like

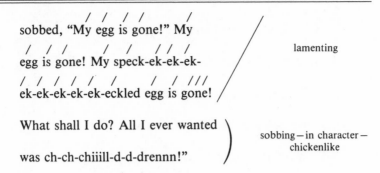

sobbed, "My egg is gone!" My

egg is gone! My speck-ek-ek-ek-

ek-ek-ek-ek-ek-ek-eckled egg is gone!

lamenting

What shall I do? All I ever wanted

was ch-ch-chiiill-d-d-drennn!"

*sobbing — in character —
chickenlike*

Problem: Someone or something is stealing Hen's egg. We know who, and we also know why.

Event sequence

    * The next day, Hen laid another egg.

She was so very pleased and not just a

little proud. She went off down the path to

tell everybody about it.

*repeat effects from * to * as
given in first sequence*

[Repeat appropriate parts of events 2

and 3 and all of 4 through 8 * in setting

*this takes the story through
another identical sequence —
a bit laborious and even
boring*

above, or narrate] "She told

Hippopotamus, and she told Elephant,

— pause

and she told Giraffe, and she told Snake.

— pause

She told everyone.

— pause

*narrate this —
to avoid going
through another
entire sequence.*

And when she got home, her egg was

— pause

gone." [If narrating, begin repeat at event

8, Hen's lines, "My egg is gone . . ."]

repeat as given previously

Day after day Hen laid her egg. And

day after day she came home to find it

gone. Finally, in a state of extreme dis-

tress, she took her problem to Spider.

Spider was known to play tricks on people,

but he was also very wise. Hen told Spider

about her trouble: about how she laid an

egg; about how she told Hippopótamus

and Elephant and Giraffe and Snake and

everyone else as well.

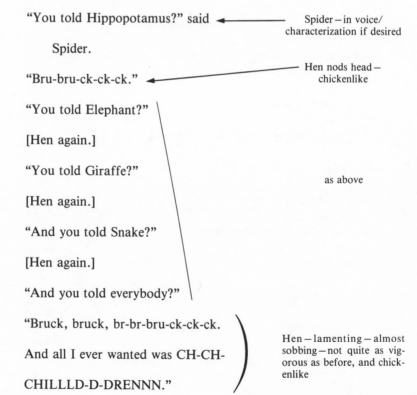

"You told Hippopotamus?" said ← —————— Spider—in voice/
characterization if desired

    Spider.

"Bru-bru-ck-ck-ck." ← —————— Hen nods head—
chickenlike

"You told Elephant?"

[Hen again.]

"You told Giraffe?"

[Hen again.]   as above

"And you told Snake?"

[Hen again.]

"And you told everybody?"

"Bruck, bruck, br-br-bru-ck-ck-ck.

And all I ever wanted was CH-CH-   Hen—lamenting—almost
sobbing—not quite as vig-
orous as before, and chick-
CHILLLD-D-DRENNN."   enlike

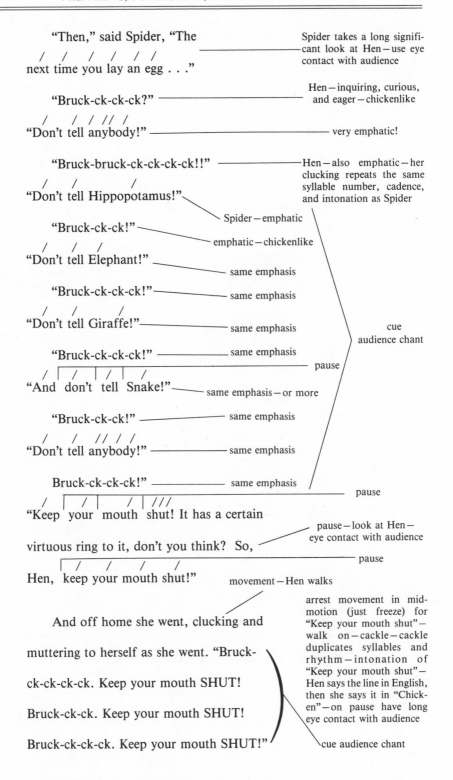

"Then," said Spider, "The
/ / / / /
next time you lay an egg . . ."

Spider takes a long significant look at Hen—use eye contact with audience

"Bruck-ck-ck-ck?"

Hen—inquiring, curious, and eager—chickenlike

/ / / // /
"Don't tell anybody!"

very emphatic!

"Bruck-bruck-ck-ck-ck-ck!!"

Hen—also emphatic—her clucking repeats the same syllable number, cadence, and intonation as Spider

/ / /
"Don't tell Hippopotamus!"

Spider—emphatic

"Bruck-ck-ck!"

emphatic—chickenlike

/ / /
"Don't tell Elephant!"

same emphasis

"Bruck-ck-ck-ck!"

same emphasis

/ / /
"Don't tell Giraffe!"

same emphasis

"Bruck-ck-ck-ck!"

same emphasis

pause

cue
audience chant

/ / / /
"And don't tell Snake!"

same emphasis—or more

"Bruck-ck-ck!"

same emphasis

/ / // / /
"Don't tell anybody!"

same emphasis

Bruck-ck-ck-ck!"

same emphasis

pause

/ / / / ///
"Keep your mouth shut! It has a certain

virtuous ring to it, don't you think? So,

pause—look at Hen—
eye contact with audience

pause

/ / / /
Hen, keep your mouth shut!"

movement—Hen walks

And off home she went, clucking and

muttering to herself as she went. "Bruck-

ck-ck-ck-ck. Keep your mouth SHUT!

Bruck-ck-ck. Keep your mouth SHUT!

Bruck-ck-ck-ck. Keep your mouth SHUT!"

arrest movement in mid-motion (just freeze) for "Keep your mouth shut"—walk on—cackle—cackle duplicates syllables and rhythm—intonation of "Keep your mouth shut"—Hen says the line in English, then she says it in "Chicken"—on pause have long eye contact with audience

cue audience chant

Event repeat begins; **substitutions** begin. Repeat events 1 through 8 in **events in setting category,** with the following changes or substitutions:

see previous notes

1. The very next morning, Hen laid

   another egg.

   same laying routine

2. [Omit "And every morning after laying the egg"]

   [Substitute Hen's speech:] "I ... I

   lai ... I laid ... I laid an ... I ...

   bruck-bru-bru-ck-ck ... I laid ...

   bruck ... I laid an ... bru-bru-

   ck ... I ... I ... a sp ... a speck ...

   speck ... bruck brruuuuck-ck-

   ck ... a speck ... a speck ...

   brrruck-ck-ck-bruuuuuuck ... ...

   essentially same as before — but Hen tries to keep from spilling the beans — she struggles not to tell

   bruck-bruuuu-bruck-ck-ck.
   / / /// ///
   Keep your mouth shut!
   / / ///
   Bruuuck bruck bruuuckkkk
   ///
   BRUCK!"

   this is chicken for "Keep your mouth shut"

   "

3. [Substitute Hen's speech as in 2 above.]

   repeat Hippo sequence — but Hen does not tell — Elephant, Giraffe, Snake — she does not tell — for each, do as in 2 above — struggle to keep from telling — on "Keep your mouth shut" Hen walks away, shaking head and muttering — do walking routine here

4.

    b.   [Substitute Hen's speech as in 2 above.]

    c.   [Substitute Hippopotamus' reply:]

        "Well! Yes, indeed, Hen. I understand perfectly." But, of course, he did not.

    d.   [Substitute Hen's speech:]

        "Bruuuck-bruck-ck-ck-ck. Keep your mouth SHUT! Bruck bruck brrruuuck BRUCK!"

as before

Note: with each animal, Hen has to keep from telling about the egg and finally must stop herself physically. Teller can slap hand over mouth, close eyes, and clench teeth or whatever to keep Hen from telling—be forceful about stopping her—the urge to blurt it out is strong.

5.

    b.   [Substitute Hen's speech as in 2 above.]

    c.   [Substitute Elephant's reply:]

        "My, my Hen! What a story! And so you did, or I did, or somebody did! I don't know. But what a delightful conversation we've had, to be sure!" But he wasn't sure at all.

    d.   [Substitute Hen's speech as in 4 above.]

as before

6.

    b. [Substitute Hen's speech as in
2 above.]

    c. [Substitute Giraffe's reply:]

       "Yes! I quite agree! I think!

       And I hope to return the

       favor, too!" But he wasn't

       certain for what.

    d. [Substitute Hen's speech as in
4 above.]   *as before*

7.

    b. [Substitute Hen's speech as in
2 above.]

    c. [Substitute Snake's reply:]

       "I sssseeeeeeeee!" But he

       didn't.

    d. [Substitute Hen's speech as in
4 above.]   *as before*

    e. [Omit:]

8. When Hen arrived home that day
and peered into her nest, there
was her egg, safe and waiting for
her.

                            chickenlike motions of
joy—rock egg in arms—
sing "Rock-a-Bye Baby" in
chicken

Event-repeat with substitutions ends.

The next morning, Hen laid another

egg. Now she had TWO SPECKLED

EGGS! And did she tell anybody? NO!   audience   coacts — chants.
                                          Ease in with hand signals —
SHE KEPT HER MOUTH SHUT! ←——————————   no more is necessary.

The next morning she laid ANOTHER   pause, establish eye contact
                                       to invite audience to join in
ONE! Now she had THREE SPECKLED
                                          allow audience to chant
EGGS! And did she tell anybody? NO!   whole routine when learned

SHE KEPT HER MOUTH SHUT!

[Continue this routine for numbers
four through nine.]

And on the last morning, she laid one

last egg. Now she had TEN SPECKLED

EGGS! And did she tell anybody? NO!   same as before

SHE KEPT HER MOUTH SHUT!

Hen sat on those eggs for eggsactly twenty-

one days. (I checked with the ag extension

office on that.) And at the end of those

twenty-one days, those eggs began to

hatch. First, there were little cracks that

appeared. The cracks widened. Then little

beaks appeared. Then the eggs cracked   add appropriate motions

open, one by one.

Hen was EGGSTATIC! There were

pause

her children! "Ten children! Ten

children!" And she counted them.

"ONE!

TWO!

THREE!

FOUR!

FIVE!

SIX!   audience coactivity—
              chant/shout/count
SEVEN!

EIGHT!

NINE!

TEN!

TEN!

TEN SPECK-EK-EK-EK-EK-EK-EK-EK-   as before

EK-ECKLED CHILDREN!"

She was so proud! She gathered her

ten speckled children about her and set   walk as before

off down the path to show everybody.

Event repeat begins; **substitutions** begin.
Repeat events 4 through 7 in **events in
setting category,** with the following
changes or substitutions:]

4.

a. And Hippopotamus called

    out, "Well! Good morning,   voice and character

    Hen! And what have we

    here?"

b. Hen was quite puffed up

about her accomplishment,

and she cackled and crowed

pridefully.

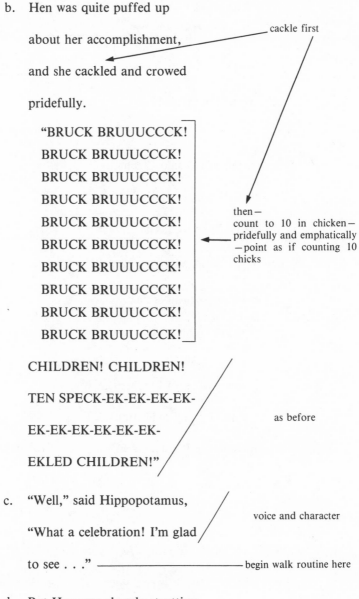

cackle first

"BRUCK BRUUUCCCK!

BRUCK BRUUUCCCK!

BRUCK BRUUUCCCK!

BRUCK BRUUUCCCK!

BRUCK BRUUUCCCK!

BRUCK BRUUUCCCK!

BRUCK BRUUUCCCK!

BRUCK BRUUUCCCK!

BRUCK BRUUUCCCK!

BRUCK BRUUUCCCK!

then—
count to 10 in chicken—
pridefully and emphatically
—point as if counting 10
chicks

CHILDREN! CHILDREN!

TEN SPECK-EK-EK-EK-EK-

EK-EK-EK-EK-EK-EK-

EKLED CHILDREN!"

as before

c. "Well," said Hippopotamus,

"What a celebration! I'm glad

to see . . ."

voice and character

begin walk routine here

d. But Hen was already strutting

away, clucking and cackling,

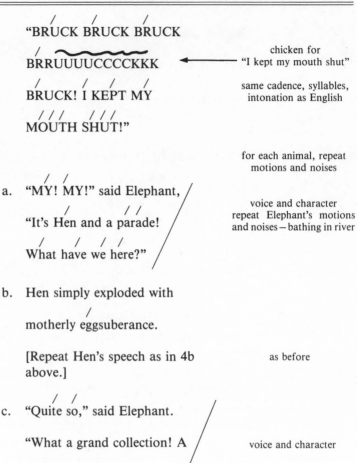

"BRÚCK BRÚCK BRÚCK

BRRUUUUCCCCKKK ←——— chicken for "I kept my mouth shut"

BRÚCK! I KÉPT MÝ   same cadence, syllables, intonation as English

MÓÚTH SHÚT!"

for each animal, repeat
motions and noises

5.

   a. "MÝ! MÝ!" said Elephant,

       "It's Hén and a parade!   voice and character
                                    repeat Elephant's motions
       What have we here?"   and noises—bathing in river

   b. Hen simply exploded with

       motherly eggsuberance.

       [Repeat Hen's speech as in 4b   as before
       above.]

   c. "Quite so," said Elephant.

       "What a grand collection! A   voice and character

       matched set! Why, I . . ."

   d. [Repeat 4d above.]   as before

6.
   a. "AH HA!" said Giraffe. "And

       what are you bringing with   voice and character

       you today, Hen?"

   b. Hen was totally without

       humility.

[Repeat Hen's speech as in 4b   as before
above.]

c.   "That is visible and verifi-

able," said Giraffe. "What an   voice and character

elegant entourage! A veri-

table . . ."

d.   [Repeat 4d above.]   as before

7.

a.   "SSSSSSOOOOOOOO-

oooooo, Hennnnnnn," said

Snake. "Whaaaat aarrrrrre   voice and character

thessssseeee?"

b.   Hen was ALMOST unforgiv-

ably arrogant.

[Repeat Hen's speech as in 4b   as before
above.]

c.   "I SSSEEEE THEMMMMM

CLLLLEARRRRLY

EEEENOUGHHHHH,   voice and character

HENNNNNN!" said Snake.

"I THHOUGHHHT . . ."

d.   [Repeat 4d above.]   as before

Conclusion

Then Hen went on through the com-

munity to introduce her brood to everyone.

And with every introduction, it was the

same. It was, at least, until she came to

Spider. "Aaaahhhh . . . ," said Spider.

"Some success, I see." Hen did not preen

or cackle for Spider. She only said, "Yes.

Ten children. All I ever wanted was

children."

chickenlike
tone and cadence

Moral

"And now you have them, Hen," said

Spider. "There is often some virtue in

keeping one's mouth shut."

The above story is a transcription of a story map with notation for many of the oral language and paralinguistic features that cannot be encoded into print. It is perhaps more detailed than most story outlines in the typical working collection, but the example illustrates the many decisions a storyteller must make in order to tell a story.

Paralinguistic elements make a story live and breathe and give it a credible reality within "story." The audience will often be able to participate ritually or coactively through the use of paralinguistic features. The teller must decide which features to use, where to insert them, and how, if at all, to involve the audience directly in their use.

Paralinguistic elements can also account for the difference between the story that is told and the story that is "told about." The told story employs such devices as movement, shape, voice, and noise, which identify the story-teller as the other and place teller and audience within story time. The teller becomes the story, and the story assumes the forms of life. The "told-about" story is not a living oral story, is not a true storytelling, and does not require a storyteller. One can tell *about* a story without crossing over into the time of the story, without entering the living framework of the tale.

> There was this hen who kept telling everybody about her eggs. So, every day, when the snake found out she had laid a new egg, he went and ate it. She always cried when her egg was gone, because she wanted to have children. One day she went to the spider for help. He told her to keep her mouth shut about the eggs, so she did. And then she laid ten eggs and had ten children. She was very happy.

The above narration is a story description, not a storytelling. Younger children often omit paralinguistic and other identifying features of the told story. They tell *about* rather then *tell*. The genuinely told story is seen from the inside, with teller and audience together experiencing its living circumstances as these "happen." The told-about story is seen from without. It is nothing more than a description set in our own time and place. It does not unbind us from daily routine because it lacks those interpretive elements that serve to transport us into "story" place and time and that build the story around us.

Practicing

Most storytellers do practice in some way before delivering a story for the first time. Outlining a story and adding interpretive notations, making decisions about language and paralanguage in the story, are a dimension of practice. Some tellers can see, hear, and do the story just by making notations and move from that activity directly to working with the audience. Other tellers prefer intermediate steps.

Tape Recordings

Experiment with both audio- and videotaped practice tellings. Use the tapes to make critical evaluations of interpretive elements and to further expand upon the oral aspects of the story. Some tellers save these first attempts. One can see how repeated tellings of the same story contribute to story evolution by comparing an original taping with the story after the story is several years old.

Mirrors

Mirrors do not work for every teller. Some tellers manage to be detached and somewhat clinical about observing their own storytelling reflections in a mirror. Others cannot. Try it. The mirror does what the tape recording does — provides concrete substance from which to critique one's interpretations and technique. Perhaps telling the whole story before a mirror is not possible. But the teller might try out some of the special effects, especially movements, just to be able to examine what an audience might see.

Car Trips

Some of the best storying can be done while the teller is alone in the car. The longer the trip, the better. Pay no attention to other drivers who stare. Do the stories. Some of the better interpretive ideas that later can enhance story imagery can be invented while driving.

Falling Asleep

Tell a story silently while falling asleep. Try to "see" the story playing in the head — a semiconscious, coherent dream that invites left and right brain integration of pattern and content. This method not only aids memory, but it allows the mind to ramble and invent. And it is better than sleeping tablets.

The Volunteer Audience

Find a person or a small group of people with whom to work out a new story. Tell them "about" the story. Tell them parts of the story. Tell them the experimental version of the story, allowing for stops, comments, and informal blurtings such as "I'm lost here," or "I always have trouble remembering this part."

Kitchens

Tell the story — and cook. Stop to read the recipe and resume the story when ready.

Gardens

Tell the story — and weed. Hoe! Dig! Chant parts of the story to the rhythms of the work.

Ironing

Tell the story—and iron. Don't leave the iron on the shirt while working out an especially vigorous part of the story requiring both arms.

Showering

Take a long, hot shower. Tell the story. Soap and scrub energetically.

Audiences

The best practice requires the audience and the formal telling. All preliminary practicings are informal and do not restrict the teller. They do not demand that the teller finish the story, or be concise, or not repeat sections, or not try several contrasting methods of saying a character's line. The formal telling does not allow the teller to stop and try some story feature over again. It pushes the teller to a fine tuning and smooth integration of all aspects of the story. The last and most important practice is the formal telling.

The story and the storytelling are situation dependent or context embedded. If practice does not take place in front of a real audience, it lacks just the dimensions of situation or context needed to engage the teller in a negotiated story construction. Making the oral story is a problem-solving exercise that is approached differently with each telling circumstance. Telling while cooking is a good preliminary exercise, but cooking and kitchens are contexts and circumstances quite different from those of a formal storytelling. The story will "come out" in a form that is influenced by the context in which it is told. Even with the most extensive of practice efforts, the storyteller cannot really know what shape his or her new story will take until that story is constructed in front of and with an audience.

Every telling of a story is a practice. The story will be different with each telling. It will evolve, largely because new circumstances—contexts—will force it to change shape. Repeated telling before an audience and repeated solving of the same problem—how to tell a given story—is the best way to learn how a story works and how to control it. The audience is a part of the story and is in the story. The teller cannot truly know the story without the audience.

Determining how much practice of the "disembedded" (out of audience context) kind is needed before going public is individual. Teller comfort, control, readiness, and story readiness (the workability of decisions made regarding oral encoding and technique) must be taken into account. A story is not ready if it has not been developed and if the teller is prepared to do nothing more than a flat recitation or a telling *about*. At the other extreme, a teller cannot indefinitely postpone going before an audience. Perhaps one reasonable measure of readiness is the degree of change in the story from one practice session to the next. When the story appears to be essentially the same product with each new run-through, with perhaps only very minor modifications, it is sufficiently developed. A story and a storyteller are always, together, a developmental package. When story and teller are no longer changing, developing, and improving together privately, the time to go to the next level has come. The audience is the ingredient needed, then, to help the story and the teller evolve.

Learning the Literary Story

The literary story is a written story. It is not an oral story encoded into print, but a story whose original form is written language. It conforms to the conventions of written, not oral, language and takes the top-level structure of written discourse. It is generally authored by one or more identifiable individuals, instead of belonging to the culture as a whole. It evolved as a product of a private composition process and cannot undergo further evolution, unless at the hands of its author and through subsequent publication.

The oral story is in a constant state of change, but the written story is whole as it is written. It is not missing any linguistic features; it is composed of exactly the language its author intended it to have.

The printed oral story lacks all of the features of oral language that cannot be encoded into print. What is missing from the oral story must be interpreted back into it for telling, while the written story has all the language features it requires for the purpose for which is was intended—to be read. It was not intended to be oral. Making it oral, then, creates some interesting problems, not the least of which is deciding whether it can or should be oral at all.

The only person with the authority to infuse the written story with its correct oral language features is the author. The author chose the written language forms; he or she would, presumably, know how these forms would "sound." The storyteller can only guess at what the author might wish the story to be in an oral form. But the teller does not have to guess at the intended shapes of sentences—the actual language of the story. The author used language with deliberation when he or she created the story. The storyteller who wishes to tell a written story *must* use the language given by the author. This requires strict memorization.

The memorized written story done orally is more a recitation—a performance—of written material than it is a storytelling. How many and which oral language features the teller adds to the recitation is limited by the consideration that the language of the story should not be changed; story "development"—changes in the language and shape of the story by the storyteller—is not proper. Story preparation is also somewhat restricted. Certainly, the storyteller must make decisions about the use of intonation and articulation. On the other hand, dialect should not be added to a written story that has none. If the narrative suggests dialect, but the written story does not encode it, the teller must determine its effectiveness and his or her capability before adding it. Expressly written dialect forms in the story should be done as they are written. If the storyteller cannot do them properly, a new problem arises, since the written story should be done as given. The best rule, though it promotes taking liberties with the story, is for the storyteller to avoid doing dialects that he or she cannot handle convincingly. The procedures for dealing with tense and linguistic garbage that apply to oral stories also apply to written.

Audience interaction with the written story should be limited to coactivity. The audience is no more at liberty than the teller to reshape the story during a telling. For that reason, the storyteller should not plan to invite the audience into other types of interactions and should discourage these if they occur spontaneously.

Paralinguistic elements do not encode in the written story. They are narrated, told about; they do not happen physically. We learn from the narrator that a character laughs. But, if the written story does not actually encode the laughter itself, the real laughter is not a part of the story. The storyteller would violate the shape of the author's writing if he or she added it. Character voice would seem to be an appropriate addition—certainly convergence of gaze, posturing, mood and tone, rate and speed, and breathing. But using the body to shape images narrated in the story or to "do" what the narrator tells about is questionable. Props would seem to be altogether inappropriate.

The recitation of the written story should not be stiff. It requires as much fluid movement and grace as the telling of the oral story. But the most appropriate movement might not be the visual picturing of the oral story. Body language for the recitation is that of speechmaking or reading aloud. The teller must make decisions about movement during preparation of the material.

The recitation of the written story is certainly not a gymnastic event. It would tend to be much more reserved and conservative than a telling of oral material. In sum, the teller cannot know what the author would intend for a recitation, or if the author would ever intend one, since the features of oral language are absent from the written story. They were never intended to be there, and the teller must be circumspect about adding them. The teller's task, then, is one of memorization, with the addition of the necessary oral language conventions of intonation, articulation, rate, speed, breathing, gaze, mood and tone, and some voice and posturing.

Memorization methods differ from teller to teller. Since the written story must be told word for word, its memorization is an exacting task. However, the teller can map the written story for structure and memorize segments of the story by associating them with and slotting them into the structure map. As the teller adds the minimum oral language features necessary to carry the story, these can also be used as benchmarks to aid memory. For instance, a facial expression can be associated with a chunk of language. The teller can also use character quotations, if these are present, to mark off sections of language to be memorized, and learn the written story from quote to quote. Then there is always the sentence-by-sentence method. This last has its drawbacks, however. Usually the "begin at the beginning and work to the end, one sentence at a time" approach results in a strong first half of the story and a weaker second half.

However the teller wishes to proceed, the written story must be memorized. The teller should be certain that the story is well in memory before attempting it before an audience.

STORY DEVELOPMENT

Story development involves a more extensive elaboration of a story than story preparation. While preparation extends the story through the addition of oral language devices and conventions during encoding, it does not expand the story itself. It takes the story as a given and makes it oral. Story development, however, makes more story by restructuring the given story from within. The storyteller begins with a (usually short) narrative that has a very limited capacity for audience involvement or in which a short narrated segment shows potential for direct interaction. The expansion is accomplished by the invention and insertion of appropriate internal structural and content detail without violating the overall shape or content of the story. The original story remains as a frame for the embedded inventions.

"The Norther and the Frogs" (Chase 1971) is a short fib, a whopper in the style of the one- and two-line tall tales typical of the liar's contest. In its original form it serves a purpose with regard to humor and commentary on the pioneer/frontier experience and fits a specific telling circumstance, but it also is a good subject for development through expansion.

THE NORTHER AND THE FROGS*

There was a man one time who could prophesy about the weather the best of anybody I ever knew. He lived out in Oklahoma, and there's a wind out there they call The Norther. This man, he could tell to the second when the weather was goin' to change. And one day late in April, he was lookin' at the clouds and sniffin' the air—and he took a notion.

Went down to a big frog pond there on his place. Sat down on a rock and started whistlin' right quiet-like, til he'd whistled every frog out of the water, and they were sittin' there on the banks whistlin' back at him. Every now and then he'd wet his finger in his

---

*In Chase 1971, p. 97.

mouth and hold it up to test the wind. And finally, he popped his hands all at once and hollered.

All the frogs jumped, and, just as they hit the water, that Norther struck. Froze the pond over solid.

The man went on home and, next morning, he came back with a scythe. The pond was covered with frogs stuck half-way down on top of the ice. So, he mowed 'em. Raked up the frog legs. Packed 'em in a little ice and shipped 'em to Chicago. Made him quite a sum of money.

Chase adds a note to this story: "I have no record of where I learned this." Like Chase, I don't know how I came upon the story. I do know that I learned it in Montana—it was set in Montana and was as short as the Chase version—and that I did not see it in print until some years later, after I had embarked—quite accidentally, in the beginning—on restorying and extending it.

THE FROGS AND THE NORTHER*

In the spring of 1882, was a man folks called Tarpaper Charlie—no more, just Tarpaper Charlie—got off the Yellowstone paddlewheeler at the Coulson landing—hadn't much in the way of possibilities along folks could see. Walked the two miles into Billings, past the tents scattered along the river opposite side of the south rim, past the Blue Grass, the Buffalo Grass, and the Bunch Grass saloons, past Olmstead and Pace Real Estate Surveyors. Staked a small claim to a piece of land west of town nobody else wanted, it being swampy, infested with frogs, and much too far away from the rest of the activity of settlement and building to be much good. He put up a board shack, about ten by twenty, with a curved "steamboat" roof, a common kind of thing, and a bit of a porch big enough to set up a rocking chair. Swaddled it up good in tarpaper. Raised that shack up right out on a piece of high ground about where 8th Street West and Central Avenue are today. Was a cutbank out in front of his place, and from there all the way to the Yellowstone was nothin' but cottonwood, a swamp, a big pond and hundreds . . . thousands of frogs.

Nobody knew where Tarpaper Charlie come from, and nobody asked, those kinds of questions not always being considered polite. However, folks discovered soon enough that he had some special developed talent where predictin' the weather was concerned. He had learned from years of observation of such

---

*Developed by Sandra A. Rietz.

natural phenomena as hail and sleet and snow storms, and cloud-busters of all kinds, plus the comings and goings of hot and cold, chinooks and sunshine, just what was in store to make life in the local environs tolerable or otherwise. He was what you might call Billings' first meterologist and was more accurate than some of them these days that have gone and got a considerable amount more schoolin'.

Now Tarpaper Charlie's specialty in the field of weather predicting, no surprise, was pinpointing the exact moment of strike of something called a Blue Norther. A blizzard is a gentle blow. A norther is a severe and prolonged wind-hail-snow-sleet-freeze kind of storm that comes on too fast for folks and critters to get out of the way, that piles up misery on the ground, collapses buildings, kills livestock, runs people out of groceries, and causes considerable trouble. A Blue Norther just delivers more of what a norther's got, quicker, longer, colder. If a blizzard drives the stock halfway to Hardin, a norther will push them into Wyoming. The Blue Norther of 1888 ran Montana cattle bawling all the way to southern Nebraska; piled them up in heaps along the fence rows. The Blue Norther, generally, is a real bankrupter.

In south-central Montana, around Billings, Blue Northers come sweeping down out of the northwest, along with black-boiling clouds, claps of thunder and lightning, howling wind. Then the trees bend half over and everything goes flat. Next comes ice, snow, and cold in generous quantity. Happens real fast. And any time of year is a good time for a Blue Norther. People around these parts know.

Tarpaper Charlie always knew when a Blue Norther was on the way—knew it before anybody else knew it. He could smell a Blue Norther in a gentle autumn breeze, feature it in the graceful bending of the prairie grasses, and mark it in the clear, unbroken blue of the sky long before it come stepping up along the north rim to say howdy.

Well, now, one lazy day toward the end of the fall of 1882—the very first year Billings ever was, and with land and railroad speculating and general opportunity running high—Tarpaper Charlie was sitting on the front porch of his modest tarpaper dwelling, rocking in the chair, just observing the pond down at the bottom of the coulee, considering the musicality of Montana's native frog population. (He had, all summer, been impressed with the tone quality and harmonic capabilities of that amphibian group, them being otherwise untrained in voice and counterpoint, and without other visible aspects of culture.) The sky was clear and blue from rim to rim and up and down the Yellowstone far as he could see. The air was warm, no breeze worth reporting, grass nodded over easy, and the yellowing leaves on the cottonwoods along the river winked slightly. But he could smell it — the Blue Norther.

He rocked and watched the bench rim-line against the sky. The wind picked up and shifted around to the north; a thin thread of black began to show to the northwest. Sky got darker, clouds boiled up a bit, and the grass rustled some. Tarpaper Charlie looked up at the north sky along the rim, got up out of the chair, scrabbled down over the edge of the cutbank, and sauntered on down to the edge of the frog pond, climbed up on a good-sized rock sitting alongside the water. He half-twisted his neck and rolled his eyes back to examine the north sky, marked the clouds boiling up higher and blacker, noted the grass laying down a bit flatter, heard the thunder, and saw the lightning. Stuck his arm right up there to test the wind with his finger — getting some wind chill. Then he leaned out over that pond, puckered his lips up good, and whistled up a little tune for them frogs.

[Whistle part of a tune here. "Ode to Joy" works well.]

All those little amphibian frog folk there in that pond, now, they liked music, and they listened, and they grinned, and they all stuck their little froggy heads up out of the water and whistled back.

[Whistle next segment of same tune.]

Then all of them little frogs swam a bit closer to Tarpaper Charlie sitting up there on that rock, and they fixed their bulgy eyes on him, and they waited.

Tarpaper Charlie sighted along the north rim again, measuring the sky, with the clouds boiling up higher, thicker and blacker. He saw the grass lay down flatter, listened to the thunder, eyed the lightning, and tested the whistling wind with his finger — his arm poked straight up over his head. Getting colder. Then he leaned out over that pond again, sucked in a lungful of air, and whistled up another little tune for them frogs.

[Whistle part of a second tune — another Beethoven is even more impressive.]

Now, all those little frog inhabitants out there in that pond, they liked music, and they stuck their little froggy heads up out of the water, and they listened careful, and they grinned. And they whistled back.

[Whistle next segment of same tune.]

All them frogs swam closer to the rock and to Tarpaper Charlie and blinked their round froggy eyes in his direction, and they waited.

Tarpaper Charlie, sitting up there on that rock, looked up at that northern sky, with the clouds rolling up like a black wall flat with the rimrock, checked the grass laid all the way down, listened to that thunder thundering and saw the lightning sparking down into the rocks at the bottom of the rims and could hear the cottonwoods start to groan and crack down along the Yellowstone. He wet his finger and lifted it up at arm's length again to test the wind—getting mighty cold. Then he leaned out over that pond and whistled them frogs up still another little tune.

[Whistle part of a third tune. "Can Can" is good.]

Them frog folk did love a good melody. They stuck their wet little froggy noses and froggy heads up out of the water, and, altogether, they demonstrated a considerable appreciation of fine music. They listened careful. Then they whistled back.

[Whistle second part of tune.]

And they all swam just a bit closer to Tarpaper Charlie on the rock, and they got him fixed square in their froggy sights, and they waited.

When Tarpaper Charlie turned round again, them clouds were rolling fast down the slope between the rimrock and the river. They come up right behind the shack, just about the same color as the tarpaper. The thunder boomed without mercy, and little bits of corn snow came pelting in sidewise, stinging where they hit Tarpaper Charlie on the face and arms. But he only stuck that arm up again to test the wind—coming' on a regular frostbiter—turned back to them frogs, and whistled up another little piece.

[Whistle part of a fourth tune. For instance, "The Star Spangled Banner."]

My, but those frogs did appreciate good music. They perked up and poked up and swam up even closer. Then they whistled back.

[Whistle second part of tune.]

They was gettin' mighty crowded 'round the bottom of Tarpaper Charlie's rock. And they waited.

Tarpaper Charlie tested the wind once more. Just stuck that moistened finger up there into the sky—nearly lost it to frostbite.

The storm decended 'round that rock with sleet, snow, hail, and rain all at once and comin' from every direction. Tarpaper Charlie looked like some kind of old-time prophet, with his shirt whippin' in the wind and his hair all on end like that. He leaned out into the dark of that blow, out toward them frogs, and whistled up one last little number.

[Whistle first part of a fifth tune—perhaps "Twinkle, Twinkle, Little Star."]

Them frogs was mesmerized. They was transfixed. They did love that music. They listened careful. Then they whistled back.

[Whistle second half of tune.]

And they swam the last little bit closer to Tarpaper Charlie, until all them frogs was sittin' on the ground, all 'round that rock, lookin' up, waitin'.
There was thousands and thousands of them.
Tarpaper Charlie looked 'round one more time. Leaned out over them frogs, then, WHOP! slapped his hands together and let out a yell sufficient to turn a stampede. And all those frogs startled, bucked, and jumped up into the air, arched over and down into the water again. And just as their little froggie arms and heads went in, the Blue Norther struck. Froze the swamp solid around their mid-sections. All them little frogs' legs stickin' up vertical out of the ice, like that.
Well, Tarpaper Charlie went back to his shack, got his scythe, came back down to the swamp, and just shaved all them little legs offn' the ice, just so. Packed 'em clean to San Francisco on the Burlington. It took not less than three box cars to do it.
Made some money. Got to speculating along with everyone else, and bought half of Billings. Still owns it, too, I hear tell.

The restorying develops the original considerably, making it unsuitable for lying and telling whoppers. However, it does make a good story for a formal telling, and it does allow audience participation. (It would tell nicely in concert with a symphony orchestra.) The expanded story does not violate the general shape and content of the original, but it does add a considerable amount of detail to it, particularly that having to do with the calling of the frogs. It creates a repetitive sequence of events that provides for audience expectation and adds internal humor in the form of the whistling.
Story development can also take the form of expansions of local histories and legends. Some of this type of material may not come in stories, but only as anecdotal bits and pieces. In such cases, the teller is a collector-historian who gathers original, unstoried material, then stories it. To do this the teller must

not only invest the material with internal structure and content but must also frame it with "story." Storying historical bits necessarily involves bending the truth and inventing beyond the "facts." But "story" is its own truth. From such inventions, legends are born.

"Wintering the Old Folks" is an example of an invented story.

WINTERING THE OLD FOLKS*

It was perfect. When I made my mind up that our family needed a retreat in the Rocky Mountains I had high expectations. However, our Taiga Sampo was better than I ever expected. We searched for years, being choosy and never finding a place that satisfied us until the real estate agent showed us five acres at the 11,000-foot elevation level. Not only five acres covered with huge spruce, ponderosa pine, aspen, and Englemann fir trees, berry bushes, rose plants, and a plethora of wild flowers, but also it had an island. Not just an island, but an incredible island. The stream flowed directly through the center of the five acres, split to form the island, and rejoined just before the thirty-foot drop. Yes, I am talking about a set of falls thirty feet high that fell over huge rock formations. The water sprayed rainbows in the sunlight and roared in the spring and roared in the fall. Melting snow from above kept the water cold and constant. A family of ouzels nested behind the falls and played in the rushing water.

The A-frame building with the big deck was perfect for cozy living. It had a wood stove for heating and cooking, a loft for sleeping just like Heidi had in my favorite book. We carried water from the stream and lit lanterns when it was dark. Altogether it was perfect. The constant music of the stream and falls, birds, and rustling leaves in the wind was peace.

We called it Taiga Sampo after the magic mill in the Finnish epic "The Kalevala." It surely was a magic mill grinding out dreams and joy. The first summer there we met most of the other residents of the valley. The old gold miners who first settled in the valley called it Happy Valley. Many of the people living there today are descendants of the original settlers. They consider the valley sacred. We felt the same way.

One of the strongest characters in the valley was a ninety-five-year-old woman called Virginia Gale. Her father had driven the stage coach that used to connect the mines and settlements in the valley. She knew the history of everyplace and everyone. She accepted us after my husband saved the life of a hot-blood who

---

*Developed by Norma Livo from the tall tale "Frozen Death" in Schwartz 1975.

drove his four-wheel-drive truck over a cliff. Virginia said, "I like a man of action. You can depend on them. And you know, Norma, you're fine as frog's hair too, because you washed the dumb bunny's blood off to see where the action was."

We didn't have to tell anyone about how George hauled the unconscious driver out of the truck, which was ready to be swept over the next set of falls. I managed to provide enough first aid to hold the vital fluids inside the body as we rushed him to the hospital. One of the neighbors in the cabin on top of Klondike Mountain saw it all and spread the word; when we came back from the hospital we found a party taking place on our deck. It was nice to be accepted with no reservations into this special fellowship.

Virginia herself was no pansy. She loved to walk in the mountains and fish, and was really the ruling matriarch of the mountains. She had two artificial knees. When she was eighty-five her arthritis troubled her to the point that she declared, "I don't understand how the blamed outhouse manages to move further away. At least it takes me longer to get there." She went to see a surgeon about getting her painful knees replaced. " 'You're too old for such an operation,' he told me," said Virginia, "but I told him, 'Don't worry, young man, I plan to outlast you and I need knees while I do it.' "

Six weeks after the knees had been replaced, Virginia was walking with the help of canes in her mountain meadow. Her recovery was a source of great pride for the surgeon, who boasted about his success. However, it was Virginia who had done it. Her determination had made his workmanship look good.

Virginia had no patience with incompetence. One of the visitors in a summer cabin got his truck stuck in a mud wallow. He had to be towed out of there by several of the valley men, and Virginia was there to supervise it. She snorted about his predicament with, "He is so dumb he couldn't find a stick with two ends." Her final insult was, "He couldn't even lead a silent prayer." She had no time for poor souls who lacked ingenuity.

After we had spent five summers in this setting, we were all talking about the previous winter. All of the cabins were closed up in late fall because the ten miles of dirt road up to our valley was not plowed. Huge snowdrifts covered the road, rocks, frozen stream, and even some cabins. Virginia put poles in several spots of her cabin to support the roof during the winter. Hardy souls got to their places in winter by skis, snowshoes, or skimobiles.

Virginia had declared, "Last winter there was only a barbed wire fence between us and the Arctic and three of the four strands of wire were down." I asked her what she did during the winter. Where did she go? That had always been a mystery to me. I always saw her '55 Chevy parked in a back yard in Eldora during the winter. She called her car Emmer Gen See because she only used it for emergencies.

Eldora was a small settlement of log cabins in a meadow near the 7,000-foot level. Electricity had made it to Eldora but that was all. The outhouses still served their function and water had to be carried in. When we snowshoed up to the cabin in winter we had to leave our Jeep in Eldora. The road ended there, but Virginia's car never showed signs of use.

When I mentioned this to Virginia, she said, "I don't have much need for a car in the winter." Again I questioned her as to where she stayed during the winter. I thought maybe one of her three daughters took her in. She said, "We couldn't make it through a winter together in her dinky apartment." Then she gave me the piercing look of an eagle about to catch a snack and quietly stated, "If you really want to know where some of us spend our winter, come up to my cabin on January ninth." I started to sputter something about the road being drifted over, but she snapped, "I didn't misjudge you, did I?"

That December was full of genuine blizzards, and one storm followed another. In the city down on the plains, we spent hours shoveling out of massive accumulations of snow. When the new year came I laughed with George about the January meeting at Virginia's cabin. We came up with dozens of reasons as to why she had said what she did. The reason we accepted was that she did not want to answer my question as to where she spent the winter.

However, the morning of January ninth was bright, sunny, cold, and full of blue sky. At breakfast George wasn't even surprised when I said, "Let's snowshoe up to the cabin today." It seemed as if we were reading each other's minds. So I packed some sliced turkey sandwiches, a thermos of coffee, and some fruit to eat at the cabin. I knew I had some dried soup up there and planned to melt snow to make some for our meal.

We parked the Jeep in Eldora (Emmer Gen See was covered with snow), strapped on our snowshoes, fixed our backpacks, and started up the mountain. We peeled off layers of sweaters and jackets as we progressed. It was hard work clomping up the drifted road. We noticed the tracks of some skimobiles ahead of us. It looked as if the same vehicle had gone up and down a few times— at least the tracks looked like only one machine.

Since the tracks passed our place, we decided to check on Virginia's cabin before we dug a trail to our cabin and cleaned the deck off so we could swing the door open. What a shock to see smoke coming from the chimney of Virginia's cabin! There were all sorts of footprints around the cabin, and there was the skimobile.

We knocked on the door and when it swung open we were greeted by Virginia herself. "Well, you did remember. I knew you would. In fact, I just won a six-dollar bet that you would make it."

Inside the warm cabin (the roof poles made space awkward) were four people our age and six people around Virginia's age. "Well, you see," she said, "the six of us come up here for the winter after the holidays. The worst part of winter is yet to come. Right now our arthritis is more than we want to live with for a while, and besides, our Social Security funds really don't cover food and medicine. That's why we choose to take it easy. Watch."

While she was talking, she poured coffee from her blue speckled enamel coffee pot for everyone. The six old folks were huddled close to the fire. One of the other four went outside several times, and after one of these trips he (it was Ted, the grandson of one of the original valley settlers) said, "It's time."

With that the six elders shook hands, hugged each other, and started to take their clothes off. They stripped down to their long johns. I stared at George, and he looked uncomfortable too. The next thing that happened left me in a panic. The old folks went outside and stretched out on their backs with their arms crossed over their bony chests. No one tried to stop them. I ran, or rather slid on the snow, over to Virginia and hissed, "Get up, Virginia! You are going to freeze. Come on, I'll help you get up."

Her words were as sharp as the winds coming over the pass: "I thought I could trust you to trust me." That stopped me cold. Meanwhile, Ted led the other three as they hauled some planks out of the storage shed and quickly nailed up a wooden box that was six feet by six feet by six feet. They dragged three bales of hay over to the box and then went inside the cabin. The six old people lay there with their eyes closed. You could see the circulation in their bodies was slowing down. It showed in the extremities first. Their noses, ears, fingers, and toes turned white. George and I went inside the cabin to plead with the others to do something before it was too late. They just said, "Virginia said we could trust you. Was she wrong?"

For some crazy reason we didn't want to let Virginia down, but at the same time how could we stand by and watch these folks commit suicide? Ted told us to sit down and have more coffee, and he stacked some pine logs on the fire. It blazed up with sparks and pops. And there we sat. Why? What was going on? What were we doing letting it happen?

Ted went outside after a while and came back with the announcement that it was time. We went outside knowing full well that those frail old bodies were indeed frozen. Funny, they all had a little smile on their faces. Ted and his brother opened one of the hay bales and spread hay on the bottom of the wooden box. Then they stacked the bodies of the old folks in layers, like cordwood, head to toe. They layered bodies and straw until the box was topped off with straw and then a rough lid. They nailed it down and then went back into the cabin. They put the fire out and closed things up. Ted made three trips down the mountain on the snowmobile with a passenger each time. His last words as he passed us on his final trip was, "Come back up on May ninth if you want to see the rest."

George and I never did stop at our cabin, let alone eat our lunch. We just plowed down the hill, silently got in the Jeep, and drove back to the city. The rest of that winter was bitter cold, and we both seemed to be suffering with the memories of what we had been part of. How could we have stood by and let it all happen? What kind of people had we become that we could still sleep peacefully at night? And so winter passed into a late spring. Up in the mountains, we knew, it was still winter until near the end of May. There we were once more, with a silent understanding, getting ready to go up to Virginia's on the morning of May ninth. It was raining in the city, but the rain was sloppy-wet snow in the mountains.

When we parked the Jeep in a dug-out area off the road, I remembered we hadn't even packed a lunch. Somehow, food was the last thing we wanted. We knew what we were probably going to see, and it left us solemn. The snow had been packed down by cross-country skiers and a snowmobile. Yes, the tracks looked like the same ones.

We didn't hurry our trip. Our cabin looked beautiful when we passed it. The snow reached up to the top of the roof on the upper hillside. We had let the winter pass without coming up once. Yep, at Virginia's there were shoveled spots by the door, smoke curling up on the breezes from the chimney, and outside the big wooden box was covered with snow. Inside the cabin was Ted and his brother and the two other fellows from January. They offered us some coffee and didn't seem surprised at all that we were there.

On the way up to Virginia's, George had mumbled that the ground would still be too frozen to dig any graves. He said that the bodies would never be buried unless someone brought up some dynamite. What haunting images flashed through my mind! It reminded me of the story Virginia had told us about the mine tunnel across the island on our land. She had told us that a determined miner had run it back in 1868 as a one-man operation. He blasted, hauled, and dug enough gold out of it to make a modest profit. When he missed his weekly trip to the town store for supplies, one of his friends became concerned. He went up to the mine to see if the miner was all right. The cabin was empty and the door was open. When he went over to the tunnel he was horrified to see blood and bones splattered all over the rock walls and ceiling. He rode his horse back into town to tell that sheriff that his buddy had blown himself to bits. They figured that the miner had made a careless move with the dynamite. However, the sheriff knew the miner to be a perfectionist and didn't believe he had had an accident. The sheriff went to the mine, carried out all the bits and pieces of the body he could find, took them to the stream, washed them off, and pieced them together. His efforts paid off, because the skull had bullet holes in it. Virginia said that the sheriff never let the case go until he had found the killer and seen him convicted for his crime.

Who would pay for the crimes of letting six old folks die? Ted shoveled the snow off the box and from around it. He then took a crowbar to the top of the box and splintered the lid off. While he was doing that, the other three were spreading clothes out to warm in front of the fireplace. They also had three copper tubs in the cabin. These copper tubs were of the large size that my mother used to boil our clothes in on washdays. People who had lived through the diphtheria epidemic were germ conscious. There were two other tubs outside. They also had big kettles of water boiling over the fireplace.

Ted and his brother lifted the first old stiff body out of the box. It hadn't changed over the winter. They balanced it in one of the outside tubs and started to pour lukewarm water over it. When it bent enough, they scrunched it into the tub and continued to pour water over it. While they did that they took turns massaging the arms, legs, and body. I couldn't help giving a Virginia-like snort and commenting, "Now is a fine time to worry about what we did." I found myself including George and me in the "we." I was not prepared for what happened next. The old body started to lose its parchment-white color and turned a pink shade. When I heard a cough coming from the body I almost believed in ghosts. There, before our eyes, the old man opened his eyes and slowly, with a slur in his voice, said, "What a nice sleep. I'm ready to warm up now." They took him inside the cabin, put him in one of the tubs there, and filled that tub up with warm water. This continued until all the old folks had been thawed out. They changed into dry, warm clothes, drank coffee, and inquired as to what the winter had been like. Virginia twinkled at me, "Now, you see what we do with old folks up in Eldora."

This story was developed by Norma Livo from a tall tale, "Frozen Death" found in *Whoppers, Tall Tales and Other Lies* (Schwartz 1975). The tale originated in a newspaper article in 1887, in Vermont. To this three-page story, details about a real mountain valley, its real inhabitants, and real mining lore were added. Invariably after a telling people quietly come up to its creator and teller and ask intently, "Is that a true story?"

A third form of story development chains one-line lies into a longer, coherent whole. The effect is rambling and does not have quite the clear-cut structural definition of a story, but the telling can be quite delightful. Such routines are very vulnerable to bantering, since they amount to monologues of exaggeration and fabrication.

*ABOUT BECOMING A MONTANAN**

I came to Montana in the fall of 1974, and after ten years in the territory might just now claim enough residence to be called a Montanan. Not that I'll ever be without a certain twinge of midwestern amazement, sometimes. At standing in some locations in Billings and looking across the city to the wheat fields beyond. Couldn't do that in Chicago. Or engaging in a friendly conversation with a perfect stranger, only to find out that we know the same people. Or seeing the cars in the grocery parking lot, all with the keys in the ignitions and motors running and their owners inside the store, because it's too cold to shut them down. Or presuming that a truck ahead of me on the highway, and going the same direction, is moving, only to find that it's parked—and in the middle of the road. Or watching a rancher land his plane on the Malta highway and taxi in to the bar at Roy's Corners for a quick one. Or seeing rows of "meters" in a parking lot that aren't meters at all, but electrical outlets instead.

On the other hand, I've been in Montana long enough to be wary of another car coming the other way on the interstate, and it on the other side of the median, too—*traffic*! And to drive through Denver on the Valley Highway with mighty sweaty palms. And to not roll up the windows and lock the doors when I see stock on the road. And to know what to do when I see a sign along the highway that says "Rough Break."

Got started learning about the environs by spending weekends with students on their ranches here and there. Fed bum lambs and calves, rode fence, and operated a rock picker. But had the best times with a fellow name of Harley A. and his wife, Beth, on their pig farm out on the benchland northwest of Billings, between Acton and Broadview. Had to turn at Acton to get there—right at

*Developed by Sandra A. Rietz.

the grain tower, but then, that *was* Acton except for the pile of railroad ties and the Stockman's Bar. (If it's got a Stockman's Bar, it's a town—post office makes no difference.) Turned off the pavement onto a road that's dirt during some seasons and gumbo during others. Came during gumbo season.

Gumbo is Montana's version of mud. It's got the consistency of Elmer's Glue, and some of its properties, too, and is the color of Grey Poupon. When you drive your rig in gumbo, you have to drag an anchor down from the front bumper to the ground or the gumbo pilin' up on the mudflaps in the rear would eventually upend the whole outfit. Some folks just sandbag the hood or put the kids out there to ride point. Passed one fella sitting out there in the middle of the road; offered him a ride. He sez, "Nope, got a perfectly good horse under me."

Harley had had a bad year on account of the gumbo. Seems like every time his pigs trotted around anywhere on the place, they picked up gumbo. It stuck to their bellies and legs, but mostly, they kicked it up behind 'em as they went along, so's it collected round their tails and caked up and dried. Most of those gumbo balls got so heavy, they stretched that pigskin backwards from the rear. Pulled it so far back and stretched it so tight, that the pigs just couldn't close their eyes no more and most of 'em died of insomnia.

That went real hard with Harley, since pigs was his livelihood. So, one evening, he hunkered down on the back stoop to do some pig callin', see if he couldn't, so to speak, beef up the herd. "SOOOUUUUUUUEEEEEEEEEE!! Sooouuu sooouuu SOOOOO-UUUUUEEEEEEEEEE!!" sez he. And "Sooouuuuuuueeeeeeeeee! Sooouuu sooouuu sooooouuuuuueeeeeeeee!!" come rumblin' back down from the rimrock. Sometime later that night, was a general commotion in the yard, when the pigs from Lavina started to come in. Then come the pigs from Great Falls and Casper. Then come the pigs from Cheyenne, Denver, and Boise. The ones from Las Vegas come in wearin' little eyeshades. But Harley kept the gate open til the porkers with the California license plates reported in, all glass packed, ridin' low, and wearin' sunglasses.*

Another time I learned how to fish Montana style, by spittin' snoose into the water. But that's another story and should be saved for later.

Tall tales, fabrications, and lies of this kind developed because the land, weather, and geographic isolation were frightening to many of the pioneers. Humor, perhaps the only solace, prevailed over the perils of the territory. Exaggeration made the experience more bearable (Brunvand 1978). Reality

---

*This pig lie is taken from Diendorfer (1980).

was nowhere near as bad, after all, as the circumstances of the lies and whoppers. When the "hoppers" came to northern Montana in "o-six" and ate everything in sight, and when they chewed the hose and aprons off the ladies who went outside to beat them off the kitchen gardens with sheets of tarpaper, and when the model T's slid off the road from rolling over those slippery bodies, it wasn't near as bad as the gutbusters and bellybenders folks could tell about "hoppers."

For the storyteller who is inclined to the telling of lies and whoppers, several good sources — other than live collection — are available. The teller might look for *The Fiddleback: Lore of the Line Camp* (Ulph 1981), *The Humor of the American Cowboy* (Hoig 1958), *Whoppers, Tall Tales and Other Lies* (Schwartz 1975), *The Hodgepodge Book* (Emrich 1972), and *America's 101 Most High Falutin', Big Talkin', Knee Slappin' Gollywhoppers and Tall Tales: The Best of the Burlington Liars Club* (Diendorfer 1980). The makings of lies can be found in such sources as *Names on the Face of Montana* (Carkeek-Cheney 1971), one of the many state place name books available, and *Western Words: A Dictionary of the American West* (Adams 1968).

Stories can also be developed from songs, particularly ballads. The ballad is a story in verse form. It lacks the conventions of prose discourse, obviously, since it is constructed using some of the forms of poetry. But it does have the general shape of "story." In a more brief rendition than a prose story, it presents a setting, problem, series of events, resolution, and conclusion, framed, usually, in meter and rhyme. A ballad can be restoried into prose form by telling the story that the ballad tells without the verse. A ballad and its restoried version follow.

THE FROZEN LOGGER*

As I stepped out one evening
To a timber town cafe,
A six-foot-seven waitress
To me these words did say.

"I see that you are a logger,
And not just a common bum.
For nobody but a logger
Stirs his coffee with his thumb.

My lover was a logger.
There's none like him today.
If you'd pour whiskey on it,
He would eat a bale of hay.

---

*In Plotz 1976.

He never shaved a whisker
From off his horny hide.
He'd just pound them in with a hammer,
And he'd bite them off inside.

My lover came to see me
One cold and wintry day.
He held me in a fond embrace
Which broke three vertebrae.

He kissed me when we parted,
So hard it broke my jaw.
I could not speak to tell him
He'd forgot his mackinaw.

I watched my lover leavin',
A-saunterin' through the snow.
Goin' gaily homeward
At forty-eight below.

The weather, it tried to freeze him.
It tried its level best.
At one hundred degrees below zero,
He buttoned up his vest.

It froze clear down to China.
It froze to the stars above.
At one thousand degrees below zero,
It froze up my logger love.

They tried in vain to thaw him,
And if you'll believe me, sir,
They made him into axe-blades
To chop the Douglas Fir.

And so, I lost my lover,
And to this cafe I've come.
And here I'll wait 'til someone
Stirs his coffee with this thumb."

*THE FROZEN LOGGER**

As you know, I never been married in this life, not that I didn't come close sometimes — once or twice in a serious manner and a time or two that I wouldn'-a chose for myself, if I had done the choosin'. One of those last kind happened back in the autumn of '88, come the end of the loggin' season at the higher elevations. I was makin' my way back to the nearest railroad to get connections for parts further west when I come upon a town — a one road in and the same one out kind of place. Boardwalks front of the saloon and general store, though.

Bein's I was hungry, I headed for the cafe, fixin' to take my entertainment later. Didn't know anybody, so I sat by myself at one of those little cafe tables, had only two chairs pulled up to it, and me in one of 'em. Up come a waitress of long and lanky proportion. I'd give her six-seven at least. "So?" sez she. (A woman of few words, it seemed.) "Coffee — black," sez I. And off she went to fetch it. When she came back with it, I commenced to stirrin' it with my thumb, as had been my custom since enterin' into the loggin' business. Now that intrigued her some, and without word nor invitation, she sat herself down on the chair opposite, to watch. Well, I proved out wrong about the few words, for she then embarked upon a somewhat extensive monologue, which I was obliged to hear out, bein's I hadn't yet paid my money.

"Logger" sez she, and didn't wait for the answer, but rambled right along. "Had a lover, once, was a logger. Remarkable man. Never be another one like that come along, I don't guess. Come breakfast time he'd order up a mess of hay bales with whiskey for topping. He'd no beard, though he coulda had one. But every day he'd take a sledge and pound the whiskers from outside to inside, then snip 'em off from the inside with bailin' wire cutters.

"I remember the last time I saw him. He'd come to see me, and after a time, had to be on his way. We hugged and kissed, and I took some immediate damage. Snapped my back in three places and broke my jawbone, besides. It was like this every time, though. I'd just lay up in bed for part of a day until I was repaired.

"Well, this time I found his mackinaw where he'd dropped it, on a chair. I waved it at him from the front porch; I couldn't talk for the jaw. But he never turned around to see, just kept on. I could hear him whistling through the crispy air. It musta been at least forty-eight below. Before he was outa sight, it dropped to a hundred below or more, and I saw him button up his vest against

---

*Restoried by Sandra A. Rietz.

the cold. Night come on, and it got down to about a thousand degrees below zero. Musta froze clear to China.

"They found him the next morning, not far from this town. Froze up. Everybody did what they could. Built a fire under him and kept it blazin' for close to two weeks. Rubbed him good and tried boilin' water, too. Wasn't any use. He was still froze solid. So they went at him with sledgehammers and chisels, and chipped him down into so many razor-sharp axe blades. Been loggin' off the Douglas Fir with the axes made from those pieces ever since, and it's been I don't know how long.

"I'm still here, as you can see. Just never found cause to pick up and go somewhere else, I guess. Been working here, just waitin' til someone like him come along. Someone who stirred his coffee with his thumb."

Now, wasn't long before I realized that I met the criterion, what with my thumb still immersed in the brew. And she looked a bit intent, too. Even though I didn't have no other plans, I thought to invent some and withdrew graceful but quick, without even a sip of that coffee.

She took off her apron and followed me, down the street and into the timber. She didn't say nothin', just kept on comin' with a deliberation that was frightening to see. Course, I managed an escape, as you can surmise by considerin' the condition of my marital status. But that's a longer story than this one, and has to be saved for some other time.

The storyteller can experiment with song-to-story reconstructions. The exercise is also useful for younger storytellers and for composition work in the classroom. Some resources include *As I Walked Out One Evening: A Book of Ballads* (Plotz 1976), *Song Fest* (Best and Best 1955), *Folksongs of North America* (Lomax 1960), *He Was Singin' This Song: A Collection of Forty-Eight Traditional Songs of the American Cowboy* (Tinsley 1981), and *Story Songs* (Seeger 1961).

Story development begins either with unstoried material, with stories that require "restorying" to suit specific purposes, or with other literary forms — e.g., the ballad or lies — that can be restoried in prose. The storyteller does some degree of constructive work with the material without violating the shape or intent of the original. The expansions and inventions that extend the developed material beyond the original belong to the teller; through the process of story development, the teller becomes an author in the oral tradition. The developed material must still be encoded with those features of oral "story" described in the section on story preparation earlier in this chapter. (See the section on copyright and the storyteller at the end of this chapter.)

STORY DELIVERY

The delivery of the story involves both construction and problem solving. With each new telling, the story will be somewhat different. The story lives only in the telling, and the telling is situation dependent and context embedded. The story will be what storyteller, audience, and total situation make of it during the telling. The teller can best insure success by having good control of the structure and content of the story and by knowing how he or she will integrate the two by slotting during the telling. He or she can build control by working out problems related to the linguistic and paralinguistic aspects of encoding before telling. In addition, the teller can plan some devices for interaction and negotiation with members of the audience in order to keep them involved and, at the same time, to make their behavior reasonably predictable.

The storyteller strives for confidence and poise through control. Control of the story begins with the storyteller and is achieved through story choice, preparation, and development. Audience control also begins with the teller. Control of the circumstances and setting for the telling is not always in the teller's hands. Unexpected situations can occur, and the teller must remain calm and be ready to handle each appropriately.

STORY CONTROL

The preceding material has covered the various aspects of story control in some detail. Before the story is told, it should be "ready." Readiness is difficult to assess. It is something the storyteller can feel. However, readiness usually does not occur until the teller has given some attention to story choice, use of language and linguistic effects, and employment of paralinguistic elements. Story readiness and control constitute the first and perhaps the most important protection against mishap. Other potential problems related to the telling can often be handled gracefully if the storyteller knows the story well. The teller who has developed an intimacy with the story, who can control it under almost any circumstances, and who can enjoy the act of telling as well will telegraph a message of confidence and comfort to the audience.

AUDIENCE CONTROL

Audience control begins with control of the story. In particular, the story-teller can plan for audience interaction. The audience that knows exactly what to do during the story, because the teller has made that determination, is less likely to do something that it shouldn't do—something unpredictable and disruptive. Good timing, smooth movement, well-executed character voices, and breathing and language that fit the story will establish audience confidence in the storyteller. The audience will be able to enter into the story more easily. When the audience is in the story, and the story is under the storyteller's control, the storyteller also has control of the audience.

Should the audience offer unexpected but story-compatible commentary, the teller can either ignore it or incorporate it. Divergent or disruptive commentary can either be ignored or redirected in order to bring the audience back to the story. Under no circumstances should the teller stop a story to discipline members of an audience. A story can be stopped if an entire audience makes clear its disinterest. (See chapter 4 on "story as game" and audience commitment.) Should that happen, the teller still need not discipline. An audience has a right to not want to hear a story. When the audience indicates an unwillingness to listen, the teller does not need to tell. A story-telling is not something to force on a reluctant group of people. The opening rituals are signals and tests designed to allow both teller and audience to take a measure of one another's willingness to get into the story and to cooperate with the telling.

Disruptive behavior can often be controlled with sustained eye contact while the teller continues to tell. Sometimes, with younger audiences, a touch on an arm or leg from the teller will stop the disruption. Again, the teller should not stop a telling. Choice of and control of the setting for the telling will also help to direct and shape audience behavior. Many potential disruptions will not occur if the setting is a good one.

Audience composition is an important consideration. The homogeneous-age-group audience is often more difficult to work with than a mixed-age audience. And, despite beginning tellers' protests to the contrary, the adult audience is the easiest of all. Adults generally are much more understanding and tolerant of teller and material than are homogeneous child audiences. The very young (preschool) audience is a difficult group simply because they do not yet have a sense of "story" and often respond only to noises and repetitious language. They are likely to lose interest in more sophisticated stories. Once interest is lost, the preschooler will often walk away, not intending to be impolite. Homogeneous groups of school-age children can be insulted by stories that, by their judgment, are immature and belittle their intelligence. At the same time, a story that is too sophisticated can cause them to lose interest. Mixed audiences are good groups for telling. The adults in the audience bring a sophistication to the experience that will make the story chosen for the young ones a good experience for the middle schooler, and the very sophisticated story is an object of much curiosity for less mature listeners. Story choice must fit audience composition. (See chapter 4.)

The storyteller can also exercise control over audience positioning. Regardless of how people arrange themselves prior to the telling, the teller can reposition them. The storyteller generally wants the audience as close as possible while still allowing enough room to move and tell. Obstructions between the audience and the teller should be avoided. Pillars, posts, tables, chairs, and the like are not conducive to good audience involvement and inter-action. Members of the audience should be close together, without violating body space or causing physical discomfort. Open spaces between clumps of people in the audience should be avoided. The teller can encourage people to fill in the spaces. If the audience is on the floor, the teller might sit on a chair or stand. If the audience is seated in chairs, the teller will probably prefer to stand. Both for control and story visibility, the storyteller should be slightly above the audience.

CONTROL OF SETTING

Whenever possible, the storyteller should discuss and/or plan the setting of the telling beforehand. The formal, ritual telling, especially, requires control of its physical space. Some tellers prefer to work with their backs to a corner. This places the audience in a ninety-degree fanlike area in front of the teller. Such an area is easy for the teller to keep in view without having to turn around or lose half the audience while focusing on the other half. It also insures that no (younger) member of the audience can crawl around behind the teller.

The area for the telling should be clear of disruptive paraphernalia. While we would like to think that the truly involved audience will always be focused on the story no matter what the outside stimulus, some "stuff" offers too much fascination and temptation. If the teller is telling in a gym, he or she doesn't need gymnastics equipment, nets, balls, etc., within easy reach of members of the audience. If the telling is held in a library, books and magazines should be cleared out of the telling area. A storytelling is not a TV show that can be watched while doing something else.

Seating is an important ingredient in control, particularly with younger, less mature audiences. If possible, all members of the audience should be seated in the same manner. If most are on the floor and two or three are on a piano bench, the makings of trouble are at hand. If most are on the floor and one or two must sit in chairs, these should be kept to the back of the group. No one should be seated too far to the side of or behind the teller. If possible, no one should be seated behind a table or at a desk.

Auditoriums, bleachers, and risers should be avoided; so should settings next to staircases that will allow an individual to stand or sit above the telling. Seating should be arranged so that members of the audience feel that they are inside the physical space of the storytelling. People who are above or outside the telling become spectators—a very awkward and uncomfortable situation for the teller and the rest of the audience. Auditoriums remove the teller from the audience to too great a degree. The storytelling is not a stage play. Bleachers place the teller below the level of the audience. Risers do the same. The only time this teller has ever had to stop a story in midtelling was in a room with risers and first-graders—an unfortunate combination. Two boys wiggled under the bottom riser so that only their upper bodies were out. They listened quietly that way, on their stomachs with chins in hands, for a time. However, when they became tired of that position and tried to wiggle out again, they found that they could not. They were stuck. They became frightened, forgot about the story, and could only think about struggling to get free. One began to cry. Five minutes, three teachers, and a janitor later, the boys were extricated. The story was forgotten by all; it could not be retrieved.

Telling outdoors, in parks, on patios, or on playgrounds, is usually much more difficult than working indoors. Acoustics can be a problem, and sound equipment might be necessary. Traffic, both people and vehicles, can cause substantial competing commotion, and park settings sometimes place the storytelling next to swings, slides, teeter-totters, and swimming pools. Children not attending the telling will occasionally run through the audience. The storyteller can control for the worst possible settings by planning the telling for the most amenable spot available and being sure that sound equipment is on hand for settings that require it. He or she should also be prepared for surprises.

CONTROL OF CIRCUMSTANCES

Before agreeing to tell stories, the teller should try to find out about the circumstances that will surround and affect the telling. If the storyteller is really being used as a baby-sitting service for parents who are being encouraged to shop downtown by a merchants' group, he or she should be prepared to tell to constant turmoil. It is difficult to tell stories in a circus atmosphere that pits the teller in one corner against a magician in another and trained dogs in still another. Telling stories in the middle of a crowded department store or in the middle of a shopping mall is difficult. If telling is part of a holiday promotion, the teller should be sure to get information from the sponsors about other aspects of the promotion. It is best to avoid having sugar plum fairies plying the audience with gumdrops in the middle of a story. If the telling is part of a Halloween party, the teller should control the situation as much as possible by determining when the storytelling will take place, where, and in competition with which other activities.

A storytelling is not a TV program, a circus act, a commercial, or a sitting service. Often, people who wish to use a storyteller to do promotions, advertising, or on-site attracting of customers do not understand how story-telling works and what conditions are necessary for a successful telling. Some situations simply are not appropriate for storytelling. The teller will have to assess each request separately and must be prepared to say no. The oral litera-ture has an integrity of its own. A setting in which that integrity cannot be maintained to a reasonable degree is not a place for telling. People who request storytellings for unworkable situations, and who do not understand the nature of storytelling, will only think badly of the teller and the oral literature if things go wrong.

PROGRAM CONTROL AND CONTRACT

The teller should discuss the program before accepting a storytelling engagement and make certain that his or her terms and expectations are clear before-hand, in order to insure that people will not make last-minute demands that cannot be met. The choice of program will depend partly on setting and audience composition.

The storyteller should also establish some degree of latitude for changing the program before the telling. Because story and telling are so very situation dependent, the real circumstances of a telling may change the program somewhat after these are assessed on site.

Experienced tellers can handle most surprises. Still, the storyteller's concentration and control are disrupted when last-minute changes are made without the teller's being consulted or informed. Surprise: The sixth grade comes instead of the first grade. Surprise: The storyteller agreed to tell for six hours, one hour for each grade, for grades 1 through 6, and is confronted instead with a six-hour schedule that combines the primary grades for an hour and the middle-school grades for an hour, in order to schedule in the junior and senior high students. Surprise: The storyteller agreed to tell to teachers at an after-school inservice and learns that the PTA is having a spaghetti dinner and a storytelling. Surprise: The school Halloween party in the gym gets loud and wild. A parent representative of the sponsoring group decides (before the telling has begun) that a storyteller cannot control the group, therefore asks the storyteller to run the projector instead. Surprise: The storyteller is invited to a party, apparently as a guest, and is informed upon arrival that he or she is the entertainment.

CONTROL OF THE GAME

Storytelling is a game. The devices of the ritual preceding and following the telling signal the game and specify the more general rules of play. The teller can keep both story and audience under control by using ritual devices and by clarifying the nature of the game. (See chapter 4.)

CONTROL OF SELF

Beginning storytellers often—understandably—concentrate all their attention upon the story and are not able to monitor themselves. However, as a story becomes more familiar and controlled, the storyteller finds that he or she also has the capacity to "watch" the telling. By observing self, story, and audience in as objective a manner as is possible during the telling, the storyteller can critique elements and devices used in encoding. Those inventions that are not successful can be modified or eliminated and replaced. Story preparation and story development become a continuous process when the teller is aware not only of the story but also of effectiveness of self as medium. The evolution of the relationship between a story and its teller is a product of teller awareness during the telling.

Conclusion

The storyteller who is well prepared, who has negotiated the circumstances of the telling, who is able to use the game devices of the ritual telling, and who is confident can also have fun with a storytelling. The audience will find joy in a story to which the teller brings his or her own genuine enjoyment. The storyteller should be able to delight in both the story and the act of telling it. The more control over all aspects of the telling a teller is able to achieve, the more he or she will be able to relax and have fun with the telling process. A teller who obviously enjoys telling extends a final dimension of game to the audience—that telling itself is a form of play. A storyteller who makes storytelling look like easy play, rather than torturous activity, is in control—although, as any experienced storyteller knows, the simpler it looks, the harder it really is.

COPYRIGHT AND THE STORYTELLER

The confusion today regarding which material belongs to the teller and which is in the public domain is a result of a meeting and mixing of printed and oral literatures. One who authors an original work owns that work, and so ownership of original written stories can be determined easily enough. Establishing clear-cut authorship of oral stories is confounded by two problems:

1. Tellers develop stories for telling that originally were in the public domain. Whether the teller finds the story in print or hears it, the teller interprets the story using the conventions of oral literature. Especially in cases in which the teller begins with printed material, the *oral* shape of the story is the original invention of the teller. Does the story, as told in that shape, then belong to the teller?

2. One of the conventions of the oral literature is story negotiability during telling. Audiences expect to be able to interact. The community ownership of the oral literature that is associated with stories that do belong to cultures and not to individuals extends very easily to oral stories that are the original works of tellers. The employment of ritual

devices around the telling of original material further invites audience sense of ownership. The oral literature is traditionally owned by groups, not single authors. How can these traditional expectations be modified to include a sense of the inviolability of an original oral work, especially when oral works are governed by the same rules of evolution and change that govern oral languages?

To prevent unauthorized use of material that a teller considers to be his or her own, the teller must specify ownership before telling. He or she can use a permission form (see appendix G) to grant use privileges to specific persons. He or she can prohibit tape recordings of tellings and get original oral stories into print. A teller can consider a story his or her invention if he or she develops an idea into a story—stories otherwise unstoried content. Storied content, however, is to be considered an expression of a given body of content. The teller who uses the given expression of a storied body of content, adding to it various oral language devices, is making a derived work. Only those additional devices invented by the teller in order to tell the story belong to the teller in such cases.

In general, only those aspects of a story that are the original inventions of the teller belong exclusively to the teller. In many instances, tellers tell stories that are amalgams of original and public-domain material. Since audiences cannot always know what belongs to whom, and because audiences are traditionally disposed to assume full ownership, tellers who are concerned about loss should specify original stories. Audiences should be aware that told stories can be original and inviolate, and that all stories, even if they are in the public domain, are, in the telling, richly infused with the original inventions of the teller. For instance, "The Barnyard Song" (Boni 1952), a common cumulative children's singing game, is in the public domain. One teller, however, makes special use of puppets when playing the game with audiences. The song itself does not belong to the teller, but the use of puppets as a device does. Another teller can use the same game without referencing the first teller, but he or she should ask permission to use and/or credit the use of the puppets if he or she intends to employ them.

To put the issue another way: Though we have carefully avoided the suggestion that storytellers perform in a theatrical sense, the problem of what belongs to whom is related to performance—delivery and the decisions regarding interpretation which are a part of it. Inasmuch as the storyteller solves a problem when encoding an oral story, especially if that story is taken from written material, the solutions—linguistic, paralinguistic, and structural—belong to the storyteller. If the storyteller invents a story, both story and elements of delivery (performance and problem solution) belong to the teller. If the teller develops a story through extension or the like, the developed aspects and the delivery are the teller's. If the teller recodes a transcribed oral story from written to oral form, the conventions of the oral language and oral delivery with which he or she invests the oral story are the property of the teller.

Storytellers who borrow from other tellers in any of the above situations should credit the original teller for an idea or method (encoding) that helps to tell a given story (solve a given problem). Even though borrowed materials or deliveries cannot be perfectly replicated, the borrower has internalized a pattern or rule invented by another teller.

More problematic is the citing of materials collected from the public domain. Such stories are, in a very real sense, still in the public domain, even though someone may have gathered some of them into a volume. They belonged to a people at the time of collection, and the fact of collection did not alter their ownership. The act of collecting and perhaps the shapes of the print on the page belong to the collector, but not the stories themselves. However, the efforts of collectors have preserved some stories and have made many more available to revivalist storytellers. A teller might want to credit a collector or a collection without also implying that the stories themselves are the exclusive property of the collector. A teller might cite a collection simply to acknowledge the origins from which his or her story developments, expansions, and encodings derived.

Copyright and the oral literature are somewhat incompatible and anachronistic with respect to one another — they create a sort of disjuncture of form and function that is difficult to resolve. For further information see Skindrud 1984.

REFERENCES

Adams, Ramon F. 1968. *Western Words: A Dictionary of the American West.* Norman: University of Oklahoma Press.

Asbjornson, Peter Christian, and Jorgen Moe. 1960. *Norwegian Folk Tales.* New York: Viking Press.

Best, Dick, and Beth Best, eds. 1955. *Song Fest.* New York: Crown.

Boni, Margaret B., ed. 1952. *The Fireside Book of Favorite American Folksongs.* New York: Simon and Schuster.

Brunvand, Jan Harold. 1978. *The Study of American Folklore.* New York: Norton.

Calvino, Italo. 1980. *Italian Folktales.* New York: Pantheon Books.

Carkeek-Cheney, Roberta. 1971. *The Names on the Face of Montana.* Missoula: University of Montana Publications in History.

Cazden, Courtney B. 1975. "Play with Language and Metalinguistic Awareness: One Dimension of Language Experience." In Charlotte B. Winsor, ed., *Dimensions of Language Experience*. New York: Agathon Press.

Chase, Richard. 1971. *American Folk Tales and Songs*. New York: Dover.

Courlander, Harold, and George Herzog. 1947. *The Cow-Tail Switch and Other West African Stories*. New York: Holt, Rinehart & Winston.

Diendorfer, Robert G. 1980. *America's 101 Most High Falutin', Big Talkin', Knee Slappin' Gollywhoppers and Tall Tales: The Best of the Burlington Liars Club*. New York: Workman.

Downing, John, and Che Kan Leong. 1982. *Psychology of Reading*. New York: Macmillan.

Emrich, Duncan. 1972. *The Hodgepodge Book*. New York: Four Winds Press.

Feller-Bauer, Carolyn. 1977. *Handbook for Storytellers*. Chicago: American Library Association.

Ginsburg, Mirra. 1973. *One Trick Too Many—Fox Stories from Russia*. New York: Dial Press.

Haley, Gail. 1970. *A Story, A Story: An African Tale*. New York: Atheneum.

Harper, Wilhelmina. 1967. *The Gunniwolf*. New York: Dutton.

Hayes, Joe. 1982. *The Day It Snowed Tortillas*. Santa Fe, N. Mex.: Mariposa.

Hoig, Stan. 1958. *The Humor of the American Cowboy*. Omaha: University of Nebraska Press.

Johnson, Edna, Evelyn R. Sickels, Francis Clarke Sayers, and Carolyn Horovitz. 1977. *Anthology of Children's Literature*. Boston: Houghton Mifflin.

Kent, Jack. 1971. *The Fat Cat: A Danish Folktale*. New York: Parents Magazine Press.

The Literature Committee of the International Kindergarten Union. 1950. *Told under the Green Umbrella*. New York: Macmillan.

Lomax, Alan. 1960. *Folksongs of North America*. Garden City, N.Y.: Doubleday.

MacDonald, Margaret Read. 1982. *The Storyteller's Sourcebook: A Subject, Title and Motif Index to Folklore Collections for Children.* Detroit, Mich.: Neal-Schuman.

McDermott, Gerald. 1972. *Anansi the Spider: A Tale from the Ashanti.* New York: Holt, Rinehart & Winston.

Pellowski, Anne. 1977. *The World of Storytelling.* New York: Bowker.

Plotz, Helen. 1976. *As I Walked Out One Evening: A Book of Ballads.* New York: Greenwillow Books.

Schwartz, Alvin. 1975. *Whoppers, Tall Tales and Other Lies.* Philadelphia, Pa.: Lippincott.

Seeger, Pete. 1961. *Story Songs.* New York: Columbia Records.

Skindrud, Michael E. 1984. "Copyright and Storytelling." *The National Storytelling Journal* 1, no. 1 (winter), 14-19.

Tinsley, Jim Bob. 1981. *He Was Singin' This Song: A Collection of Forty-Eight Traditional Songs of the American Cowboy.* Orlando: University Presses of Florida.

Ulph, Owen. 1981. *The Fiddleback: Lore of the Line Camp.* Salt Lake City, Utah: Dream Garden Press.

Wiesner, William. 1972. *Happy-Go-Lucky.* New York: Seabury Press.

4

Working with Audiences

Storyteller: Let's tell another story.
               Let's be off!
Audience: Pull away!
Storyteller: Let's be off!
Audience: Pull away!

(Ritual opening, origin unknown)

In what way can storytelling be considered a game?

In what way is storytelling a ritual?

How does the storyteller initiate and operate the game and the ritual?

How can a storyteller assess an audience?

What kinds of stories and deliveries are appropriate for various groups?

What factors are important clues to audience interest and capability?

How can a storyteller expand audience interest and capability?

The storytelling audience does not watch a performance; it becomes directly involved in the construction of a literary experience. The storyteller does not give the audience a finished product, but rather the promise of a cooperative negotiation. The teller contributes a memory of story structure and content and a set of oral language conventions for encoding; the audience contributes a set of expectations for "story" and a sense of cultural ownership. Then audience and teller together make the story. Storytelling and storying are processes, not products.

The process of making a story during a storytelling requires that both teller and audience know what to do and enter into a mutual agreement to do it. The teller will lead ("I'm going to tell a story"), and the audience will agree to follow ("Pull away!"). The storyteller plans and prepares a negotiation in which the audience will participate both spontaneously, through coaction and prediction, and under teller direction, through a more controlled involvement in such ritual, repetitive, and inventive devices as the storyteller has chosen to include in the story. (See chapter 3.) For audience and teller, the object of the exercise is the successful building of the story and the shared pleasure and sense of community and belonging that is a part of storying. A storying is not the exclusive province of the storyteller, nor is it meant to be a competition in which audiences interfere with the making of the story.

Many modern audiences do not know what is expected of them during a storytelling. They do not know how to behave. Most of us have learned how to spectate—at sporting events, at the theater, at a concert, in front of a TV set, or at a movie. We understand that at some of these "performances" we must be quiet and watch and listen. We know that at others we may cheer, yell, heckle, criticize, talk through, or walk away. In all cases, however, we are observers. While the players play, we watch. We are only indirectly and vicariously involved in the play itself, and we may or may not have any investment in its outcome.

In storytelling, the storying is the play. The teller is only a medium who brings the play and controls and conducts it. The audience is in the story and therefore is in the play. This is quite a different kind of entertainment from that to which we are accustomed. We cannot sit silently and let the storyteller do a show. On the other hand, we are not invited to treat the storytelling as if it were a game to be cheered or booed from the sidelines. The story is not a movie or TV program, in which the players neither see nor respond to the audience or know what the audience is doing. The storyteller is live and in the close, immediate presence of the audience, not removed to a "stage." The members of the audience are "players" in the making of the story.

Because the audience is in the play, the story is a game. As with any other game that is fun to play, an audience may ask to play again—for the teller to repeat the story. Unlike a TV show, which is fun the first time and of much less interest thereafter, a story can be told over and over again with no loss of excitement. Indeed, as the audience learns to control elements of the story, interest and involvement often increase.

BRINGING THE AUDIENCE IN

The uninitiated audience must learn how to act during a storytelling, how to negotiate, and how to do its proper part in story construction. Audiences accustomed to spectating may be reluctant to interact, fearing that their direct involvement is impolite. Some less mature audiences, given the invitation to interact, may not understand the limits to audience interaction or the cooperative nature of a storytelling and compete with or interfere with the telling.

As a mutual and cooperative kind of play, storytelling has its rules, like any other game. All members of the audience must agree to the rules and agree to play, or the play will break down. One member of the audience cannot refuse to play without undoing the play for the others. The "beginner" audience must learn the rules and how to play by them. They must understand that the storyteller establishes the boundaries and directs the play. The rules are not to be violated for the private pleasure of one individual. (This observation is not intended to suggest that the storyteller should "teach" and "enforce" a rigid set of rules or admonish or punish people for not following the rules. Audiences learn game rules by playing games, and storytelling rules by being in storytellings.)

STORYING AS GAME

Although a storyteller cannot and should not force members of any audience into a storytelling experience they are reluctant to join, the circumstances of the storytelling do make agreement to play necessary. The storyteller tells the audience into another time and place, and the ritual of the storytelling releases the audience from the binding of present time. The members of the audience must agree to enter into the play, or the "other" reality that the storyteller brings with the story and telling cannot come to exist. The audience cannot watch from the perspective of present time while the teller moves into another reality. Safety from "story"-time consequences impinging upon the real-time real lives of members of the audience is established and maintained when the audience joins the play. Because of the invocation of the ritual, members of the audience understand the difference between reality and fantasy, or daily and story reality, daily and story truth.

(Much modern "entertainment" has used frightening degrees of violence, sex, destruction, and other such titillating topics in the absence of ritual. This is dangerous. The ritual clarifies relationships—real and not real, my world and other world, my time and other time. The ritual insures safety and distance. It reassures by reminding members of the audience of the separation between themselves and "story." In the ritual storytelling, the audience crosses over into the storytelling and the story. When the telling ends, the audience crosses back, to safety, and to a time and place that the circumstances of the story cannot touch. No such arrangements exist in movies, TV, and rock video. No storyteller/medium conducts the audience safely into and out of whatever dangers or consequences might exist in the story. People need ritual to clarify the differences between reality and fantasy, between what they can and cannot do in their daily lives, between real and imagined dangers and consequences. Some of the newer forms of "entertainment" remove the audience from any kind of proximity to the players. They do not invite the audience to play, and, in fact, abuse and violate the nature of play. They have no identifiable rules and present few if any familiar, traditional archetypes. They often use some of the conventions of story structure to frame exaggeratedly sensational and somewhat disconnected activity and abandon the psychological safety of the traditional story experience, offering up uncertainty and confusion instead. The loss of the ritual from these "stories" is profound, and could have—perhaps is having—serious social consequences.)

A storying has rules. The "meta" rules—the general rules for story-telling—are those that govern all games. All participants play. They all play together under the same set of restrictions. The rules which apply to one apply to all. No one, for any reason, is allowed to play from outside the jurisdiction of the rules. The rules of the storying have to do with transporting participants from one time and space into another, in which a different but equally valid truth pertains—the truth of "story." They also have to do with the nature of negotiation of the story: that the teller brings a shape to the play in the form of story structure and content and types of interaction invited. Each teller and each story will require the operation of different specific rules within a story. The audience takes cues from the teller as to which rules to follow for a given story and does not violate these. Even the wildest bantering session is still under teller control, and the object, no matter how diverse the editorial commentary, is to make the story.

SIGNALING THE GAME

The storyteller can both teach the rules and signal the game by making use of a variety of devices that audiences come to associate with the play of storying. Rather than "explaining" and lecturing, the storyteller can bring an audience into proper rule-governed play by doing. Once audiences learn to associate these devices with the play of story building, they generally regard them as sacred to storytelling activity. Doing the ritual, then, will automatically bring the audience into the storytelling and bring storying rules into play. (Younger audiences, especially, can become devoted to protocol and ritual, and may come to regard an omission in or misuse of the devices of protocol and ritual as an intolerable violation of process.) The storyteller must remember that once an audience learns to prepare for a storying by observing a set of rituallike behaviors, those behaviors then belong to the telling experience. Such ritual devices should not be abused by using them for something else—to coerce a reluctant group of children into doing a workbook page, for example. Storytelling rules that are misplaced and misused will lose their effectiveness, not only for the workbook page, but also for the storytelling.

Ritual devices that signal the beginning or ending of a storytelling call for audience commitment to the success of the activity. Additional devices serve to identify the person of the storyteller as "storyteller" (the "other" one) and to make the person of the storyteller transparent. Other devices bring the audience into the story itself. Still more devices establish the physical setting for the telling or signal the participants to come to a storytelling. Through the use of these operations, the teller and all the members of the audience join together to make a story. They understand that they have made an investment, a ritual contract governing a form of play, and they understand the nature of the game.

Ritual devices also clarify the relationship between the storytelling and the story. The storytelling is a ritual game that frames the story. The story is told inside the storytelling. In order to get an audience into a story, the teller must first initiate the framework for it — the storytelling. Then the story can be told.

Ritual Openings and Closings

The ritual openings and closings begin and end the game. They mark the time of "story," when the rules of storying are in force. They also often ask for verbal acknowledgment from the audience that the game has begun or ended. They call the audience over into game and story. Implicit in many openings is the giving of consent. The audience agrees to play by the rules of the game by entering into a verbal contract that is binding until the closing is given. The storyteller's call to the audience to "come over" requires audience response indicating willingness.

Audience Participation Rituals

Perhaps the most successful and compelling openings and closings are those that require audience response. These devices are themselves small games. The ritual allows the audience to play, but the play is initiated by the storyteller and comes back to the storyteller. The storyteller is always in control.

"A Story, a story. Let it come. Let it go" is an opening that is a form of play. The storyteller begins: "A story, a story." The audience chants the reply: "Let it come. Let it go." The teller calls, offering the storytelling and asking the audience to come. The audience accepts the storytelling, agrees to play the game, and crosses over into "story" time. Then the story begins. The sequence is teller — audience — teller, or, from the storyteller's point of view, my turn — your turn — my turn. Younger audiences, especially, understand taking turns.

Without much more introduction than that required to explain the nature of openings and to teach one specific opening, the younger audience especially will respect the order of turn taking. The final turn, which goes to the teller, is really the turn that belongs to the story. The above opening is even more effective if repeated more than once, with each successive repetition being quieter until storyteller and audience are mouthing the words. This employment of the opening simultaneously extends the game of turn taking, allows more participation by the audience, clearly establishes the contract or commitment, and quiets the audience for the story. It provides a much more effective method for readying the audience and getting audience attention than yelling, demanding, or begging.

Other turn-taking openings and closings include:

Storyteller: Cric!

Audience: Crac!

    (Haitian ritual opening—done loudly)

Storyteller: Let's tell another story. Let's be off!

Audience: Pull away!

Storyteller: Let's be off!

Audience: Pull away!

    (Origin unknown—done with vigor)

Accompanying closing:

Storyteller: And now, I have finished my story.

Audience: Yes! Yes!

Storyteller: Tomorrow you may dig potatoes! [Verb and object are teller's choice.]

Storyteller: I'm going to tell a story.

Audience: Right!

Storyteller: It's a lie.

Audience: Right!

Storyteller: But not everything in it is false.

Audience: Right!

    (Sudanese ritual opening—done with vigor)

Storyteller: Hello!

Audience: Helloooooooooooo!

   (Yoruba ritual opening)

Storyteller: One day . . .

Audience: A day will never end.
                 A day continues to be.

   (Yoruba ritual opening)

Storyteller: Once upon a time . . .

Audience: Time never ends.
                 There is no end to any time.

   (Yoruba ritual opening)

Accompanying closing: Storyteller ends with a song, then leaves the story-telling circle while singing. Audience remains until teller is gone.

Nonparticipatory Rituals

Some ritual openings and closings initiate the storytelling without audience response. Many of these are extended metaphors that establish the special reality and mystical nature of the storytelling and certify the teller as other. By using these openings, the teller operates a ritual invocation, taking all present into "story" time and "story" reality.

The audience is released from "story" time and reality by the use of the ritual closing. The closing ends a story*telling* and brings the storyteller back from the role of medium and other to self.

   "We do not really mean . . .
   We do not really mean . . .
   That what we say is true."

      (Asanti ritual opening)

Accompanying closings:

   "This is my spider story which I have told.
   Let it come. Let it go.
   If it is sweet,
   If it is not sweet,
   Some you may take as true,
   And the rest you may praise me."

"This is my spider story which I have told.
Let it come. Let it go.
If it is sweet,
If it is not sweet,
Take some elsewhere,
And let some come back to me."

"Under the Earth I go.
On the oak leaf I stand.
I ride on the filly
That was never foaled,
And carry the dead in my hand."

    (Celtic ritual opening)

"Now listen carefully and keep quiet.
Otherwise, who knows what might happen!
The stove could fall on top of you.
So could the ceiling!
And you would have to leap out of the window
And run far away—
If you were still in one piece.
So! Pay attention!"

    (Russian ritual opening; Hamlyn 1975)

"Three apples fell from heaven.
One for the teller,
One for the listener,
And one for all the peoples of the world."

    (Armenian ritual closing; Belting 1953)

"Three apples fell from heaven.
One for the one who asked for the story.
One for the one who told it.
And one for the one who gave ear to it."

    (Armenian ritual closing; Belting 1953)

"Hah! Old age is coming on,
And it's dark in the world.
Let's drink!"

    (Slavic ritual closing)

"And now you can have your supper,
And say your prayers, and go to bed.
Morning is wiser than evening."

(Russian ritual closing)

"Leaves are green for a little while.
Then they fade to yellow,
Fall to earth and wither,
And become dust."

(Anglo-Saxon ritual closing)

Ritual Story Beginnings and Endings

Story beginnings serve a different purpose than ritual openings. The ritual openings initiate story*tellings*. The story beginnings start the stories themselves. They establish "story" time by (usually) setting the story in a past so far distant that it predates anything we know. When the story setting is identified in the ritual beginning, it is far away, in a place that can no longer be reached by ordinary means and therefore can only be accessed via the mystique of the telling. Ritual beginnings remind us that the story is old and that it contains archetypes. We understand that the "facts" in the story may not be verifiable in our own time and reality, but that the story is a truth in its own time and reality. Perhaps the most familiar story beginning, at least for many stories in the English language, is "Once upon a time. . . ."

Ritual endings mark the end of a story, but not the end of the story*telling*. The ending to a given story only releases the audience from that story in order that it may enter into another.

"Once there was and once there was not . . ."

(Armenian beginning)

Accompanying ending:

"And so they achieved their heart's desire.
May you thus achieve your heart's desire."

"Once upon a time . . ."

(Origin unknown)

Accompanying ending:

"And they lived happily ever after."

"Once upon a time, when chickens still had teeth,
And horses still had feathers . . ."

   (Origin unknown)

"Somewhere beyond the Red Sea,
Beyond the Blue Forest,
Beyond the Glass Mountain,
And beyond the Straw Town,
Where they sift water and pour sand,
There was . . ."

   (Russian beginning; Hamlyn 1975)

"In a faraway land,
Where the goose thrashes the corn with its wings,
And the goat grinds the flour with its chin,
There was . . ."

   (Russian beginning; Hamlyn 1975)

"The sparrow flew swiftly, just as an arrow,
Across the sea from east to west,
Til in a far land it came to rest.
And in this land . . ."

   (Russian beginning; Hamlyn 1975)

Accompanying ending:

"And I am glad that we have come to the end
of this story, and I can have a rest."

Accompanying ending:

"This happened a long time ago.
Believe it or not, it is absolutely true."

"Once upon a time,
When bears had tails as big as their heads,
And willows bore a fruit juicy and red,
There lived . . ."

   (Rumanian beginning)

Other endings:

> "And it would never happen again,
> Even if potatoes should begin to grow on trees,
> And corn ripened in snowdrifts."

> "Snip, snap, snout!
> And now the tale is out!"

One other story beginning and ending is amusing to young children. The storyteller uses any sequence of rituals desired to initiate the telling. Then, when ready to tell a story, he or she says,

> "Now I am ready to tell my story.
> And, if you don't listen,
> Your ears will turn green and fall off."

To end the story, after using a ritual story ending, the teller looks at everyone's ears and says,

> ". . . and I am glad to see that you all still have your ears."

Combining Rituals

Audiences like ritual. Extended ritual operations before a storytelling are often as much fun as the stories themselves. Participation rituals, especially, give the audience a chance to work out some energy. Using more than one ritual to begin or end a telling can be quite effective.

One way to combine ritual openings might be to use one participation ritual followed by one nonparticipation ritual, then a story beginning.

Storyteller:	A story, a story.
Audience:	Let it come. Let it go.
Storyteller:	We do not really mean . . . We do not really mean . . . That what we say is true.
Storyteller:	"Once upon a time . . ."

The participation ritual confirms audience commitment. The nonparticipation ritual establishes the storyteller as other, and the story beginning ritual places the story in the time and place of the other reality. Each ritual in turn helps to bring the audience farther into the experience.

A combined ritual ending might consist first of the story ending, then of the ritual closing. The story ending returns the audience from the reality of the story to the reality of the storytelling. The ritual closing returns the audience from the storytelling to their own time and place.

Storyteller: . . . It all happened a long time ago,
                And, believe it or not,
                It is all absolutely true.

Storyteller: And now, you can have your supper,
                And say your prayers,
                And go to bed.
                Morning is wiser than evening.

Ritual Devices and Artifacts

Aspects of setting, storyteller dress, and personal paraphernalia, as well as use of objects, can become part of the storytelling ritual, identifying the teller as other and signaling the beginning of the game. Some items might belong exclusively to the ritual of telling. Others might be attached to the person of the storyteller and help to announce the identity and function of the teller. Still others might be connected to specific stories.

Ritual Settings

Settings that audiences associate with storytellings are those reserved exclusively for the purposes of telling stories. When the setting conveys the expectation for storytelling, the person who tells the stories is partly identified by the setting. Anyone may act as the storyteller if he or she takes the designated place in the storytelling setting. The presence of the teller within the setting is a signal that the game is about to begin.

Schoolrooms and libraries can provide a permanent storytelling setting without elaborate preparation. Association is the most important ingredient. The telling should always be done in one location. That location should be prepared, initially, by eliminating distractions and physical obstructions and by setting aside a place for the teller to work and for the audience to sit comfortably. As storytelling activity continues over a period of time, audiences will begin to associate the location with storytelling. For younger audiences, especially, such associations are strong. Stories told in another location are not quite right. Eventually, the storytelling place will accumulate artifacts that go along with storytelling, specific storytellers, and favorite stories.

Hangings of various kinds—appliquéd, painted, embroidered, or macraméd—make good backdrops for storytelling settings. They mark the place for the storyteller to stand or sit. They also can lend character to the area. Backdrops can consist of places where artifacts representing specific stories are hung. A curtain, a rolling bulletin board, an upright painted pegboard, or cardboard will also work.

Rugs or other demarcations on the floor can be used to indicate the space in which the audience can sit and still be in the storytelling. Individuals who are not within the space thus defined are not in the telling and therefore are not in the game.

Some storytellers keep all of their storytelling-related paraphernalia in the storytelling area, pulling it out with some ceremony when they are ready to begin a storytelling. The storage of these storytelling devices helps to mark the storytelling location.

A special chair, bench, log, stool, or other seat for the storyteller can either help to identify a storytelling area or can be used as a portable telling center. The location of the portable seat then becomes the storytelling area, if the audience learns to associate the activity with the chair or bench.

One fairly elaborate permanent storytelling area in a city library contains two banks of felt appliquéd draperies that meet in a corner, a carved stump for a storyteller's chair, a modest spotlight, and a large, round carpet. A teacher who learned to tell regularly to her second-graders created an area defined by a throw rug, with a macramé hanging upon which she tied various artifacts to represent her stories. She kept a common classroom chair in the area to sit on while telling. Eventually the children associated that chair with storytelling and would not allow it out of the area to be used for more mundane purposes. It had become "sacred." So certain were the children that the chair had powers of its own that they took up storytelling themselves, but would only tell if seated in the chair.

A good home setting for storytelling need not be intricate. One special place, a soft chair or special corner, can quickly become *the* storytelling location, if that is the place where stories are always told. My grandfather told stories to all of the grandchildren using the simplest of devices: an out-of-the way kitchen corner (the one behind the door to the parlor and in front of the coat hooks), an old felt hat, and his tobacco pouch. Storytelling time was when Grandpa sat in that place to roll and smoke cigarettes. The grandchildren would come and gather on the floor in front of him. He would not tell a story until he had rolled a cigarette (one-handed), and he took perverse pleasure in prolonging the process. I learned later that Grandma had restricted his in-house smoking to that corner and was annoyed that the grandchildren were always there to watch. After these many years, the now middle-aged grandchildren remember that corner more vividly than any other place in the house.

Time as Setting

Special times can be established for storytelling. Those times then become "sacred" and should not be used for other activity. Many cultures place restrictions on the times when stories may be told. Many Native American cultures allow storytelling only when snow is on the ground. If special storytelling times are identified, expectations for stories at those times will develop. Those expectations should not be violated.

Since the oral literature is a literature in its own right, an important human heritage, and a rich source of information, it deserves adequate time. If a special time cannot be set aside for the oral literature, owing to school schedules and the demands of various curricula, storytelling may have to be done when time permits, but such sessions should be sufficiently long when they do occur. Under no circumstances should the telling of stories be used to keep children busy or to fill in the extra minutes that sometimes present themselves on a Friday afternoon before the buses come. Once a storytelling is begun, it must be finished—made whole. Storytelling time should be planned such that stopping midway will not be necessary. Interrupting a telling because a bell rings teaches the wrong lessons about the purposes and importance of ritual, play, and literature.

The Sacred Circle

Many cultures identify the storytelling setting as a "magic circle" or a "golden ring." Circles and the spaces within circles have, throughout much of human history, been associated with religious and sacred ceremony and special activity. The connection of storytelling with such circles suggests that story-telling may once have been intimately associated with or integrated with sacred ritual. Certain stories may have been told only in association with specific ceremonies and only as part of a larger liturgy or ritual.

Storytelling audiences seem to have some deep memory regarding the importance of the circle in storytelling, even if the stories are no longer connected to some yearly ritual calendar. Audiences "feel" the circle. Even six- and seven-year-old children understand being "inside" and "outside" the story-telling. "Inside," by their definition, is roughly circular and defines a space with a certain proximity to the teller. A certain distance away, they say, is too far away, and therefore "outside." With limited degrees of variance, the children define that distance to within a difference of a foot or two. In an otherwise undocumented, informal experiment with preschool children, a librarian made a circle on the floor with a yellow rope and placed her preschool audience within it. She told them that the story she was going to tell them lived inside the space defined by the rope. Unlike other sessions in which the children sometimes crawled away (they had no sense of story and lost interest), they stayed inside the roped boundaries.

The circle is probably the space or area that the storyteller can hold within the dynamic of the storytelling. People who are too far away from the teller simply do not feel that they are a part of the experience. They are inclined to watch the audience participate but to accept no responsibility of their own for the successful completion of the story. Furthermore, physical obstructions of any kind inside the story space sometimes disrupt the power of the story within the circle. One library storytelling area is bounded on one side by free-standing chest-high bookshelves that serve to separate that space from the rest of the library. Even though people who stand behind the shelves and lean on them to listen to a storyteller are physically closer to the teller than some individuals in the audience within the storytelling area, they clearly consider themselves to be outside the limits of the activity. These people regard both audience and storyteller as spectators would watch a stage play. And they do not make any effort to join in.

Preschool, kindergarten, and primary school audiences don't always understand the physical space that the storytelling encompasses – the concept of circle – without the use of some concrete marker to signify the boundaries. A long piece of rope can be used to mark the circle with such younger audiences. The ritual marking of the circle by passing the rope around the outside and behind the backs of the individuals at the back of the audience, and the formal knotting of the ends of the rope behind the storyteller, become a part of the initiating ceremony. Audiences who have become accustomed to this procedure will not begin a storytelling without it. Older audiences do not need ropes to indicate the circle within which the power of the story and the dynamic of the storytelling are in control.

Audience placement is an important aspect of making the circle work. The storyteller is at risk, certainly, during a telling. That risk increases to the degree that members of the audience do not feel responsible for the story and do not participate. (Individuals within a game are living by game rules. They are always vulnerable to others within the same game who do not feel bound by the rules.) The storyteller uses ritual and audience placement to share out the responsibility for the storytelling and extend the jurisdiction of the rules of the storytelling to all of the players. The closer an audience is to the teller, the more vulnerable it is and therefore the more likely to feel a responsibility for the success of the experience. Spaces between members of the audience should be closed in. Empty chairs, if the audience is seated in chairs, should be removed. The story is a bit like electricity. It cannot jump across gaps in what should be a closed circuit.

The circle also is in force when a group of storytellers tells to one another. While some sharing sessions between storytellers use the audience-with-teller-in-front arrangement, many tellers choose to sit in a circle to do a group storytelling. Turn taking is usually still random, but the arrangement is sometimes less intimidating than approaching an "audience" of storytellers. This arrangement also helps reduce anxiety among students in storytelling classes and among children who wish to tell stories. When the storytellers sit in a circle, the circle itself marks the boundaries of the game. The integrity of the circle is best maintained if no empty chairs are allowed in it. Should an individual have to leave the circle, his or her chair should be quietly removed and the space in the circle closed off. Should a teller arrive late, a handy empty chair can be unobtrusively slipped into the circle. The circle suggests an equality that encourages a special kind of closeness and story negotiability. Monitoring the occasional comings and goings of participants by inserting and removing chairs keeps the circle whole and the game unbroken.

Ritual Objects

The storyteller can make use of objects to help initiate and end a storytelling, incorporating these into a larger ritual protocol that might also include ritual openings and closings. In one form or another, passing objects around and through an audience for everyone to touch, and by touching to commit to the experience, is a very old practice. Some ideas for modern audiences are listed below.

Ropes. A soft, thick nylon rope can be passed into the audience with instructions that each individual tie a knot into it. Each knot tied represents a commitment to the storytelling. The fully knotted rope, when returned to the storyteller in a lumpy, tight ball, is a physical embodiment of the closeness and community of the audience during the game. To close the storytelling, the teller can again send the rope out into the audience, this time for the knots to be untied. To avoid misunderstandings among members of younger audiences, the storyteller might direct that each individual is to untie a knot, but not necessarily the same knot he or she tied at the beginning. A nylon rope that will not hold knots permanently, and in which knots cannot be pulled tight, is best.

Stones. Stones have quite literally been around from the beginning of time. They are as old as the universe is old, and they have much to tell. Certainly on this planet they contain many stories in their composition and distribution. Perhaps they hold or can hold other stories as well. A storyteller can invest a favorite storytelling stone with stories. All of the stories that a teller knows, in fact, can be kept in a stone, to be brought out for telling one at a time. Such an arrangement would be consistent with the mystique of both stones and stories. The stone can be introduced to the audience at the beginning of a telling, then passed around for touching and "warming up" before the first story is told. The touching and especially the body heat given to the stone are the commitment to the storytelling.

Bones. See chapter 8.

Blankets, quilts, shawls, and rugs. Some storytellers employ such objects as blankets, rugs, and the like in a variety of ways to bring an audience together into a storytelling. An audience can gather around the edges of a blanket or shawl, each individual touching or holding a part of it for a moment. They can all sit on a rug or quilt. Any like device will serve to illustrate the community of the telling in a very concrete manner.

Clothing and accessories. Objects such as hats, knotted or beaded necklaces or cords, embroidered vests, shirts, and skirts can "hold" stories. The teller simply invests his or her stories in the object, then uses the object during the initiation of a storytelling to call forth the stories. In the cases of such items as beaded clothing, knotted cords, embroidered quilts, and carved sticks, each story can be represented by a bead, a knot, an embroidered picture or symbol, or a carving. Members of the audience can request a given story by identifying it on the clothing, cord, quilt, or stick. Possibilities are listed below.

1. Hats—beaded, with buttons sewn on, painted, embroidered, or with small artifacts attached to represent stories

2. Shirts, skirts, aprons, vests, scarves—see item 1

3. Necklaces—knotted, beaded, crocheted, macraméd, with representative items knotted or beaded in or hung from

4. Shirts or other items of clothing with holes, each hole representing a story. The more holes, the more stories a teller knows. The biggest, most worn, oldest holes are the oldest, best, most favorite stories.

5. Sticks—carved, painted, with items attached, with nails pounded in, each representing a story

6. Seats, logs, rocks—see item 5

7. Curtains—see item 1

8. Rugs—hooked, braided, woven, with designs, shapes, or knots representing stories

9. Aprons—see item 1; also, with pockets containing story-related items

10. Fishing tackle boxes or nut-and-bolt boxes with tiny sliding drawers—can be used as containers for story-related items

11. Bags, sacks, pouches—can be filled with story-related items. Audiences can reach into these to pull out stories to tell.

12. String or yarn—tie a piece, one for each story, to an article of clothing, a hanging, a stick, a hat.

Special inventions. Many students in storytelling classes have developed clever applications of old ideas. One student used a telescope through which she could "see" her stories. Another used a pair of glassless spectacle frames. She was able to "see across time, space, and distance" and "find" all of her stories in the far-away places where they lived. Numerous others have used animals—live, dead, and stuffed—to contain their stories. Knapsacks of various sizes, shapes, and colors have appeared with stories housed within and sewn, embroidered, painted, tied, and glued on without. Bowls, baskets, and bags of yarn have appeared, as have old spool, button, and bead collections. Music boxes and other old childhood treasures have also served the purpose of ritual story repository.

Storyteller as "Other" Rituals

The ritual routines and objects thus far mentioned tend to be somewhat generic, in that they are associated with stories and storytelling rather than an individual teller. However, the individual storyteller can also adopt a "habit." The habit is some clearly identifiable item of clothing or some artifact or object that belongs to the teller and signals that the teller is ready to be the storyteller—the "other." The teller wears, carries, or otherwise displays the item to initiate the telling and makes appropriate use of it throughout, even if such use amounts only to leaning it against a wall or setting it on the floor.

The habit becomes a signal associated with a storytelling, given when the teller puts it on, picks it up, or places it in a special location. The signal does not need to be overly obvious to have an effect. In keeping with the notion of storyteller as medium rather than as performer, the habit should be modest. Too much of a habit could distract audience attention from the telling and the stories by making the teller too visible, too ostentatious. Too spectacular a habit could also encourage expectations for a performance that will not be fulfilled in the telling. Keep it simple.

The habit, because it contributes to the identity of an individual as story-teller, can be an intimate object, something of personal significance to the teller. A hat, a cane, a necklace, a shirt, a scarf, or a pair of old shoes will suffice—not to hold the stories, but to hold the identity of "other" for the teller. Some tellers have more than one such object. When the teller employs the object, he or she is ready to tell. He or she has already committed to the game and entered into that other reality. The storyteller must make the first move toward the time and place of "story" in order to be able to conduct the audience into "story" and into the game. The use of the personal ritual object also serves the purpose, then, of readying the storyteller for a storytelling.

Some storytellers operate like some athletes, in that they regard their habit as sacred and lucky. They would not consider telling a story without it. It has a private ritual importance for the teller aside from its role in identifying the teller for the audience. Rather than making a deliberate effort to locate such a habit, the storyteller should let it evolve. Serendipity often strikes; the right thing identifies itself. Occasionally a storyteller will tell stories for some time without having identified a habit, only to discover that one has crept into his or her storytelling practice. It will be something that always somehow seems to be there during a telling.

One teller always told with a ring of keys fastened about her waist on a cord. These turned out to be keys that she had saved from all of the places she had lived as a child. The keys had considerable personal importance to her, and they made her feel comfortable when she told her stories. They also became a trademark of sorts with her schoolchildren. They learned that when the keys went on, the stories were ready. The keys otherwise bore no relationship to the stories she told. Another teller always wore a Pueblo frog fetish on a silver chain—an accident of repeated application rather than of deliberate choice. However, the association eventually became so regular that the teller felt naked and unprotected without it. If the frog failed to make its appearance, audiences would inquire as to its absence. Still another teller always told in blue clothing. The color became the habitual signal. When questioned about this curiosity, the teller said that blue made him feel good and more in control of the entire telling situation. A fourth teller, a first-grade teacher, wore braids. She developed the habit to the degree that she could sit anywhere in her classroom and begin to braid her hair and the children would come for stories.

Habits should feel good and natural and should fit the person of the storyteller. They should be used easily, often without explanation. The habit becomes a part of the storyteller as other. The person who does the storytelling does not otherwise wear or use the item. Eventually, the item itself will become associated with the experience of a storytelling, first for the teller and later for the regular audience. Once the association is made, the item can sometimes be handed to another individual without loss of audience expectation, extending its significance to more than one storyteller.

The Storytelling Liturgy

Using ritual devices in combination is a common practice in storytelling. A teller might choose to use a ritual opening and a ritual object (rope, stone, etc.) to initiate the telling, usually using the object first. He or she might also use some other device—a pouch containing artifacts or a beaded hat to represent the stories themselves. At the same time, the teller might carry or be wearing a personal habit that identifies him or her as other. Each story might begin with a ritual beginning and perhaps contain some kind of ritual participation.

The Importance of Ritual

The storytelling is filled with ceremony. Traditionally, a storytelling was/is a ceremony and required/requires the ceremonial employment of the proper rituals. By using rituals in combination, the teller creates a ritual protocol that brings the audience into the game, that signals the beginning of another time, that binds the audience into a different reality, that frees the audience from real-time inhibitions, and that allows negotiation. Ritual protocol, in addition, feels right and good.

Unless a teller is responsible to a traditional protocol that he or she has inherited, protocol can be borrowed, assembled, and invented. The storyteller who works with different audiences and rarely sees the same group more than once will have to develop and teach his or her protocol to each new audience in turn. The fortunate teller who works with the same group or groups repeatedly can develop the beginnings of a ritual sequence and allow the audience to contribute to its further development. Children especially enjoy making ritual, and adults find comfort and security in it. Once a ritual sequence or protocol is established, regular audiences will do it with relish. Woe be to the storyteller who forgets even one precious and sacred operation or who, even more unforgivably, deliberately leaves out a part of the sequence to save time.

Our lives are bound by ritual. We remember because ritual provides a framework for remembering. We know how to behave because ritual specifies the acceptable boundaries for our behavior. Ritual supplies comfort, security, propriety, and satisfaction. It brings closure, a sense that something is whole. And we can make successful predictions regarding the world around us because ritual (or convention) provides us with reliable patterns of expectation.

Storytelling is a literary ritual. It uses the conventions of oral language to structure the storytelling. We have, at least traditionally, had expectations for the manner in which a storytelling should work. Those expectations have included ritual routines or sequences that are liturgical in nature. A storytelling follows a protocol that is negotiated by and agreed to by all participants. That is one of the special characteristics of an oral literature. We expect the structure and the ritual. We do it, and it feels good.

A Sample Ritual Sequence

The teller wears an old vest that belonged to his grandfather. He never talks about the vest unless asked, but always has it with him. The teller tells in a storytelling center in a library. The center contains a specially designed hanging and chair. The teller has the vest hanging in the center on an old free-standing coat rack. The hanging is kept rolled up when it is not in use.

1. The audience is waiting.

2. The teller enters the center and puts on the vest.

3. A member of the audience is chosen to unroll the hanging.

4. The teller takes his seat.

5. The teller rearranges the seating pattern of the audience if necessary.

6. The teller begins the storytelling with a rope knotting.

7. The teller uses a ritual opening to finish the initial ritual.
    Teller: A story, a story.
    Audience: Let it come. Let it go.

8. The story begins with, "Once there was, and once there was not . . ."

9. The story contains both ritual and coactive participation. The audience repeats a long cumulative list.

10. The structure of the story is regular and very predictable.

11. The story ends with a ritual story ending: "And if he ain't moved away, he's a-livin' there still."

12. The teller uses a ritual ending to close the telling: "Tomorrow you may peel potatoes and eat soup."

13. A member of the audience rolls up the hanging.

14. The teller removes his vest and hangs it on its hook.

ASSESSING THE AUDIENCE

Most storytelling programs are designed, at least in part, before the fact of a telling, but not without some knowledge on the storyteller's part of the audience with whom he or she will tell. When the storyteller's services are engaged, the teller should gather information regarding the nature of the audience, the length of program desired, and the setting in which the telling will take place. All these factors will have some effect upon audience behavior during a telling and upon the kinds of stories that will be best received.

NATURE OF THE AUDIENCE

Audience Age

Audience age is perhaps the most important factor in planning the story-telling program and, if necessary, tailoring stories for a given telling. Homogeneous audiences are often the most difficult to work with, since their levels of literary development tend to be restricted. The storyteller cannot use some materials, perhaps, because no members of the audience will be able to appreciate them and/or apprehend their significance. The story that makes use of figurative language to convey humor and meaning, or that makes subtle social commentary, or that uses the editorial aside to carry an important message about some aspect of the story will probably not work with younger audiences. Story structure, too, can confound the younger audience if it is too complex and/or unpredictable. In general, the less conventional the material and the more adult the content and humor, the less comprehensible a story will be to an audience of young children. Interestingly enough, older children, who also lack certain dimensions of literary development, might regard the same material as too unsophisticated and reject it.

While the stories told to the homogeneous child audience should not be restricted entirely to shapes the children can predict — they do need exposure to more mature literature — the storyteller should keep one educator's axiom in mind: Children need to have experiences in which they can succeed (to levels of between 80 and 90 percent). This requirement suggests that children should be presented with materials for which they already have relatively high levels of expectation and that, therefore, they will be able to control to a great extent. They will then be able to integrate new information — content, story structure, and literary convention — into patterns of memory already stored. (Teachers have sometimes mistakenly thought that they should teach what children do not know. In fact, we often cannot retain what we do not know, precisely because we know nothing about it. But if we are presented with information that we can already control, plus a smattering (10 to 20 percent) of new, related material, we will be able to integrate the new into the old. What we already know provides a framework for saving new information.) The story-telling program for the child audience should be designed to insure audience success. A storytelling is a cooperative venture, a negotiation, and should not make individuals feel inept.

The Very Young Audience

For the toddler, preschool, and perhaps even kindergarten audience, highly predictable, exceptionally conventional stories will help the children learn "story," predict the manner in which stories structure information, and participate collectively in a group game and negotiation. The best stories are those that contain repetitive motion, noise, and language—activity the children can do and chant. While the children are developing a sense of "story" and learning storying process, they will be able to participate fully with internal aspects of the story. "The Fat Cat" (Kent 1971) is a good example of the type of material that can be used successfully with small children. The content is presented in fairly simple language within a story structure that contains one setting, one problem, one sequence of events, and one resolution. There are no unexpected episodes. The primary vehicle, since the story is cumulative (winding and unwinding), is repetitive language which the children can chant and (sometimes) shout.

In planning and preparing the story for the very young audience, the storyteller should include as much immediate activity as possible: chanting, singing, movement and motion, clapping, exclaiming, and facial expression. Repetitive language is especially important for children whose primary task is still language development. Play with language within story context provides opportunities for learning control of various linguistic forms without making a formal exercise out of the experience. The language remains transparent; the story content is opaque (Cazden 1975).

The storyteller should not be surprised if very young children do not always respond to the whole story. They may focus on a motion or a noise and remember that feature clearly, while not being able to recall more "important" story content. More than one storyteller has had small children ask for a story to be retold, only to discover that the children had little interest in the story. They wanted another opportunity to learn to control the repetitious language in the story by repeating it and playing with it again.

Because they offer the most extensive language play opportunities, cumulative-type stories, especially those that both wind and unwind, are popular with very young audiences. Noncumulative stories with event-repeat sequences also can allow language play, providing that the storyteller tailors the story to include it. Stories that slot content into very simple structural arrangements are also among the best choices. Children who do not yet have a sense of "story" can learn it more easily from stories that present one clear setting, one obvious problem, one sequence of events leading directly to problem solution, and one clear-cut resolution.

Props that help organize story events, present characters, or show aspects of story structure (one prop for each event in an event sequence) will help the children remember the story itself and develop (map) memory for story structure. Interactive props are those that allow the children to work out the story physically. The children become a part of the story and "act" in the story in order to do a given task with a prop. Simple activities such as holding up pictures or bringing items forward to give the teller at the appropriate moment will be very successful. Examples of prop use with selected stories follow.

1. "The Fat Cat" (Kent 1971): A series of pictures sequencing the cat growing fatter teaches size relationships and sequencing. A series of pictures of the characters eaten by the cat also teaches sequencing and aids memory for the repetitive language in the story.

2. "Stone Soup" (Brown 1947b): A pot, a wooden spoon, a stone or two, and selected vegetables distributed to children in the audience teach identification and naming. Each child brings his or her vegetable to the pot when its name is called.

3. "Why Mosquitoes Buzz in People's Ears" (Aardema 1975): A clothesline, clothespins, and cutouts of the characters named in the repetitious language are used. As the children hang the character cutouts on the line when these are named, they learn names and sequence and are provided with a set of cues for remembering the repeat language.

4. "The Very Hungry Caterpillar" (Carle 1970): Cutouts of the items the caterpillar eats, and in the given quantity, are attached to sticks. As the storyteller names and specifies the quantity of each item, the children to whom these were distributed hold them up for all to see. This activity teaches naming and numbering.

5. "Drummer Hoff" (Emberley 1967): Hats representing the characters, or cutouts for a felt board to build the cannon, are used. The storyteller switches hats or builds the cannon during the telling. The children can help with both, under direction, learning sequencing and naming in the process.

Selected stories for toddler, preschool, and kindergarten audiences include:

"The Pancake" (Johnson et al. 1977)

"Titty Mouse and Tatty Mouse" (Jacobs n.d.)

"Once a Mouse" (Brown 1947a)

"Too Much Noise" (McGovern 1967)

"The Three Wishes" (Galdone 1961)

"The Gingerbread Boy" (Galdone 1975)

"Henny Penny" (Galdone 1968)

"The Turnip" (Domanska 1977)

"The Three Billy Goats Gruff" (Arbuthnot 1961)

"The Three Little Pigs" (Literature Committee 1950)

"Speckled Eggs" (see chapter 3)

"Little Red Riding Hood" (Grimm and Grimm 1969)

"The Little Red Hen and the Grain of Wheat" (Haviland 1972)

The Primary School Audience

In general, first- and second-grade audiences are very much like preschool audiences, in that they like highly predictable, very conventional material that has been tailored to allow a maximum amount of direct interaction. They are still very much involved with primary language development, and language play will aid in the building of language competence. Many of the stories that are appropriate for preschoolers will also be favorites of primary schoolers. The difference lies in the respective levels of literary development evidenced by the two groups.

While many preschool children do not know "story" and respond primarily to play within the story (noises, language, motions), the primary school child usually is aware of "story" and "story" as game. He or she has developed a sense of "story" through experience with stories at the preschool level and is ready to respond to story structure frameworks as well as to internal content. The primary school child can predict story structure and content and can slot content into story pattern. Where the preschooler will exhibit limited or no expectation for the features of "story" itself, the primary schooler will have a set of expectations regarding how a story should work. Sometimes these expectations are rather parochial, in that they often do not admit special twists, figurative language punch lines, internal complications of plot, or unconventional features (an ending that is not of the "happily ever after" variety, for example).

Both first- and second-graders are able to do most within-the-story play that a teller might ask, usually without the extra prompting and urging that is sometimes required with preschoolers. They lack the beginning of social awareness that might inhibit them from participation and will join in without hesitation, regardless of the activity. Third-graders are a different sort of group. They have enough self-awareness to be suspicious of a storyteller's requests to interact (they might look silly if they do) and are a bit slower to become involved in the story. They are beginning to think consciously about appearances and might be somewhat inhibited.

Third-graders need the language interactions of cumulative and event-repeat stories but will sometimes regard these story structures as "baby stuff." The stories are, of course, anything but babyish. Still, nine- to ten-year-old children make certain associations. These types of highly conventional stories can be tailored to meet the interests and social needs of the third-grade group by including appropriate editorializing, internal joking, and graphic description that is appealing to that population. Many of the interactive props that are so necessary with younger audiences may not be necessary with third-graders. Some of the effects invented to hold the interest of the preschooler may also not be necessary, since nine- to ten-year-olds can focus on structure and make very sophisticated predictions. In general, the storyteller should ask: "If I used this effect with sixth-graders, would they be offended?" If the answer is yes, third-graders will be offended, too.

Perhaps because print is the newer tool, and because we make such a fuss over it in the school curriculum, we tend to think of the oral literature as a lesser literature—less sophisticated, something "for children." Third-graders, certainly older children, do not class themselves as children. (They will preface some reminiscences with, "When I was a kid. . . .") They can be made ready for some of the most sophisticated literary play that the oral literature can make available, with the exception of some adult humor. They can be very willing participants, provided that they do not think that the teller, the stories, or the storytelling are insulting their intelligence. Some third-grade children are ready to learn to tell stories; for these few, "story" is becoming opaque. With this growing awareness of "story" and storying, children can make the kinds of conscious decisions about telling a story that are necessary to do the oral literature.

If the storyteller is planning a program for a nine- to ten-year-old audience, he or she should include some stories that would be appropriate for older children and deliver them as if to the older group. Cumulative and event-repeat stories also belong in the program, with adjustments to make them appeal to the more sophisticated audience. It should be noted, however, that the appeal of a story depends to a large extent upon the storyteller's attitude and expectation. If the storyteller regards the individuals in the audience as intelligent and respects their abilities, no matter how limited, he or she is less at risk of delivering insult along with the story. If the teller thinks of the people in the audience as "babies"—in the derogatory sense—he or she will inevitably reveal this attitude. Perhaps third-graders have simply become more aware of and more intolerant of the attitudes of some adults toward children. They can be very particular about how they are treated. They very much dislike patronization in any form, even when it sneaks out in the way the teller pitches words and sentences, or the way he or she tries to coerce the audience into an interaction designed more for a preschool group. Story choice, development, and delivery should reflect the storyteller's genuine appreciation of the adult in each and every child in an audience.

Selected stories for the primary school audience include:

"The Gunniwolf" (Harper 1967)

"The Hedgehog and the Hare" (Grimm and Grimm 1969)

"The Wide-Mouthed Frog" (see chapter 2)

"The Five Chinese Brothers" (Bishop 1938)

"One Trick Too Many" (Ginsburg 1973)

"The Brementown Musicians" (Johnson et al. 1977)

"The Old Woman and Her Pig" (ibid.)

"The Fisherman and His Wife" (ibid.)

"The Three Goats" (Literature Committee 1950)

"The Straw Ox" (ibid.)

"La Hormiguita" (Hayes 1982)

"Anansi the Spider" (McDermott 1972)

"Soap, Soap, Soap" (Chase 1948)

"The Twistmouth Family" (Haviland 1972)

"The Tailypo: A Ghost Story" (Galdone 1977)

The Middle School Audience

Most middle school audiences can handle adult stories, with the possible exceptions of some forms of adult humor and social commentary. They certainly do not need to be "protected" from story content and are ready for many complicated story structures. They will generally respond as will an adult audience, and, unlike younger children, will regard the conclusion and moral as the most important part of the story. They understand that the story is both fun in its own right and a vehicle used to deliver a larger message. They also are developing an appreciation of the language play in figurative usage. Some aspects of their understanding of "story" and language remain literal, but a sense of the metaphoric is present. They quite plainly enjoy tricks of plot and logic, the memory games of sophisticated cumulative play, and stories that poke fun at social custom. They are beginning to recognize archetypes as archetypes and take pleasure in justice done to those who deserve it. They have developed a sense of the omniscience and power of the observer and can thus play the storytelling game with a better awareness of the relationship between reality and fantasy in "story" and storytelling.

The middle school child has also developed a level of literary awareness that allows him to appreciate not only the story but the way in which the teller tells it. He can separate technique from story structure and content and will often say to the storyteller, "I like the way you did that." Because aspects of the art of storytelling have become opaque, or as tangible as the story itself, children in this group are ready, often eager, to learn to tell stories. They realize that telling a story requires the development of some skill, and that the storyteller has learned to control something. Just as younger children are developing language competence by learning to control many language forms, the middle schooler is ready to take the first steps in control of top-level structure of the established oral literature through formal storytelling.

The middle school storytelling program can contain some of the language and motion play of the stories for younger children; however, this play should be set in stories that are more sophisticated in their structure and content. Middle schoolers' predicting abilities are better challenged with chronicle-type structures in which events are logically related but less repetitive. They particularly enjoy stories in which their predictions of outcome are led in one direction by the action, only to be foiled by the surprise ending or twist in plot. They moan and groan over figurative-language punchlines, like to play with tongue-twisting language, and delight in the cleverness of tricksters and quick-witted interactions between characters. The exaggerated, preposterous, and ridiculous is good fare. They are ready for mythologies and epic stories and can handle tales in which the characters have to solve more than one problem or in which the problems, not the language, are cumulative. They respond well to stories that comment on social situations they can understand—friends, parents, brothers and sisters—and have a special appreciation of justice meted out where it is due. They are, overall, ready for most adult content, but prefer it with surprise elements, a touch of clever slapstick, and a smattering of the impossibility of the tall tale.

The teller who develops and tailors a story for the middle-grade audience should plan to eliminate some primary-level props, ritual interaction, and coactivity from the delivery. While these audiences will participate in ritual and coactive interactions that are sophisticated enough to challenge (a story such as "The Fat Cat" does not) they are eager to interject some views of their own. Unlike the younger child, who will more than likely talk off topic if given the chance, the middle schooler will banter in a story-related manner, beginning with the inevitable editorial groan, moan, or "Oh, No!" Props that are appropriate for younger children are generally not necessary for upper elementary students. (Flannel boards are often viewed with suspicion, and the examples for audience interaction using props given for preschoolers are inappropriate.) They do like to sing, dance, and invent chantings for stories, provided that their intelligence is respected, that they do not feel coerced, and that they are able to assume some control of the situation. A story that is delivered with props, ritual chantings, and noisemakings and overtly encourages and cues coactivity for younger children might be quite acceptable to the upper elementary age group if told "straight" or with the addition of limited editorial and figurative language.

The middle school group understands language with more than the narrow literal capability of the younger child. Their understanding of the story, therefore, is enriched by their appreciation of metalinguistic language play (using knowledge about language to play with language): puns (the silliest possible), alliteration (tongue-twisters—lengthy ones preferred), metaphor and simile (especially if ridiculous), and hyperbole (the more preposterous, the better). Upper elementary is the group that plays the "How big was it?" ("It was soooo big that . . .") or "How hot was it?" ("It was soooo hot that . . .") game with the storyteller with much earnestness, leaning forward for the answer and hoping for the most impossible exaggeration.

While middle schoolers are more appreciative of such language play, and less interested in simple repetitive play, they still view the act of story*telling* literally. This is understandable, since storytelling is a higher-level "top-level structure" than the single story within it. One sixth-grader was interested in the use of artifacts to document stories and in how the storyteller might use these to convince a (younger) audience that the stories were absolutely true. I replied that, in the case of my story artifacts, I was present when the event took place and kept each artifact as a souvenir. "I was hiding behind a rock, and I saw it all," I repeated as I described the acquisition of each of several artifacts I was holding (a feather from Quail's tail, the bell from the collar of the littlest Billy Goat Gruff, and a shell that Fox shook out of his fur). The boy replied, "Lady, people would believe you better if you said that you hid behind a bush or a tree sometimes, too." While the middle school audience would often prefer not to use ritual objects (stones, bones, and ropes) in a telling ritual, the other aspects of the storytelling opening and closing are serious matters indeed, often understood literally rather than for their figurative relationship to the game.

Finally, middle schoolers clearly understand that the stories are fantasy and are beginning to apprehend "story" truth as well. They know, in some rudimentary way, that the stories exist in some other time and place, and that, in that time and place, the stories are real. Perhaps their special excitement over further exaggeration of the fantastic helps them to establish the relationship between real time and "story" time. Every audience moan and groan originates in a real-time frame of reference and confirms audience understanding of "other" time. In a way, one "time" confronts the other during the telling, so that members of the audience can come to a full understanding of the nature of the game of storytelling.

Through the play of storytelling, children in the middle grades work toward a consciousness and awareness of the relationship between reality and fantasy in their worlds. Because they seem to be involved in such a problem solving, the use of the ritual is important. Hands-on, concrete ritual is fun and creates safety for younger children. A more sophisticated, formal, abstract ritual (formal and more philosophical openings and closings) becomes a vehicle for achieving a level of literary awareness for middle schoolers.

Selected stories for the middle school audience include:

"The Liar's Contest" (Courlander and Prempeh 1957)

"The Hungry Spider and Turtle" (Courlander and Herzog 1947)

"Younde Goes to Town" (ibid.)

"The Singing Tortoise" (ibid.)

"The Messenger to Naftam" (ibid.)

"Guinea Fowl and Rabbit Get Justice" (ibid.)

"How Soko Brought Debt to Ashanti" (ibid.)

"The Monkey and the Crocodile" (Johnson et al. 1977)

"The Husband Who Was to Mind the House" (ibid.)

"From Tiger to Anansi" (ibid.)

"The Goat Well" (ibid.)

"The Silly Goose War" (ibid.)

"The Frog's Saddle Horse" (Hardendorf 1968)

"The Day It Snowed Tortillas" (Hayes 1982)

"Coyote's Needle" (Courlander 1970)

"The Beetle's Hairpiece" (ibid.)

"Sea Frog, City Frog" (Van Woerkorn 1975)

"The Hobyahs" (Fenner 1943)

"Happy-Go-Lucky" (Wiesner 1972)

Also include collections of American tall tales and folklore (Rounds 1976; Malcolmson 1941; Leach 1958; Haviland 1979; McCormick 1936; Chase 1943, 1948, 1950, 1951; Emrich 1972; Tidwell 1956; Botkin 1951a, 1951b; *Life* 1961; Polley 1978; Malcolmson and McCormick 1952; Jagendorf 1949; Felton 1958; Gorham 1952), the Uncle Remus stories (Rees 1967; Harris 1883, 1920, 1941, 1948, 1955), and Coyote tales (Hayes 1982; Curry 1965; Robinson and Hill 1975; Cothran 1954; Dolch 1956; Courlander 1970; Matson 1968; Brown 1979; Jones 1974).

The Secondary School Audience

When secondary school students are included in an adult audience, they accept stories like adults. When they are isolated in their own age groups, they require adult treatment and adult stories. This is because secondary students, particularly the younger ones, are quite certain that they are not children and do not react positively to stories delivered in the manner of a primary school storytelling. But they are not convinced that they are grown up, and they doubt their credibility as adults daily. As so many texts on human growth and development point out, it is a confusing and difficult age, in which identity is uncertain. The stories chosen for this group, and the manner in which they are delivered, will either confirm or deny the adult status of the secondary student.

The adult audience has some degree of confidence in its own adulthood and does not doubt its credibility. For that reason, adults enjoy a preschool story. They know that they are mature people and that they are appreciating the story because they remember their own childhoods, because they are sharing the experience with their own young children, or because they are learning to be storytellers. They have an appreciation of the story that is directly related to their purposes for listening to it. They come to the story with an adult task in mind: remembering, parenting (or "teachering"), or "storytellering." Their experience with the story simply reinforces their adult identities and roles.

When included in an adult audience, the secondary student shares adult purposes in the storytelling. His or her adulthood is confirmed. When the student is isolated with peers in a storytelling audience, his or her role as an adult in the audience is far from certain. Therefore, the content of the storytelling—ritual, stories, and delivery—must be handled in as adult a manner as possible. And, if the telling takes place in a school setting, a secondary adult reason for being in the telling might be identified: study of the literature, consideration of the oral language conventions of the literature, or learning to tell to younger audiences. The intent is not to suggest that the oral literature is less worthy than the written, but to assure the student that he or she is an adult and can have adult reasons for listening. This is especially important in a culture such as our own, in which the written literature is viewed as a mature and adult endeavor, but the oral is often not. In a culture in which the oral literature is still a primary literature, a sufficient number of adult role models for the appreciation of the oral literature exist, and the oral literature does not appear to be the exclusive province of children.

With secondary students, the storyteller must assume that he or she is telling to an adult audience that is listening with no other purpose than to hear the stories. Perhaps considering how stories would be told at a private dinner that is not also a workshop or class and that includes no teachers, librarians, or children will help clarify the task. Props, if any are used, must be adult in nature. So must language. Ritual participation must not insult. Story structure must challenge the literary capabilities of the adult listener. Coercion in order to insure interaction is usually not well received, though some storytellers (using humor) do it well and get away with it. Coactivity should be voluntary. Bantering, also voluntary, should be encouraged when appropriate by the insertion of adult editorial commentary. Figurative language, play with political, social, economic, and personal circumstance, play with the structure of the story, and more sophisticated story structures are acceptable. The over-exaggerated, preposterous, and foolish touches that so please the middle school child will also please the secondary student, if done tastefully and without the hint of slapstick.

The teller as person is important to consider with secondary students. They, more than any other age group, have difficulty disassociating the person of the teller from the story. No matter how accomplished the storyteller, many secondary students will see the teller as a personality as clearly as the story during the telling. Perhaps the student sees the teller as opaque because the student often feels so painfully opaque during the telling. A good teller will be able to reduce these feelings of vulnerability in the audience through self-assurance, composure, confidence, control of the situation, and, most importantly, a clear (though unstated) belief in the worth of the oral literature and in storytelling. The storyteller will also telegraph his or her awareness of the adulthood of the audience in the manner in which the audience is handled and the story is told. (Consider doing a telling for the local school board.) Most importantly, the storyteller must remember that he or she is conducting a literary experience for people who are watching adults as role models with serious intent and purpose. The storyteller must always be an adult who is telling a story.

Selected stories for the secondary school audience include:

"The Two Donkeys" (Wolkstein 1978)

"The Two Old Women's Bet" (Chase 1951)

"The Frogs and the Norther" (Chase 1971)

"Gudbrand of the Hillside" (Asbjornsen and Moe 1960)

"The Seventh Father of the Seventh House" (ibid.)

" 'Good Day, Fellow.' 'Axe Handle!' " (ibid.)

"The Squire's Bride" (ibid.)

"The Princess Who Always Had to Have the Last Word" (ibid.)

"The Land Where One Never Dies" (Calvino 1980)

"Jack and the Three Sillies" (Chase 1950)

"The Three Sillies" (Jacobs 1967)

"Wali Dad the Simple-Hearted" (Lang 1949)

"The Goat Well" (Johnson et al. 1977)

"Molly Whuppie" (ibid.)

"Anansi's Fishing Expedition" (Courlander and Herzog 1947)

"The Cow-Tail Switch" (ibid.)

The Adult Audience

Some adults — parents, teachers, librarians — attend storytellings because they wish to learn to tell stories. The adult audience in a storytelling class has a purpose for listening other than to simply hear the stories. Likewise, adults in mixed (adult and child) audiences often attend to do more than listen for their own private enjoyment. They often come to enjoy the responses of the children in the audience. Program and delivery for the adults in such audiences takes on the character of a workshop/demonstration, though the teller need do no more than tell. Programs can be prepared deliberately to include stories that contain content, structure, humor, language, and interaction suitable for a variety of types of child audiences. Adults who plan to tell stories to children and those who come to listen with children will most often delight in the experience. The stories and the nature of the delivery will match adult needs, since these are related to understanding and appreciating the child audience. The adults, because they are confident of their maturity, will also be able to appreciate the stories and the storytelling privately, for personal reasons.

Homogeneous adult audiences who attend tellings to listen and enjoy for themselves alone should be treated to stories tailored for them with respect to content, structure, humor, language, and interaction. Delivery should accommodate the level of social development of the adult listener, and story choice the concomitant level of literary development (sense of "story").

Adults will enjoy many of the stories that the storyteller also tells for younger audiences. The stories themselves cannot be grouped into age-appropriate categories. But because adults have a more extended set of expectations for story behavior and structure, the teller can tell stories that might not be appropriate for younger audiences. Structural complications, story length, number of episodes and internal problems to be resolved, twists on logic, and story coherence present fewer restrictions to story choice for the adult audience. And even if a story is not particularly sophisticated structurally — for example, "The Hedgehog and the Hare" (Grimm and Grimm 1969) — the level of social and literary development of the adult audience insures an awareness of and appreciation of the archetypal features of the story and of the timeless message embedded therein. Adults can apprehend the play in the shape of the story, the play in the storytelling, and the inferred parablelike nature of the experience.

Almost any story can be told to adults provided that it is prepared, developed, and delivered in a manner appropriate for adults. Some aspects of content, perhaps some types of interaction, and employment of props designed for younger audiences would best be eliminated; the teller must use his or her discretion. Certainly, adults do not need to be coerced into an interaction. Participation in a story should be a matter of choice. Bantering should be allowed and encouraged. Editorializing is also a way in which a story can be made into adult material. Adult stories are not stories that contain sex, violence, and dirty jokes. They can be the same stories told to children but rendered adult through tailoring. "Speckled Eggs" seems to be a very success-ful story, a favorite with five-year-olds and also among graduate students. They listen to it once for professional reasons and thereafter request retellings for adult reasons. The adult nature of the story lies in the preparation and delivery.

Preparing and delivering a story for the adult audience cannot be described in a discrete listing of dos and don'ts. Once again, the storyteller should attend many tellings and observe a variety of stylistic approaches used with the adult audience. Watching stand-up comedians can also help the teller learn to tailor stories for adults. The storyteller need not aspire to be a stand-up comedian, but such entertainers have learned how to interact intimately with adult audiences in much the same way storytellers do. Comedians can provide good demonstrations of deportment and manner that can help tellers learn how to approach the adult audience with the same story that might, if delivered differently, be a delight for the middle schooler.

Many storytellers are intimidated by the adult audience. Tellers who learn to tell in order to work with children are sometimes especially fearful of the prospect of telling to adults. Perhaps that concern stems from the understand-ing that the adult audience is more sophisticated. Sophistication, however, makes the audience easier to handle, not more difficult. The more extensive the experience of the audience in terms of story structure, language, content, humor, and interaction, the less the teller needs to use concrete illustration and interaction, the fewer the required activities for the audience, and the more appreciative the listeners of nuances of language and humor. Perhaps the size of preschool children is a comfort to the storyteller. After all, how can human beings of such limited physical stature possibly be a difficult audience? In fact, the younger the listeners, the more difficult the task for the teller. The less sophisticated the listeners, the fewer the features of "story" and storying that will be apprehended, understood, and therefore appreciated.

Perhaps the storyteller who fears the adult audience really views the audience as a jury of peers. The teller should remember that he or she is not doing a performance. The teller is not opaque. The story is the visible entity. The audience is there to enter into the experience, not to watch the teller's gymnastics from a distance. Adult audiences generally have a better under-standing of their role and a greater willingness to play than many child audiences. They are usually very compliant, less self-conscious, and not so inclined to compete with the storyteller as some child groups. Moreover, they know how to control themselves and routinely monitor their own behavior. They can be trusted. They offer more safety to the teller than does any other group. All the teller need do is relax, assume a degree of self-confidence, remain in control of self and situation, abandon self-consciousness and embarrassment, and be an adult telling to peers.

The oral literature is an adult invention intended for adult entertainment. It is an old invention. We use it widely with children primarily because the oral language is so universally accessible, and because the oral literature is such an essential preliminary experience in the development of control of the conventions of written language and literature. But the oral literature has not lost its adult character; the shape of its play, story structure, and content are still very adult in nature. Children do not make stories like those in the literature (Sutton-Smith 1981). Children attending a storytelling are learners making discoveries about how adults behave. Adults already know how.

The Mixed-Age Audience

Mixed-age audiences are perhaps the most workable and the most delightful. They are certainly the most natural. Traditional storytellings generally did not group audiences by age. The literature was the creation of a culture. It belonged to all the people, young and old. Everyone attended the storytelling. The stories were not changed or censored because children were present. They helped the children learn how to live and be in their respective communities and confirmed the rightness of a way of living and being for the adults. The adults served as models for appreciation of the literary experience, and the oral literature brought people together.

Storytelling is still one of the most powerful devices available for confirming belonging and community. Modern society has witnessed the dissolution of the extended family and institutionalization of homogeneous groupings. "Child" is an adult invention that isolates children as a special social class requiring special and different treatment. Children require adult models and experiences with adults yet are separated from them and from engaging cooperatively with adults in mutually important activity. Stories and storytelling will be important to children if children can see adults enjoying the experience. The oral literature is "dumb" if adults never participate, if they watch while the children "have to do it," or if the children are always confined to an audience of their peers. If adults avoid experiences with the oral literature, children cannot be blamed for deciding that the oral literature is only for children, and that they will be more adult if they, too, avoid it. We identify what we value by making choices that others can see.

Children watch adults closely. Their primary task, after all, is to become adults. They will be reluctant to choose the oral literature if adults do not also choose it. In the mixed-age audience, children see adults choose to participate in a literary experience and can learn how to participate themselves. Adult presence makes the storytelling socially safe for the children. Adults also provide children in the audience with language and literary instruction through adult interaction with the story and the storyteller. Adults respond to elements within the story—content, humor, language—that children miss. The adults demonstrate additional levels of sophistication in the story to the children as they respond to the experience. Children will often ask an adult, usually a parent, what was so funny or what this or that meant. For their part, adults watch their children, perhaps remembering, perhaps seeing the world again as children see it, by experiencing the stories with children.

Each individual in the mixed-age audience has something special to add to the storytelling that will be an important part of the experience for everyone else, including the storyteller. After all, the story is the cooperative product of all present and includes even the explosive vocalizations of the prelinguistic infant. The mixed-age audience has a greater capacity to expand the shape of the story than any other type of group, because the story is able to live through the understandings of so many different levels of development and appreciation. Each individual in the audience contributes something to everyone else's awareness of the story. The five-year-old—even the ten-month-old—contributes no less than the adult.

The variety of literary sophistication in the mixed-age audience makes story development and delivery and program planning easier for the teller. The teller can include interactions, repetitions, and play appropriate for the children because the children are there. Adults will do the activity because the children are present. The teller need not eliminate the more adult aspects of story shape and delivery such as editorializing, social commentary, and figurative-language play. The children will be more aware of these elements because the adults will respond to them.

The storytelling program for the mixed-age audience can include stories for very young children and stories for adults. Each story can contain something for everyone. The stories become a vehicle through which people can learn, discover, remember, and appreciate by watching one another interact with the literature. With the mixed-age audience, the stories are whole. They are more fully negotiated and appreciated by the mixed group, and they better fulfill their community and literary function.

During delivery, the teller accustomed to telling primarily to children should avoid the temptation to confine his or her eye contact and recognition of the audience to the children present. The adults are there for their own reasons, not necessarily having to do with the children. Even if the adults are attending because of the children, they will become just as personally involved in the telling as the children if the storyteller acknowledges their presence as separate and unique. Likewise, the teller who tells primarily to adults should remember to recognize the children and encourage their contributions to the building of the story by looking at them during the telling.

The storyteller who will be telling to the mixed-age audience must still inquire beforehand about the circumstances of the telling and try to learn something about the character of the audience. But the mixed-age audience makes the teller's job easier, allowing for a variety of story choice and a flexible approach to story delivery.

School Combination Audiences

Quite often, the storyteller who tells in public schools is obliged to accommodate the storytelling program to the school schedule. Different grade levels must sometimes be combined. Some combinations work more easily than others, only because the children themselves make associations. If the teller is allowed some control of the groupings, precautions can be taken that will help the teller plan and present suitable programs for each group. For example:

Combine preschool and K.

Combine K and 1.

Combine 1 and 2.

Combine 3 and 4.

Combine 4, 5, and 6.

Combine 5 and 6.

Combine 6 and 7.

Combine 8 and 9.

Combine 9 and 10, 11 and 12, or 10, 11, and 12.

Do *not* combine 2 and 3.

Do *not* combine 7 and 8 unless 9, 10, 11, and 12 are also present.

Do *not* combine nonconsecutive grade levels (3 and 5 or 6 and 2) unless all grades in between are also included in the group. (To have a workable 3-5 combination, for instance, grade 4 should also be present.)

A sufficient number of adults in any of these groups, perhaps making up one-third of the audience, will make concern for combining grade levels unnecessary. The presence of adults seems to neutralize children's fear of looking "stupid" if grouped with younger children. (Teachers do not count as adults, because they "have to" be there. Other staff and parents do count.)

GENERAL OBSERVATIONS

About Explication

Explication must be avoided. The stories do not require it. The message is embedded in the story. Members of the audience who are ready to understand the message will understand it and do not require formal instruction, before or after the telling. Members of the audience who are not ready to understand the message will not understand it, even if told about it later. Furthermore, neither the stories nor the storytelling is designed for formal literary study. Such study, if it is necessary, should be done at some other time. If the stories are to be the objects of study, the middle of the storytelling is neither the time nor the place to undertake it. The storytelling is a game—another reality. Study disrupts the game and violates the other reality.

Literary study is no substitute for experience with the literature. One cannot know the story or the storytelling by studying *about* it. One has to do it or be in it first before one can talk about it. As with language learning, we must take care not to assume that teaching *about* something will make people more able to *do* that something. People learn precisely what they are taught. If they are taught *about* a literature, they will learn *about* it. If they experience that literature, they will learn the literature itself. Storytelling will provide literary learning which will not be enhanced by literary study. In addition, people cannot know *about* something that they do not already know. Story-telling provides the basis for a primary "knowing" of literature (of "story" and storying). One cannot study "story" and storying until one has gained a primary knowledge of them through direct activity. The first appreciation of a literature comes from experience with it. A secondary level of appreciation, founded upon the first, can be accomplished through study—later.

Children should not be required to study stories and storytelling. Storying is something to *do*, not to pick apart. If a child wants to know something *about* a story or *about* storytelling, he or she will make those needs clear enough by asking specific questions. (When the child asks questions, they should be answered. Before the child formulates the questions, he or she will not be interested in the answers.) Fifth- and sixth-graders are quite often interested in storytelling. They want to learn to tell stories. That is the time to supply some metaliterary-type (literary study) information, but only as much as is requested. If a child does not ask about-the-literature types of questions, he or she is probably not thinking about-the-literature sorts of thoughts and would not, in any case, be ready to appreciate the worth of the information.

After a storytelling is completed, the teller might ask the audience questions that have no right-answer responses and that allow the listeners to evaluate their own interactions with the material, for example, "What did you think about _____? If you had been _____, would you have done _____?" The culmination of a storytelling, however, is not meant to be an examination, no matter how open-ended. Such questions are often rhetorical and sound patronizing. They can spoil rather than enhance a telling. Stories traditionally were intended to teach without formal instruction. The story generally does the telling; the listener does not need to be told again after the story is finished.

About Lecturing

Lecturing is unnecessary and counterproductive. The teller should tell the stories and operate the ritual. These devices say far more and more powerfully than the most informed of well-intentioned lectures. Story ritual is undone by lecturing.

About Repeating Stories

Audiences learn to love certain stories and like to hear them again and again. Child audiences often request repetitions because they are using particular stories to learn and confirm their hypotheses regarding the operations of literature and language. Such requests should be honored. Stories are much more profound than television reruns. Audiences recognize the timelessness in story structure and archetype. New stories can be introduced into a program of old, familiar material: "I remember that you liked that story, so I will do it again. And, because you liked it, I remembered another one that I thought you would also like." Stories provide important dimensions of awareness, "truth," sense of self and others, and confirmation of community. We need to be reminded and comforted again and again by hearing stories. The more familiar the story, the more comforting it is. The more we hear it, the more we discover in it. The more we discover in it, the farther we extend our literary capacities.

About Maintaining Variety in the Program

Variety in the program is valuable. Even the youngest audiences should hear some sophisticated stories. Of course, the young audience will love the more conventional and simpler stories and the ones that offer the greatest opportunity for direct interaction. Younger listeners, like older ones, appreciate what they can successfully predict and control. But they will eventually learn to control more sophisticated material if they have the opportunity to hear it. Slightly more complex material should be included in the simple program. The confidence children develop as a result of experiencing control of one story can carry over to the next. Audiences learn to expect that they can control a story and will put those expectations to work, even with more difficult material.

About Being an Adult

The storyteller is an adult and more—the storyteller is the "other" or "the ancient one." The teller, then, is not to assume inappropriate—particularly childish—mannerisms and habits when telling stories. Even the most rudimentary stories require adult treatment. The youngest of audiences will recognize and be disturbed by the absence of a certain degree of adult dignity in the telling.

About Pitch

The pitch (tone) of the voice carries meaning in isolation of the articulated language that it usually accompanies. A high, especially an exaggeratedly high, pitch insults audience intelligence by itself and apart from the content of the story. High pitch is (at least in English) associated with the early stages of language learning during which adults pitch high over language forms to which they wish a very young listener to attend. Children, in particular, are insulted by frequent use of high pitch. They rightly associate it with "instruction." They say such things as, "She talks like we were babies."

Follow the pitch contour diagrams below, and read the sentences aloud.

Hello, boys and girls.

Welcome back to school.

You are all looking well.

I hope that you had fun this summer.

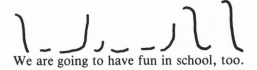

We are going to have fun in school, too.

Today we have a storyteller.

He has come to tell you some stories.

Won't that be fun?

Good storytellers introduced to audiences in high pitch have to undo the damage and make up for the loss of their own credibility. The storyteller who utilizes high pitch in an "instructive" manner runs the risk of alienating the audience. (The only audience that would not be alienated is the one too young to understand the story.) We have all witnessed well-meaning storytellers meet school audiences, hit the high pitch, and lose control:

Hello.

I'm here to tell you stories.

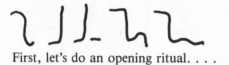

First, let's do an opening ritual. . . .

I once watched an eighth-grade group develop that glazed look that says "I'm not here" when a storyteller hit the high pitch in her introduction. She told the story, but the students refused to hear it. The user of high pitch sends a blatant message regarding his or her assumptions about listener intelligence. If emphasis of a language form is needed, stress can be used.

OTHER FACTORS REGARDING THE AUDIENCE

Although factors such as cultural origins, language, and socioeconomic background are not as critical as age in terms of literary readiness, they do have some impact upon audience reaction to and interaction with stories. Many audiences of western European extraction can enter into negotiations more readily if stories are set in patterns of three. Native American audiences can relate to the Slavic fox stories, since these are similar to the Coyote tales. Non-English-speaking audiences can still understand a story done in English if it is accompanied by sufficiently clear paralinguistic interpretation and props. A story with versions existing in several different language groups and that is well known to the audience can be understood easily in a language foreign to the audience and can even be used for second-language instruction. English-speaking primary school children follow German versions of "The Three Little Pigs" and "Little Red Riding Hood" without any difficulty, provided that the storyteller includes a sufficient number of non-language-specific cues in the form of intonation, props, characterization, noise, motion, and voice.

Previous experience with language and literature is also an important consideration. Audiences that have never experienced a storytelling will need to learn how to play the game and will very likely require more direct effort by the storyteller to accomplish interactions. Just as reading readiness grows directly from experiences with printed material, story readiness is the product of experiences with stories. An audience that has had little contact with stories will not be as ready to listen, predict, slot content, and appreciate as an audience that has heard stories many times before. Social development can affect story choice and delivery, too. One of the most critical changes in social development and self-awareness occurs between the second and third grades. An occasional second-grade group will exhibit the social behaviors of older children. Their tastes will be somewhat more sophisticated, and they will be more reluctant to participate, at least initially.

Audience purpose can also affect the shape of the storytelling program. The teller can make some preliminary determinations of audience purpose when he or she is asked to do a storytelling. The setting—school, church, home, library, public park—will help to clarify purpose. Occasion is also a significant factor. A storytelling for a birthday party implies different audience purpose than a telling for a college-level public speaking class, for a storytelling workshop, for a campfire program, for a civic group, or for a holiday celebration. Further, the promoter or organizer of a storytelling event might have quite a different purpose in mind than the individuals who sit in the audience to listen. While the teller can ask the promoter or organizer why the telling is being organized and what it is intended to accomplish, he or she cannot know the purposes for which the audience will listen. Listeners set their own purposes. These remain a hidden agenda until the teller meets the audience. Many audiences will telegraph their purposes or the lack of them. By far the most difficult audience is the one with no purposes at all save the requirement that they attend. School audiences, especially older ones, often come to a telling without purpose, but with the certainty that they do not share the purposes of teacher or school, whatever these might be. Immediately before and during the telling, the teller will be able to sense audience purpose. Some adjustments in story choice, story tailoring, and delivery can be made to accommodate. The shape of the ritual will certainly be affected by audience purpose.

An organizer's or promoter's purposes for the storytelling will affect the nature of the audience, aspects of setting, and, therefore, the program. The teller must make sufficient inquiry regarding the expectations of the promoter. Some promoters *think* they want a storyteller when they really want a juggler, a mime, a magician, or a clown. A storyteller might not be the best attraction to promote a sale in a department store or to entertain children while parents shop. The storyteller may be obliged to help a promoter understand that he or she does not really want or need a storyteller. A storytelling serves purposes related to its literature. If the circumstances of the telling are such that these purposes cannot be served, the telling will probably not be successful. If the arrangements are conducive to a telling, information regarding circumstances and the promoter's purpose will help to identify the nature, interests, and purposes of the audience.

Storytellers tell for reasons, also. The storyteller accepts a storytelling engagement for given purposes. While the teller may have little control over conditions affecting the audience's presence at a telling, he or she can set private purposes for telling that are very much affected by the nature of the audience, the setting, and the occasion. A storyteller's private purposes for telling are often related to development of repertoire and technique. Each telling represents an opportunity to expand capacity, and the storyteller must consider the circumstances of the storytelling as a chance to reprocess his or her own material under a new set of constraints. Otherwise, a teller's purpose is related to his or her role as other during the telling. The "other" brings the other reality, the other truth, the mirror, the sense of community and belonging. The purpose of the storytelling, in addition to game playing and having fun, has to do with the reasons for which the oral literature developed and for which all people need stories. These last purposes are those which the teller should convey to the audience indirectly through the telling. Audiences understand and accept these reasons for storying, even audiences who come to the telling under pressure and/or with no purposes of their own.

WATCHING THE AUDIENCE

The experienced storyteller watches audiences carefully both before and during a storytelling. Observation before the telling helps the teller make last-minute adjustments and decisions about story choice, use of devices within stories, technique for delivery, types of interactions to include, and ritual openings to choose. More than one teller has looked at an audience and completely scrapped a carefully planned program. (Many tellers do not "plan" programs, but arrive on site with alternatives and options in mind.)

Observation during the telling can also lead to alterations in program and delivery while the telling is in process. Information about the circumstances of a telling that is gathered before the teller meets the audience, and even just before the telling, lacks the "sizing up" that only a direct confrontation can provide. Interaction and negotiation between teller, audience, and story gives the storyteller the most intimate understanding of the nature of the audience.

The storyteller learns situation-specific information about an audience and the circumstances of a telling from each storytelling encounter. This information can provide the teller with collective, in-memory patterns of audience readiness, needs, expectations, and behavior that can be used to predict the capabilities of future audiences and to plan material for possible future storytelling circumstances.

Observations before the Telling

The teller can sometimes gather information about an audience long before the fact of the storytelling — its age and language and cultural background, for example. Such information, while it should not be used restrictively for program development and choice of stories (an audience's capabilities should not be underestimated), can provide some guidelines. Readiness, social development, general literary sophistication, and disposition toward the storytelling experience are conditions of the telling itself and generally cannot be determined until the teller meets the audience. A storyteller might want to arrive early to become familiar with surroundings and people, gather impressions, and quickly reassess his or her program. (This teller has had many teachers deliver warnings regarding the dispositions of junior and senior high school groups. The students, however, were better barometers of their inclinations toward the storytelling than were the predictions of the teachers.)

Observations during the Telling

The sensitive storyteller will be "reading" an audience throughout a telling. The manner in which an audience reacts to the teller, the story, and the interpretive elements can affect the shape of subsequent program and delivery. Audience interaction during story negotiation can be particularly revealing. An audience will make its willingness to participate clear. It will send messages specifying its interest in types of interaction, types of stories and story structure, characters, language and language play, and paralinguistic interpretation. It will also reveal its purposes for attending the telling — its own hidden agenda.

An audience "reading" is situation specific. Few generic rules can tell a storyteller how to "read" an audience and make immediate application to the process of telling. Some very general rules specify the teller's maintenance of sensitivity to the audience, poise, control, steadfastness of purpose (clear understanding of self as "other"), and flexibility. A teller will eventually tell the same story to more than one kind of audience and under more than one set of circumstances. Even the same group of people will be a different kind of audience from one telling to the next. And as we have said, no two tellings of the same story are absolutely alike. The one story that the teller knows is, in fact, many stories — the same story constructed differently each time as it is influenced by circumstance.

Developing Flexibility from Observation

Repeated telling of the same story under different storytelling conditions allows the storyteller to try out a variety of internal changes in the interpretation of aspects of the story, to experiment with delivery and technique, and to work with several ritual sequences. Although the storyteller is the "other," he or she is also an outside observer who examines the impact of delivery, technique, and interpretive devices on the audience. The teller watches himself or herself and the audience simultaneously, noting the quality and willingness of audience interaction and the overall effectiveness of the negotiation.

Since audiences and circumstances affect the telling experience, the teller will be reconfiguring material with each telling. Each additional telling will provide the storyteller with still another way of telling a story and will, therefore, add a new dimension to the map for the story in the teller's memory. As the map expands and the possible combinations of effects within the same story increase, the teller's capacity for meeting the needs of a specific audience is enhanced. By watching the audience, and by knowing about audience background, the teller can begin to develop a set of expectations for audiences themselves. With experience, the teller will be able to make predictions about audiences reliable enough to sustain story choice, development, interpretation, and program construction.

Audience reactions to specific devices within a story are also good indicators of the workability of those effects. An audience, for instance, will verify the credibility of a characterization or the use of a character's voice, a motion, a noise, or the use of chanted repetitious language. An effect within a story that is a delight for five-year-olds may not be so warmly received by fifth-graders, although the story itself might be told successfully with both groups. The teller will learn how to tell the story to each of several different audiences by evaluating audience reactions to stories and devices within them. Stories are improved, over time and with repeated telling, not only because the telling becomes more polished with practice, but because the story takes on a shape that is appropriate to and dictated by the audience itself.

A caution for storytellers evaluating audience responses: audiences are responding to the story, not to the person of the teller. The story is the whole product of all the effects that the teller has chosen to employ. If audience response suggests that a given effect is inappropriate, the response is not directed at the teller. It is an interaction with a single aspect of the story and a measure of the momentary weakness of the story for that audience under that set of circumstances. An alternative device might be substituted for the weak one—developing a new character voice, trying a different facial expression or movement, eliminating interpretation and using narrative instead, abandoning an ineffective attempt at dialect—or the weak device might be used again with a different kind of audience to determine its range of acceptability. (Even the most inexperienced storyteller can sense that a given device has fallen flat.) The object is the successful telling, the creation of a credible story reality with seeming lack of effort through the transparent medium of the teller. The teller, by watching audience responses to the various devices of delivery, can become a more effective medium and can learn to be even more transparent during telling.

BUILDING LITERARY COMPETENCE

Audiences come to a storytelling with various listening capacities: abilities to follow story structure, to predict and slot story content, to play with language, to appreciate archetypal features, and to accept techniques and devices used for delivery as credible and fitting within the story. Audience capacity is a collective reflection of individual in-memory maps for "story," of individual previous experiences with stories and storytelling—of individual overall literary competence.

The oral literature is a genuine literature. It has its own top-level structure, its own evolution, and its own collection of linguistic conventions. It is not a watered-down version of a written literature. Its proper medium is oral language. Storytelling is its formal, official vehicle. The storyteller is the vessel or medium. Experiences with the oral literature, its language, its vehicle, and its medium are equivalent to reading a literature, in which written-structure and written-language conventions prevail, print is the vehicle, and the book (etc.) is the vessel. Just as sequences of experiences with written literature can be designed to introduce people to an ever-greater scope of literary form and function, sequences of experiences with stories and other forms of the oral literature (see chapter 7) can extend memory for the operations of the oral literature. Oral literature competency, an important dimension of overall literary competency and a necessary beginning for control of the written literature, can be developed through planned experiences with storytelling.

While it would be a violation of storytelling tradition to commit the story-telling experience to the formal "scope and sequence" device of education with a capital E—those things often become more confining and absolute than the guidelines they are usually meant to be—audience experiences with stories can be planned and guided.

When planning for the development of literary competence, storytellers must remember that the oral literature is best learned through experience, not through study. The oral literature represents a more sophisticated (top-level) organization of oral language. Just as people learn an oral language through exposure, hypothesis formation, trial and error, and practice, they will learn the rules that govern the shapes of the oral literature by having experiences with stories. We do not examine stories to learn them; we tell them.

DEVELOPMENT OF THE RITUAL

The storyteller who has the good fortune to work repeatedly with the same audiences can gradually introduce a variety of ritual devices and combinations of devices. The ritual play experienced as a series of experiments with ritual forms can lead to a more sophisticated understanding of the purpose of the ritual and of the nature of storytelling as a form of play. Development of audience expectations for more than one set of ritual operations can also help the audience see the contrast between time and "story" time, truth and "story" truth, teller as person and teller as other. The ritual forms clarify the relationship between reality and fantasy. The storyteller can plan and develop sequences and combinations of ritual forms for introduction to audiences of a variety of levels of readiness, gradually building audience capability by moving to new operations and combinations.

DEVELOPMENT OF STORY READINESS

As with any other kind of instruction, development of literary competence must begin with the known level of story sense of any given audience. Readiness can be assessed through telling. The storyteller can use stories that he or she knows are favorites for certain types of audiences and/or include interpretive devices of known popularity to determine audience response. The teller might want to test the effectiveness and acceptability of chanting, language play, figurative language, and use of different types of props and interactions. Audience capability will surface in the form of successful prediction and control of story and within-the-story play.

A storytelling sequence for extending expectations for story shape, content, and behavior will begin with stories for which the audience exhibits the greatest amount of control. Those stories will very likely become favorites precisely because the audience has already mapped them. These, then, can provide the foundation for further development.

An oral literature sequence might take several shapes. It might be organized according to levels of humor and language play. It might be built with the intention of introducing new and more complex story structures or expanding expectations for sets of episodes, people, or things from threes to fours, fives, and sevens. It might extend audience awareness of motif across cultures by presenting the same story as it is told in many different parts of the world. It might demonstrate the cross-cultural application of the same structural devices by including a sequence of stories from many cultures that all employ essentially the same pattern of organization. It might provide the audience with insights about cross-cultural treatments of a topic, a theme, a given archetype (e.g., the youngest child or the poor but honest man), a character, a type of animal (dragon, frog, rabbit, cat), or a human circumstance (opportunity, poverty, loneliness). It might introduce various forms of the oral literature: story, song, singing game, singing dance, chant, rhyme, riddle, ballad, epic, lie, tall tale, myth, fable, legend, finger play, street chant or song, or jump-rope rhyme or jingle. It might demonstrate a collection of creation and origin stories. The sequence, whatever its specific focus, will begin with the development of a foundation for audience expectation and control, then build and extend by adding new stories and forms to the familiar. The following topics would make good sequences for the development of audience listening and literary ability:

1. Extending structural competence

2. Extending number set competence

3. Extending motif experiences

4. Extending archetypal experiences

5. Extending cross-cultural experiences with one story structure

6. Examining stories from a single ethnic origin

Audiences are composed of people. People today, no less than their predecessors in earlier or more distant storytelling audiences, need stories. They also need the binding together of the community, and the other reality and time of the storytelling experience. Though today's audience may not know how to *be* at a storytelling, the storyteller can be comforted by the certainty that these needs exist and proceed with the task of reeducation in order to conduct mutual negotiation of a literature. Once an audience learns the rules of the play, the experience of story making, because it is a community effort, conveys the understanding of extended ownership. It gives both teller and audience together a power through doing, controlling, and emerging self-knowledge.

REFERENCES

Aardema, Verna. 1975. *Why Mosquitoes Buzz in People's Ears*. New York: Dial Press.

Arbuthnot, May Hill. 1961. *The Arbuthnot Anthology of Children's Literature*. Glenview, Ill.: Scott, Foresman.

Asbjornsen, Peter Christian, and Jorgen Moe. 1960. *Norwegian Folk Tales*. New York: Viking Press.

Belting, Natalie. 1953. *Three Apples Fell from Heaven*. New York: Bobbs-Merrill.

Bishop, Claire H. 1938. *The Five Chinese Brothers*. New York: Coward-McCann.

Botkin, Benjamin A. 1951a. *A Treasury of American Folklore*. Garden City, N.Y.: Garden City Books.

_____. 1951b. *A Treasury of Western Folklore*. New York: Crown.

Brown, Dee. 1979. *Tepee Tales of the American Indian*. New York: Holt, Rinehart & Winston.

Brown, Marcia. 1947a. *Once a Mouse*. New York: Scribner.

_____. 1947b. *Stone Soup: An Old Tale*. New York: Scribner.

Calvino, Italo. 1980. *Italian Folktales*. New York: Pantheon Books.

Carle, Eric. 1970. *The Very Hungry Caterpillar*. New York: Collier.

Cazden, Courtney B. 1975. "Play with Language and Metalinguistic Awareness: One Dimension of Language Experience." In Charlotte B. Winsor, ed., *Dimensions of Language Experience*. New York: Agathon Press.

Chase, Richard. 1971. *American Folktales and Songs*. New York: Dover.

_____. 1951. *Wicked John and the Devil*. Boston: Houghton Mifflin.

_____. 1950. *Jack and the Three Sillies*. Boston: Houghton Mifflin.

_____. 1948. *The Grandfather Tales: American and English Folktales*. Boston: Houghton Mifflin.

_____. 1943. *The Jack Tales*. Boston: Houghton Mifflin.

Courlander, Harold. 1970. *People of the Short Blue Corn: Tales and Legends of the Hopi Indians*. New York: Harcourt Brace Jovanovich.

Courlander, Harold, and George Herzog. 1947. *The Cow-Tail Switch and Other West African Stories*. New York: Holt, Rinehart & Winston.

Courlander, Harold, and Albert Kofi Prempeh. 1957. *The Hat-Shaking Dance and Other Tales from the Gold Coast*. New York: Harcourt, Brace.

Curry, Jane Louise. 1965. *Down from the Lonely Mountain: California Indian Tales*. New York: Harcourt, Brace and World.

Dolch, Edward W., and Margaret P. Dolch. 1956. *Pueblo Stories*. Champaign, Ill.: Garrard.

Domanska, Janina. 1977. *Best of the Bargain*. New York: Greenwillow.

Emberley, Barbara, 1967. *Drummer Hoff*. Englewood Cliffs, N.J.: Prentice-Hall.

Emrich, Duncan. 1972. *Folklore on the American Land*. Boston: Little, Brown.

Felton, Harold W. 1958. *New Tall Tales of Pecos Bill*. Englewood Cliffs, N.J.: Prentice-Hall.

Fenner, Phyllis R. 1943. *Giants, Witches and a Dragon or Two*. New York: Knopf.

Galdone, Joanna. 1977. *The Tailypo: A Ghost Story*. New York: Seabury.

Galdone, Paul. 1975. *The Gingerbread Boy*. New York: Seabury.

_____. 1968. *Henny Penny*. New York: Seabury.

_____. 1961. *The Three Wishes*. New York: McGraw-Hill.

Ginsburg, Mirra. 1973. *One Trick Too Many — Fox Stories from Russia*. New York: Dial Press.

Gorham, Michael. 1952. *The Real Book of American Tall Tales*. Garden City, N.Y.: Garden City Books.

Grimm, Jacob, and Wilhelm Grimm. 1969. *The Hedgehog and the Hare*. Cleveland, Ohio: World.

The Hamlyn Publishing Group, Ltd. 1975. *Russian Fairy Tales*. London: Hamlyn.

Hardendorff, Jeanne B. 1968. *The Frog's Saddle and Other Tales*. Philadelphia, Pa.: Lippincott.

Harper, Wilhelmina, 1967. *The Gunniwolf*. New York: Dutton.

Harris, Joel Chandler. 1955. *The Complete Tales of Uncle Remus*, ed. Richard Chase. Boston: Houghton Mifflin.

_____. 1948. *The Favorite Uncle Remus*, ed. George Van Santvoord and Archibald C. Cooledge. Boston: Houghton Mifflin.

_____. 1941. *Brer Rabbit: Stories from Uncle Remus*, ed. Margaret Wise Brown. New York: Harper and Row.

_____. 1920. *Uncle Remus, His Songs and Sayings*. New York: Appleton.

_____. 1883. *Nights with Uncle Remus: Myths and Legends of the Old Plantation*. Boston: Houghton Mifflin.

Haviland, Virginia. 1979. *North American Legends*. New York: Collins.

_____. 1972. *The Fairy Tale Treasury*. New York: Coward, McCann and Geoghagen.

Hayes, Joe. 1982. *The Day It Snowed Tortillas*. Santa Fe, N. Mex.: Mariposa.

Jacobs, Joseph. 1967. *English Fairy Tales*. New York: Dover.

_____. n.d. *English Folk and Fairy Tales*. New York: Putnam.

Jagendorf, M. 1949. *The Marvelous Adventures of Johnny Darling*. New York: Vanguard Press.

Johnson, Edna, Evelyn R. Sickels, Francis Clarke Sayers, and Carolyn Horovitz. 1977. *Anthology of Children's Literature*. Boston: Houghton Mifflin.

Jones, Hettie. 1974. *Coyote Tales*. New York: Holt, Rinehart & Winston.

Kent, Jack. 1971. *The Fat Cat: A Danish Folktale*. New York: Parents Magazine Press.

Lang, Andrew. 1949. *The Olive Fairy Book*. New York: Longmans, Green and Co.

Leach, Maria. 1958. *The Rainbow Book of American Folktales and Legends*. Cleveland, Ohio: World.

The Life Treasury of American Folklore. 1961. New York: Time-Life Books.

The Literature Committee of the International Kindergarten Union. 1950. *Told under the Green Umbrella*. New York: Macmillan.

Malcolmson, Anne E. 1941. *Yankee Doodle's Cousins*. Boston: Houghton Mifflin.

Malcolmson, Anne E., and Dell J. McCormick. 1952. *Mister Stormalong*. Boston: Houghton Mifflin.

Matson, Emerson N. 1968. *Longhouse Legends*. Camden, N.J.: N. J. Nelson.

McCormick, Dell J. 1936. *Paul Bunyan Swings His Axe*. Caldwell, Idaho: Caxton Printers.

McDermott, Gerald. 1972. *Anansi the Spider: A Tale from the Ashanti*. New York: Holt, Rinehart & Winston.

McGovern, Ann. 1967. *Too Much Noise*. Boston: Houghton Mifflin.

Polley, Jane, ed. 1978. *American Folklore and Legends*. New York: Reader's Digest Association.

Rees, Ennis. 1967. *Brer Rabbit and His Tricks*. New York: Young Scott.

Robinson, Gail, and Douglas Hill. 1975. *Coyote the Trickster: Legends of North American Indians*. New York: Crane Russak.

Rounds, Glenn. 1976. *Ol' Paul the Mighty Logger*. New York: Holiday House.

Sutton-Smith, Brian. 1981. *The Folkstories of Children*. Philadelphia: University of Pennsylvania Press.

Tidwell, James N. 1956. *A Treasury of American Folk Humor*. Bonanza Books.

Van Woerkorn, Dorothy O. 1975. *Sea Frog, City Frog*. New York: Macmillan.

Wiesner, William. 1972. *Happy-Go-Lucky*. New York: Seabury Press.

Wolkstein, Diane. 1978. *The Magic Orange Tree and Other Haitian Folktales*. New York: Knopf.

5

Story Resources

I really feel that stories are not just meant to make people smile, I think our life depends on them.
(Nigerian writer Chinua Achebe)

Do some common characteristics occur in stories from different countries?

How can local folklore be developed into stories?

How can autobiographical material be developed for storytelling?

The resources for storytellers are rich and varied. A tremendous number of the stories from the oral tradition have been captured for us in print or sound recordings. But many lie dormant, awaiting discovery by the imaginative researcher.

A cross-section of the former is examined here to illustrate the range and variety of the existing story repertoire. Stories can be clustered in many ways; often stories from different cultures and periods will exhibit similar characteristics, such as structure, topic, or genre. The arrangement in the first part of this chapter shows some of the patterns or groupings that occur. The categories are not exclusive: a same-structure story may also be an example of a certain genre, and so forth.

The second part of this chapter is intended to encourage individuals to research the legends and traditions of their own communities and families — to rediscover old folk stories and to create new ones.

TYPES OF STORIES

SAME-STORY VARIANTS

There are many stories for which a variety of versions can be found. The German "Rumplestiltskin" (Tarcov 1973) is the same story as the English "Tom Tit Tot" (Ness 1965), the Scottish "Whippety Stourie" (Ratcliff 1976), the Arabian "Fareedah's Carpet" (Larson 1966), the Japanese "The Ogre Who Built a Bridge" (Uchida 1965), and the Cornish "Duffy and the Devil" (Zemach 1973). The Norwegian tale "The Pancake" (Asbjornsen 1908) is the same as the English "The Gingerbread Boy" (Haviland 1972) and "The Johnnycake" (Stobbs 1973), the Russian "The Bun" (Brown 1972), and the Scottish "The Wee Bannock" (Steel 1962). Cinderella tales are told throughout the world, and there are more than 500 European variants alone. (Some versions have young male heroes, or Cinderfellers.)

In the process of telling these tales throughout the centuries and in many different places, the tellers have left their individual marks on the stories. Thompson (1965) gives an exacting analysis of the many variants of the well-known "star husband" tale (for one version see Mobley 1979). His explanations are fascinating, and he provides sources for all the different versions. Several outstanding reference works that present information on same-story variants are listed in the bibliography.

"La Llorona"

"La Llorona" (weeping woman), the best-known folk story in the American southwest, is still actively being told and can be found worldwide in a variety of forms. The skeleton of the story is quite simple. A young woman married to an older man wants to dance and have fun but must stay home to tend her children and husband. One night in a fit of petulance, she decides that to enjoy life she must run away from her husband. She then drowns her children in a stream. That is why children who are out at night or who have been naughty hear wailing and moaning and screaming along waterways or at wells. It is La Llorona, who has been sentenced to search throughout eternity for her children, and she takes away any children she can find.

This story has a strong effect on children. An article on folk legends in the October 9, 1983, *Rocky Mountain News* drew a letter to the editor from Dennis Gonzales of Pueblo, Colorado, that read in part:

> I remember when I was young, my parents would tell me about the story of "La Llorona," and I tell you, if I wasn't a good boy I was convinced that she would come and take me away.
>
> Anyway, when I was 13 years old, one of my friends was over at my house and I told him the story of "La Llorona." When it was time for him to go home, he was so scared that my mother had to drive him. He lived down the block. To this day, I can still hear her crying by the river.

The details of the story vary with each teller, and usually—even today—the teller will swear that he or she knows exactly where it happened and that the story is true. Here are some of the variations and details, gathered from oral sources.

A Colorado woman reported a version heard by her family in which a lady and her family were camping by a big stream when their two boys fell into the stream and drowned. The lady looked desperately for her children. She ran along the riverbank screaming. She went crazy while looking for them, and that is why you still hear the screams of the lady today.

The Colorado woman also stated that when she was young, she and some other children were playing hide-and-seek at their farm when they all heard screams. The screams seemed to be just hanging in the air. The children ran to the house and told her mother, who said, "Yes, I heard the Llorona." Their dog heard the screams too and came dashing in and hid under the bed. The teller said, "We did hear those screams. A lot of people around heard them."

Another version from Sopris, Colorado, twelve miles west of Trinidad, involved three children ages two, four, and six. There was no mention of a father. One day the bedroom caught fire. The neighbors formed a bucket brigade, but the children died. The mother died of heartache, and on the anniversary of the children's death her crying can be heard from the river. People know the abandoned house where it happened and have seen a light flickering in the windows and have heard her wails.

In Santa Fe, New Mexico, a version tells of the mother doing laundry in the river; the children, who were playing along the shore, fell into the river and drowned.

In Laredo, Texas, the story goes that the woman had to take in washing to keep her three children fed because her husband partied all the money away. When her husband left her for another woman, she drowned her children in despair and spends the rest of eternity crying for her children. In another Texas version the husband came back for his wife but would not allow her to bring the children, so she drowned them. Yet another Texas story has the lady pregnant with an illegitimate child. Her father was very ashamed of her, so when the child was born he drowned him in the river. The mother is there at night crying for her child.

A Guatemalan version also involves an illegitimate child. This time the mother kills the child.

A Venezuelan version is a bit different. In this one, a woman was accused of being a witch and was burned at the stake. At night she roams the streets looking for children, because she was killed before she had the chance to have children of her own.

People from Brazil, El Salvador, Mexico, and New Orleans have similar versions to tell. There is a Mexican story about an Aztec goddess who sacrificed babies and then disappeared shrieking into a lake. Another Mexican version involves a mother who murdered her own children born out of wedlock when her lover married a woman of his own social status. Another Aztec story tells of the Aztec goddess Chihuacothuatl, who found her baby missing from its cradle. In the cradle was an arrowhead shaped like the Aztec sacrificial knife. At night, the goddess would shriek and weep through the streets lamenting her dead infant.

Gus Arriola, the creator of the "Gordo" comic strips, told the story of La Llorona in a series of twenty-three of his daily strips in February and March 1977.

Among Mexican Americans, La Llorona has been characterized as either a kidnapper of infants (in retribution for the child she lost in its infancy) or as a mourner of dead infants. She is viewed either as a threat to infants or a solace for grieving parents, depending on the tale itself. She is always described as wearing white, flowing garments. The father is either not existent or immaterial to the story.

The La Llorona stories are not strictly New World imaginings. The lady is found in Spain in story and song. She can be traced also to English and Scottish ballads through Child's ballad number 20, "The Cruel Mother," from 1776 (Bronson 1959). A variation of this ballad is found all over Germany and Denmark. The ballad then comes back over the ocean to Nova Scotia and Newfoundland. The Newfoundland version, "The Cruel Mother" (Bronson 1959), was sung by Mrs. Theresa Corbett at Conception Harbour, Newfoundland, on October 24, 1929, from the restored manuscript by Maude Karpeles. In it, a fair maid is walking by a stream and sees two babes playing ball. She says that if they were hers, she would dress them up in fine silks. The babes call her "mother" and tell her she killed them and as punishment she must roll a stone, stand alone, ring a bell, and stay in hell for seven years each.

All of these folk versions of story and song have several levels of meaning. Parents use the story to emphasize the dangers of being out after dark, playing near the water, and not obeying their parents. These are always the conditions present when La Llorona is searching for her children or other children to take their place. Other levels of meaning warn adults to cherish their children, be faithful, and avoid pre- and extramarital sex, and they predict the punishment if this advice is not heeded. The story has lasted until the present because its original folk message was so strong. The message has been adapted for the places the story has traveled and has assumed details to fit the new location. Its influence has been felt through the ages and continues to be passed on today.

As one educated woman said with terror in her eyes, "I know you will think I am a bit mad, but La Llorona is in my house. She is trying to capture my children and I just came from a real estate office. I put my house up for sale."

If you want to see or hear a printed version of the story that has been honed by a gifted storyteller, see the story collection by Hayes (1982) or listen to his tape (Hayes 1981) of the "La Llorona" story.

SAME-THEME VARIANTS

What do Chinese brothers, African spiders, a Russian fool, Finnish brothers, and a French-Canadian boy from New Brunswick have in common? Magic, of course, as well as unique attributes that form the motif for some favorite folktales. These qualities are utilized in a variety of ways to save someone or to win a prize.

In "The Five Chinese Brothers" (Bishop and Wise 1938) each boy has a remarkable characteristic. The first can swallow the sea, the second has an iron neck, the third can stretch and stretch and stretch his legs, the fourth cannot be burned, and the fifth can hold his breath indefinitely. These distinctive assets are vital to the story and the eventual decision that saves the life of one of the brothers. The book has been attacked, however, as "rampant with negative stereotypes of the Chinese" (Schwartz 1977).

Many librarians have removed the book from their shelves or have substituted another version. One such version is "The Six Chinese Brothers" (Hou-tien 1979), in which the unique features of the brothers are cleverness, arms that can stretch to either end of the world, a head so hard that steel bounces off it, skin like iron, the ability to withstand great heat, and legs that can stretch for miles and miles. This variant utilizes the talents of the sons to save their father.

One of the best-known stories involving magical characters is "Anansi the Spider" (McDermott 1972). In this Ashanti folktale, Anansi has six sons with novel gifts—seeing trouble a long way off, building roads, drinking rivers, skinning game, throwing stones, and being very soft. When Anansi gets into trouble, his sons combine their gifts to save him.

In "The Fool of the World and the Flying Ship" (Ransome and Shulevitz 1968), a Russian folktale, the Fool meets and befriends a man who can hear all that is being done in the world, one who can cross the world in a single stride, another who can shoot bird or beast vast distances away, a fellow who eats enormous amounts, a man who can drink endlessly, a peasant with wood that can spring into a whole army of soldiers, and finally a man with straw that when scattered in the very hottest time of summer can turn the weather so cold there is snow and frost. The extraordinary companions of the Fool help him win the daughter of the czar in marriage.

A Finnish version, "The Ship That Sailed by Land and Sea" (Bowman and Bianco 1936), is quite similar to the Russian tale. Noki, the hero, picks up Meat-Eater, Wine-Drinker, Far-Runner, and Heat-Cooler. The tale differs from the Russian in that it is a king, not a czar, who offers his daughter's hand in marriage, and the magical ship is presented to the hero in a different way. Also, the Finnish version involves a chant as charm and a magic whistle that are not part of the Russian story. (These elements are similar to those found in the Finnish epic "The Kalevala.")

Marie E. Powers, a student at Lesley College in Cambridge, Massachusetts, has shared a folktale from New Brunswick, Canada, which she had heard from her French-Canadian mother. Of course, her mother had heard it in turn at her grandmother's. To date, this version has not appeared in print.

PIERRE AND HIS MAGIC CULOTTES

In a tiny cottage beyond the clam flats and the marsh hay, but near enough to the sea to feel the stiff salt breeze and watch the seagulls wheel and cry, lived Pierre and his mother. They had a poor farm with one old cow (Bessie), twelve hens and one rooster, and an old horse named Dick.

They were almost starving due to last summer's drought, so Pierre decided to face his rich, stingy uncle — Oncle Maxime — and plead for some money Pierre knew rightly belonged to his mother. Pierre left home for his uncle's prosperous farm, a day's journey away, with a few of the last bits of bread and cheese.

Pierre took a shortcut through the woods. Partway through he took a rest, and as he rested he discovered he was not alone, for there was a lean-looking fox eyeing him across a clearing. Pierre commented, "*Petit renard*, is your uncle rich and mean too? Your thin body is like mine." The fox responded, "I'm so tired I can't run another yard. Could you carry me for a while now that you are rested?" Pierre laughed and said, "Jump into my culottes here," and he held open his right pocket.

In fact, these were magic culottes made for Pierre by his mother from cloth given to her by an old Indian trader in exchange for a night's lodging. "Whosoever wears this cloth will always have room for whatever is needed, no matter how big," the Indian had said. Pierre and his mother had forgotten about this promise until the day Pierre stuffed his pockets with hazelnuts to grind and found no matter how many he crammed in, his pockets did not bulge or feel any heavier than before.

With the fox in his pocket, Pierre continued on the journey until near noon, when he decided to rest and eat. He sat down on a fallen log and carefully unwrapped his meager piece of cheese and hard bread. A spindly bear, scrawny from a long winter's nap, left his den to follow the scent of Pierre's food. Pierre saw the bear and said, "*Pauvre ours*, no honey or salmon have filled your stomach."

The bear replied, "Help me find my way to the cold running stream where the fish jump."

"Gladly — jump into my culottes." Pierre motioned to his left pocket, for he knew the fox was fast asleep in the right.

"Thin as I am, I cannot possibly fit in there," moaned the bear.

"Yes, you can," Pierre insisted, "for these are magic culottes."

The weary bear climbed in doubtfully, but to his surprise, he disappeared into Pierre's left pocket. Pierre headed for the part of the forest where he remembered a cold running stream in which the fish jumped all the time. The walk was long and hot, and all three traveling companions were quite thirsty. Fox and bear were peering out of Pierre's pockets, eagerly intent on finding the cool, inviting water.

When the trail turned to the left and dropped downhill, before Pierre could cry, "*L'eau*," the fox and bear had sprung out of his pockets and tumbled and scampered to the stream below. Pierre was surprised, when he got down to the water, to watch the bear swipe his paw in the water and start on the fish course of his meal.

Pierre himself cupped his hands, splashed water on his flushed face, and slurped several handsful of water. As he squatted by the stream he thought he heard a silvery, bubbly voice say, "Good, isn't it?" He looked all around but only saw the fox lapping water and the bear fishing. Then Pierre heard the voice again. "I have been of service to you and your friends, and now it is your turn to help me. Could you help me move to the granite cliff so I can flow faster and easier and renew my strength?"

"Of course," Pierre promised, as he turned his rear pocket toward the stream. "Jump into my culottes. Would you please make yourself as small as possible? Wet culottes are none too comfortable in April." The stream allowed a slow dribble into the pocket of the magic culottes.

Pierre roused the fox, who had gone to sleep, and the bear, who was still licking his paws after gorging himself in the fish-rich stream. "We must hurry if I am to reach my uncle's farm before dark," warned Pierre.

As it was, it was dusk when Pierre and his companions reached the plowed, fertile fields and the well-tended farmhouse. All was at peace in the quiet, newly painted henhouse. No sounds came from the barn. Pierre observed that even the well-oiled gate swung noiselessly as he started up the path to the house. Then it happened! Pierre stumbled on the top step of the porch and thumped into the heavily paneled front door, which had an ornate brass knocker at the same level as his head.

Before Pierre had time to collect himself, the door opened and Pierre faced a menacing, heavyset man with a black hat on his head and a scowl on his face. "What are you doing here at this time of night, boy?" he snapped.

"I am your nephew Pierre, and I have come to ask for gold to help my mother and me. We need food for ourselves and our tired animals. We only ask what rightfully belongs to us."

Oncle Maxime went into an absolute rage at the thought of giving any gold coins to this wretched boy. "Impudent, lazy boy! Who do you think I am — the money lender?" He grabbed Pierre by the back of his shirt and jerked him toward the henhouse. "Maybe after a night in here with the chickens you will think twice before you come on such a fool's errand again!" he roared as he shoved his nephew into the chickenhouse.

Three roosters started to peck Pierre unmercifully. Startled and in pain and terror, Pierre cried out, *"Renard, aidez-moi!"* (Help me, fox!)

The fox needed no convincing as he faced the makings of a feast he had only dreamed of. He leaped out of Pierre's pocket. The roosters were crowing, hens were cackling, feathers were flying, and Pierre was shouting. All the noise brought Oncle Maxime to the henhouse, his red nightshirt flapping in the cool night air.

I will fix you for trying to destroy my flock. I will put you in the barn with the bulls," bellowed the uncle as he flung Pierre into the barn. As Pierre bounced past the tethered bulls, they broke loose from their stalls, intent on crushing and trampling him.

"Ours, aidez-moi!" (Bear, help me!) screamed Pierre. The drowsy bear, catching the sound and smell of danger, made straight for the nearest snorting bull. Once again Oncle Maxime rushed from the house, just in time to watch the stampeding bulls, being chased by a bear, of all things, disappear across his newly planted field.

With his anger completely out of control, he roughly tied Pierre to one of the stalls and set fire to the hay. At this Pierre cried out, *"L'eau, aidez-moi!"* (Water, help me!) The stream swelled to a flood as it poured out of Pierre's rear pocket. Not only did it quench the flames, but its torrent caught Oncle Maxime, bulls, plow, fences, and water trough and washed them all over the hill and out of sight.

Pierre freed himself and headed for his uncle's elegant house. Once inside, he found many gold coins. He counted out only as many coins as he considered fair and wrapped them carefully in his kerchief. He could not resist sitting down at his uncle's well-scrubbed kitchen table and eating a fat slice of bread with gobs of honey and drinking some cool milk. As he ate, he thought about how his mother would smile when she heard the stories of his adventures and saw the gold coins.

SAME-TOPIC VARIANTS

Just as no two people are alike, no two groups are alike. If you are telling stories to the same group over a period of time, it can be quite helpful to investigate a particular subject that interests the group. One year, one of the authors taught a group of youngsters that was dragon happy. Three-dimensional dragons were created, original dragon plays and puppet shows were presented, dragon games were invented, and of course dragon stories and songs abounded.

There are many topics that can be developed into a series of stories. For example, dragons, elephants, spiders, dinosaurs, mice, and, as will be demonstrated later, frogs and rainbows are possible topics with a multitude of material available. These topics can be explored as long as interest in them is evident. You can easily detect group interest as more stories are requested or volunteered.

Included in appendix A are two topics that have been explored with the idea of integrating them into the daily school curriculum. The ideas developed around the topics of frogs and rainbows demonstrate the range of activities available. The resource lists provided show the tremendous wealth of material that is available. They are not all-inclusive, however; it is amazing what youngsters can create when given the freedom to explore a topic that interests them.

SAME-CHARACTER STORIES

Yet another pattern of organizing stories exists aside from those already discussed. Stories about one character enable the teller to expand on character traits, voices, and mannerisms and to build a continuing cycle of stories. When Richard Chase (1943) collected the Appalachian Jack stories he provided a gold mine of same-character material.

The Jack collection is a classic. New tellers discover the stories regularly. However, just because the stories are already collected does not ensure their survival. At a recent conference the well-known storyteller Jackie Torrence told several Jack stories and a very intelligent librarian remarked afterward, "I never knew how good those stories were before. I have read them, but they did not appeal to me. Now that I have heard Jackie tell them I need to go back again." This is another example of the power of oral telling to make a story come alive for the listener.

Other characters, either in collections already or ripe for collection, include raven, coyote, spider woman, Anansi, and fox. It is relatively easy to collect enough stories on any of these characters to plan a series of programs.

SAME-STRUCTURE STORIES

Stories with entirely different themes and topics may still be built upon similar structures. There are many such structures (see chapter 2), but the cumulative is perhaps the predominant one in the folk literature. It is believed by many that cumulative tales are really preserved remnants of religious rituals and incantations. Whatever their origins, they are repetitious in a variety of ways.

Cumulative story grammar can include repeating events, substituting events, single- and two-to-several-problem plot stories, and stories within stories. A minimum of plot in cumulative stories is enriched by a maximum of rhythm. The action moves neatly, logically, and quickly.

A child's first experience with repetition in word or phrase comes when some adult chants the toe-counting rhyme:

> This little piggy went to market
> This little piggy stayed home
> This little piggy had roast beef
> This little piggy had none
> This little piggy went *wee wee wee* all the way home.

Another verse with repeated words, generally classified as a nursery rhyme, is:

> There was a crooked man,
> and he went a crooked mile;
> He found a crooked sixpence
> against a crooked stile;
> He bought a crooked cat,
> which caught a crooked mouse,
> And all lived together
> in a little crooked house.

The story "The Teeny-Tiny Woman" (Galdone 1984; Jacobs 1892) repeatedly uses the word *teeny-tiny* to describe everything. It tells of a teeny-tiny woman and the events of her day.

The first cumulative stories a child generally encounters are chants such as "The House That Jack Built" (Frasconi 1958) and "The Old Woman and Her Pig" (Jacobs 1892). Some scholars believe they are related to the Hebrew chant that begins:

> A kid, a kid, my father bought
> For two pieces of money,
> A kid, a kid.
> Then came the cat and ate the kid
> That my father bought
> For two pieces of money,
> A kid, a kid.

The chant continues with the sequence of dog, staff, fire, water, ox, butcher, then the angel of death and the Holy One. This chant is recited as part of the Passover liturgy and is probably older than "The Old Woman and Her Pig." It is felt that the chant symbolizes the Hebrew people and their enemies at the time of the Crusades (Eckenstein 1906, 81).

These stories add characters one at a time, build up slowly, and are then resolved quickly. "The Old Woman and Her Pig" ends with:

> As soon as the cow had eaten the hay, she gave the old woman the milk, and away she went with it in a saucer to the cat. As soon as the cat had lapped up the milk, the cat began to kill the rat; the rat began to gnaw the rope; the rope began to hang the butcher; the butcher began to kill the ox; the ox began to drink the water; the water began to quench the fire; the fire began to burn the stick; the stick began to beat the dog; the dog began to bite the pig; the little pig in a fright jumped over the stile; and so the old woman got home that night.

The build-up to this end is at least six times this long as the old woman asks each character to help her.

The Danish folktale "The Fat Cat" (Kent 1971) is similar in structure to "The Old Woman and Her Pig" and "The House That Jack Built." Other stories of this type are "Henny-Penny" (or "Chicken Little"; Jacobs 1892) and "Plop," a Tibetan story (Withers 1965). "Plop" involves six rabbits who hear a ripe fruit fall into the water and flee from "Plop." A deer, pig, buffalo, rhinoceros, elephant, and other animals run wild until a lion identifies the fearful "Plop."

"The Three Little Pigs" (Jacobs 1892), "The Bremen Town Musicians" (Grimm and Grimm 1944), "The Three Billy-Goats Gruff" (Asbjornsen and Moe 1888), "Jack and the Beanstalk" (Jacobs 1892), and "The Story of the Three Bears" (Southey 1849) are repetitional and sequential but have evolved to include a well-rounded plot. The characters of these stories are exaggerated and one-dimensional in true folktale tradition. In these stories there are repeat events.

In "The Three Little Pigs" both phrases and events are repeated as the wolf goes to the first pig's house made of straw, the second pig's house made of furze (a prickly evergreen shrub), and the third pig's house made of bricks. In the Jacobs (1892) collection the story also includes events in which the third pig outwits the wolf three times before the chimney scene.

When we think of being rewarded for our efforts at work we must all be reminded of the story "The Little Red Hen" (Zemach 1983). For centuries this story taught the value of work and reaping the benefits of our labors. In the story no one will help the Little Red Hen plant the wheat, harvest the wheat, thresh the wheat, take the wheat to the mill to be ground into flour, or bake the bread. However, everyone wants to share in the eating of the bread. The Little Red Hen recounts (in cumulative fashion) what they would not do before, and declares as she has throughout the story, "Then I'll do it." And she and her chicks eat all the bread.

There are several modern versions of cumulative tales. Wolkstein's (1977) "The Visit" is an adventure story of a little ant on a journey to visit her friend. The language is rhythmic as it traces the ant's trip through the world of giant stones, leaves, and branches.

Other modern cumulative stories include "Ask Mr. Bear" (Flack 1932); "Millions of Cats" (Gag 1928); and "One Was Johnny" (Sendak 1962).

SAME-GENRE STORIES

Epics

The epics are made up of a cycle of stories built around one hero. This hero is a human being, not a god. The hero pursues legendary adventures, meets setbacks, and begins again. Epics endow the hero with traits that are strongly national in origin, thus contributing to an understanding of national ideals of behavior and to an ideal of valor and nobility. They glorify man and his striving. It has often been said that if you study the epic hero of a nation you can identify the moral code of that particular time and place. The epic heroes dare to do great things, are courageous, full of sagacity, suffer without complaining, and endure staunchly to the end. Some of the various epic heroes and epics are listed below.

Hero	Epic	Literary tradition
Roland	*Song of Roland*	French
Siegfried	*Niebelungenlied*	Middle High German
Sigurd	*Sigurd the Volsung*	Norse
Beowulf	*Beowulf*	English
Robin Hood	*The Merry Adventures of Robin Hood*	English
King Arthur	*The Death of Arthur*	English
Cuchulain	*Cuchulain, the Hound of Ulster*	Irish
Rama	*Ramayana*	Indian
Pakaa	*Pakaa and His Son Ku*	Hawaiian
Odysseus	*The Odyssey*	Greek

The Kalevala

The national folk epic of Finland, *The Kalevala* (land of heroes), is lyrical yet full of tall-tale extravagance and homely realism. It was composed over the centuries by Finnish and Karelian folk singers and passed on in the oral tradition. *The Kalevala* is the longest epic in the world, with 22,975 lines. One could say it became "frozen" in print in 1835, when the "Old Kalevala" (Lonnrot 1835) was published, followed by an 1849 edition (Lonnrot 1849) with additional material. As for so much of our oral literature, print has been both a blessing and a curse. The blessing, of course, is that the material is available to read and study; there is no need for a teller who remembers and can tell it. The curse is that no further embellishments and variations will be added. The story has come to an end. Even native Finnish speakers are losing many of the meanings for rich, obsolete idioms and losing contact with the older culture. *The Kalevala* has become history and has also lost touch with today's Finnish culture.

The folk traits discovered in analyzing *The Kalevala* include some basic human values. The hero Vainamoinen, singer of the magic songs, is respected for his wisdom. He is referred to as the eternal sage, yet he is also recognized for his pranks. His brother Ilmarinen is appreciated for his craftsmanship and ingenuity. He discovers bog iron and is called upon to forge the magic Sampo, which grinds out things to eat, money, and things to sell. He is a perfectionist. Present-day Finns alluded to this discovery and refinement of iron when they nicknamed one of their recent Olympic winners "The Ironman."

Then there is Lemminkainen, the boastful, reckless one. He is full of thoughts of pretty girls and claims a bride for whom he must perform incredible tasks. While off to perform one of these tasks, he is "hacked into five pieces and hewed into eight fragments," which are sent floating down the river of hell. Lemminkainen's old mother knows there is something wrong and finds out from the sun what happened. She orders Ilmarinen to forge a rake for her with which she will rake the river. Piece by piece she rakes up all that is left of her son, fits the pieces together, knits the veins, and binds them using skill, prayer, and magic spells. She then calls upon the bird of honey, the bee, to bring her back honey from the pots of Ukko the Creator. She anoints her son's body with it and restores him to life.

In Lemminkainen's mother we discover the persistence, wisdom, and powers the women of *The Kalevala* possess. The Finnish tradition assumes that females can accomplish and succeed as well as males.

The Kalevala contains jousts of wisdom, monsters, magic, and a great variety of charms. There are charms for bewitching, for ransom, against disease, to prevent misadventure, and for banishment. There is also a story of the creation of the world and the origin of snakes and bears. Throughout this epic we can discover peasant beliefs and images of domestic life along with the intellectual sorcery. All the way through the narrative a love of nature is clearly evident. There is a poetic, lyrical mood. This is because the stories were originally passed on orally by folk singers, accompanied by a kantele, which is a type of harp.

Traditionally two singers would sit facing each other on a bench with their right hands clasped together. The first singer would tell one of the stories, and when he was finished he would lean back and the other singer would retell the same story. He would try to outdo the first teller by inventing his own descriptions incorporating lyrical rhymes, proverbs, and magical charms. It was a poetic duel. In this way the stories were preserved and traveled across Finland.

The Kalevala has influenced not only Finnish art and music (Sibelius based his music on *The Kalevala*) but American literature as well. Longfellow used the meter of the Finnish epic in *Hiawatha*. Many Finns settled in the North Woods area of our country, and Paul Bunyan's Babe the Blue Ox might be a variation of Vainamoinen's huge blue elk and Ilmarinen's giant ox. It appears that *The Kalevala* has had bits and pieces transported to America. Maybe we can put the pieces together as Lemminkainen's mother did.

Epics provide continuing material for the storyteller to choose from and allow the teller to close each telling with a "teaser" for the next session — for example, "Next time, you will hear about how Vainamoinen searches for his lost harp made from a pikebone and finds a solution while having a conversation with a birch tree." Many epic stories do not have a particular order, so the storyteller is free to pick and choose. Using epic material is helpful in maintaining continuity in telling stories to the same group.

Tall Tales

American literature has evolved and developed a specific type of folktale, the tall tale, which seems to express an attitude typical of our country. Tall tale characters are bigger and stronger than life. The tales weigh the delicate balance between truth and untruth in favor of untruth. There is just enough truth to make good story material, and vast exaggeration imaginatively improves on actual happenings. The tales tend to be told as firsthand accounts, with liberal doses of local color and circumstantial detail. They generally involve bragging and boasting and are rich in colorful language. The heroes are poker-faced and swagger with a great show of reason and accuracy seasoned with lunacy.

Tale tale heroes include Pecos Bill, Paul Bunyan, Joe Magarac, Stormalong, John Henry, Mike Fink, Annie Christmas, and many others. Rounds (1978, 1984, 1985) has a flair for writing tall tales.

A colorful tale made up in 1875 by John Thomas O'Keefe, a sergeant in the U.S. Army Signal Corps, is a favorite of Colorado storyteller John Stansfield. O'Keefe served atop Pikes Peak when Colorado was still the Colorado Territory. His story was made up in cahoots with a local journalist and got picked up on May 28, 1876, by the *Rocky Mountain News*. From there it spread across the country and subsequently was picked up by the foreign press. Here is the article as it appeared on the front page of the *News*.

Killer Rodents on the Rampage!

An Awful and Almost Incredible Story — A Fight for Life With Rats on Pikes Peak — An Infant Child Eaten!

The vast number of rats inhabiting the rocky crevices and cavernous passages at the summit of Pikes Peak have recently become formidable and dangerous. These animals are known to feed upon a saccharine gum that percolates through the pores of the rocks, apparently upheaved by some volcanic action.

Since the establishment of the government signal station on the summit of the peak, at an altitude of nearly 15,000 feet, these animals have acquired a voracious appetite for raw and uncooked meat, the scent of which seems to impart to them a ferocity rivaling the fierceness of the starved Siberian wolf.

The most singular trait in the character of these animals is they are never to be seen in the daytime. When the moon pours down her queenly light they may be seen in countless numbers trooping around among the rocky boulders that crown the barren waste, and during the warm summer months they may be seen swimming and sporting in the waters of the lake, a short distance below the peak, and on a dark, cloudy night, their trail in the water is marked by a sparkling light, giving the lake a bright and silvery appearance.

A few days since, Mr. John T. O'Keefe, one of the government operators at the signal station upon the peak, returned to his post, taking with him upon a pack animal a quarter of beef. It being late in the afternoon his colleague, Mr. Hobbs, immediately left with the pack animal for the Springs. Soon after dark, while Mr. O'Keefe was engaged in the office, he was startled by a scream from Mrs. O'Keefe, who had retired for the night to an adjoining bedroom, and who came rushing into the office screaming: "The rats! The rats!"

Mr. O'Keefe immediately encircled his wife with a scroll of zinc plating, such as is used in roofing, which prevented the savage creatures from climbing upon her person, and although his own body and limbs were being covered with them, he succeeded in encasing his legs each in a joint of stovepipe, and then with a heavy war club, preserved at the station with other Indian weapons captured at the battle of Sand Creek, began a desperate struggle for the preservation of his life.

Hundreds of animals were killed on every side by the rapid and well-aimed blows of the murderous bludgeon, yet still they seemed to swarm in with increasing numbers from the adjoining room, the door of which had, by a fatal oversight, been left open. The entire quarter of beef was devoured in less than five minutes, but it seemed only to sharpen their appetites for still fiercer attacks upon Mr. O'Keefe, whose hands, face, and neck were already terribly lacerated.

In the midst of the warfare, Mrs. O'Keefe managed to reach a coil of electric wire hanging near the battery, and being a mountain girl, familiar with the throwing of the lariat, she hurled it through the air, causing it to encircle her husband, making unnumerable spiral waves along which she poured the electric fluid from the heavily charged battery with all the fullness of its power.

In an instant the room was ablaze with light, and whenever the rats came in contact with the wire they were hurled through the air to an almost instant death.

The sudden appearance of daylight, made such by the coruscations of the heavily charged wire, caused the ravenous creatures to abandon their attack and take refuge in the crevices and caverns of the mountain, making their exit by way of the bedroom window through which they had forced their entrance.

But the saddest part of this night adventure upon the peak is the destroying of their infant child, which Mrs. O'Keefe thought she had made secure by a heavy covering of bed clothing. But the rats had found their way to the infant (only two months old), and left nothing of it but the peeled and naked skull.

Doctors Horn and Anderson have just returned from the peak. It was thought at first that the left arm of Sergeant O'Keefe would have to be amputated, but they now believe it can be saved.

The more a researcher gets into folklore tall tales and their newspaper accounts, the easier it is to become a cynical, unbelieving newspaper reader.

Storytellers can adapt tall tales and tell them as if they were actual fact, with local, personal touches included. One Colorado storyteller enjoys listeners' reactions when she tells her version of "Frozen Death" (Schwartz 1975), changing the setting from Vermont to Eldora, Colorado, including people she "knows" in the mountains, and expressing her horror at the events she "witnessed" only a few months before (see chapter 3).

The Droll or Fool Folktale

The droll or fool folktale is a gentle form of humor that is found universally and has served to poke fun at absurd behavior for thousands of years. These stories of astonishing simpletons, sillies, numskulls, dolts, noodleheads, and ninnies are not as popular as other folk stories. This is probably because the events, however improbable, are painfully possible. In folktales in which the silly character is an animal, we can laugh at the character's follies; however, when the character is human, we may feel uncomfortable. Every nationality has stories with these sillies—for example, "Clever Elsie" (Germany; Jacobi 1952); "Clever Elsie and Her Companions" (Italy; Thompson 1968); "Fearless Simpleton" (Italy; Calvino 1980); "The Nine Crying Dolls" (Poland; Pellowski 1980); "Gudbrand on the Hillside" (Norway; Thompson 1968); "Mr. Vinegar" (Norway; Jacobs 1967); "Seven Silly Wise Men" (Finland; Bowman and Bianco 1970); "Goha the Simple or The Wisdom of Folly" (Arab countries; Makhlouf 1982); "Lazy Jack" (England; Jacobs 1967); "Epaminondas" (American Black; Bryant 1907; Merriam 1968); "The Mixed-Up Feet and the Silly Bridegroom" (Yiddish; Singer 1966); "Why Wisdom Is Found Everywhere" (Africa; Courlander 1957); "Simple Ivanushka" (Russia; Morton 1967).

The triumph of the good simple soul is a pattern in many of the droll stories. The amusing character is rewarded when his or her silly antics make the princess laugh or is misjudged as wise by a suitor or observer.

The droll characters are perceived as fools. However, some of them turn out to be the most exceptional of people in spite of their eccentric behavior.

After all, fools rush in where angels fear to tread, or as the Hasidic poem says, "A man must descend very low before he can rise up again."

Within a country, people tell with gusto about fellow countrymen and their silly ways. In England, it is the men of Gotham; in Switzerland, it is the folk of Meiringen; in Finland, it is the "wise" men of Holmola; in the United States, it is the hillbillies; in Yiddish stories, it is the fools of Helm (or Chelm).

Helm is a small town located in the deep forests of Poland and populated by very religious Jews. Some believe that the reason there are so many fools in one area is because an angel carrying a sackful of foolish souls to heaven for repairs got lost in a storm while flying over Helm. As the angel struggled through the storm, the bottom of the sack ripped, and all the damaged souls spilled out and fell into Helm, where they have stayed to this day. How foolish are these Helmites?

- Helmites built a wall around the city to keep the cold out.

- Helmites say the sea is salty because of salty herring.

- Helmites came up with a way to make their town bigger — push a mountain out of the way.

- Helm community spokesman and respected scholar woke up one morning with a terrible toothache. He made his dentist prove his skill — he had to find the bad tooth on his own. Ten pulled teeth later, the dentist hit on the troublesome tooth and it was pulled, leaving the respected scholar with two teeth. He praised the dentist for good workmanship in finding the correct tooth.

Droll tales and characters can be found in modern versions — for example, the writing of James Thurber, Andy Rooney, and Shel Silverstein; the comic strips "Dagwood Bumsted" and "Drabble"; and the television shows "All in the Family" and "M*A*S*H."

FINDING STORIES ALL AROUND US

FOLKLORE

Legends, beliefs, and superstitions about individuals, regions, institutions, and occupations are plentiful. From this folklore has sprung a wealth of stories.

The belief in Tommyknockers, mine-dwelling gnomes prominent in Cornish mining lore, provides an example of the prolific material folk beliefs can engender. Tommyknockers, allegedly withered, dried-up little creatures the size of two-year-olds, with big ugly heads, ungainly limbs, faces like old men, and beards that reached to the floor, dressed in leather jackets, peaked hats, and water-soaked boots, exerted a powerful influence on Cornish and later American miners.

One belief said Tommyknockers had the habit of knocking or tapping on the walls of tunnels and mine shafts just before a cave-in. It was believed that the first miner to hear the tapping of the Tommyknockers would be the first to die in the disaster. Usually these knockings were heard from midnight to 2 a.m., and this was also the time when most mine deaths occurred. Another, less gruesome theory was that when a sleeping miner was awakened by a Tommyknocker between midnight and 2 a.m. the miner would come upon a strike if he moved in the direction of the knock.

An additional prevailing notion concerning Tommyknockers was that they were essentially benign but became vindictive whenever they were neglected or abused. Among the evil practices attributed to the Tommy-knockers was their habit of kicking out the rungs of ladders to block the escape of entrapped miners. One Mexican variant had a "step devil" in the mines who gouged out notches in the timbers with an enormous, powerful toenail.

Many old miners recall having seen small Tommyknocker effigies made of clay placed by the entrance to a tunnel. The belief in a guardian spirit of the mine was so strong that an effigy, once placed, often remained undisturbed for years. Tommyknockers were also fashioned from clay and carried as candle-holders, often with pipes in their mouths and eyes made of match heads. Some of the Cornish miners settled for a ball of clay attached to their helmets for their good luck Tommyknocker charm.

If a miner carried a facsimile of a Tommyknocker in his pocket and it started to move, that indicated his spouse was being unfaithful. Along this line, the lore goes that if a miner's candle went out three times or fell off a ledge or wall, somebody was home with the miner's wife. Some mines blew their whistles after accidents to prevent the terrific battles that resulted when miners unexpectedly returned home from sudden mine shutdowns to find male visitors in their homes. It was decided that two long blasts would enable such visitors to make a hasty exit.

Other stories showed the knackers (another term) were considered to be exceedingly playful, but a demureness came over them when they were being watched. This theory of the freakish friendly elf leading miners to rich veins or rich mines is reminiscent of the little characters in *Snow White and the Seven Dwarfs*.

Old World versions of Tommyknockers had the tradition that they lived in rich, productive areas and attracted industrious, pious, or deserving miners to the precious lodes. Three knocks were considered a favorable omen.

Belief in the Tommyknockers inhabiting the Cornish mines was dying out in Cornwall itself in the 1860s but seems to have thrived in its transplanted American soil for decades longer. Most of them seem to have emigrated to America. Thirty years ago one might have expected almost any miner here to be conversant with the terms and traditions of Tommyknockers.

Why are there no Tammyknockers? The lack of feminine mine lore may be due to the fact that women had other, nonadvertised responsibilities, or more likely, it was due to the strong miner superstition about women in mines bringing bad luck. If Tommyknockers were bad news bringers, a Tammyknocker would be a disaster. Even now many miners will leave a mine if they see a woman underground.

One theory attributed the presence of Tommyknockers to the spirits of dead miners or sinister forces at work in the mine. This notion that Tommyknockers were spirits of dead miners was probably more prevalent in America than it ever was in the homeland. (The dead miner was said to return to work the shift on which he was killed.) These Tommyknocker spirits exist in many stories of mining. In one story, a ghost that looked exactly like a man would be seen riding on ore cars; then he would hop off and with a friendly gesture disappear into the sidewalls (ribs) of the tunnel. At an old mine in Gold Hill, Utah, there is a legend that a dead miner can still be heard, or could be some years ago, at certain times of night "single jacking" in the face of the drift, which was following the gold vein.

One Colorado oldtimer told of a ghost miner tommyknocking in the number 9 stope of the Perigo Mine. The *pick-pick-pick* sounded like a man using a pickax, but an investigation revealed the sounds to be those of water dripping on a dinner pail. Another story reported the mysterious ringing of a hoisting signal at Colorado's Pittsburgh Mine when all mine hands were eating lunch in a shaft house. This led to the immediate deduction that a ghost was pulling the bell rope from below, but further investigation traced the phenomenon to a cave-in in the shaft that caused timbers to hurtle against a signal rope.

Probably the most complete and exciting story related to a Tommyknocker ghost was collected by the W.P.A. Writer's Project, 1936-1942. The mine in "The Ghosts of the Mamie R. Mine" was reported to have had an unusually large incidence of tommyknocking, with knocking almost every night. The mine also had several fatalities, including an unexplained blast at the 375-foot level in which a miner was blown to bits. Around 1894, a manager was taken ill with mountain fever and died. On Thanksgiving night, the foreman and boarding boss heard the signal bells for the hoisting bucket ring all sorts of signals. They went down the shaft and through the workings but did not find anyone. A few days later, a worker on the 375-foot level said he believed a man had just been killed in his drift because he had seen someone walk directly into the charges he had just placed, lit, and shot off. The miner, foreman, and boarding boss went to investigate after the smoke had cleared and saw a man come out of the drift with blood streaming from several gashes on his head. Not only that, but the wounded man had had an arm blown off, and he carried this mangled arm over the other shoulder. When one of the men reached out to grab the grisly stranger, he clutched only air. The boarding boss then poked at the walking wounded man with a drill, which also just went through air. As the three men watched, the stranger calmly walked to the shaft, got in the bucket, pulled the bell cord, and went up. They saw him do all this as he still carried his shattered arm on his shoulder.

When the amazed miners got to the surface, they were told by the engineer that no one had come up the shaft. After that, no one would work in the 375-foot level. As usually happens, people gradually returned to their normal operations. Then on Christmas Eve at midnight, when no one was scheduled to be in the mine, the signal bell rang, the cable began to wind on the spool, and the engineer, the foreman, and the boarding boss saw the manager who had died of mountain fever, with his yellow, pinched face and staring eyes, get out of the bucket. The dead manager was followed by the blood-splattered one-armed man who still had a shattered stump where an arm used to be. These two apparitions reached back into the bucket and lifted out the body of a man who was lashed to a plank. After the plank was placed on the ground, the one-armed man leaned over the bucket again, lifted out his tattered arm, and put it on top of the body. The two ghosts raised the plank to their shoulders, walked out over the edge of the dump, and disappeared into the inky black night.

This time the engineer saw it all, along with the foreman and boarding boss. However, that was not the end. The next midnight the hoisting cable slipped off the frame, and one of the coils of cable caught the foreman around the neck and sliced his head off. The Mamie R. Mine closed down about one month later.

Legends and folk stories unique to various areas or people of the United States abound. Researching this folklore can be an exhilarating and rewarding process, leading to the discovery of old folk stories and the development of new ones. Local newspapers provide a rich source of stories. Periodically they publish stories about local characters or legends that can easily be developed into great oral presentations. Microfilms of old newspapers can hold exciting discoveries. Newspapers might be termed "literature in a hurry." All the elements are there: love, violence, humor, bravery, cowardice, mystery, joy, pain, the rich royalty in their castles, the poor peasants in their huts, terrible battles, and wishes that come true. Certainly these stories can provide ideas for the storyteller. Olesker (1979) gives examples of story ideas taken from newspapers.

Appealing articles can be clipped and filed for moments when fresh story-telling ideas are needed. Embellishing and imagining "what if" are good ways to come up with some successful original material. The following newspaper articles would be excellent for eliciting stories. The article about the hitchhiker could be used as a basis for students to write and tell stories about what happened to the unique hitchhiker on his trip. Whom did he meet? What were some of his adventures? What would be a good ending for such an epic story?

Another idea for a group activity might be to have each person choose among a collection of selected articles, read the chosen article, and then extemporaneously tell a story incorporating the material in the article.

A profile of a rigid hitchhiker

By ANTHONY POLK
News Staff

Herman the Hitchhiker is missing.

Just 115 miles from accomplishing his goal of hitchhiking from Evergreen to the San Francisco area, he has vanished, leaving his admirers fretful and worried.

Truckers, travelers, policemen and reporters have come to love him over the last two months. They won't exactly weep if he's not found — yet all pray the remarkable journey of this heartless, rigid man isn't over.

Herman, you see, is a wooden dummy hitchhiker who managed to find his way from near Evergreen to Turlock, Calif., before disappearing several weeks ago.

His story begins in the mind of an Evergreen man named Robert G. Foster. Foster, a remodeling contractor, wanted to travel to California this summer to visit a friend, Mike Leydon of Menlo Park,

GRAPHIC BY DAN GIBSON

was a supply of stamped, self-addressed postcards, enabling those who met Herman along the way to keep Foster posted about his progress.

On Sept. 2, the 32-year-old Foster and some of his friends held a "bon voyage" party for the novice traveler. The next day, Foster set him up on Interstate 70, just west of the Evergreen exit on Colorado 74.

At first things looked good. Three days after he bid adieu to Herman, Foster received a card from a traveler who'd taken Herman from Tabernash to Granby. But the mail two days later brought grim tidings.

'People just played along with it to the hilt'

whom he'd known since kindergarten. But time wouldn't permit the trip.

So, in a fit of creativity, Foster made a wooden dummy to make the journey in his place. He made an outline of himself on a piece of plywood, cut the figure out and painted it to resemble himself.

Herman was a thin, 6-foot-4 cutout with brown hair and beard and an oversized thumb jutting from his right side. He wore a good natured grin, bib overalls and a white turtleneck sweater.

A brief description of his background and destination were written on a piece of paper attached to his back. Along with it

Herman had been arrested for illegal hitchhiking and vagrancy and was sentenced to two days in the Hot Sulphur Springs jail, according to the Grand County sheriff's department. The hard-headed cut-up frustrated authorities when they tried to take his fingerprints.

Eventually, the deputies admonished Herman and sent him on his way. Next, he made it to Little America, Wyo., where he was picked up by a Lakewood man, Tommy Dye, who was driving a truck for the Mayflower World-Wide Moving.

Dye and a fellow driver, identified only as George from Texas, sent Herman to Salt Lake City. But Herman then disappeared for two weeks.

So impressed was Foster at Herman's ability to catch rides, he himself set out on the road for a hitchhiking vacation for the first time in seven years.

"I got kind of inspired by Herman," said Foster. "I figured if a plywood dummy could make it so could I."

On his return from Telluride, Foster learned his creation had become a celebrity.

"Herman is a TV star," wrote television reporter Craig Wood of KUTV in Salt Lake City. "After being found in the weeds all covered with dirt, he was interviewed, cleaned up and is again on his way."

Other postcards arrived, placing Herman in different towns west of Salt Lake City, mostly along U.S. 80. One traveler sent Foster a photograph of Herman at the Utah-Nevada border, standing under the famed, 40-foot cowboy statue which points the way to Nevada.

"Herman runs into an old comrade," reads the note on the back of the photo, taken in Wendover, Nev., where the peripatetic traveler tried his luck at the slot machines, hoping to win a Jeep to make his traveling easier.

The final postcard was mailed Sept. 27, placing Herman in Turlock, 30 miles south of Stockton. Foster is convinced that Herman remains there. If word of Herman's whereabouts doesn't come soon, Foster plans to send a plywood detective after him.

Foster says the response to Herman's travels has "just floored me . . . just knocked me cross-eyed.

"People just played along with it to the hilt. It showed me that people in the heartland still have a good eye for a goof," Foster said.

If Herman turns up or makes his way to Leydon's home in Menlo Park, Foster intends to have him shipped back to Evergreen. There, he'll be greeted with a proper celebration. All who helped Herman will be invited.

"I'm going to have a hero's welcome for him. . . . I'll have a ticker-tape parade down the main street of Evergreen," Foster said.

"A profile of a rigid hitchhiker." 16 October 1979. Reprinted from the *Rocky Mountain News*, Denver, Colorado.

Dogged dolphin stays with boy in ocean ordeal

PERTH, Australia (UPI) — A dolphin protected an 11-year-old boy in shark-infested waters off the Cocos Islands for four hours last week after the young surfer was swept out to sea, said the boy's father.

The boy, Nick Christides, said after his rescue that the dolphin never left his side during his ordeal in waters off the islands, 800 miles southwest of Singapore in the Indian Ocean.

He had been surfing with friends in the Cocos Island Lagoon when a wave tossed him off his board, his father Tony told the West Australian News by radio telephone Friday.

The strong current dragged him out, and boats from the island couldn't find him in the rough seas.

An Air Force P-3 Orion aircraft on the island being prepared to take off for Diego Garcia in the Indian Ocean was diverted to the search and located the boy for the search boats. "Nick may never have survived if the dolphin had not stayed with him. He was very very lucky. We were sure we would never see him alive again," said Christides, who lives on the island.

He said Nick told him after the rescue that when he first saw the dolphin, "he thought it was a shark, but then it started blowing water and Nick knew it wasn't.

"The dolphin just stuck with him, either swimming beside him or going around in circles. He must have realized Nick was in trouble and that the boy was being pulled out by the northerly current because he just followed him and stayed with him all the time."

Nick "kept his head and didn't panic. That's what got him out of it. That and the dolphin," Christides said.

"Dogged dolphin stays with boy in ocean ordeal." 15 August 1982. Reprinted from the *Rocky Mountain News*, Denver, Colorado.

Other ideas for uncovering old and new stories are listed below.

- Investigate the superstitions and beliefs connected with gems. For example, opals were regarded during the Middle Ages as evidence of the presence of demons. In Russia, if a merchant saw an opal among the goods, he would stop trading for that day. Some English people fear opals; hence most of the Australian opals are sold in America or on the continent.

- Investigate some of the beliefs and legends related to flowers. For instance, how did forget-me-nots get their name?

- Report on the stories of Paul Bunyan. What stories are told about the name Bunyan? How do people explain the name?

- Try to predict future folk heroes or heroines. Observe celebrations such as Lowell Ferguson Days in Buffalo, Wyoming, to honor the pilot who landed a Boeing 737 at the town's one-runway airport, thinking that he was in Sheridan, Wyoming. Is there a new tall tale legend developing there?

- Interview some older folks in your area — friends, relatives, or nursing home residents — and collect local stories from them. These stories could be published in a school newspaper or exhibited in a hall display.

- Interview people in your community who were not born in the United States and collect stories from their native countries.

- Ask your parents or older family members to tell you the story that was their favorite in their childhood.

- Investigate occupations to see if there are any superstitions, humor, myths, or practical jokes involved with them. Stage performers are notorious for their superstitions.

- Discuss why Albert Einstein prescribed "Fairy tales, more fairy tales, and more fairy tales" as the way to develop imagination. Create a new folktale or tall tale for your community.

THE FAMILY ORAL LITERATURE

Most history books are almost devoid of human details, feelings, and thoughts. We lose touch with the past rapidly.

Family oral literature includes such details — social customs (such as marriages, birth, death), clothing, types of homes, superstititions, folk remedies, folk speech, and games.

A rewarding way to preserve your family characters, stories, and history is to make taped "oral autobiographies" of parents, grandparents, children, and other relatives. Besides providing a personal link with the past, these tapes can serve as the basis for developing original stories.

If you intend to collect stories in this manner, develop a series of questions that call for more than a "yes," "no," or "maybe" answer. Use pictures, letters, or recollections of your own to help elicit rich, colorful details from the people you interview. The booklet *Instant Oral Biographies* (1969) contains seventy questions to prod even the most reticent person into sharing stories.

It is far better to feel overwhelmed with oral material than to wish you had recorded oral reminiscences while the person was alive. Our own lives and the lives of our families are diminished and deprived when we permit important people to go mute to their graves.

Here are some questions for discussion and sharing:

1. From where did your family originally come to this country?

2. What are some first names that are passed on from father to son or from mother to daughter in your family?

3. How did your grandparents meet and marry?

4. How has history affected your family? For example, what did your family do during the Depression?

5. Are there any stories about how a great fortune was lost or almost made in your family?

6. Does your family hold reunions? Are there any traditional foods, customs, or activities at the reunions?

7. Do you know where your family name came from? What is its history and what does it mean?

8. What are some of the family traditions you treasured?

9. What are some of the treasures stored in the family attic? Were there things there you enjoyed playing with?

In turning family anecdotes into stories, there are some things to consider. How will you establish time, place, and personality in the story? What mood do you wish to develop—distant, intimate, humorous, wishful, fanciful?

For instance, in the simple recollection of a pet that disappeared when you were a youngster, tell:

— why the pet was special to you. What did it look like? act like? What were its habits?

— where you lived and some possible reasons for the pet's disappearance.

— what you and your family said. Did you want to look for the pet and thereby be late or miss school? How did your parents feel about that?

— where you looked for the pet. How did you feel while you were looking?

— whether you found the pet. If not, how did you feel and what did you do next? If you did find the pet, how did you feel and what did you do next?

— what finally happened to the pet.

All good anecdotes can be turned into effective stories. It is important to remember to convey events through conversations and actions rather than straight narration. Some other recommendations include:

1. Start with an exotic opening. Few listeners can resist a story with a good beginning.

2. Expand on the anecdote and possibly develop it into an extended story. After all, "The Arabian Nights" were created one story at a time.

3. Share the story and evaluate what worked and why. What didn't work? Why?

4. Refine the story based on these evaluations.

5. Identify sound effects that belong naturally to the anecdote.

6. Give the anecdote a satisfying ending.

AUTOBIOGRAPHICAL TALKINGS AND TELLINGS

Events in your own life can be turned into stories. For example, think of the time in your life when you were most embarrassed. All people have experienced similar joys, fears, and feelings of being different while growing up. Developing autobiographical stories about some of these moments in your life can trigger a sympathetic understanding in your listeners. The columnist and author Erma Bombeck has made a living (and a fortune) turning personal feelings and incidents into humorous vignettes.

In developing ideas for autobiographical talkings or tellings, a personal history is also valuable. Making a timeline of major events in your life can be the start of such a personal history. What is meaningful, important, valuable in your life? If you were to make a time capsule of your life, what things would you include in the collection?

- As a youngster, what was your favorite meal or dish? Do you have the recipe for it?

- What happened on your first day at school?

- What was good about your "good old days?"

- How did you learn to drive? Where? What was your first car like?

- What historical event that has taken place during your lifetime do you remember most vividly?

- What was your first job for wages?

- What are the five most significant incidents in your life?

- What was the happiest moment in your life?

- If you could spend a day exactly as you liked, how would you begin?

- If your house were on fire and you had time to save only three possessions, what would they be?

- What/where is your favorite spot in all the world?

- What are some things you were sure of but have changed your mind about?

- What era would you choose (past, present, or future) in which to live your life?

- Almost all parents can recall in great detail the events of the day of the birth of a child. What happened the day you were born? (You also might want to look back in newspaper files and see what was happening in the world on your birthday.)

- What were some things you liked to collect?

REFERENCES

Asbjornsen, Peter Christian, and Jorgen Moe. 1888. "The Three Billy Goats Gruff." In *Popular Tales from the Norse*. Translated by Sir George Webbe Dasent. Edinburgh: David Douglas.

Bishop, Claire Huchet, and Kurt Wise. 1938. *The Five Chinese Brothers*. New York: Coward.

Bowman, James Cloyd, and Margery Bianco. 1936. "The Ship That Sailed by Land and Sea." In *Tales from a Finnish Tupa*. New York: Albert Whitman.

Bronson, Bertrand Harris. 1959. *The Traditional Tunes of the Child Ballads*. Volume 1. Princeton, N.J.: Princeton University Press.

Brown, Marcia. 1972. *The Bun: A Tale from Russia*. New York: Harcourt Brace Jovanovich.

Bryant, Sara Cone. 1907. *Epaminondas and His Auntie*. Boston: Houghton Mifflin.

Calvino, Italo. 1980. "The Fearless Simpleton." In *Italian Folktales*. New York: Harcourt Brace Jovanovich.

Chase, Richard. *The Jack Tales*. 1943. Boston: Houghton Mifflin.

Child, Francis James, ed. 1965. *English and Scottish Popular Ballads*. Volume I. New York: Dover Publications.

Courlander, Harold. 1957. "Why Wisdom Is Found Everywhere." In *Hat-Shaking Dance and Other Ashanti Tales from Ghana*. New York: Harcourt, Brace and World.

Dorson, Richard. 1959. *American Folklore*. Chicago: University of Chicago Press.

Eckenstein, Lina. 1906. *Comparative Studies in Nursery Rhymes*. London: Duckworth.

Flack, Marjorie. 1932. *Ask Mr. Bear*. New York: Macmillan.

Frasconi, Antonio. 1958. *The House That Jack Built*. New York: Harcourt, Brace and World.

Gag, Wanda. 1928. *Millions of Cats*. New York: Coward-McCann.

Galdone, Paul. 1984. *The Teeny-Tiny Woman*. New York: Clarion Books.

Grimm, Jacob, and Wilhelm Grimm. 1944. *Grimm's Fairy Tales*. Translated by Margaret Hunt. New York: Pantheon.

Haviland, Virginia, ed. 1972. "The Gingerbread Boy." In *The Fairy Tale Treasury*. New York: Coward-McCann.

Hayes, Joe. 1984. "Tales of the Southwest" (audio tape). Weston Woods Storytelling Circle.

Hayes, Joe. 1982. "La Llorona." In *The Day It Snowed Tortillas*. Santa Fe, N. Mex.: Enchanting Land Books/Mariposa Publishing Co., pp. 50-57.

_____. 1981. "The Day It Snowed Tortillas" (audio tape). Available from Joe Hayes, Have Stories, Will Travel, 700 Amherst, N.E., Albuquerque, NM 87106.)

Hou-tien, Cheng. 1979. *The Six Chinese Brothers*. New York: Holt, Rinehart & Winston.

Instant Oral Biographies. 1969. New York: Guarionex Press (Write Guarionex Press, 201 West 77th Street, New York, NY 10024.)

Jacobi, Frederick, Jr. 1952. "Clever Elsie." In *Tales of Grimm and Andersen*. New York: Random House.

Jacobs, Joseph. 1967. "Lazy Jack" and "Mr. Vinegar." In *English Fairy Tales*. New York: Dover.

_____. 1892. *English Fairy Tales*. New York: Putnam.

Kent, Jack. 1971. *The Fat Cat*. New York: Scholastic Books.

Larson, Jean Russell. 1966. "Fareedah's Carpet." In *Palace in Bagdad: Seven Tales from Arabia*. New York: Scribner.

Lonnrot, Elias. 1849. *The Kalevala*. Helsinki: Snomalaisen Kirjallisuuden Seura.

_____. 1835. *The Kalevala or Old Karelian Songs from the Ancient Times of the Finnish People*. Helsinki: Eemil Nestor Setala.

McDermott, Gerald. 1972. *Anansi the Spider*. New York: Holt, Rinehart & Winston.

Makhlouf, Georgia. June 1982. "Goha the Simple or the Wisdom of Folly." *The Unesco Courier*, 26-27.

Merriam, Eve. 1968. *Epaminondas*. Chicago: Follett.

Mobley, Jane. *The Star Husband*. 1979. Garden City, N.Y.: Doubleday.

Morton, Miriam, ed. 1967. "Simple Ivanushka." In *A Harvest of Russian Children's Literature*. Berkeley: University of California Press.

Ness, Evaline. 1965. *Tom Tit Tot*. New York: Scribner.

Olesker, J. Bradford. August 1979. "Ten Ways to Start." *The Writer*.

Pellowski, Anne. 1980. *The Nine Crying Dolls*. New York: Philomel Books.

Ransome, Arthur, and Uri Shulevitz. 1968. *The Fool of the World and the Flying Ship*. New York: Farrar, Straus and Giroux.

Ratcliff, Ruth. 1976. "Whippety Stourie." In *Scottish Folk Tales*. London: Frederick Muller.

Rounds, Glen. 1985. *Washday on Noah's Ark*. New York: Holiday House.

————. 1984. *The Morning the Sun Refused to Shine*. New York: Holiday House.

————. 1978. *Mr. Yowder and the Giant Bull Snake*. New York: Holiday House.

Schwartz, Albert V. 1977. "The Five Chinese Brothers: Time to Retire." *Interracial Books for Children Bulletin* 8, no. 3.

Sendak, Maurice. 1962. *One Was Johnny*. New York: Harper and Row.

Singer, Isaac Bashevis. 1966. "The Mixed-Up Feet and the Silly Bridegroom." In *Zlateh the Goat*. New York: Harper and Row.

Southey, Robert. 1849. "The Story of the Three Bears." In *The Doctor*, ed. J. W. Warter. London.

Steel, Flora Annie. 1962. "The Wee Bannock." In *English Fairy Tales*. New York: Macmillan.

Stobbs, William. 1973. *The Johnny-Cake*. New York: Viking.

Tarcov, Edith. 1973. *Rumplestiltskin*. New York: Four Winds Press.

Thompson, Stith. 1968. "Clever Elsie and Her Companions." "Gudbrand on the Hillside." In *One Hundred Favorite Folktales*. Bloomington: Indiana University Press.

————. 1965. "The Star Husband Tale." In *The Study of Folklore*, edited by Alan Dundes, 414-74. Englewood Cliffs, N.J.: Prentice-Hall.

Uchida, Yoshiko. 1965. "The Ogre Who Built a Bridge." In *The Sea of Gold and Other Tales from Japan*. New York: Scribner.

Withers, Carl. 1965. *I Saw a Rocket Walk a Mile*. New York: Holt, Rinehart & Winston.

Wolkstein, Diane. 1977. *The Visit*. New York: Knopf.

Zemach, Harve. 1973. *Duffy and the Devil*. New York: Farrar, Straus and Giroux.

Zemach, Margot. 1983. *The Little Red Hen*. New York: Farrar, Straus and Giroux.

ADDITIONAL RESOURCES

SAME-STORY VARIANTS

Espinosa, Aurelis M. 1910. "New Mexico Spanish Folk-Lore I and II." *Journal of American Folklore* 23, 395-418.

Janvier, Thomas A. 1905. *Legends of the City of Mexico*. New York: Harper.

MacDonald, Margaret Read. 1982. *The Storyteller's Sourcebook: A Subject, Title, and Motif Index to Folklore Collections for Children*. Detroit, Mich.: Gale Research Co.

Nelson, Mary Ann. 1972. *A Comparative Anthology of Children's Literature*. New York: Holt, Rinehart & Winston.

Paredes, Américo, ed. and trans. 1970. *Folktales of Mexico*. Chicago: The University of Chicago Press.

Ross, Elinor P. April 1979. "Comparison of Folk Tale Variants." *Language Arts* 56, no. 4, 422-26.

Trujillo, Luis. Summer/Fall, 1984. "La Llorona, the Most Famous Southwestern Hispanic Folktale." *Alma*, 44-47, 77-78.

Western, Linda E. April 1980. "A Comparative Study of Literature through Folk Tale Variants." *Language Arts* 57, no. 4, 395-402, 439.

THE DROLL OR FOOL FOLKTALE

Ausubel, Nathan. 1948. *A Treasury of Jewish Folklore*. New York: Crown Publishers.

Bowman, James Cloyd, and Margery Bianco. 1970. *Seven Silly Wise Men*. Chicago: Albert Whitman.

Carlson, Bernice Wells, and Ristiina Wigg. 1973. *We Want Sunshine in Our House*. Nashv...e: Abingdon Press.

Celek, Cris. December 5, 1979. "Humor in the Classroom." *Denver Post*.

Donelson, Ken. March 1974. "Humor in Literature." *English Journal.*

Jacobs, Joseph. 1967. "The Wise Men of Gotham." In *More English Fairy Tales.* New York: Dover Publications.

Monson, Dianne. February 1977. "What's So Funny?" *Early Years*, 342-45.

Zemach, Margot. 1963. *The Three Sillies.* New York: Holt, Rinehart & Winston.

FINDING STORIES ALL AROUND US

Dittmer, Allen E. September 1972. "Using the Newspaper to Stimulate Innovative Writing." *Media and Methods.*

6

"Nonstory" Resources

There's cheese and crackers on the upper shelf. If you want more singin', you can do it yourself.
(Common song ending)

What is the "nonstory" oral literature?

How do games in the literature work?

How does the storyteller find suitable games for the storytelling program?

Of which internal game features should the storyteller be aware?

How does the storyteller integrate the games into a storytelling program?

How does the storyteller control the games during a storytelling program?

What games belong to the folk traditions of children?

The resources for storytellers are not limited to stories. Much of the oral literature consists of songs, ballads, singing games, singing dances, chants, finger plays, riddles, rhymes, jingles, and jokes, many of which do not tell stories as stories are commonly defined. Selected items from the "nonstory" literature can add structural variety to a storytelling program and can provide for increased audience participation. The kinds of items to use will depend upon the nature of the audience, the physical capabilities of the setting, and the purposes for which the storytelling is taking place.

Although the use of "nonstory" material allows for a change of pace in a storytelling program, the material is easily integrated into such a program, for it shares many of the characteristics of stories, which have been discussed in depth in chapters 1 through 3. Like stories, "nonstory" materials are all forms of game-playing. The material involves rule-governed ritual and has a reality and truth of its own into which the participants enter. (The shouts of "No fair!" heard on school playgrounds are protests that the ritual and "truth" have been violated.)

Unlike stories, which are more likely to have tellers and audiences and to include play through negotiation, the "nonstory" material often requires the full and equal participation of all. The participants are players who physically construct the experience together. The games are supremely democratic, in that they do not require a leader (unless they have to be taught); they are simply *done* by a group of people who know what to do and consent to play.

"Nonstory" materials can be located in reference works and collections, the best of which also provide musical notation and directions for play. These materials, however, are derived from the actual practice of the song and game forms of the literature on playgrounds and streets, in homes and houses of worship, and at other public gatherings. The storyteller who is looking for such materials to add variety to a storytelling program or for a specialty program can get the best understanding of how to use the printed versions of the songs and games by attending programs and parties where these are used.

TYPES OF "NONSTORY" MATERIAL

Like stories, songs, games, and other forms of "nonstory" play are conventional, rule-governed structures. Many of the songs and singing games are event-sequence patterns stripped of the other conventions of story framework. Unless they are ballads, they have no setting, problem, resolution, or conclusion. The event-sequence type is recognizable, however.

CUMULATIVE SONGS AND GAMES

Like cumulative stories, cumulative songs and games are listings that wind and unwind. They provide memory and sequencing play and are sometimes cyclic. The cumulative devices of these activities make use of the many possible orders and positions in which language and items can be added to a list.

End-of-the-String Winding and Unwinding

The following songs and games employ the most common cumulative operation — addition of items to the end of a list. Repetition and unwinding are done from the end of the list backward. "Children, Go Where I Send Thee," (Langstaff 1971, 1982; Ritchie 1952 [as "Little Bitty Baby"]) is a typical example. With each verse, a new item is added to the cumulative list (winding), then all are repeated back in sequence (unwinding).

Children, go where I send thee.
How will you send me?
I'm going to send thee one by one.
One for the little, bitty baby,
Wrapped in swaddling clothing,
Lying in a manger.
He was born, born, born in Bethlehem.

Children, go where I send thee.
How will you send me?
I'm going to send thee two by two.
Two for Paul and Silas,
One for the little, bitty baby,
Wrapped in swaddling clothing,
Lying in a manger.
He was born, born, born in Bethlehem.

Children, go where I send thee.
How will you send me?
I'm going to send thee three by three.
Three for the Hebrew Children,
Two for Paul and Silas,
One for the little, bitty baby,
Wrapped in swaddling clothing,
Lying in a manger.
He was born, born, born in Bethlehem.

Four for the four come a-knockin' at the door

Five for the gospel preacher

Six for the six who couldn't get fixed

Seven for the seven who went to heaven

Eight for the eight who stood at the gate

Nine for the nine who got left behind

Ten for the Ten Commandments

Other cumulative songs and games are listed below.

SONGS

"The Wind Blew East" (Seeger 1948)

"Bought Me a Cat" (ibid.)

"By'm Bye" (ibid.)

"On This Hill" (Richards 1973)

"Drummer Hoff" (Emberley and Emberley 1967)

"The Green Grass Grows All Around" (Winn 1974; Mitchell and Biss 1970 [as "The Tree in the Forest"])

"Hi Ho the Rattlin' Bog" (Langstaff 1969)

"There's a Hole in the Bottom of the Sea" (Winn 1974)

"When I First Came to This Land" (Brand 1974)

"The Ford Song" (oral tradition)

"The Barnyard Song/I Had a Little Rooster" (Boni 1952)

"There Was an Old Lady" (Adams 1973; Yolen 1972)

"She'll Be Comin' Round the Mountain" (Hart 1982)

"Old MacDonald" (Quackenbush 1972)

"The Twelve Days of Christmas" (Wildsmith 1972; Boni 1947)

"The Twelve Apostles/Green Grow the Rushes-Ho" (Boni 1947; Mitchell and Biss 1970; Landeck 1950 [as "Story of the Twelve"])

GAMES

"My Aunt Came Back" (oral tradition)

"The Greenwood Tree/I Had a Little Cat" (Langstaff 1971)

"Come and Follow Me" (Richards 1973)

The familiar operation of the end-of-the-string winding and unwinding cumulative pattern makes songs of this type highly predictable. Players can invent songs of their own that make use of the winding and unwinding device or that parody well-known songs. The following version of "The Twelve Days of Christmas" evolved in an undergraduate language arts class on a hungry day:

> On the first day of Christmas, my true love gave to me
> A pickle in a Diet Pepsi.
>
> Second day — Two apple strudels
>
> Third day — Three chili dogs
>
> Fourth day — Four frosted doughnuts
>
> Fifth day — Five Hershey bars
>
> Sixth day — Six Hostess cupcakes
>
> Seventh day — Seven bean burritos
>
> Eighth day — Eight swedish meatballs
>
> Ninth day — Nine sausage pizzas
>
> Tenth day — Ten Quarter-Pounders
>
> Eleventh day — Eleven peeled bananas
>
> Twelfth day — Twelve Alka-Seltzers

End-of-the-String Winding/
Front-of-the String Unwinding

A second type of cumulative device adds new elements at the end of the string (winding), but repeats the string from the front (unwinding). This game is a bit more difficult to play, as it violates the more common back-to-front order. "Mommy, Buy Me a China Doll" (Zemach 1966) and "The Judge" (Zemach 1969) are good examples of this variation.

> Mommy, buy me a china doll, do, Mommy, do.
> What shall we buy it with, Eliza Lou?
> We could trade our Daddy's feather bed, do, Mommy, do.
>
> Trade our Daddy's feather bed?
> Then where would our Daddy sleep, Eliza Lou?
> He could sleep in the horsie's bed, do, Mommy, do.

Trade our Daddy's feather bed?
Daddy in the horsie's bed?
Then where would the horsie sleep, Eliza Lou?
He could sleep in Sister's bed, for a day or two.

Trade our Daddie's feather bed?
Daddy in the horsie's bed?
Horsie in your sister's bed?
Then where would your sister sleep, Eliza Lou?

Front-of-the-String
Winding and Unwinding

A still more complicated form of cumulative play involves the addition of new elements to the front of the cumulative string (winding) and a front-to-back repetition (unwinding). "The Ladies in the Harem of the Court of King Carraticus" (Winn 1974) incorporates nonsense and tongue twisting along with the additive sequence.

Verse 1 — The ladies in the harem of the court of King Carraticus were just passing by.

Verse 2 — The noses on the faces of the ladies in the harem . . .

Verse 3 — The boys who put the powder on the noses on the faces . . .

Verse 4 — The scintillating witches put the stitches in the britches of the boys who put the powder . . .

This type of cumulative play so violates back-to-front expectations that it is a difficult form of play for young children. However, children in the upper grades find it challenging and fun.

Unwinding Only

Some cumulatives incorporate reverse additions. That is, they involve the removal of one element at a time from an initially complete verse. Sometimes clapping, stomping, nodding, sniffing, or other movement is substituted for each newly removed element. "The Horse Went Around" (Winn 1974), "My Hat It Has Three Corners" (Best and Best 1955), "Bingo" (Hart 1982), and "Little Cabin in the Wood" (Gelineau 1974) are examples of this type of play. "The Horse Went Around," sung to the tune of "Turkey in the Straw," eliminates one word from the end of the string (sentence) with each repetition, substituting claps for syllables.

Oh, the horse went around with his foot off the ground

[Repeat each verse four times]

Oh, the horse went around with his foot off the *clap*

Oh, the horse went around with his foot off *clap clap*

Oh, the horse went around with his foot *clap clap clap*

Oh, the horse went around with his *clap clap clap clap*

Oh, the horse went around with *clap clap clap clap clap*

Oh, the horse went around *clap clap clap clap clap clap*

Oh, the horse went *clap clap clap clap clap clap clap clap*

Oh, the horse *clap clap clap clap clap clap clap clap clap*

Oh, the *clap clap clap clap clap clap clap clap clap clap*

Oh, *clap clap clap clap clap clap clap clap clap clap clap*

Clap clap clap clap clap clap clap clap clap clap clap clap

This exercise and others like it look simple, but they are not. They require a deliberate level of game awareness and concentration, without which successful participation is impossible. Older children and even adults must work and think in order to play. "My Hat It Has Three Corners" and "Little Cabin in the Wood" substitute movement sequences for the omitted words, doubling the memory work involved and requiring careful attention to task.

Winding Only

The winding-only type of cumulative play is often an exercise in sentence expansion and provides for manipulation of various within-the-sentence structures. This device allows the development of longer and longer language sequences of types specified by each game. "You Can't Have Any of My Peanuts" (Landeck 1954 [as "Whoever Shall Have Peanuts"]) is an adjective-embedding expansion. "By'm Bye" (Seeger 1948) accomplishes expansion through subject/verb construction and addition of prepositional phrases. In both cases, each new expansion is longer than its predecessor.

In "My Peanuts," players invent a substitute phrase for the word *peanuts* and insert their inventions into the proper slots in the verse. Tongue twisters are common and a part of the play.

You can't have any of my _____ 'til your _____ are gone.

You can't have any of my *peanuts* 'til your *peanuts* are gone.
You can't have any of my *peanuts* 'til your *peanuts* are gone.
'Til your *peanuts* are gone.
'Til your *peanuts* are gone.
You can't have any of my *peanuts* 'til your *peanuts* are gone.

You can't have any of my *Firestone radial tires* . . .

You can't have any of my *plastic space cadet rings from Cracker-jacks boxes* . . .

You can't have any of my *brass monkeys from the ancient secret crypts of Egypt* . . .

In "By'm Bye" (Landeck 1950; Seeger 1948), the invention is constructed on a subject/verb pattern by adding conditions such as *where, how, when,* and *why.* Descriptive adjectives can also be used.

By'm bye.
By'm bye.
_____ _____. [insert subject and verb]
Number one.
Number two.
Number three. [Count to desired number]
Good Lord.
By'm bye. By'm bye.
Good Lord. By'm bye.

The same song will allow front, back, and both-ends accumulations.

By'm bye.
By'm bye.

Twelve fish swimming   [or]

Twelve speckled fish swimming   [or]

Twelve speckled sharp-toothed fish swimming   [or]

Twelve speckled sharp-toothed fish with glasses swimming

    [and/or]

Fish swimming in the water   [or]

Fish swimming in the water in the bathtub   [or]

Fish swimming in the water in the bathtub because they are too big
    for the fishtank   [or]

Fish swimming languidly in the water in the bathtub because they
are too big for the fishtank.

Number one.
Number two.
Number three . . .
Good Lord!
By'm bye. By'm bye.
Good Lord!
By'm bye.

While many of the previously mentioned games, songs, and stories in
other cumulative categories are conventional, that is, the language to be
repeated is given, songs in this last category require the insertion of audience-
invented language into a fixed pattern. With each new playing, the invented
language can be entirely new, but the framework into which it is fitted remains
the same.

Cumulative Action
(Nonwinding and Non-unwinding)

A song such as "There Was a Man and He Was Mad" (Seeger 1948) is a
special case of cumulative play. The game is contained in the building of a
couplet rhyme scheme in which the rhyming word in one verse determines the
problem for construction of the rhyme in the next.

There was a man, and he was mad.
And he jumped into the pudding bag.

The pudding bag, it was so fine
That he jumped into a bottle of wine.

The bottle of wine, it was so clear
That he jumped into a bottle of beer.

The bottle of beer, it was so _____
That he jumped into _____.

Players can invent the entire sequence — for example:

The bottle of beer, it was so smelly
that he jumped into a bowl of jelly.

The bowl of jelly it was so green
that he jumped into a submarine.

The submarine it dived so deep
that he jumped into a flock of sheep.

"The Farmer in the Dell" (Hart 1982) and "Hush Little Baby" (Winn 1974) play essentially the same game.

THE BARNYARD SONG*

There was a little rooster by the barnyard gate.
And that little rooster was my playmate.
And that little rooster sang,
COCK-A-DOODLE-DOO-DLE-DOO-DLE-EE-DOO-DLE-EE-
    DOO-DLE-EE-DOO.

There was a little chicken by the barnyard gate.
And that little chicken was my playmate.
And that little chicken went cluck, cluck cluck.
And that little rooster sang,
COCK-A-DOODLE . . .

There was a little goose by the barnyard gate.
And that little goose was my playmate.
And that little goose went honk, honk honk.
And that little chicken went cluck, cluck cluck.
And that little rooster sang,
COCK-A-DOODLE . . .

Pig—Oink, oink oink.

Cow—Moo, moo moo.

Horse—Neigh, neigh neigh.

Cat—Meow, meow meow.

Dog—Rouf, rouf rouf.

Goat—a-a-h-h-h, a-a-h-h-h a-a-h-h-h.

(Add and invent.)

HOLE IN THE BOTTOM OF THE SEA**

There's a hole in the bottom of the sea.
There's a hole in the bottom of the sea.
There's a hole, there's a hole, there's a hole in the bottom of the sea.

---

*In Yolen 1972 as "I Had a Little Rooster."

**In Winn 1974.

There's a log in the hole in the bottom of the sea.
There's a log in the hole in the bottom of the sea.
There's a hole, there's a hole, there's a hole in the bottom of the sea.

There's a bump on the log in the hole in the bottom of the sea.
There's a bump on the log in the hole in the bottom of the sea.
There's a hole, there's a hole, there's a hole in the bottom of the sea.

There's a frog on the bump . . .

There's a hair on the frog . . .

There's a flea on the hair . . .

There's an atom on the flea . . .

PATTERN-REPEAT SONGS AND GAMES

Pattern-repeat songs and games contain lines or verses that are sung, chanted, danced, or clapped over and over again. The frequency of repetition can provide the quantity and regularity necessary for language learning. Many of the pattern-repeat activities also use cumulative, counting, and other play devices. A list of such songs and games follows.

"There's a Little Wheel A-Turnin' in My Heart" (Hart 1982)

"Roll That Brown Jug" (Seeger 1948)

"Over in the Meadow" (Keats 1971)

"Such a Getting Upstairs" (Seeger 1948)

"About Whales" (Best and Best 1955)

"Johnny Hammered with One Hammer" (Glazer 1973 [as "Peter Hammers"]; Grayson 1962 [as "Johnny's Hammer])

"The Wind Blew East" (Seeger 1948)

"Green Sally" (Richards 1974)

"Sally Go Round the Sun" (Hart 1982)

"Oats, Peas, Beans" (ibid.)

"The Tide Rolls High" (Seeger 1948; also called "Sailing in My Boat")

"Three Blind Mice" (Hart 1982)

"How Many Miles to Bethlehem" (Richards 1974)

"Draw a Bucket of Water" (Chase 1972)

"Do, Do, Pity My Case" (Seeger 1948)

"Juba" (ibid.)

"She'll Be Comin' Round the Mountain" (Hart 1982)

"Little Bird, Little Bird" (Seeger 1948)

"Hot Cross Buns" (Hart 1982)

"Pease Porridge Hot" (ibid.)

"Walk Along, John" (Seeger 1948)

"Sweet Water Rolling" (ibid.)

"Old Mister Rabbit" (ibid.)

"The Three Craws" (Winn 1974)

"Mary Wore Her Red Dress" (Seeger 1948; Landeck 1950)

"Clap Your Hands" (ibid.)

"A-Hunting We Will Go" (Hart 1982)

"This Old Man" (Seeger 1948)

"Oh, Oh, the Sunshine" (ibid.)

"Down Came a Lady" (ibid.)

"The Eency Weency Spider" (ibid.)

"Here We Are Together" (ibid.)

"The Mailboat Song" (traditional)

"London Hill" (Winn 1974)

"The Green Grass Grew All Around" (Winn 1974)

"The Keel Row" (Best and Best 1955)

"Old Roger Is Dead" (Gomme 1967)

"Milking Pails" (ibid.)

"Where Has My Little Dog Gone?" (Cano 1973)

"A-Hunting We Will Go" (Richards 1973)

"Maple Swamp" (ibid.)

"I'm Going to Town" (ibid.)

"Come and Follow Me" (ibid.)

"The Juniper Tree" (Seeger 1948)

"Skip to My Lou" (ibid.)

"The Closet Key" (ibid.)

"Green Gravel" (Gomme 1967)

"Three Dukes A-Riding" (ibid.)

"Poor Mary Sits A-Weeping" (ibid.)

"The Farmer in the Dell" (Cano 1973)

"Jimmie Rose He Went to Town" (ibid.)

"Adam Had Seven Sons" (ibid.)

"All around the Kitchen" (ibid.)

"Scraping Up Sand" (ibid.)

"The Little Pig" (ibid.)

"Johnny Get Your Hair Cut" (Richards 1973)

"Throw in a Stone" (ibid.)

"Come and Follow Me" (ibid.)

SUBSTITUTION SONGS AND GAMES

Substitution songs and games provide given language and fixed structure that players manipulate by substitution of words, phrases, or clauses into specific positions in a line or verse. The list of substitution-play songs provided below indicates substitution types, functions, and positions for each song or game. While the storyteller's reasons for using these games should have to do with program variety and audience interest, and should never be used to teach grammar, a hidden bonus for the language learner is embedded in the play. Adults who use these materials with children can make deliberate game choices that meet the language development needs of the child audience.

"Over in the Meadow" (Keats 1971) — object of preposition, subject, verb, and pronoun

"There Was an Old Lady" (Adams 1973) — direct object

"One Wide River to Cross" (Emberley 1966) — subject, prepositional phrase, adjective clause, and whole clause, usually subject/verb/object

"The Green Grass Grew All Around" (Winn 1974) — subject and object of preposition

"Mommy, Buy Me a China Doll" (Zemach 1966) — subject and adjective

"The Ford Song" (oral tradition) — subject and object of preposition

"Gather My Gold Together" (Langstaff 1971) — adjective

"Who Killed Cock Robin?" (Boni 1952) — subject and adverb phrase

"There Was a Man and He Was Mad" (Seeger 1948) — noun phrase as subject, subjective complement, verb phrase, object of preposition

"The Ant Song" (Freschet 1973) — adverb phrase and verb

"She'll Be Comin' Round the Mountain" (Hart 1982) — subject, direct object, verb and adverb phrase

"Old Aunt Kate" (Seeger 1948) — verb and direct object

"There's a Hole in the Bottom of the Sea" (Winn 1974) — subjective complement and object of preposition

"The Three Craws" (Winn 1974) — adjective and direct object

"This Old Man" (Seeger 1948) — adverb, direct object, and object of preposition

"Here We Are Together" (ibid.) — nominative and objective case and possessive pronouns

"Adam Had Seven Sons" (ibid.) — noun phrase as direct object

LANGUAGE INVENTION SONGS AND GAMES

Like substitution play, the songs and games that fit this play category involve making language substitutions in specific locations in sentences within the game. The songs and games listed below, only a small selection from the many available in the literature, require the players to invent words, phrases, or whole sentence patterns for insertion into prescribed positions in the play.

Word or Phrase Invention
Songs and Games

"I Love My Shirt" (anon.) — noun or noun phrase as direct object

"Mary Wore Her Red Dress" (Seeger 1948) — subject and noun or noun phrase as direct object

"Circle Left" (Richards 1973) — verb/adverb — imperative construction

"Frog's in the Meadow" (ibid.) — noun or name as subject

"Here We Are Together" (ibid.) — object of preposition

"Sally Go Round the Sun" (ibid.) — noun or name as subject

"Down Came a Lady" (Seeger 1948) — noun or name as subject

"Jim along Josie" (ibid.) — verb

"Here Sits a Monkey" (ibid.) — noun or name as subject

"Clap Your Hands" (ibid.) — verb and noun as direct object

"All around the Kitchen" (ibid.) — verb and noun as direct object

"Little Bird, Little Bird" (ibid.) — subject

"Walk Along, John" (ibid.) — noun or name as subject

"Old Mister Rabbit" (ibid.) — verb and noun or noun phrase as direct object

"Who's That Knocking at My Window?" (ibid.) — noun or name as subject

"The Barnyard Song" (Boni 1952) — adverb and subjective complement

"A-Hunting We Will Go" (Hart 1982) — verb

"The Mailboat Song" (anon.) — noun or name as subject

"London Hill" (Winn 1974) — direct object

"Galloping Horses" (anon.) — verb

"When I First Came to This Land" (Brand 1974) — direct object and adverb phrase

"The Greenberry Tree" (Seeger 1948; also called "Bought Me a Cat") — direct object and adverb

"You Can't Have Any of My Peanuts" (Landeck 1954; also called "Whoever Shall Have Peanuts") — noun phrase as subject/direct object

"Oh, Watch the Stars" (Seeger 1948) — verb and direct object

"The Wind Blow East" (ibid.) — direct object

"Such a Getting Upstairs" (ibid.) — verb

Phrase, Line, or Whole-Pattern Invention Songs and Games

"There's a Little Wheel A-Turnin' in My Heart" (Hart 1982)

"I Got a Letter This Morning" (Seeger 1948)

"Roll That Brown Jug" (ibid.)

"Old Molly Hare" (ibid.)

"Sweet Water Rollin' " (ibid.)

"This Old Man" (ibid.)

"Toodala" (ibid.)

"By'm Bye" (ibid.)

"What Shall We Do When We All Go Out?" (ibid.)

"Oh, Oh, the Sunshine" (ibid.)

"Juba" (ibid.)

"Hop, Old Squirrel" (ibid.)

"Do, Do, Pity My Case" (ibid.)

Whole-Story Invention Songs and Games

"Skip to My Lou" (Seeger 1948)

"The Train Is A-Comin' " (ibid.)

"When the Train Comes Along" (ibid.)

"Deep Blue Sea" (oral tradition)

"The Tide Rolls High" (Seeger 1948; also called "Sailing in My Boat")

COUNTING SONGS AND GAMES

Counting play is usually most appropriate for younger audiences. Counting-up play is less challenging than counting backward. Some songs are less restrictive and allow counting invention, such as counting by twos, threes, fives ("The Tide Rolls High"). Counting play that appeals to older audiences is often the tedious, repetitious, nonsensical reverse-counting activity that can continue monotonously for long periods of time ("There's 100 in the Bed," "100 Bottles of Beer on the Wall"). The challenge in this latter form of play has little to do with learning to count. It seems to be more related to endurance and perversity.

"One Bottle Pop" (Winn 1974)

"Over in the Meadow" (Keats 1971)

"Five Little Monkeys" (Bennett 1981)

"Johnny Hammered with One Hammer" (Glazer 1973 [as "Peter Hammers"]; Grayson 1962 [as "Johnny's Hammer"])

"One Wide River to Cross" (Emberley 1966)

"Gather My Gold Together" (Langstaff 1971)

"By'm Bye" (Seeger 1948)

"The Ant Song" (Freschet 1973; also called "The Ants Go Marching")

"The Three Craws" (Winn 1974)

"This Old Man" (Seeger 1948)

"Down by the Greenwood Sidey-O" (ibid.)

"Down Came a Lady" (ibid.)

"The Tide Rolls High" (Seeger 1948; also called "Sailing in My Boat")

"100 Bottles of Beer on the Wall" (Best and Best 1955)

"100 in the Bed" (ibid.)

"Who Built the Ark? Noah! Noah!" (ibid.)

QUESTION-AND-ANSWER (SWAPPING) SONGS AND GAMES

Question-and-answer, or swapping, play provides audiences with direct, formal interaction and language learners with manipulation of the question transformation operation. A question-and-answer game is always a welcome addition to a storytelling program. Choice of the proper game depends more upon the additional play in the song—level of humor, social commentary, balladlike construction, cyclic story.

For Younger Audiences

"Who's That Knocking at My Window?" (Seeger 1948)

"What Shall We Do When We All Go Out?" (ibid.)

"How Old Are You?" (ibid.)

"Billy Barlow" (ibid.)

"Did You Go to the Barney?" (ibid.)

"Blow, Boys, Blow" (ibid.)

"Old Molly Hare" (ibid.)

"Mommy, Buy Me a China Doll" (Zemach 1966)

"The Button and the Key" (Richards 1973)

"Milking Pails" (Gomme 1967)

"Who Built the Ark? Noah! Noah!" (Seeger 1948)

"Jenny Jenkins" (Silber and Silber 1973)

For More Mature Audiences

"There's a Hole in the Bucket" (Winn 1974)

"What Shall We Do with a Drunken Sailor?" (Best and Best 1955)

"Who Killed Cock Robin?" (Boni 1952)

"Billy Boy" (Hart 1982)

"Soldier, Soldier, Won't You Marry Me?" (Boni 1952)

"Buffalo Boy" (Winn 1974)

"The Deaf Woman's Courtship" (ibid.)

"Henery My Boy" (oral tradition)

"The Cutty Wren" (Tyson and Fricker n.d.)

THERE'S A HOLE IN THE BUCKET

Henry:	There's a hole in the bucket, dear Lisa, dear Lisa. There's a hole in the bucket, dear Lisa, a hole.
Lisa:	Well, fix it, dear Henry, dear Henry, dear Henry. Well, fix it, dear Henry, dear Henry, well, fix it!
Henry:	With what shall I fix it?
Lisa:	With a straw.
Henry:	The straw is too long.
Lisa:	Then cut it.
Henry:	With what shall I cut it?
Lisa:	With an axe.
Henry:	But, the axe is too dull.
Lisa:	Then sharpen it.
Henry:	With what shall I sharpen it?
Lisa:	With a stone.
Henry:	But the stone is too dry.
Lisa:	Then wet it.
Henry:	With what shall I wet it?
Lisa:	With water.
Henry:	With what shall I fetch it?
Lisa:	With a bucket.
Henry:	But there's a hole in the bucket.

HENERY, MY BOY

Ma: Where ya been all the day, Henery my boy?
Where ya been all the day, my pride and joy?

Henery: In the woods, dear Mother.
In the woods, dear Mother.
Mother be quick, I'm gonna be sick
And lay me down to die.

Ma: What'd ya do in the woods all day, Henery my son?
What'd ya do in the woods all day, my pretty one?

Henery: I ate, dear Mother.

Ma: What'd ya eat in the woods all day, Henery my boy? (pride and joy)

Henery: Eels, dear Mother.

Ma: What color was them eels, Henery my son? (pretty one)

Henery: Green and yeller.

Ma: Them eels was snakes, Henery my boy. (pride and joy)

Henery: Bleeecccchhhhh, dear Mother.

Ma: What color flowers do ya want, Henery my son? (pretty one)

Henery: Green and yeller.

BUFFALO BOY

She: When are we gonna git married, git married, git married?
When are we gonna git married, dear ol' buffler boy?

He: I guess we'll marry in a week, in a week, in a week.
I guess we'll marry in a week. That is if the weather be good.

She: How will you come to the weddin', to the weddin', to the weddin'?
How will you come to the weddin', dear ol' buffler boy?

He: I guess I'll come in my oxcart, in my oxcart, in my oxcart.
I guess I'll come in my oxcart. That is if the weather be good.

She: Why don't you come in your buggy, in your buggy, in your buggy?
Why don't you come in your buggy, dear ol' buffler boy?

He: My ox won't fit in my buggy, in my buggy, in my buggy.
My ox won't fit in my buggy, not even if the weather be good.

She: Who will you bring to the weddin', to the weddin', to the weddin'?
Who will you bring to the weddin', dear ol' buffler boy?

He: I guess I'll bring my children, my children, my children.
I guess I'll bring my children, that is, if the weather be good.

She: I didn't know you had children, had children, had children.
I didn't know you had children, dear ol' buffler boy.

He: Oh, yes, I have five children, five children, five children.
Oh, yes, I have five children, six if the weather be good.

She: There ain't gonna be no weddin', no weddin', no weddin'.
There ain't gonna be no weddin', not even if the weather be good.

THE DEAF WOMAN'S COURTSHIP

1: Old woman, old woman, will you go a-shearing?
Old woman, old woman, will you go a-shearing?

2: Speak a little louder sir, I'm rather hard of hearing.
Speak a little louder, sir, I'm rather hard of hearing.

1: Old woman, old woman, are you good at spinning?
[Repeat]

2: [See 2 above]

1: Old woman, old woman, can you do fine weaving?
[Repeat]

2: [See 2 above]

1: Old woman, old woman, will you darn my stockings?
[Repeat]

2: Speak a little louder, sir, I think I almost hear you.
[Repeat]

1: Old woman, old woman, why don't we get married?
[Repeat]

2: Lord-a-mercy on my soul, I'm sure that now I hear you.
[Repeat]

AWFULNESS, SILLINESS, AND NONSENSE

Songs that classify as unpleasant to crazy fit the "awful" category. The content of this material sometimes irritates adults, making it all the more attractive to audiences between the ages of about eight and twelve or thirteen. In order for a song or game to qualify as nonsense, it must be so utterly ridiculous that singing it seems to be a positively useless pursuit. (Its very uselessness makes it worthwhile.) The ad nauseam countdowns of the "100 Bottles of Beer" (Best and Best 1955) type are good examples. Others are the literal screamers ("The Cow Kicked Nellie in the Belly in the Barn," Best and Best 1955), the silly-content songs ("The Tattooed Lady," "On Mules We Find," Best and Best 1955), tongue twisters, and anything that is purely disgusting. The following lists present a very limited selection; the category is quite extensive. This type of oral literature is often the invention (and certainly the delight) of children and, although they do not hold exclusive rights to it, they sometimes resent its widespread adoption by adults.

Irritating Songs and Games

"Mrs. Murphy's Chowder" (Winn 1974)

"The Tattooed Lady" (Best and Best 1955)

"On Mules We Find" (ibid.)

"Pink Pajamas" (ibid.)

"The Hearse Song" (ibid.)

"My Bonnie" (ibid.)

"There'll Be a Hot Time in the Old Town" (Quackenbush 1974)

"The Cow Kicked Nellie" (oral tradition)

"Johnny Vorbeck" (Best and Best 1955)

"The Pig and the Inebriate" (ibid.)

"Ol' Joe Clark" (ibid.)

"The Ship Titanic" (ibid.)

"Throw It Out the Window" (ibid.)

"Junior Birdman" (oral tradition)

"My Nuthouse" (oral tradition)

"Do Your Ears Hang Low?" (Hart 1982)

Infuriating Songs and Games

"Green Bottles" (Winn 1974)

"100 Bottles of Beer" (Best and Best 1955)

"The Ant Song" (Freschet 1973)

"100 in the Bed" (Hart 1982; also called "Roll Over")

"The Ford Song" (oral tradition)

"My Peanuts" (oral tradition)

"The Ladies in the Harem" (Winn 1974)

"The Horse Went Around" (ibid.)

"Pink Pajamas" is an example of a nonsense tongue-twister game that, sung to excess, can exhaust adults, while remaining fresh and fun for children.

PINK PAJAMAS

I wear my pink pajamas in the summer when it's hot.
I wear my flannel nightie in the winter when it's not.
And sometimes in the springtime, and sometimes in the fall,
I slip right in between the sheets with nothing on at all.

Glory, glory, what's it to ya.
[Repeat two more times.]
If I slip right in between the sheets with nothing on at all.

One grasshopper jumped right over the other grasshopper's back.
[Repeat three more times.]

They were only playin' leap frog.
[Repeat two more times.]
When one grasshopper jumped right over the other grasshopper's
    back.

One mosquito bit the other mosquito's skeeter bite.
[Repeat three more times.]

They were only bein' friendly.
[Repeat two more times.]
When one mosquito bit the other mosquito's skeeter bite.

One flea fly flew up the flue, the other flea fly flew down.
[Repeat three more times.]

They were only playin' flue fly.
[Repeat two more times.]
When one flea fly flew up the flue, the other flea fly flew down.

One pink porpoise popped up the pole, the other pink porpoise
    popped down.
[Repeat three more times.]

Goodness, isn't that peculiar?
[Repeat two more times.]
When one pink porpoise popped up the pole, the other pink por-
poise popped down.

(Tune: "Battle Hymn of the Republic.")

WHOLE-STORY PLAY—BALLADRY

Ballads are stories in verse. They employ the conventions of "story" but
"tell" in rhymed and metered form. The restrictions of poetic language and
structure represent a game aside from the game of storying. Making a ballad
requires slotting of story content according to a new and very limiting set of
rules. The rhythms, rhymes, and musical shapes of the ballad structure the
memory for content and language. Perhaps many stories and histories were
sung and/or chanted because of the memory-fixing framework of tune, shape,
and cadence.

The addition of a ballad to a storytelling program lends variety, especially
in the form of structure and delivery. Ballad singing or saying tends to be more
of a performance than a telling, since the language of the ballad is a given.
Ballads with choruses can be taught to the audience in order to extend participation, and the teller can invite people to join in if they already know the song.
A program that includes too many ballads, however, will severely limit
audience participation and ownership of the telling.

Ballad delivery is governed by the same general rules as story delivery.
The ballad should be opaque, the teller transparent. For this reason a
storyteller need not be concerned if he or she does not have a fine singing voice
or cannot play a musical instrument. The song itself is the focus of attention;
the teller merely brings the play to the audience. Unless the teller's style attracts
attention to the teller, or the delivery is unintelligible, performance quality
need not be a concern.

Just like the stories, the ballads must be done live. Though ballads make a
good addition to a program, they should not be included if they are recorded
and played back for the audience. Regardless of the capabilities of the

storyteller, the audience would rather hear the teller than a tape or a record. Storytellers who are reluctant to sing ballads or other singing games might want to talk them out instead. A ballad with a regular and heavy rhythm can be chanted, clapped, or beat out on the knees as well as sung. A teller who begins ballad delivery through talking can eventually make the transition to singing when confidence grows.

Choosing ballads is very much like choosing stories. The storyteller's capability and interest will govern the development of the repertoire perhaps more than any other factors. The requirements of the program can also influence choice, provided that the teller has ample time to prepare the material. Ballads must be committed to memory word for word. The storyteller has little if any flexibility for invention or ad-libbing during delivery; lapses of memory are glaringly obvious. Before the teller brings the ballad to the audience, overlearning to the point of automaticity is necessary to prevent panic forgetting.

Perhaps the most common memory technique for learning verse is the cumulative process: learn the first line, add the second, then the third, etc. The method works, but the verses or lines at the end of the ballad tend to be weak, since they are repeated less frequently than those at the beginning. Another method, using the principles of cloze procedure (Iverson and Sebesta 1975), involves preparing copy from which key words are eliminated, then repeating the verse(s) again and again, adding in the missing words. At intervals, copy is prepared from which more words have been removed, until only structure words (articles, conjunctions, interjections, prepositions, and the like) are left. An example follows.

> As I stepped out one evening,
> To a timber town cafe,
> A six-foot-seven waitress
> To me these words did say.

[Chant verse aloud several times, then remove one or two key words—nouns, adjectives, adverbs, or verbs—per line.]

> As I _____ out one evening,
> To a timber town _____,
> A six foot _____ waitress
> To me these _____ did say.

[Chant verse aloud again, inserting missing words. Then remove an additional one or two key words per line.]

> As I _____ out one _____,
> To a _____ town _____,
> A _____ foot _____ waitress
> To _____ these _____ did say.

[Chant, insert missing words, then eliminate additional key words.]

As I _____ _____ one _____,
To a _____ _____ _____,
A _____ foot _____ _____
To _____ these _____ did _____.

[Chant, insert, eliminate additional words.]

As _____ _____ _____ one _____,
_____ a _____ _____ _____,
A _____ _____ _____ _____
To _____ _____ _____ did _____.

[Same procedure.]

Eventually, the only remaining cues in the copy are punctuation marks. Some storytellers simply sing or chant the ballad repeatedly in its entirety, distributing such practice over time until the material is acquired as a whole. The special value in this method is related to slotting content into structure during memory making. The teller will learn the ballad in bits and pieces in a natural manner, the most important parts being the first to "stick."

The storyteller who wishes to add balladry to his or her program should listen to ballads, recorded or live, to develop a sense of delivery and phrasing. Many fine collections of ballads are available on tape or record and in print. A teller will find his or her own favorites. Collections of ballads from a variety of regions, cultures, nationalities, and industries can be found in the following sources: Baird and Baird 1981; Best and Best 1955; Fife and Fife 1969; Finger 1923, 1927; Glass and Stinger 1966; Jackson and Bryan n.d.; John 1978; Korn and Rainbolt n.d.; Larkin 1963; Lingenfelter and Dwyer 1968; Lomax 1947, 1960; Lomax and Lomax 1934, 1938, 1941, 1947; Moore and Moore 1964; Ohrlin 1973; Plotz 1976; Sackett and Scott 1967; Sandburg 1927; Seeger 1961; Sharp 1932; Silber and Robinson 1967; Silber and Silber 1973; Silverman 1974, 1975; Smiley et al. 1966; Thorpe 1966; Tinsley 1981; Tyson and Fricker n.d.; Watson n.d.; Watson and Watson n.d.; Weavers 1960; Wells 1950; and White 1975. A limited number of favorite story songs are included here.

THE GREENLAND WHALE FISHERY

We can no longer stay on shore
Since we're so far in debt.
So a voyage to Greenland we will go,
Some money for to get, brave boys,
Some money for to get.

Now when we lay in Liverpool,
Our goodly ship to man;
Twas then our names were all wrote down,
And we're bound for Greenland, brave boys,
We're bound for Greenland.

In eighteen hundred and twenty-four,
On March the twenty-first day,
We heisted our colors to our topmast high,
And for Greenland bore away, brave boys,
For Greenland bore away.

And when we reached that icy shore
With our goodly ship to moor,
We wished ourselves back safe at home again,
With our friends upon the shore, brave boys,
With our friends upon the shore.

The bo'sun went to the mast head,
A spyglass in his hand.
"There's a whale! There's a whale! There's a whale," cries he!
And she blows on every spring, brave boys.
And she blows on every spring.

The captain stood on the quarter deck,
And a very good man was he.
"Overhaul, overhaul your boat tackle all,
And launch your boats to sea, brave boys.
And launch your boats to sea."

The boat's been launched, and the hands got in,
And the whale fish appeared in view.
Resolv-ed was that whole boat's crew
To steer where the whale fish blew, brave boys,
To steer where the whale fish blew.

And when this whale we did harpoon,
She gave one slap with her tail.
She capsized the boat; we lost five men,
Nor did we catch that whale, brave boys,
Nor did we catch that whale.

Bad news unto our captain brought,
That we had lost his precious boys.
He hearing of this dreadful news
His colors down did haul, brave boys,
His colors down did haul.

The losing of this whale, brave boys,
Did grieve his heart full sore.
But the losing of his five brave men
Did grieve him ten times more, brave boys,
Did grieve him ten times more.

"Come, weigh your anchors, my brave boys,
For the winter star I see.
It's time we should leave this cold counteree,
And for England sail away, brave boys,
And for England sail away.

"Heist the sails, and away," cries he.
Let us leave this cold counteree.
Where the whale fish does grow,
And the stormy winds do blow,
And the daylight's seldom seen, brave boys,
And the daylight's seldom seen.

For Greenland is a barren place.
Neither light nor day to be seen.
Just ice and snow where the whalefishes blow,
And the daylight's seldom seen, brave boys,
And the daylight's seldom seen.

FARMER'S CURST WIFE

There was an old man lived over a hill
If he ain't moved away he's a-livin' there still
Singin' fa de ing ding dide ing ding da de ing ding dide ing ding da
      de ing ding dide ing day

[Or hi diddle I diddle I fi, diddle I diddle I day]

Devil come up to his house one day,
Sez one o' your family I'm gonna take away.

"Take my wife with all of my heart,
And I hope by golly that you never ever part."

He took the old lady up on his back,
He looked like an eagle skeered of the rack (And down the road he
      went clickity clack)

He set her down in the fork in the road
And sez "Old lady, you're the devil (one hell) of a load."

He got her to the gates of hell,
Said "Poke up the fire, we'll scorch her well."

In come a little devil with a ball and chain
She up with her foot and she kicked out his brain.

Nine little devils climbing up a wall
Sez "Take her back, Daddy, she'll murder us all."

The old man peepin' out through a crack.
He saw the ol' devil a-bringin' her back.

They found the old man sick to bed,
She up with the butterstick and paddled his head.

Says "Here's your wife all safe and well,
If I'd kept her there longer she'd uv ruint hell."

Says "I've been in the devil business most all my life,
And I never been in hell till I met your wife."

The old man went whistlin' over the hill,
"If the devil won't have her, darned if I will."

This one thing women have over the men,
They go down to hell and come back again.

THE GREY GOOSE

Oh, last Monday mornin', Lord Lord Lord.
Oh, last Monday mornin', Lord Lord Lord.

The preacher went a-hunting, Lord Lord Lord.
Oh, the preacher went a-hunting, Lord Lord Lord.

He took along his shotgun, Lord Lord Lord.
He took along his shotgun, Lord Lord Lord.

He was hunting for the grey goose, Lord Lord Lord.
He was hunting for the grey goose, Lord Lord Lord.

The grey goose came a-flyin', Lord Lord Lord.
He was real high a-flyin', Lord Lord Lord.

Well, he pulled that trigger way back, Lord Lord Lord.
The hammer went a click clack, Lord Lord Lord.

And the grey goose came a-fallin', Lord Lord Lord.
He was six weeks a-fallin', Lord Lord Lord.

Then he put him on the wagon, Lord Lord Lord.
And took him up to my house, Lord Lord Lord.

Then you did, and I did, Lord Lord Lord.
We had a feather pickin', Lord Lord Lord.

He was six weeks a-pickin', Lord Lord Lord.
Then we put him on to parboil, Lord Lord Lord.

He was six weeks a-parboilin', Lord Lord Lord.
Then we put him on the table, Lord Lord Lord.

The knife couldn't stick him, Lord Lord Lord.
And the fork couldn't prick him, Lord Lord Lord.

So we throwed him to the hog pen, Lord Lord Lord.
And he broke those jerries' jawbones, Lord Lord Lord.

So we put him on the sawmill, Lord Lord Lord.
He broke that saw's teeth out, Lord Lord Lord.

Well, the last time we seen him, Lord Lord Lord.
He was flyin' 'cross the ocean, Lord Lord Lord.

With a long string o' goslins, Lord Lord Lord.
And they all went a-quick quack, Lord Lord Lord.

BOW DOWN (The Barcher Tragedy/Rollin' A Rollin')

There was an old lord by the north countree.
Bow down (derry down, down).
There was an old lord by the north countree.
The boughs they bend to me.
There was an old lord by the north countree,
And he had daughters one, two and three.
I will be true, true to my love.
Love, and my love will be true to me.

[Italicized lines are repeated in following verses.]

A handsome young man came a-courtin' there.
He chose the youngest for she was most fair.

He brought the young one a beaver hat.
The eldest she thought hard of that.

He brought the young one a gay gold ring.
The eldest he brought not a single thing.

The eldest said, "Sister, let's walk the sea shore,
And see the ships as they sail o'er."

Two little sisters side by side.
The eldest one for the young man cried.

Two little sisters walkin' downstream.
The eldest one pushed the young one in.

The youngest said, "Sister, please give me your hand."
The eldest said, "No, I'll not give you my hand.
I will have your lover and I'll have your land."

The youngest sank down and away she swam.
She floated on down to the miller's dam.

The miller he took her by the hand.
And pulled her safely back to the land.

The miller took off her gay gold ring.
And pushed her back into the water again.

The miller was hung from the gallows so high.
The eldest sister was hung close by.

This endeth my tale of the north countree.
'Tis known as the Barcher Tragedy.

SINGING DANCES AND GAMES — THE "PLAYPARTY"

Many singing games, folk games, dramatic activity play, and dance play had their origins in the routine work, the ritual, and the beliefs of an older culture. The common rhythms and activities of daily living presented natural cadences, interactions, and cycles that could be "played," transformed into games that mimicked life's common circumstances and revealed their universal aspects and that set chores and experiences to music.

Singing, gaming, and playing are natural extensions of all other human undertaking. The rhythms of pounding, hoeing, spinning, and milking can be made into language activities and sung. Perhaps the natural integration of game, music, and play occurred first during daily work and made work into play. Later, games and play that represented work and other human activity evolved. In these games, song and action go together; human activity becomes a dance, and participants affirm the significance of even the smallest aspects of daily living.

Children's singing games sometimes played out ancient, often forgotten ceremony ("We're Marching round the Valley," Cano 1973) using a combination of song, dance, and dramatic action. Some were historic reminiscences ("The Grand Old Duke of York," Chase 1972; "Roman Soldiers," Gomme 1967; "Captain Jinks," Collins 1973) that used drama and movement to act out the memories of a community. Some were the games of daily living, the singing and movement that mimicked and accompanied daily chores ("I Want to Be a Farmer" and "Oats, Peas, Beans," Collins 1973). Still others, those classed as "playparty," were figure or country dance games that combined some of the patterns of adult figure dances (square dances, progressive rounds, line dances, quadrilles, and contredanses) and dramatic activity with singing (Chase 1967). Playparty games evolved in communities where some musical instruments — most notably, banjo and fiddle — and some instrumental music and instrumentally accompanied dances were considered wicked. The people solved the problem by eliminating the instrumental accompaniment and by singing to the same dance figures that otherwise would have been forbidden (Chase 1967).

The more encompassing genre of folk game can include the playparty game, children's singing games and dances, dramatic games, and a variety of nonmusical games involving circle and line activity, chanting, question-and-response play, skill and strength testing, and running and tag play, as well as games that incorporate the use of balls, blankets, sticks, ropes, or string and other physical objects.

Each play or game is a special kind of reality complete with rules, sequences, cycles, objectives or goals, signals for repeating, and sometimes "story" and role playing. In "Oats, Peas, Beans" (and an alternative in Vinton 1970) and "I Want to Be a Farmer" (Collins 1973), part of the agricultural cycle is acted out. Implicit in such games is the wish for a good harvest. "Old

Roger" (Chase 1967) remembers the ancient custom of planting trees on the graves of the dead. "Captain Jinks" (Collins 1973) is a bragging game of Civil War origin that incorporates some square dance movement. "Blackberry" combines a common food-gathering chore with a version of "Pom Pom Pull Away" (Vinton 1970).

While many western European games may once have been ceremonial, or reiterations of ceremony or daily activity whose immediate implications have been forgotten, some Native American games have retained their direct ties to ceremony, especially to the rituals connected with the seasons. Both "Ptarmigans against Ducks" and "Shoving Winter Out" are examples of seasonal ceremony as play. In both, the people express their wishes regarding seasonal duration and change (Vinton 1970).

Game playing was spontaneous and informal, deliberate and formal, and sometimes a ceremonial activity. However conceived, the playing of games was a collective undertaking that represented some deliberate form of group agreement, and it was generally intended to be high-spirited and fun, often partylike.

The playparty itself, while not a new idea, was a phenomenon of the American frontier. Though it is regularly associated with the Great Plains, it was a part of the settling of the country when Ohio was "out West" and the Rocky Mountains were rumors. It was as much a social activity of Spanish colonials in northern New Mexico as it was of the British families who migrated to the sand hills country of western Nebraska or of the Germans from Silesia who settled in south-central Montana. It emerged out of the silence of the country, the great distances, the loneliness, and the need to be together. Before the advent of town "entertainments" and the eventual westward migration of so-called cultured activities, whole families gathered in response to word-of-mouth invitations, arriving at a centrally located homestead by a variety of human and animal-powered transportation, with babies in arms and a change of clothing and a contribution of food packed in somehow. The chosen soddie, dugout, cabin, or perhaps even "house" was emptied of its furnishings and swept clean. Furniture, set out in the front yard, was used to display food, to sleep on, and to lean on while gossiping. Dancing and singing-and-dancing games were done indoors. Running games and activities requiring more space were played outside.

On the American frontier, where people lived at great distances from one another and lacked easy or regular communication, the playparty was a means of establishing and reaffirming community. It allowed people an opportunity to engage in essential social commerce. Participation in the games provided a sense of belonging, the various shapes of the play acting as devices for the development of other relationships.

The games today are a valuable cultural and human heritage. Like stories, they serve to organize information and to help people understand themselves individually and in the larger frames of reference of community and culture. In their more ceremonial habit, the games are paradigmatic, reminding us through play of the larger schemata into which we have integrated ourselves and what we know. They allow us to play out our work and our social activity, to confirm the existence of community and the rightness of the common shapes of our lives. Through the play, we are able to laugh at our circumstances and develop perspective. The games are equalizers; everyone is "in" the play and must play by the same rules. And, most importantly, people are provided with a socially acceptable, controlled, nonthreatening way of touching and looking at one another and establishing social intimacy.

While we often do the games with children, our legacy of traditional play is not the exclusive property of any single age group, time, or culture (Collins 1973). Game playing and the making of games out of living is universal, crossing all human boundaries. When we do the "old" games together, they are new again, and even the youngest among us senses the timelessness of the play.

Storytelling programs can successfully include singing dances and games. A few modest precautions will preserve both the pleasure of the experience and the storyteller's control of the circumstances. First, the teller must know the song/dance as a physical exercise—not only the directions, but its real on-the-floor configuration. Development of control will require memory of the song, the music, the sequence of movement, the directions, *and* actual trial experiences with teaching and conducting the game. The storyteller might want to borrow friends for the preliminary work in order to become accustomed to directing a dance and moving people about. Second, the storyteller should choose a game that is appropriate for the audience. Unlike the story, which does not have to be fully comprehended for participation, the singing dance must be understood by the players in order for it to work. Most of the game resources available include some recommendations about age group. If the storyteller is unsure, he or she should test the game on a group of adults, considering the difficulty of the directions, the amount of repeated movement, the complexity of movement, the memory work required to do a full sequence of movement, and the body size (length of arms and legs) required to do a given motion. Third, the teller must arrange to do the game at a time in the storytelling program when it will not detract from the rest of the agenda. The game will require that the audience get up to play, do the play, then return to the storytelling area. The logistics of such an operation are more complicated than one would assume, particularly if the game is lively and the following story is not. The teller might consider doing a full program of such games, or saving the games for the end of the storytelling. Fourth, the storyteller must pay attention to space. An area that will serve adequately for telling stories might not work for singing dances. The games require open space—a playground or gymnasium. The storytelling audience takes up little room, but the same group spread out for a circle or line game requires three to four times the area. Conducting a game in inadequate space could result in injury. Fifth, the storyteller must consider audience dress. The games require running, skipping, hopping, making bridges, and crawling through spaces. Some members of an audience might be improperly dressed for such activity. The wrong shoes together with the wrong game can lead to injury. An audience in evening dress may not care to play a game that requires lying on the floor. Sixth, the teller must allow members of the audience the option not to play. In the traditional playparty, players were able to participate at will. A long program can exhaust some members of an audience.

Some favorite singing dances and games are included below. Other singing dances and games can be found in Bley 1982; Cano 1973; Chase 1967, 1972; Collins 1973; Gelineau 1974; Gomme 1898, 1967; Gomme and Sharp 1976; Jamieson n.d.; Jones n.d.; McMorland n.d.; Nancrede 1940; Newell n.d.; Opie and Opie 1984; Richards 1973, 1974; Sweeney 1973; Vinton 1970; and Warran 1973.

WILLOWBEE* — reel-type dance

1. This way you willowbee, you willowbee, you willowbee.
   Oh, this way you willowbee, all day long.

2. Dancing down the alley, the alley, the alley.
   Dancing down the alley, all day long.

MOVEMENT

1. All players choose partners.

2. Partners face each other such that two long lines are formed.

   STEPS 1-2-3-4

3. Partners hold hands and extend their right feet forward so that their right feet are touching, outside foot to outside foot.

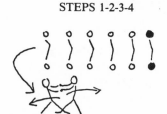

4. Verse 1—Partners rock forward and back like a see-saw to the beat of the music. Sing and rock through two repetitions of verse 1.

5. Verse 2—Head couple keeps hands joined while other couples let go of their partner's hands. Head couple *slides* down the center of the line. Other players clap.

   STEP 5

---

*In Landeck 1950.

When the head couple reaches the foot of the line, they also drop hands. Each head couple player leads his/her line around to the outside and back up to the head-of-the-line position. (One head player turns right, the other left at the foot of the line.)

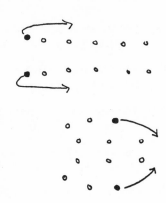

When each head player reaches the head of the line, he/she turns once again, this time to the inside, and marches down to the foot-of-the-line position.

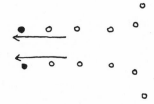

All the other players stay in line and follow their head player.

As the two head players lead the others up and down the line, they may walk, jump, hop, skip, or make any motion that they choose. The other players must do whatever motion their leaders do as they walk up and down the line.

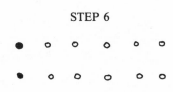

Repeat verse 2 as many times as is necessary to get both lines back to place.

6. Since each lead player chooses his/her own motion for his/her line to imitate and follow, one line may get back to place before the other. The first line back to place claps and sings until the other is back to place.

STEP 6

7. Begin again with new head couple.

*OLD ROGER** — dramatic movement

1. Old Roger is dead and gone to his grave.
   HI HO Gone to his grave.

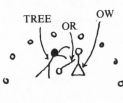

2. They planted an apple tree over his head.
   HI HO Over his head.

3. The apples were ripe and ready to drop.
   HI HO Ready to drop.

4. There came an old woman a-picking them up.
   HI HO Picking them up.

5. Old Roger jumped up and he gave her a knock.
   HI HO Gave her a knock.

6. Which made the old woman go hippety hop.
   HI HO Hippety hop.

MOVEMENT

1. All players stand in a circle, facing the inside.

2. The leader chooses individuals to play Old Roger, brings these players, one at a time, to the center of the circle, gets them to lie down and play dead.

3. For each Old Roger, the leader chooses a player to play the apple tree. The leader positions each apple tree beside an Old Roger and arranges the apple tree in a posture.

4. The leader chooses one "old woman" for each Old Roger, practices bent-backed walking with the old women, and places each old woman next to an Old Roger.

5. All other players face center, cross hands and arms over chests, and sing all verses, bowing from the waist to the beat of the music.

6. Players in the center listen to the verses and act out their parts as the singers cue them. (When the apples are ready to drop, the apple trees drop apples. The old woman hobbles about picking up apples in verse 4. Old Roger jumps up and knocks her in the head in verse 5. She hops about in verse 6.)

---

*In Gomme and Sharp 1976.

7. When the song is finished, the players in the center return to the circle. New players are chosen to play the parts of the tree, the old woman, and Old Roger. When the new center players are in place and the players in the circle are ready to sing, play begins again. Play can continue until every player has had the chance to be one of the center characters.

WIND UP THE APPLE TREE* — line/crack the whip game

1. Wind up the apple tree, hold on tight.
   Wind it all day and wind it all night.

2. Stir the soup til the pot boils over.

MOVEMENT

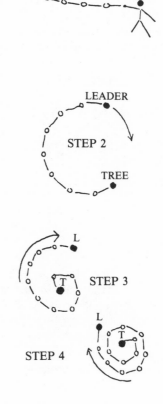

1. One player stands steady in a central space. This person is the apple tree. All other players form a straight line extending out from the tree, holding hands. The leader stands at the opposite end of the line from the tree.

2. Verse 1 — All players sing entire verse over and over while the leader walks/ leads/pulls the line in a circle around the tree. (The tree stands still — does *not* rotate as the line comes around.)

3. Verse 1 — The leader wraps the line up around the tree like a piece of string around a twig.

4. When the line is fully wound — i.e., the leader is also standing in a wound-up position — all players stop.

---

*In Chase 1967.

5. Verse 2—All players sing verse over and over. Leader walks away from the tree in a straight line, pulling the line of players out from around the tree. Now the tree spins in the center of the wound-up line.

6. Verse 2—Leader pulls harder and walks faster. The line is pulled tighter about the tree and the tree spins faster. Leader pulls until the full line has been pulled out.

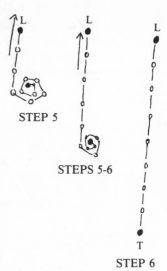

STEP 5

STEPS 5-6

STEP 6

(When the leader pulls out the line, the line will be stretched and the players in the wound-up line pulled into a tighter and tighter knot around the tree. The entire knot of people will spin. If the leader winds the line too tightly around the tree during verse one, the line will have no give and will break apart. Best for the leader to wind so that there is a bit of space between bodies as the line is wound.)

THE ALLEY-ALLEY-O* — line/crack the whip game

Oh, the big ship is sailin' through the alley-alley-o.
The alley-alley-o.
The alley-alley-o.
Oh, the big ship is sailin' through the alley-alley-o.
Through the alley-alley-o.

MOVEMENT

STEPS 1-2

LEADER   ROCK

1. One player is a "rock." This player stands fast in one location. The rock might be located so he/she can hang onto something (a pipe or pole) with one hand.

2. All other players line up in a long, straight line next to the rock and join hands. The leader goes to the end of the line opposite the rock.

---

*In Chase 1967.

3. All players sing verse over and over for the duration of play. The leader leads the line (walking) back around onto itself until the leader is facing the space between the rock and the first player in the line. These two raise their joined hands to make a bridge. The leader leads the entire line under the bridge.

4. The leader leads the line back out and around again, this time around to the space between player 1 and player 2 (counting out from the rock). These two players raise their joined hands. The leader leads the line under the bridge, out and around again. The leader repeats this procedure until all of the players in the line are wound up.

5. At this point, all players should have their arms pulled tightly across their chests, left over right and right fist (holding another player's hand) jammed under the left armpit. All players hold this position.

6. The action that follows is a more and more rapid crack the whip. Players may not want to sing. (Sometimes, even though they try, players are too busy hanging on to sing.) The leader is *pulled under* the arms of the last *two* players. (The player holding onto the leader *yanks* the leader through.) Then the second-last player pulls both the last player and the leader through. With each succeeding round, the next player in line pulls the player to his/her immediate outside under his/her left arm, pulling the entire line through.

7. Play continues until entire line has been unwound.

STEPS 3-4-5

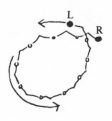

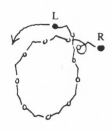

STEP 5

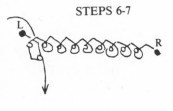

STEPS 6-7

*I WANT TO BE A FARMER** — bridge making

1. I want to be a farmer, a farmer, a farmer.
   I want to be a farmer and by my lady stand.

2. With a pitchfork on my shoulder, my shoulder, my shoulder.
   With a pitchfork on my shoulder and a sickle in my hand.

3. I'll harvest wheat and barley, and barley, and barley.
   I'll harvest wheat and barley and corn from all my land.

MOVEMENT

1. Choose partners. Couples stand in a circle facing each other. (The back of one partner should be to the inside of the circle, the back of the other to the outside.)

2. Add one extra person to the inside circle (designated on diagram by black dot).

STEPS 1 & 2

3. Verse 1—Inside circle faces right, walks right (clockwise). Outside circle faces left, walks left (counterclockwise). Both circles continue marching until the end of the first verse. On "stand" all players stop and grab a partner. Inside players must grab a partner from the outside circle. One inside player will be left without a partner.

STEP 3

4. Verse 2—Couples are once again standing in a circle, with the back of the inside partner to the inside of the circle, the back of the outside player to the outside. Partners join hands to make bridges. The extra player (the farmer) from the inside circle walks under the bridges during verse 2. At

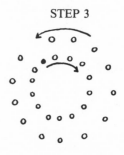

STEP 4

*In Collins 1973.

the end of the verse, on "hand," the bridge nearest the farmer catches him/her.

5. Verse 3—The farmer and the players in the bridge that captured him/her join hands to make a circle of three. These three skip in a circle for verse 3. Other players clap.

6. On "land," players stop. The farmer takes the two players who caught him/her by their hands—plants them in the center of the ring. The planted players are "out." (This is a reverse catch.) The farmer instructs the caught players as to how to stand, sit, etc.—tells these players what kinds of plants they are to be: corn, beans, watermelon, etc.

7. Begin play again. (The last round of the game is done with only three people—two in the inside circle and one in the outside. All of the others are planted.)

STEP 5

STEPS 6 & 7

*OATS, PEAS, BEANS** — circle/choosing game

1. Oats, peas, beans and barley grow.
    Oats, peas, beans and barley grow.
    Can you, or I, or anyone know
    How oats, peas, beans and barley grow.

2. First the farmer plants his seed.
    Then he stands and takes his ease.
    Stamps his feet, claps his hands
    And turns around to view the land.

3. Looking for a partner,
    Looking for a partner.
    Open the ring; select one in,
    And then we'll sing and dance again.

---

*In Collins 1973.

MOVEMENT

1. Players stand in one large circle, facing clockwise. One single player (the farmer) stands in the center facing counterclockwise.

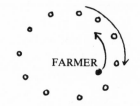

STEPS 1-2

2. Verse 1—Players march in the circle clockwise. Farmer marches in a smaller inside circle, counterclockwise. On "grow," players stop and face center. Farmer may face in any direction.

3. Verse 2—Players stand and pantomime the motions cued in the verse.

4. Verse 3—Players resume marching as in verse 1. On "select one in," the farmer reaches out and pulls one person from the outside circle into the center. Both circles continue marching to end of verse.

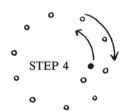

STEP 4

5. Play begins again with verse 1 with two farmers. During the next round of play, each farmer selects a partner. Farmers march in the inside circle. The inside circle gets more populated as the game continues. Play is ended when all of the players are in the inside circle.

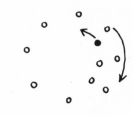

6. To play again, choose a new farmer.

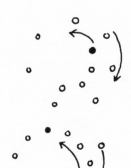

PTARMIGANS AGAINST DUCKS* — seasonal team game

This calendar custom of the Eskimo peoples (also played by the Haida, Tlingit, and other Northwest coast peoples under the name "Summer vs. Winter Born") has its equivalent in western European games — "Tug-of-War" and "Pom Pom Pull Away." It is designed to predict the severity of the coming winter. In the fall, all of the people gather to play.

PLAY

1. Players divide into summer people and winter people according to birthdays. Unless determined by another custom, the summer born can be those whose birthdates fall between the spring equinox (March 20) and the fall equinox (September 20). The winter born can be those whose birthdays fall between September 20 and March 20.

2. The summer people line up along one end of a long rope, the winter people on the other. Each group pulls against the other, trying to pull a mark on the rope over a line drawn onto the ground.

3. If the summer people win, the winter will be mild. If the winter people win, it will be severe.

SHOVING WINTER OUT** — seasonal team game

A calendar custom found in Tierra del Fuego, this game is played at the end of winter and expresses the desire of a people to begin with spring.

PLAY

1. Players divide into two groups. Winter people and summer people can be chosen by birthdates or by clan groups.

2. Players draw a large circle on the ground, bisecting the circle in the middle with a straight line.

3. The winter people stand or sit in one half of the circle; the summer people stand in the other. The object of the game is for the summer people to push the winter people out of their half of the circle.

---

*In Vinton 1970.
**In Vinton 1970.

4. All players fold arms over chests. Summer people advance into the winter people's half of the circle. (Winter people do not advance on the summer people.) Summer people push, shove, bump the winter people to the outside of the circle. Summer people may not strike winter people, but may only use their sides, backs, and shoulders to shove the winter people out.

5. Winter people must also keep their arms folded. They may otherwise resist by sitting down, but may not crawl around the summer people to avoid the shoving. Once a winter person is shoved outside the circle, he/she may not reenter as a winter person, but must join the summer people in pushing the remaining winter people out. The game is vigorous and sometimes a bit rough, but fighting (aggression and active resistance) is not a part of it.

6. Sometimes summer and winter people color their faces or wear colored clothing to identify themselves (white for winter and green for summer).

CHĒ WEH*

This is an American Indian game.

SONG

Chē weh, chē weh
Mocah cameh yan.

PLAY

1. Players form a circle and all face to the center, extending arms forward and at angles to each side, hands in fists. Players hold arms steady.

2. The lead player brings his or her fists together, one on top of the other, in front of his or her body. This begins a signal that the lead player then sends to the players to his/her immediate left and right by putting his/her left fist on top of the right fist of the player to the left and his/her right fist on the left fist of the player to the right.

3. The players to the immediate left and right of the lead player bring their fists together in front of them, then send the signal to the player next to them (away from the lead player). As each new player gets the signal, he/she brings his/her fists together, then sends the signal on.

---

*In oral tradition.

4. Players send the signal while singing the verse through four times. The signal pulses along to the beat of the music — fists together, fists apart. (Note: Only the players who have the signal and are passing it along bring their fists together. Other players stand with fists out waiting.)

5. After the signal has been passed around the circle for four verses, action stops. Two players will be "caught" with the signal. These players become the runners for the second part of the game. The runners must choose who will chase the other first.

6. While runners stand, all other players sing one verse through, taking four giant steps in any direction while singing. After the fourth step, these players yell "Freeze," and they freeze into statues of trees.

7. "Trees" sing four more verses while runners chase each other through the trees. The runner who has agreed to be the first chaser runs after the other runner. If he/she tags the other runner, the other runner becomes the chaser. The runners play exchange tag during the singing of the verses.

8. The runner who is the chaser when the singing ends has the signal. (The tag involved passing the signal back and forth). This runner begins the signal when all players reform the circle and begin a new game.

BLACKBERRY* — seasonal team game

This is a game from the American and Canadian Middle West.

CHANT

Runners: Blackberries, blackberries on the hill.
How many buckets can you fill?

Catchers: Briars are thick and briars scratch,
But we'll get all the berries in the blackberry patch!

PLAY

1. Players form two long facing lines. The lines should be about twenty to thirty feet apart.

2. Several players are chosen to be catchers or pickers. The catchers or pickers stand between the lines, in the center space.

---

*In Vinton 1970.

3. Players in the lines (the blackberries) chant "Blackberries, black-
    berries on the hill. How many buckets can you fill?"

4. Players in the center answer, "Briars are thick, and briars scratch, but
    we'll get all the berries in the blackberry patch!"

5. All players chant "One berry, two berries, three berries!" On "three
    berries" the players in the two facing lines run forward. They must
    dodge the catchers in the center and run across the opposite line
    without getting caught. Caught runners become catchers and stand in
    the center when play resumes.

6. The play repeats until all runners are caught and are in the center.

7. The last runner to be caught becomes the "head catcher" and may
    choose two assistants to be catchers. All other players form two lines
    and the game begins again.

OTHER PLAY FORMS

Riddling, rhyming, chanting, street cries, finger plays, string and hand
games, Mother Goose play, and lying contests can add variety and dimension
to a storytelling program. Chanting can be incorporated into songs and
stories, or the audience can learn and join in chanting activities initiated and
directed by the storyteller. One chanting game involves dividing the audience
into small groups or teams and teaching each group a different chant. Chants
that have the same cadence should be chosen (see chants below) and each
group set to chanting its own chant in time to the chanting of the other groups.

DADDY SHOT A BEAR

Daddy shot a bear.
Daddy shot a bear.
Shot him through the keyhole,
And never touched a hair.

GREEN SALLY

Green Sally up. Green Sally down.
Green Sally baked her possum brown.
I asked my mother for 15¢,
To watch the elephant climb the fence.
He climbed so high, he touched the sky,
And didn't come down til the Fourth of July.

SALLY GO ROUND

Sally go round the sun.
Sally go round the moon.
Sally go round the chimney pot every afternoon. Hey!!

PEASE PORRIDGE

Pease porridge hot.
Pease porridge cold.
Pease porridge in the pot nine days old.

Some like it hot.
Some like it cold.
Some like it from the pot nine days old.

THE KEEL ROW

As I went down to Sandgate, to Sandgate, to Sandgate.
As I went down to Sandgate,
I heard a lassie sing.

Oh, weel may the keel row, the keel row, the keel row.
Oh, weel may the keel row that my laddie's in.

He wears a blue bonnet, blue bonnet, blue bonnet.
He wears a blue bonnet, a dimple in his chin.

He's comin' home tomorrow, tomorrow, tomorrow.
He's comin' home tomorrow, and he'll be mine again.

HOT CROSS BUNS

Hot cross buns! Hot cross buns!
One a penny! Two a penny! Hot cross buns!
If you have no daughters, give them to your sons!
One a penny! Two a penny! Hot cross buns!

THREE BLIND MICE

Three blind mice! Three blind mice!
See how they run! See how they run!!
They all ran after the farmer's wife.
She cut off their tails with a carving knife.
Did you ever see such a sight in your life as three blind mice!

Question-and-answer or response chants can be arranged from familiar songs, or chant responses can be invented in which the audience answers the storyteller by saying "Oh, yes" or "Let's go" or "Me, too" (Graham 1979). The familiar spelling chant — "Give me a D!" "D!" — can be directed by the storyteller. Some songs make good chants ("Mrs. Murphy's Chowder," "The Cow Kicked Nellie in the Belly in the Barn"), and the teller can direct the audience through whispering, talking, and shouting variations. Jump-rope rhymes also make good chanting and clapping exercises. The storyteller might begin to accumulate rhythm instruments and kazoos to distribute to the audience to create an accompaniment to the chant. Chanting invokes the ritual "my turn, your turn" game that we all understand.

The audience can also be led in clapping patterns and cadences alone or to accompany songs or chants. The audience can be divided into groups, and each group taught a body noise (clapping, slapping, snapping fingers, clicking tongues, blowing, huffing, puffing) and a rhythm for each. The noises can be combined into a noisemaking "composition."

"The Rain Song" (oral tradition) is a special cumulative finger and hand play noisemaking game. The audience is divided into four groups and each group instructed to follow the storyteller, making exactly the same motions as the teller when so directed. A group is not to stop making a motion until the teller indicates that they may. The teller begins by facing the group to his or her immediate left and showing the group their first motion — rubbing the thumbs against the fingers of the hand. The storyteller then turns to the next group to the right, indicating that they, too, are to make the motion, then the third group is directed to begin, then the fourth. The teller turns back to the first group to direct the next motion — rubbing the palms of the hands together vigorously. Each group in turn is cued to do this motion and continue to do it until the teller gives them a new motion. The teller introduces the next motion, left to right — slapping knees with the palms — and then the last motion — foot stomping along with the knee slapping. When all groups are slapping knees and stomping feet, the teller directs each group in turn to return to knee slapping only, in the next round to hand rubbing, in the next to finger/thumb rubbing, and finally to silence. The effect of the winding and unwinding of motion and sound is reminiscent of the coming and going of a rainstorm.

Street cries were originally invented to help merchants sell wares. Audiences might be taught street cries (Gibbons 1968 and Langstaff 1978). If the audience can chant and sing several street cries at once — grouping again — they might be able to simulate the sound of a London street of 500 years ago. Once the audience understands the purpose of street cries and has learned to phrase, sing, and chant them, they might enjoy inventing modern street cries for today's merchandise. Street cries can also be used as an entree to dramatic play for younger children.

String figures (Ball n.d.; Jayne 1962; Pellowski 1984) hold a special fascination. For the storytelling program, the teller might want to develop string stories. However, more informal circumstances can be used to hold string figure contests in which players match and compare figure for figure.

Finger plays, body motion songs, and hand plays (Glazer 1980, 1973; Brown 1980; Grayson 1962) are associated most often with very young children. Appropriateness of finger or hand play, however, is related to content. A storyteller can find plays that are appealing to older children (for example, "Do Your Ears Hang Low?" [Glazer 1980], "Eyewinker" [Glazer 1973], "I'm Upright Inright Outright Downright,"* "Junior Birdmen"* and "If I Weren't Sixth Grader"*). Directions for one familiar hand game follow. (See illustration on p. 320.)

1. Put your palms flat together, fingers and thumbs matching, in prayer position.

2. Keeping the palms flat, fold the middle fingers over. (Fold the right middle finger foward at a ninety-degree angle to the right palm. Fold the left middle finger forward similarly. Be sure that the right finger is *in front of* the left finger.)

3. Keeping the palms flat and touching, fingers folded over but otherwise unmoving, rotate the left hand toward you, the right hand away.

4. Palms are now together, but with tips of right fingers touching bottom of left palm, tips of left fingers touching bottom of right palm. Middle fingers — still at right angles to their respective palms — are now sticking up (right) and down (left) in good wiggling position.

---

*In the oral tradition.

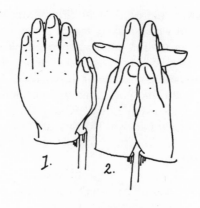

1.   2.

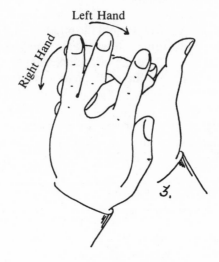

Left Hand

Right Hand

3.

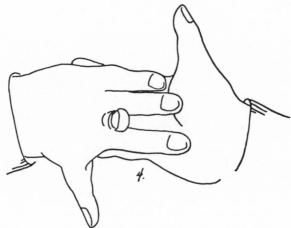

4.

Special inventions can be done with Mother Goose forms or other given sentence structures (Lee 1975; Koch 1970). Lee's play with poetic form uses many of the familiar cadences of Mother Goose as starters for poetic invention and chanting. His title poem, "Alligator Pie," has an infectious rhythm:

> Alligator Pie! Alligator Pie!
> If I don't get some, I think I'm gonna die.
> Give away the green grass,
> Give away the sky,
> But don't give away my Alligator Pie!

The same rhyme scheme and rhythm can be tried for Alligator Skin, Alligator Goop, Sweet Potato Pop, or Helicopter Glop. "Hickory Dickory Dock" can also be used as the basis for invention.

> Zippety zappety zot!
> Stir up the soup 'til it's hot.
> The mere touch of the steam
> Will make us all clean
> And our sweatshirts and shoes will all rot.

"Zappety, zappety zee," "Zip zipper zipper zip zip," or "Rumple dee dumpledee do" are other possibilities.

Other Mother Goose play sets the rhymes themselves in a larger game framework. "Throw It Out the Window" (Best and Best 1955) is a song that frames the Mother Goose rhymes.

> Old King Cole was a merry old soul,
> And a merry old soul was he.
> He called for his pipe,
> And he called for his bowl,
> And *threw them out the window, the window,*
> *The second story window.*
> *If you can't sing a rhyme and sing it in time,*
> *Throw it out the window.*

The rhymes must be sung to the tune of "Throw It out the Window." This game can be played with teams, each team singing a new rhyme when its turn comes around. Each team must choose the rhyme it will sing and all members of the team sing together. No rhyme can be repeated. Once a rhyme has been sung it cannot be used again, even by another team. The last line of the rhyme must be fitted to the song. If any of these rules is violated, a team is eliminated.

Riddling, like the liars' contest, involves the full interaction of an audience. Once the teller does a riddle, others in the audience will be ready with riddles of their own. Members of the audience might begin to riddle with one another. Riddling is a good circle game; there is an equality in it that eliminates the need for a leader. At the close of a telling the storyteller might use the riddle hand game. Directions follow. (See illustration below.)

1. Write *push* on the back of each hand. Draw an arrow pointing down from the word to a dot drawn below. (The dot is a button to push.)

2. Write a riddle question on the palm of the right hand.

3. Write the answer on the palm of the left hand.

4. Make a fist of the right hand, extending it to someone in the audience. That individual is to follow the directions written on the back of the hand and push the button. After the individual pushes the button, open the hand, showing the riddle on the palm. Allow ample time for the audience to answer the riddle. If they cannot, present the back of the left hand as a fist. When someones presses the button, show the answer to the riddle.

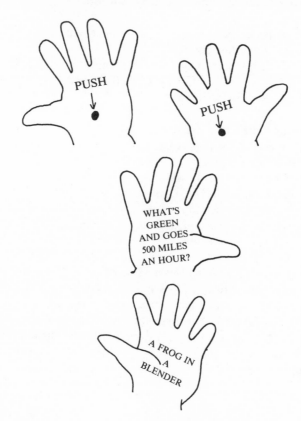

THE INVENTIONS OF CHILDREN

Children own and maintain a truly oral literature of their own. That literature is passed on from one generation of children to another (yes, we did our part), along with those changes that occur across time and from region to region. It is primarily a singing, rhyming, riddling, joking, gaming literature, and much of it is the kind that adults might find frivolous, if not offensive. Knapp and Knapp (1976) have collected much of this material and have provided notation as well as, in some cases, comparative forms. *Jump Rope* (Skolnik 1974) is a catalog of jump-rope rhymes collected from children.

While collecting and explicating is of interest to adults, the rhymes, riddles, and games themselves are kept alive through the activities of children. This kind of activity is not foolishness, though its content might seem foolish. The rhymes and games teach the rules of literary invention, help children to learn to work with and invent within the frameworks of a variety of top-level structures, teach the conventions of literary play, and contribute to language learning. Children themselves have little interest in studying their own literature, and they collect it for the purpose of playing. Their collections, in the purest of oral traditions, are held in memory and done orally. If a story-teller includes any such material in a telling program, he or she might be treated to a host of wonderful contributions from the audience. Children are in control of their own literature. Two eager children offered these rhymes:

> Boys use muscles.
> Teachers use brains.
> Girls use sex, so they win all the games.
>
> (Boy, age 6)

> So, so, suck your toe
> All the way to Mexico.
> While you're there, eat a pear.
> Stuff it down your underwear.
>
> (Girl, age 4)

LANGUAGE DEVELOPMENT
THROUGH PLAY

Most of the singing games, songs, dances, finger plays, and other "nonstory" forms use highly repetitive and relatively simple language patterns. In addition, many provide play with counting, word or phrase substitution, rhyming, and language invention.

An oral literature game challenges the player first to learn and then to demonstrate the ability to play. Because a player's focus is on development of skill and achievement on the level of the whole game, he or she generally does not recognize that language is also an object of play. Language usually remains transparent — a tool by which one plays the game itself. Knowledge *about* language is usually not a requirement for play. (Players sometimes learn language rules because these are game rules.) Interest in learning to play successfully, and subsequently in experiencing the private reward of successful play, often compels players to choose to play a game again and again. The inevitable repetitions of and play with language forms within the game satisfy the natural requirements for language learning: quantity and regularity of language forms within the language learner's environment, safety to make mistakes — to learn through trial and error — and interaction with other language users to confirm the shape of the language. Play is a primary vehicle for language learning.

For every item in a language development list of skills, there is a language game in the oral literature that presents the form repeatedly for the purposes of manipulation and play. Teachers, parents, librarians, and friends of children can help language development by playing singing and dancing language games. Since each game makes use of many language forms embedded into the play, a game (fortunately) prevents the disembedding and isolation of a single language form for the purposes of instruction. The form must be employed within the larger framework of the whole language of the game. However, teachers and others assure the manipulation of the specified form, and consequently focus on the development of a single aspect of language competence, by recognizing and identifying the language development capabilities of the songs and games. These capabilities can be coordinated with the language development skills scope and sequence.

The following sample songs/language games are accompanied by explications that identify sentence (structure) pattern play, extent and type of expansion of basic sentence pattern, use of grammatical morphemes, use of substitutions into positions (functions) within sentences, opportunity for language invention, figurative language, sight words (for chanting and reading), type of play (counting, cumulative, etc.), use of pronouns, and other special features. The language feature profiles of the songs/games illustrate the rich use of language in the "nonstory" literature and demonstrate the instructional potential of "nonstoried" material.

YOU CAN'T HAVE ANY OF MY PEANUTS

You can't have any of my _____ 'til your _____ are gone.
You can't have any of my _____ 'til your _____ are gone.
'Til your _____ are gone.
'Til your _____ are gone.
You can't have any of my _____ 'til your _____ are gone.

PATTERN PLAY

Subject — verb — object
Subject — verb — adverb

PATTERN EXPANSIONS

Negative transformation
Complex construction
Phrase embedding in direct object function
Subordinating conjunction — "until"
Possible adjective embedding in direct object function

OTHER FEATURES

Contraction — "can" and "not"
Auxiliary verb — "can"
Pronoun in nominative case as possessive adjective — "my" and "your"
Prepositional phrase — embedded
Present tense irregular verb form — "have"

SIGHT WORDS

you	of
can	my
not	(un)til
can't	your
have	are
any	

OTHER PLAY FEATURES

Cumulative (winding only)
Invention — noun phrase in direct object function
    embedded adjective(s) in direct object function
    same in subject (agent) function
Silly imagery
Tongue twister
Possible alliteration

OLD MOLLY HARE

Old Molly Hare, what're you doin' there?
Runnin' through the cotton patch as fast as I can tear.

[question repeats]

[answers:]

Sittin' at my fireplace a-smokin' my cigar.

Sittin' on a haystack, a-shootin' at a bear.

Sittin' on a butter plate, a-pickin' out a hair.

PATTERN PLAY

Subject — verb — object
Subject — verb — adverb phrase
Subject — verb

PATTERN EXPANSIONS

Question transformation
Clause embedding as adverbial
Phrase embedding as adverbial
Adjective embedding in object of preposition location

OTHER FEATURES

Present progressive tense — "ing"
Contraction — "what" and "are"
Prepositional phrase — location/manner in which — in final position on
    pattern
Possessive pronoun — "my"
Comparison — simile
Auxiliary verb — "are"
Compound words
Proper noun usage

SIGHT WORDS

old	doing	the	a
what	there	as	my
are	run	fast	at
you	running	I	on
do	through	can	out

OTHER PLAY FEATURES

Invention—declarative—answer to question
        verb and adverbial phrase, embedded clause
        use of embedded adjective or compound word or simile
Rhyming
Chanting
Question/answer
Possible cumulative (winding and unwinding)

JOHNNY PLAYED WITH ONE HAMMER

Johnny played with one hammer, one hammer, one hammer.
Johnny played with one hammer. Then he played with two.

Johnny played with two hammers, two hammers, two hammers.
Johnny played with two hammers. Then he played with three.

[Count three to four, four to five, etc.; then count down]

Johnny played with two hammers, two hammers, two hammers.
Johnny played with two hammers. Then he played with one.

Johnny played with one hammer. Then he played with none.

PATTERN PLAY

Subject—verb.

PATTERN EXPANSIONS

Adjective embedding
Phrase embedding as adverbial

OTHER FEATURES

Regular past tense—"ed"
Regular noun plural and change from singular to plural—"s"
Prepositional phrase—manner in which—in final position on pattern
Proper noun usage

SIGHT WORDS

play(ed)	three
with	four
one	five
then	none
two	

OTHER PLAY FEATURES

Substitutions — proper name in subject function
    noun as object of preposition
    embedded adjective
Counting — up and down
Cumulative (winding and unwinding)

WHEN I FIRST CAME TO THIS LAND

When I first came to this land, I was not a wealthy man.
So I got myself a pig.
I did what I could.
And I called that pig Not So Big.
But the land was sweet and good.
I did what I could.

cow . . . No Milk Now

horse . . . Lame, of course

PATTERN PLAY

Subject — verb
Subject — verb — indirect object — direct object
Subject — linking verb — subjective complement

PATTERN EXPANSION

Embedded clause — direct object function
Negative transformation
Complex construction
Subordinating conjunction — "when"
Adjective embedding — in subjective complement function
Inversion transformation
Compound subjective complement
Phrase embedding as adverb

OTHER FEATURES

Locational preposition — "to"
Irregular verb forms — "did," "got"
Prepositional phrase — locational — in final position on the pattern
Coordinating conjunctions — "so," "and," "but"
Adverb (modal) — "could"

SIGHT WORDS

when	was	myself	but
I	not	did	the
first	a	what	
came	man	could	
to	so	and	
this	got	that	

OTHER PLAY FEATURES

Invention—noun as direct object
                rhyme
Cumulative (winding and unwinding)
Possible prop play
Pattern repetition

WHO'S THAT KNOCKIN' AT MY WINDOW?

Who's that knockin' at my window?
Who's that knockin' at my door?

_____'s knockin' at your window.
_____'s knockin' at your door.

PATTERN PLAY

Subject—verb

PATTERN EXPANSION

Question transformation
Phrase embedding—adverbial
Clause embedding in subjective complement function

OTHER FEATURES

Contractions—"who" and "is" and invented noun (name) and "is"
Present progressive tense—"ing"
Locational preposition—"at"—prepositional phrase—location—final
     position
Possessive pronouns—"your" and "my" in objective case

SIGHT WORDS

who	that	my
is	at	your
who's		

OTHER PLAY FEATURES

Sitting circle game
Invention — naming children — proper noun in subject function
Question/answer
Motion game
Dramatic invention

An enterprising teacher can database the linguistic features of songs and language games to provide a collection of information regarding the language development capabilities of the materials. A cross-referenced system of data would allow retrieval of a list of songs and games according to language features. If a teacher needed a list of oral language activities that would allow students to play with, manipulate, and learn to control the use of objective case pronouns, he or she could call such a list out of the database by using *objective case pronouns* as a code phrase. All the songs and games that contained play with that specific language feature would be filed under that code phrase. (A computer would help.) Careful examination of the songs and games can make their potential for language development available for classroom and other purposes evident.

REFERENCES

Adams, Pam. 1973. *There Was an Old Lady*. New York: Grosset and Dunlap.

Baird, Pancho, and Marie Baird. 1981. *Songs of the Southwest*. Golden, Colo.: Lloyd Shaw Foundation.

Ball, Rouse W. W. N.d. *Fun with String Figures*. New York: Dover.

Bennett, Jill, ed. 1981. *Tiny Tim: Verses for Children*. New York: Delacourte Press.

Best, Dick, and Beth Best, eds. 1955. *Song Fest*. New York: Crown.

Bley, Edgar S. 1982. *The Best Singing Games for Children of All Ages*. New York: Sterling.

Boni, Margaret B., ed. 1952. *The Fireside Book of Favorite American Folk-songs*. New York: Simon and Schuster.

———. 1947. *The Fireside Book of Folksongs*. New York: Simon and Schuster.

Brand, Oscar. 1974. *When I First Came to This Land*. New York: Putnam.

Brown, Marc, ed. 1980. *Finger Rhymes*. New York: Dutton.

Cano, Robin E., ed. 1973. *Game Songs*. Boston: Houghton Mifflin.

Chase, Richard, ed. 1972. *Old Songs and Singing Games*. New York: Dover.

_____. 1967. *Singing Games and Playparty Games*. New York: Dover.

Collins, Fletcher, Jr., ed. 1973. *Alamance Playparty Songs and Singing Games*. Norwood, Pa.: Norwood Editions.

Emberley, Barbara. 1966. *One Wide River to Cross*. Englewood Cliffs, N.J.: Prentice-Hall.

Emberley, Ed, and Barbara Emberley. 1967. *Drummer Hoff*. Englewood Cliffs, N.J.: Prentice-Hall.

Fife, Austin E., and Alta S. Fife. 1969. *Cowboy and Western Songs: A Comprehensive Anthology*. New York: Potter.

Finger, C. J. 1927. *Frontier Ballads*. Garden City, N.Y.: Doubleday.

_____. 1923. *Sailor Chanties and Cowboy Songs*. Girard, Kans.: Haldeman-Julius.

Freschet, Bernice. 1973. *The Ants Go Marching*. New York: Scribner.

Gelineau, R. Phyllis. 1974. *Songs in Action*. New York: McGraw-Hill.

Gibbons, Orlando, ed. 1968. *Cryes of Londontown*. New York: Putnam.

Glass, Paul, and Louis Stinger. 1966. *Songs of the West*. New York: Grosset and Dunlop.

Glazer, Tom. 1980. *Do Your Ears Hang Low? Fifty More Musical Finger-plays*. Garden City, N.Y.: Doubleday.

_____. 1973. *Eye Winker, Tomtinker, Chinchopper: Fifty Musical Finger-plays*. Garden City, N.Y.: Doubleday.

Gomme, Alice B., ed. 1967. *Children's Singing Games*. New York: Dover.

_____. 1898. *The Traditional Games of England, Scotland and Ireland*. London: Davis Nutt.

Gomme, Alice B., and Cecil J. Sharp. 1976. *Children's Singing Games*. New York: Arno Press.

Graham, Carolyn. 1979. *Jazz Chants for Children: Rhythms of American English through Chants, Songs and Poems*. New York: Oxford University Press.

Grayson, Marion F. 1962. *Let's Do Fingerplays*. Washington, D.C.: Robert B. Luce.

Hart, Jane. 1982. *Singing Bee: A Collection of Favorite Children's Songs*. New York: Lothrop, Lee and Shephard Books.

Huizinga, Johan. 1980. *Homo Ludens: A Story of the Play Element in Human Culture*. Boston, Mass.: Routledge and Keagan Paul.

Iverson, William J., and Sam Leaton Sebesta. 1975. *Literature for Thursday's Child*. Chicago: Science Research Associates.

Jackson, George P., and Charles F. Bryan, eds. N.d. *American Folk Music*. Princeton, N.J.: C. C. Birchard.

Jamieson, S. N.d. *Playparties from Anglo-American Tradition*. Washington, D.C.: Office of Museum Programs, Smithsonian Institution.

Jayne, Caroline Furniss. 1962. *String Figures and How to Make Them*. New York: Dover.

John, Timothy, ed. 1978. *The Great Song Book*. Garden City, N.Y.: Doubleday.

Jones, B. N.d. *Children's Games from the Afro-American Tradition*. Washington, D.C.: Office of Museum Programs, Smithsonian Institution.

Keats, Ezra Jack. 1971. *Over in the Meadow*. New York: Four Winds Press.

Knapp, Herbert, and Mary Knapp. 1976. *One Potato, Two Potato: The Secret Education of American Children*. New York: Norton.

Koch, Kenneth. 1970. *Wishes, Lies and Dreams*. New York: Vintage Books/ Chelsea House.

Korn, Michael, and Jo Rainbolt. N.d. *When the Work's All Done This Fall*. Missoula, Mont.: Montana Folklife Project.

Landeck, Beatrice, ed. 1954. *More Songs to Grow On*. New York: William Sloan.

_____. 1950. *Songs to Grow On*. New York: William Sloan.

Langstaff, John, ed. 1982. *The Christmas Revels: Wassail! Wassail! An American Celebration of the Winter Solstice*. Cambridge, Mass.: Revels Records.

_____. 1971. *Gather My Gold Together*. Garden City, N.Y.: Doubleday.

_____. 1969. *Hi! Ho! The Rattlin' Bog and Other Folksongs for Group Singing*. New York: Harcourt, Brace and World.

Larkin, Margaret. 1963. *Singing Cowboy*. New York: Oak Publications.

Lee, Dennis. 1975. *Alligator Pie*. Boston: Houghton Mifflin.

Lingenfelter, Richard E., and Richard A. Dwyer. 1968. *Songs of the American West*. Berkeley: University of California Press.

Lomax, John. 1960. *Folk Songs of North America*. Garden City, N.Y.: Doubleday.

_____. 1947. *Songs of the Cattletrail and Cowcamp*. New York: Duell, Sloan and Pierce.

Lomax, John A., and Allan A. Lomax, eds. 1947. *Folksong USA*. New York: Duell, Sloan and Pierce.

_____. 1941. *Our Singing Country*. New York: Macmillan.

_____. 1938. *Cowboy and Other Frontier Ballads*. New York: Macmillan.

_____. 1934. *American Ballads and Folksongs*. New York: Macmillan.

McMorland, A. N.d. *Children's Games from British Tradition*. Washington, D.C.: Office of Museum Programs, Smithsonian Institution.

Mitchell, Donald, and Robert Biss, eds. 1970. *The Gambit Book of Children's Songs*. Boston: Gambit.

Moore, Ethel, and Chauncey O. Moore. 1964. *Ballads and Folksongs of the Southwest*. Norman: University of Oklahoma Press.

Nancrede, Edith de, and Gertrude Madeira Smith. 1940. *Mother Goose Dances*. Chicago: H. T. Fitzsimmons Co.

Newell, William V. N.d. *Games and Songs of American Children*. New York: Dover.

Ohrlin, Glenn. 1973. *The Hellbound Train: A Cowboy Songbook*. Champaign-Urbana: The University of Illinois Press.

Opie, Iona, and Peter Opie, eds. 1984. *Children's Games in Street and Play-ground*. Oxford, England: Oxford University Press.

Pellowski, Anne. 1984. *The Story Vine*. New York: Macmillan.

Plotz, Helen, ed. 1976. *As I Walked Out One Evening: A Book of Ballads*. New York: Greenwillow Books.

Quackenbush, Robert. 1974. *There'll Be a Hot Time in the Old Town Tonight*. Philadelphia, Pa.: Lippincott.

Richards, Mary Helen. 1974. *The Music Language: Part Two*. Portola Valley, Calif.: Richards Institute of Music Education.

_____. 1973. *The Music Language: Part One*. Portola Valley, Calif.: Richards Institute of Music Education.

Ritchie, Jean. 1952. *The Swapping Song Book*. Fairhaven, N.J.: Oxford University Press.

Sackett, Samuel J., and William R. Scott. 1967. *Cowboys and the Songs They Sang*. N.p.

Sandburg, Carl, ed. 1927. *The American Songbag*. New York: Harcourt, Brace.

Seeger, Pete. 1961. *Pete Seeger Story Songs*. New York: Columbia Record Company, C11668.

Seeger, Ruth Crawford, ed. 1948. *American Folksongs for Children*. Garden City, N.Y.: Doubleday.

Sharp, C. 1932. *English Folksongs from the Southern Appalachians*. New York: Oxford University Press.

Silber, Irwin, and Earl Robinson. 1967. *Songs of the Great American West*. New York: Macmillan.

Silber, Irwin, and Fred Silber. 1973. *The Folksinger's Wordbook*. New York: Oak Publications.

Silverman, Jerry, ed. 1975. *Folk Song Encyclopedia, Volume II*. New York: Chappell Music Company.

_____. 1974. *Folk Song Encyclopedia, Volume I*. New York: Chappell Music Company.

Skolnik, Peter L. 1974. *Jump Rope*. New York: Workman.

Smiley, Marjorie B., Richard Corbin, and John J. Marcatante, eds. 1966. *Stories in Song and Verse.* New York: Macmillan.

Sweeney, Sister Fleurette. 1973. *Experience Games through Music for the Very, Very Young.* Portola Valley, Calif.: Richards Institute of Music Education.

Thorpe, N. Howard "Jack," Austin Fife, and Alta Fife, eds. 1966. *Songs of the Cowboys.* New York: Gardner.

Tinsley, Jim Bob. 1981. *He Was Singin' This Song: A Collection of Forty-eight Traditional Songs of the American Cowboy.* Orlando: University Presses of Florida.

Tyson, Ian, and Sylvia Fricker, eds. N.d. *Ian and Sylvia: Greatest Hits.* New York: Vanguard Recording Society, VSD 5/6.

Vinton, I. 1970. *The Folkways Omnibus of Children's Games.* Harrisburg, Pa.: Stackpole Books.

Warran, Margaret. 1973. *Experience Games through Music for the Very Young.* Portola Valley, Calif.: Richards Institute of Music Education.

Watson, Doc, ed. N.d. *Doc Watson.* New York: Vanguard Recording Society, VSD 79152.

Watson, Doc, and Merle Watson, eds. N.d. *Ballads from Deep Gap.* New York: Vanguard Recording Society, VSD 6576.

Weavers, The, eds. 1960. *The Weavers Songbook.* New York: Harper and Bros.

Wells, Evelyn K., ed. 1950. *The Ballad Tree.* New York: Ronald Press.

White, John I. 1975. *Git along Little Dogies: Songs and Songmakers of the American West.* Champaign-Urbana: University of Illinois Press.

Wildsmith, Brian. 1972. *The Twelve Days of Christmas.* New York: Watts.

Winn, Marie, ed. 1974. *The Fireside Book of Fun and Game Songs.* New York: Simon and Schuster.

Yolen, Jane, ed. 1972. *The Fireside Songbook of Birds and Beasts.* New York: Simon and Schuster.

Zemach, Harve. 1969. *The Judge.* New York: Farrar, Straus and Giroux.

_____. 1966. *Mommy Buy Me a China Doll.* Chicago: Follett.

ADDITIONAL RESOURCES

Abisch, Roz. 1969. *'Twas in the Moon of Wintertime*. Englewood Cliffs, N.J.: Prentice-Hall.

Aliki, ed. *Hush Little Baby: A Folk Lullaby*. Englewood Cliffs, N.J.: Prentice-Hall.

Botkin, B.A. 1951. *A Treasury of American Folklore*. New York: Crown.

_____. 1937. *The American Playparty Song, with a Collection of Oklahoma Texts and Tunes*. Omaha: University of Nebraska.

Brunvand, Jan Harold. 1978. *The Study of American Folklore*. New York: Norton.

Bryan, Ashley. 1974. *Walk together Children — Black American Spirituals*. New York: Atheneum.

Cramer, Carl, ed. 1942. *America Sings*. New York: Knopf.

Crane, Walter. N.d. *The Baby's Bouquet: A Fresh Bunch of Old Rhymes and Tunes*. London: Frederick Warne and Co.

_____. N.d. *The Baby's Opera: A Book of Old Rhymes with New Dresses*. London: Frederick Warne and Co.

Diendorfer, Robert G. 1980. *America's 101 Most High-Falutin', Big Talkin', Knee Slappin' Gollywhoppers and Tall Tales: The Best of the Burlington Liar's Club*. New York: Workman.

Emrich, Duncan. 1972. *The Hodgepodge Book*. New York: Four Winds Press.

Flint Board of Education. 1981. *Ring-a-Ring-O'-Roses*. Flint, Mich.: The Flint Public Library.

Fluegelman, Andrew, ed. 1976. *The New Games Book*. Garden City, N.Y.: Doubleday.

Glazer, Tom. 1982. *On Top of Spaghetti*. Garden City, N.Y.: Doubleday.

Harrop, Beatrice. 1983. *Sing Hey Diddle Diddle: 66 Nursery Rhymes with Their Traditional Tunes*. London: A. C. Black.

Hindman, Darwin A. N.d. *1800 Riddles, Enigmas and Conundrums*. New York: Dover.

Johns, Malcolm, ed. 1980. *Jumbo: The Children's Book. The Best of Children's Music*. Miami Beach, Fla.: Hansen House.

Karasz, Ilonka, ed. 1949. *The Twelve Days of Christmas*. New York: Harper and Brothers.

Langstaff, John, ed. 1978. *The Christmas Revels*. Revels Records.

_____. 1978. *Hot Cross Buns and Other Street Cries*. New York: Atheneum.

_____. 1974. *Oh! A-Hunting We Will Go*. New York: Atheneum.

_____. 1972. *The Golden Vanity*. New York: Harcourt Brace Jovanovich.

_____. 1972. *Soldier, Soldier, Won't You Marry Me?* Garden City, N.Y.: Doubleday.

Langstaff, John, and Nancy Langstaff, eds. 1970. *Jim along Josie*. New York: Harcourt, Brace and World.

Opie, Iona, and Peter Opie, eds. 1951. *The Oxford Dictionary of Nursery Rhymes*. Oxford, England: Oxford at the Clarendon Press.

Parker, Robert Andrew. 1978. *Sweet Betsy from Pike, a Song from the Gold Rush Days*. New York: Viking Press.

Poulsson, Emilie. N.d. *Finger Plays for Nursery and Kindergarten*. New York: Dover.

Prieto, Mariana. 1973. *Play It in Spanish: Spanish Games and Folksongs for Children*. New York: John Day.

Quackenbush, Robert. 1976. *Pop! Goes the Weasel and Yankee Doodle*. Philadelphia, Pa.: Lippincott.

_____. 1975. *Skip to My Lou*. Philadelphia, Pa.: Lippincott.

Schackberg, Richard. 1965. *Yankee Doodle*. Englewood Cliffs, N.J.: Prentice-Hall.

Schwartz, Alvin, ed. 1979. *Chin Music, Tall Talk and Other Talk*. Philadelphia, Pa.: Lippincott.

_____. 1975. *Whoppers, Tall Tales and Other Lies*. Philadelphia, Pa.: Lippincott.

Society of Brothers, eds. 1968. *Sing through the Day: Ninety Songs for Younger Children*. Rifton, N.Y.: The Plough Publishing House.

Vogel, Malvina G., ed. 1978. *The Big Book of Jokes and Riddles*. New York: Playmore.

Wessells, Katherine Tyler. 1945. *The Golden Songbook*. New York: Simon and Schuster.

Winn, Marie, ed. 1970. *What Shall We Do and Allee Galloo! — Play Songs and Singing Games for Young Children*. New York: Harper and Row. .

Wylder, Robert C. 1947. *A Comparative Analysis of Some Montana Folksongs*. Master's thesis, University of Montana.

Yolen, Jane, ed. 1977. *Rounds about Rounds about Rounds*. New York: Watts.

7

Storytelling at Home and School

*Storytelling is a kind of music with
the storyteller as the instrument.*
> (Massachusetts storyteller
> Jay O'Callahan)

How can storytelling be used in the home?

How does storytelling fit into the K-12 curricula?

What are some storytelling activities that can be used
in the classroom?

STORYTELLING AT HOME

From the moment a baby is born, there are golden opportunities for storytelling. Infants are ready listeners to lullabies and nursery rhymes. They need to hear the melodies of our voices in song and chant as well as conversation. This period lays the foundation for all complex language development.

Parents need to build a climate of words, to take the child places and then talk about what he or she has seen, heard, smelled, tasted, and touched. The basis of storytelling is good talk. Wolkstein's (1977) *The Visit* is the simple story of an ant going for a visit and what it sees and does.

Children should hear their parents tell stories often. Reading books is important but quite different from storytelling. The parent is a model as well as the child's first teacher.

The establishment of story pattern through parental telling will serve as a guide for youngsters to make up their own stories. For example:

1. The child is dirty (problem).
2. The child tries three times to get a bath (no water, no soap, got the bath).
3. The warm water makes him or her so drowsy that he or she falls asleep.
4. The child's mother dries him or her with a soft towel and puts him or her to bed (and they all live happily ever after).

Everyday stories can be invented about things the youngster does using this pattern. Once children get the understanding of it, they have a useful framework for their own stories.

Young children enjoy hearing stories made up for them and about them and about things they see and do. A classic story, *Carrot Seed* (Krauss 1945), is a wonderful ego-building story for a small child; it is the story of a youngster who finds a seed and, despite the advice of everybody in his family, plants it, waters it, weeds it, and finally harvests it.

One storyteller's children were particularly fond of *Carrot Seed*, and today her two-and-one-half-year-old grandson, no doubt influenced by his father's interests, his own story of how he and his dad planted a garden, digging the soil, adding fertilizer, scratching rows, planting the seeds, covering them, and watering the garden. Stories and storytelling are already a part of his everyday life.

One evening a week devoted to storytelling can help reacquaint family members with each other. Involvement of each family member is important. However, if such extended time is not possible, a natural time for storytelling is just before bed. Telling a story to youngsters helps punctuate the day as well as calm them down for sleep. No television program can substitute for a caring adult personally sharing storytime with a youngster.

The following article by Jim Sanderson, part of his syndicated column "The Liberated Male," appeared in the *Denver Post* on July 21, 1984.

Jim Sanderson The Liberated Male

Stories for Kids

Magic in the telling

QUALITY TIME, they call it. All too often it turns out to be Guilt-and-Frustration Time. You break your back to get home from a high-pressure job to spend a few precious hours with your kids, but — for a hundred different reasons — the emotional connection just isn't made.

You're there, and so are they, but somehow it doesn't mean anything. You can't get in touch with them that fast.

I remember one terrible year when I'd just started a business of my own and felt a little panicky that I wasn't going to make it. Although I had three little kids under 7, I came and went in the house like a ghost — until I realized that I needed them as much as they needed me.

Like many working parents today, I tried to make something out of the bedtime hour, laughing and tickling and roughhousing a little before I tucked them in to read a story.

But reading some book didn't really help us to connect, I decided. A primitive campfire enchantment remains in *telling* the story: a magic that belongs to a chief, or a wizard, or a wise and all-knowing father. Especially when young heads are snugly bedded in a quiet, half-dark room.

One night in desperation I invented a brainy black cat named Tomkins, who just happened to have the same names as my kids. As they went to bed the kids let him out to have an adventure.

I had no idea of a plot. I was vamping as I told how Tomkins explored a new house going up in our block. He jumped over heating pipes and walked along roof beams in a location the kids could visualize. Then, since this started out as an animal saga, I decided that another animal should be in trouble.

So in the basement of the house Tomkins found a big animal who had escaped from the zoo. "What kind of animal?" I wondered aloud.

"A tiger," my youngest shouted. There he was cowering, swishing his striped tail and afraid to come out. What was his problem? I waited, beginning to get the idea that if you let them, the kids sometimes will write the story for you, just the way they want it.

My son knew: The tiger was lost and afraid of scaring people if he kept trying to get back to the zoo. Well, Tomkins had to give this a good think. So did old Dad — where was this story going?

Stalling for time, I threw in a bunch of sound effects. The tiger roared until Tomkins gave him a box on the ear. Then he whimpered. Tomkins' tail went s-w-i-s-h, s-w-i-s-h, and his mind, in deep thought, went b-u-z-z/b-l-o-o-p, b-u-z-z/b-l-o-o-p.

The kids loved it, and I checked the bedroom door to see if my wife was listening. Sometimes it ain't easy for a grown man to get down to making sounds that tickle a 5-year-old.

Anyway, because he was the world's smartest cat, Tomkins found a can of black paint to cover the tiger's fearsome stripes, and put him in a taxi back to the zoo. (My oldest daughter had just had her first cab ride home from a visit to the dentist.)

It seems rather simple-minded as I summarize it, but consider the audience. I became an instant legend on our street, and had to retell that story for the next six nights, because we had all kinds of neighbor kids sleeping over.

TV teaches that once you've got a formula, stick with it. Tomkins solved the problems of many animals: a honey bear with a sweet tooth who couldn't stand bee stings, a kangaroo tangled in a sheet who scared adults witless as a shroud-covered apparition bounding 30 feet at a hop, and a depressed giraffe who recovered his self-esteem when, under Tomkins' guidance, he stretched his long neck up to a burning house so some children could slide down safely. Etc.

Tomkins pretty much carried me through that year until I could become a normal father. If any of you harassed working parents want to borrow him, you're welcome. It looks like it will be a while yet before I become a grandfather.

Besides bedtime, another natural time for family storytelling is while traveling in the car. One family developed ongoing, original stories while on long vacation trips about a character named Dopey Duck — what adventures he would have on the trip and what would happen to him when he got to their destination. Everyone had a turn at creating another episode in Dopey Duck's saga. These youngsters, now grown up, have been overheard sharing fantastic stories of Dopey Duck with their own children. A tradition has been developed.

Sometimes adults chuckle when they observe children with their precious possessions, but we should be aware of how important they are to children. Once four adults gathered outside the bedroom door of a friend's four-year-old son and listened as he told his beloved towel everything that had happened that day. The adults stifled giggles as they eavesdropped on the boy's innermost thoughts. It wasn't until one of the adults had a son of her own who told his stories to his blanket, and yet another son who crawled into the dog's house and confided in the dog, that she realized how important these outlets are to youngsters.

A favorite stuffed animal, imaginary friend, or other precious object can become central elements of stories woven by children and adults.

A set of experiences with a homemade hand puppet exposed one storyteller who was a first-grade teacher to some of the possibilities for involvement with objects.

The teacher had made a large papier-mâché Bassett hound head with long velvet ears and had attached white flannel fabric to cover her arm. She intended to use the puppet to tell stories about her own Bassett hound at home. The class voted to name the puppet Boo-Boo. Boo-Boo told the children stories, left notes in their desks and on the chalkboard, and became a fixture in the classroom. One day the class "bully" and the class "nice kid" had a big fight in the schoolyard after lunch. The gym teacher sent the whole class back to the classroom. After the two offenders had given their garbled versions of what had happened, the "bully" asked the teacher to get Boo-Boo out, and the boys told the dog a complex story of how each had been hurt by the other. They worked their problems out themselves as they expressed their feelings to Boo-Boo, who listened carefully but said not a word.

THE ORAL LITERATURE IN THE CURRICULUM

WHY SHOULD ORAL LITERATURE BE INCLUDED IN THE CURRICULUM?

In our electronic-media age, it is easy to forget that storytelling gives meaning to our lives, incorporating as it does the feelings and doings of real people. Stories bring us closer to the human heart and its symbolic conditions. The mental imagery storytelling evokes creates a theater of the mind. The listener must add color to the scenes and characters sketched by the storyteller.

Some further advantages of storytelling (besides simply aiding academic skill development) are listed below.

- It provides a much-needed opportunity for adults and students of all ages to interact on a very personal level.
- It develops in the student storyteller an awareness of and sensitivity to the thoughts and feelings of the listeners.
- It stimulates imagination and visualization.
- It helps develop poise in the student storyteller.
- It improves discrimination in choice of books and stories and fosters increased knowledge of literature.

"ESSENTIALS OF ENGLISH" AND ITS IMPLICATIONS FOR STORYTELLING

Essentials of English (National Council of Teachers of English 1982) is a document intended to provoke reflection and dialogue. Its stated purpose is "to identify the ways in which the study of English contributes to the knowledge, understanding, and skills of those who will make up the society of the future." The sections on literature, speaking, listening, reading, writing, and creative thinking have important implications for storytelling in the schools.

Literature

Through their study and enjoyment of literature, students should

- realize the importance of literature as a mirror of human experiences, reflecting human motives, conflicts, and values
- be able to identify with fictional characters in human situations as a means of relating to others; gain insights from involvement with literature
- become aware of important writers representing diverse backgrounds and traditions in literature
- become familiar with masterpieces of literature, both past and present
- develop effective ways of talking and writing about varied forms of literature
- experience literature as a way to appreciate the rhythms and beauty of the language
- develop habits of reading that carry over into adult life

Certainly, storytelling is a powerful technique to realize the importance of literature as a mirror of human experience, reflecting human motives, conflicts, and values. As individuals tell stories, they can convey with immediacy the commonalities of lessons taught in them.

Folktales provide models for what behavior is rewarded (after all, modest, well-behaved Cinderella did win the prince) and what behavior is punished (Cinderella's selfish stepsisters got their just deserts). In fact, you might say folktales are recipes for studying human motives, conflicts, and values. For further convincing, read Bettelheim's (1976) *The Uses of Enchantment*.

As the teller interprets each story character, he or she gives insights into human relationships and character development. How can the storyteller best indicate to listeners the wicked witch? the heroine? the hero? the powerless victim? What character traits, behaviors, and mannerisms are appropriate to each? It is the challenge of the teller to help the listener visualize each of the characters in the story. To do this requires a personal understanding of each character.

Obviously storytelling is one of the best ways to appreciate the rhythm and beauty of the language. As children chant the refrain, "hundreds of cats, thousands of cats, millions and billions and trillions of cats" with the storyteller (Gag 1928), they are sharing a natural multisensory experience with rhythm in language. They are hearing it as they are saying it. This is also a satisfying way to be playful with concepts of huge numbers. What would it be like to see "hundreds of cats, thousands of cats, millions and billions and trillions of cats?" Using words and gestures, how can the storyteller translate the vastness of that many cats?

At the more advanced levels of the elementary grades, students can listen for figurative language in stories. They can be encouraged to listen for and identify similes, metaphors, alliteration, personification, and hyperbole. As they tell their own stories they can be guided to add interesting figures of speech. (One youngster telling a story changed the word *manure* to *sophisticated hay*.)

The maturing of literary imagination is encouraged in homes and schools where parents and teachers tell stories. Especially if these adult models also invent new stories, children will see this as an approved activity and will respond to the fantasy by actively engaging in it themselves.

Speaking

Students should learn

- to speak clearly and expressively about their ideas and concerns
- to adapt words and strategies according to varying situations and audiences, from one-to-one conversations for formal, large-group settings
- to participate productively and harmoniously in both small and large groups
- to present arguments in orderly and convincing ways
- to interpret and assess various kinds of communication, including intonation, pause, gesture, and body language, that accompany speaking

Learning takes place best when there is a real purpose involved. Storytelling can help students practice speaking clearly and expressively about their ideas and concerns. How can a storyteller convince the listeners that the little boy in "Abiyoyo" (Seeger 1964) is petrified of the monster and yet confident enough to face him down and save his town and all the people in it? How many different ways can students demonstrate this?

There is no better way to interpret and assess the various kinds of communication, including intonation, pause, gesture, and body language, than in storytelling. These features of language are to the storyteller what hammer and nails are to the carpenter.

Listening

A good storyteller needs the support of a good listener; well-developed listening skills are crucial. *Essentials of English* points out what students should learn as listeners.

Students should

- learn that listening with understanding depends on determining a speaker's purpose

- learn to attend to detail and relate it to the over-all purpose of the communication

- learn to evaluate the messages and effects of mass communication

Students should have the opportunity to hear many stories and many tellers of stories. In this way they can develop discrimination and the ability to evaluate strengths and weaknesses of a variety of storytelling styles and story genres.

Each student needs to evaluate his or her own effectiveness as a listener. To draw attention to the role of the listener, one student may be assigned to observe and record listener reactions as another student tells a story. Such reactions might include verbal comments, facial expressions, attention, or body movements. These observations could be shared with the storyteller and class. It is just as difficult to be an efficient listener as it is to be an effective storyteller. It requires concentration and cooperation. Just because we do so much listening each day does not necessarily mean that we are proficient at it.

Reading

Storytelling contributes to reading and writing development. To again refer to *Essentials of English*:

Students should

- recognize that reading functions in their lives as a pleasurable activity as well as a means of acquiring knowledge

- learn from the very beginning to approach reading as a search for meaning

- develop the necessary reading skills to comprehend material appearing in a variety of forms

- learn to read accurately and make valid inferences

- learn to judge literature critically on the basis of personal response and literary quality

Writing

Students should

- learn to write clearly and honestly

- recognize that writing is a way to learn and develop personally as well as a way to communicate with others

- learn ways to generate ideas for writing, to select and arrange them, to find appropriate modes for expressing them, and to evaluate and revise what they have written

- learn to adapt expression to various audiences

- learn the techniques of writing for appealing to others and persuading them

- develop their talents for creative and imaginative expression

- recognize that precision in punctuation, capitalization, spelling, and other elements of manuscript form is a part of the total effectiveness of writing

As students search print material for stories to develop for storytelling, they are certainly "learning to judge literature critically on the basis of personal response and literary quality." They are also learning to compare and contrast stories. Probably the most important decision of the storyteller is to pick a story he or she likes. If the teller does not like the story, neither will the audience. Tellers unconsciously communicate their enthusiasm about each story they tell; besides that, why should anyone learn a story they dislike? Each subsequent telling of the story will compound the teller's lack of interest with it, and listeners will sense the negative attitude.

Another step, after hearing stories, telling stories, and reading stories, is for students to write their own. This involves learning "ways to generate ideas for writing, to select and arrange them, to find appropriate modes for expressing them, and to evaluate and revise what they have written." Then, the child must transform his or her written story into an oral experience.

Creative Thinking

Aside from these language arts skills, students are learning to think creatively as they engage in storytelling.

Students should learn

- that originality derives from the uniqueness of the individual's perception, not necessarily from an innate talent

- that inventiveness involves seeing new relationships

- that creative thinking derives from their ability not only to look, but to see; not only to hear, but to listen; not only to imitate, but to innovate; not only to observe, but to experience the excitement of fresh perception

These creative thinking skills are integral to all aspects of storytelling. As tellers and listeners share the storytelling experience, they exemplify the creative thinking abilities. Obviously, "that creative thinking derives from their ability not only to look, but to see; not only to hear, but to listen; not only to imitate, but to innovate; not only to observe, but to experience the excitement of fresh perception" speaks directly to what storytelling does so naturally.

THE PROCESS OF STORYTELLING

When dealing with storytelling in the classroom it is necessary to establish the distinction between process and product. Process involves the whole procedure of hearing or reading stories, appreciating them, selecting a story to try out, developing and refining the telling of it, and acquiring confidence in both the story and one's style of telling it. Product is the finished telling and implies evaluation. We evaluate written stories, composed music, art, and storytelling. We need to be mainly concerned with the process of storytelling, for that is where the learning is internalized and personalized. The process of storytelling is more important in educational situations than the product. Any evaluation by the teller or listener should be done for self-improvement.

A word of caution is necessary here. Storytelling should not be undertaken with reading and writing improvement as its primary purpose. Would you use the Mona Lisa to teach facial expression primarily? Or Beethoven's Fifth to teach pitch primarily? Storytelling is an art, and the whole is much more than the sum of its parts.

Children naturally tell stories, beginning stories, as they explain to parents how they scraped their knee or lost their first tooth. Story is the conventional way to share information. As children's linguistic abilities grow (because of more concrete experiences with things and more names or labels applied to things with understanding), their abilities to deal with abstractions expand. They learn to generalize information. *Daddy* becomes a specific person; *men* becomes a category of specific people. They learn to distinguish between fact and fantasy.

With literary experience children learn there are patterns for stories; they learn the variety of stories. Folktales are wonderful starting material. Children can identify cumulative stories (maybe not by name but certainly by comparing and contrasting them with other cumulative stories), talking beast tales, droll or humorous tales, realistic tales, religious tales, romance, and tales of magic.

Cumulative stories enable youngsters to recognize the adding-on feature. Such stories include "The Old Woman and Her Pig" (Jacobs 1892), "The Fat Cat" (Kent 1971), "The House That Jack Built" (Frasconi 1958), and ballads such as "When I First Came to This Land" (Brand 1974), and "The Green Grass Grows All Around" (Hoffmann 1968). Memory is exercised in these stories as each additional phrase is added.

Talking beast tales are stories in which the characters are really us in furs or feathers. Droll and humorous tales help youngsters appreciate humor. Then the child's experiences with realistic tales, religious tales, romance, and tales of magic give them a wide range of story types to draw on. Children need to hear these stories told and read, and then they will be ready to tell and read them themselves.

Many high school students are resistant when they hear the word *story-telling*—it connotes something childish to them. An easy entree to storytelling for this age group is to use the urban legends and folktales. *The Vanishing Hitchhiker* (Brunvand 1981) is full of modern youthful folklore. Among the stories are the well-known "The Boyfriend's Death," "The Death Car," "The Philanderer's Porsche," "The Vanishing Hitchhiker," "The Hook," "The Alligators in the Sewers," "The Solid Cement Cadillac," "Ghost Truckers," and "The Ghost Airliner." Once you invite high school students to share stories they know, there is usually a constant flow of stories, and generally someone will state emphatically that they know exactly where that happened or who it happened to.

Storytelling is play in which the teller and listener agree to participate together. As the storyteller creates mental images, sounds, and characters and uses refrains, the play continues. Riddles and humorous stories are many times the seeds for word play, as are alliteration, repetition, and figurative language. This of course requires sophistication and familiarity with linguistic elements for full meaning, as well as self-confidence.

Teachers and students should realize that it is natural to be nervous before telling a story. Some of the most famous storytellers feel nervous before they perform, as the following remarks illustrate (Graber 1984).

"The nervousness seems to differ. Sometimes it will be a very quiet kind of nervousness. Sometimes, if the setting, the environment, and the people are all totally unknown, I feel more nervous. But sometimes it's just the hope that the show goes well." (Jay O'Callahan, Marshfield, Massachusetts)

"By and large, I am more confident with children than adults. I've had more experience with them, for one thing. Also, my material for adults is more personal so I'm more nervous." (Pat Spaulding, Portsmouth, New Hampshire)

"You do develop a certain confidence. I'm very comfortable working with children now, and rarely get that nervous. I feel comfortable working in tandem, as part of West of the Moon; by myself I get more nervous and when I'm performing for adults, especially new or original material, I tend to be nervous." (Ellen Block, West of the Moon Storytellers, Somerville, Massachusetts)

"I don't regard the nervousness as something that's necessarily bad. It's a natural thing. It helps people be on their toes." (Tim van Egmond, Windsor, Vermont)

Students should also be aware that even the most experienced storytellers need to prepare for each telling. Each has his or her own favorite way to warm up (Graber 1984):

"What I do is a lot of singing exercises that are ritual. It is the doing of the same thing every time that relaxes me. I use some scenes in my story where I have to stretch my voice a lot—a very loud part, or a very soft part—and as part of the singing I do some stretching exercises. It relaxes my body, and gives me something physical to do. After the singing exercises, it depends a lot on how I feel. Sometimes I'll pace, and sometimes I'll just be quiet." (Jay O'Callahan)

"I try to take a little quiet time, sit down, breathe deeply, and concentrate on relaxing. I really attune myself to the people in the audience, see them as friends, and think of the performance as an opportunity to be of help, a chance to really give them some sort of gift." (Tim van Egmond)

"Beginning with a ritualized introduction helps me to center. I'll start with my most solid material—that builds my confidence. Then after I've warmed up with something familiar, I'll go on to other material. I definitely do some deep breathing, sometimes stretching. Some people I know have to be alone and center themselves; since Laura and I perform together, we don't isolate ourselves before a performance. On our way there, we naturally go through things and talk to each other." (Ellen Block)

"I tend to do physical stuff to warm up. I find a corner somewhere away and do a lot of body movement and shake myself out a little. I try to concentrate specifically on that show or those stories, to bring myself into the present and get all the distractions out. If I'm confident of the material and if the audience begins to respond, I generally don't stay nervous. Sometimes in a new situation, I just kind of get set and put my mind set on experiment. I try to remember that the world is not dependent on this one concert, and go with the experiment clause." (Pat Spaulding)

CLASSROOM ACTIVITIES

The following suggested storytelling activities are teaching tools for all curriculum areas. These ideas are appropriate for all levels—K-12+. Storytelling is alive with opportunities for the use of creativity and imagination. Try to use the delightful idea of storytelling to make your classroom a more interesting and challenging place to learn. (For additional activities to use in the classroom, see appendix A.)

Warm-ups

It is helpful to develop storytelling warm-up activities for use before tellings. There are many useful possibilities.

- Play a twenty-questions game. Pin a tag on each student's back, each tag with one of the following names on it:

Snoopy	Cinderella	King Kong
Mickey Mouse	Dracula	Snow White
Wizard of Oz	Pinocchio	Frankenstein
Donald Duck	Grumpy	Sleeping Beauty
Tin Woodsman	Hansel	Superman

Have the students find out what name is pinned on their backs by asking questions of the others.

- Have the group imitate bacon sizzling in the pan. How would it move?

- Put the names of popular books on slips of paper. Divide the group into two teams and have each team take turns drawing a slip from a hat. The team then is to act out in charades clues for the title of their book. The other team tries to guess the title.

- Have the students act out the actions of a pan of popping corn as it heats and starts to pop.

- Have the students imitate an egg being cracked.

- Have the students try to show an ice cube melting. How many different dramatizations can the students develop?

- Have one person begin telling a story. Ring a bell at a random moment and have another person continue that story. Continue on around the group until the story is completed or returns to you. A long piece of heavy string with knots in it at intervals can be rolled into a ball and passed around, with each person adding to the story as he or she unwinds the ball and comes to a knot in the string.

- Hold readers theatre performances and choral readings.

- Divide the students into pairs. One person chooses a phrase or an object and the other must create a story about the phrase or thing.

- Pick one of the Jack tales. (Chase 1943) and assign different people to pantomime different actions. How would Jack walk down a dusty road with two loaves of bread under his arms? How would Jack capture turkeys in his bag? How would Jack eat his supper? Have the remaining students guess what actions the pantomimist is performing.

Developing Story Ideas*

- Have the students prepare unusual plot or situation, character, problem, and setting ideas. Write them on slips of paper and place them in boxes marked Plot or Situation, Character, Problem, Setting. Have the students take turns drawing an idea from each box and developing a spontaneous story using the selected ideas.

- Have the students find any newspaper article that interests them and use it as the basis for creating a story.

- Have the students read several folktales and choose one to tell from the point of view of one of the characters. For example, how would "The Three Pigs" sound as told by the wolf?

- Have the students create their own cumulative story to tell or sing.

- Make a Möbius strip, which is a surface with only one side, formed by giving a half twist to a narrow, rectangular strip of paper and then pasting its two ends together. Such a Möbius band is a perfect example of the form of continuous stories. Have the students write stories that loop back from the end to the beginning. As an example of a continuous poem/story, read Edna St. Vincent Millay's poem "Renascence." It begins,

---

*(For additional story idea activities, see chapter 5.)

"All I could see from where I stood,
Was three long mountains and a wood.
I turned and looked another way
And saw three islands in a bay."

and ends with

"Back to where I started from,
And all I saw from where I stood
Was three long mountains and a wood."

- Organize a liar's contest. (Have the students read "The Liar's Contest" in Courlander and Prempeh 1957 in preparation.) Assemble a panel of three judges (to avoid tie votes). Develop as many categories of winning stories as possible aside from the overall blue ribbon winner. Such categories might include silliest, most unique, saddest, most surprising, shortest, longest, etc.

  Be prepared with a story of your own. You might also want to provide liar's labels for the students to wear as badges. On a big chart (chalkboard, overhead, etc.) place two columns of words, for example,

Adjectives	Nouns
bad	bellybender
double	blanket stretcher
hard	gallyflopper
outlandish	liar
outrageous	sidebuster
triple	tonguewagger
severe	whopper
	windie

  Instruct the students to combine an adjective and a noun to make individual badges. The first part of the contest might be to see who can come up with the most atrocious label.

- Investigate myths as the encyclopedias of scientific information of preliterate societies. Classify and organize these stories into topics—creation, technology, morals, explanations of natural phenomena, etc. Have the students develop their own categories. Then have them write an original explanation of a topic (for example, how might a preliterate society member explain the geysers in Yellowstone Park?) and tell their stories to classmates—or make arrangements for the students to try out their stories with some elementary school children.

- Choose a town in your state that you want to know more about. What facts and legends concerning this town can you and the students find? How did the town get its name? Develop these findings into an original story about the town and its first citizens. This project then could be developed into a storytelling contest to choose whose story is the most original and intriguing.

- Have students collect stories from older family members. Put transcriptions of these stories into a booklet for family members. The booklets could be mailed to other relatives who live out of state, with the request that they return a tape of family stories they remember.

- Have the students construct a book using their own collection of stories they have told and written.

- Have students keep a journal of important events in their lives for a month. How could these events be woven into a story that would be a personal history for someone hearing it fifty years from now?

- Have students, working in pairs, share any information or stories they know about the last name of each—how it came to be, what it means, where it came from, etc. Interesting stories can be shared with the whole group.

- Have students, working in pairs, share stories about some natural phenomena they have experienced—earthquakes, blizzards, floods, tornadoes, windstorms, and lightning, as well as gentle events like rainbows. Ask them to share some of these stories with the whole group. It is fun to watch a storytelling partner tell his or her partner's story.

- A storytelling class at Lesley College in Cambridge, Massachusetts, went to the Boston city zoo for its final project. The instructor had made previous arrangements with the zoo curator as to what stories each student would tell, and the curator prepared a follow-up. For instance, after a student told a story about a dragon, the curator brought in a live iguana to talk about. The habits, diet, and habitat of the creature were discussed. In this manner, each story, fanciful or not, had a real-life nature experience attached.

Learning Storytelling Techniques

- Invite a storyteller to your class. Have him or her tell some stories and explain the process of developing a story. Do not forget to include old-timers with good stories among your guests.

- Have the students listen to a storyteller with special attention to how he or she deals with characterization, mood, atmosphere, setting, and style.

- In family living classes, introduce storytelling (one African god decreed no couple could have children until each of them knew at least 100 stories). Have the students practice some stories with youngsters of different ages. (This exercise will also help them in babysitting.)

- Demonstrations involving the audience actively in the story are effective teaching techniques. If you are telling a story about a dragon, you might pass around a large pearl to the listeners so they can experience the pearl every grandfather dragon has at his throat. Children can be led to be part of stories as they repeat refrains ("hundreds of cats, thousands of cats, millions and billions and trillions of cats") and chants. They can also contribute sound effects. These might include rubbing their hands to create the sounds of grass, slapping their hands on their knees for footsteps, blowing like the wind, or squeaking like a mouse. They also could physically act out the actions of characters as the story progresses. A beginning lesson for practicing this might be to write a short, action-packed story and designate sounds to be made when the particular character or object is named in the story. (Melodramas use this device effectively, with boos and hisses for the villains and sighs and cheers for the heroine and hero contributed by the audience.) The class or group could write their own story and invent the sound effects to go with it. The object or character and the related sound effect could be written on cards and taped to the wall or chalkboard to remind the students what to do (see below).

An example of such a story follows.

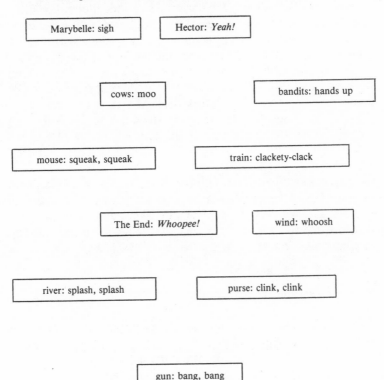

```
┌─────────────────────────┐   ┌─────────────────────────┐
│   Marybelle: sigh       │   │   Hector: Yeah!         │
└─────────────────────────┘   └─────────────────────────┘

      ┌──────────────┐              ┌──────────────────────┐
      │  cows: moo   │              │  bandits: hands up   │
      └──────────────┘              └──────────────────────┘

 ┌──────────────────────────┐   ┌──────────────────────────┐
 │  mouse: squeak, squeak   │   │  train: clackety-clack   │
 └──────────────────────────┘   └──────────────────────────┘

    ┌────────────────────────┐    ┌────────────────────┐
    │  The End: Whoopee!     │    │  wind: whoosh      │
    └────────────────────────┘    └────────────────────┘

 ┌──────────────────────────┐   ┌──────────────────────────┐
 │  river: splash, splash   │   │  purse: clink, clink     │
 └──────────────────────────┘   └──────────────────────────┘


          ┌──────────────────────┐
          │  gun: bang, bang     │
          └──────────────────────┘
```

MARYBELLE was traveling out west to marry her childhood sweetheart, HECTOR. HECTOR had promised his delicate MARYBELLE that she would live in luxury and charm. The TRAIN was crossing the dry prairie and it was hot. MARYBELLE looked out the windows and saw COWS munching on the grasses. Suddenly the TRAIN came to a screeching halt and MARYBELLE heard BANDITS ordering everyone off the TRAIN. When they saw beautiful MARYBELLE, the BANDITS grabbed her PURSE and told her they planned to kidnap her for ransom, for she must be very rich. They threw her PURSE into their burlap bag. When the TRAIN started again with a clang, clang, MARYBELLE saw across the tracks a whole field of COWS. She snatched the GUN from one of the BANDITS and ran down to the RIVER and hid behind a large tree. The WIND was howling with an impending storm and the BANDITS were searching for her. They wanted to get her before it got dark. You could hear the TRAIN in the distance along with the WIND, COWS, and the water flowing in the RIVER. MARYBELLE raised the GUN in fright when a MOUSE scurried out of a hole in the ground by the tree. But then she remembered the BANDITS and spared the MOUSE. Now it was nightfall, and the WIND became so strong it blew her into the RIVER, where she remembered the cardinal rule, "Feet first" and rode the waves down the RIVER that way until she rounded a bend, heard the TRAIN coming, jumped out of the RIVER, ran over to the TRAIN, stood in the tracks facing the oncoming TRAIN as the WIND blew, the RIVER flowed, and more COWS munched peacefully in a nearby field. MARYBELLE stopped the TRAIN, explained her plight, gave the GUN to the Wells Fargo agent, and traveled the rest of the way on the TRAIN to meet HECTOR and to live a life full of luxury and comfort. THE END.

As you read (or better yet, tell) the story, after each of the sound effects has been used twice, remove the cards so the audience can be weaned from the visual clues. This will help develop listening skills, as the students will have to pay attention to catch the next cue. This idea could also be extended by having the listeners call out a whole new set of sound effects or cues.

Evaluating Storytelling

Students should be encouraged to participate in ongoing objective evaluations of storytelling. If possible, videotape a storyteller telling a story and have the students evaluate the teller and discuss their findings. (It would be preferable to view the tape once for enjoyment and then a second time for the evaluation.)

Have the students develop a checklist for their evaluations. If essential items are omitted by the students, add them to the list yourself. A good checklist might read as follows:

The storyteller was (1) able to, (2) sometimes able to, (3) not able to:

	(1)	(2)	(3)
motivate the audience to listen			
convey action vividly			
convey sequence of events clearly			
assume characters' point of view			
express human motives			
express human conflict			
express human values			
establish mood			
use figurative language			
use language rhythmically			
speak clearly and distinctly			
utilize varied intonation			
utilize appropriate gestures			
utilize eye contact effectively			
end the story gracefully			

Analyzing Stories

- Have the students search through collections of folktales (African and Asian folktales are particularly good for this) to find examples of discrepancies between traditional written language and spoken language (repetition, language reversals, sentence structure). Another way to illustrate this point: Tape a storyteller telling a story, then transcribe it. The differences between oral and written language will be clearly depicted.

- Have the students read several versions of the same folktale as told by different cultures. In all good folktales, the stories include familiar mannerisms and customs of the people and place where they are set — even the plants, clothing, and food are parts of the authentic detail of the culture they belong to. Then have the students

   — identify what cultural names, places, objects, or customs are unique to each story

— make a chart showing how two of these stories are alike and how they are different

— develop and tell a version of the same story incorporating places, names, artifacts, and customs specific to where you live

- Type a short story, preferably one page long, in chunks of story events. Make a second copy of the story. Cut the story events apart, mix them up, and place them in an envelope. Do this for three stories. Divide the class into three groups. Give each group one of the envelopes with instructions to put the events into the correct story order. When each group has completed this, give its members the uncut copy of the story to self-check their results. In the course of this activity, have the students evaluate their version. Is it the same as the uncut version? If not, are the differences logical? When the group finally reconciles any story differences, instruct its members to reread the story in preparation for telling it.

  The next step is to have a member from each of the three story groups join a new group. Students will tell the story they worked on to the new listeners.

Curriculum-related Activities

Social Studies

- Have the students locate and develop for telling a story from a culture they are studying.

- In studying the economics and history of an area, bring in someone from the community—rancher, millworker, banker, etc.—to share his or her experiences and stories with the class. These abstract subjects will be made real by people and their firsthand stories.

- A high school in Boulder, Colorado, is currently experimenting with a study of presentation of historical material. Storytellers present material in dramatic context to the students, and group discussion follows. Students are encouraged to read further. Other classes are involved in traditional research/report techniques. The study at this stage indicates that the material presented by the storytellers has much more interest and personal impact than the traditional method. Also, students in the storytelling classes are using more library materials than the traditional groups. Long-term retention of the material is yet to be evaluated.

- Most elementary school students study Japan. Start out by telling the students the Norwegian story "Why the Sea Is Salt" (Lang 1965). After your students have had several chances to retell the story and act it out, have them rewrite it into a Japanese version. What names, places, holidays, and events would have to be changed? For instance, incorporate the Japanese tradition of giving bean cakes as a gift to children before they leave a party. Build in the older brother catching the younger brother using the mortar to make some bean cakes but not seeing or hearing the ritual to stop the mortar. After the students have developed their Japanese version, listen to Jay O'Callahan's taped telling of "The Magic Mortar," or read the story in Sakade (1959). How was the student-developed story like the O'Callahan telling?

Language Arts

- Use vocabulary words from stories heard in class or told by the students as spelling words.

- For an initial writing experience, have each student select a favorite folktale. Then have the students rewrite the story in a different form — in a modern setting, in the future, as science fiction, as poetry, in an interview form, or in reader's theater format. New story endings might be devised. These products, after editing and proofing, could be included in a class booklet. This transition activity from familiar folktales to a revised, retold version will demonstrate how an author can take an idea and create something new from it.

- Episodes from the students' own lives could be written in story form. To guide them in this project, remind the students that the common characteristics of stories told in the United States include a setting, an action that starts the story, an emotion related to this action, an attempt to alter the action or reach a goal, consequences of this attempt, and an emotional response to this consequence. These story components will develop an anecdote into a full-fledged, well-developed story.

- Have the students write fictional stories about what they will be doing twenty years from now. These individual stories — illustrated, perhaps — could be collected into a class book to be placed in the school library for reading as well as future reference.

- The humor of Garrison Keillor on the National Public Radio program "A Prairie Home Companion" is an example of good storytelling, translated into written form and then into radio format. Have the students listen to Keillor's stories of the people in his mythical hometown of Lake Wobegon and study the style and humor used. Have the students invent an imaginary setting based on their own environment and humorous stories to populate the place.

Science and Math

- Have the students find and share an interesting story about some scientist or event they are studying in science.

- Have the students locate stories to liven the mathematics classes. For instance, what standard of measurement was used for foot? yard? inch?

Expressive Arts

- Have the students paint and trim a special chair or stool to be the official storyteller's magic spot.

- Have the students make a banner or flag to be used to indicate upcoming storytelling time. It could be art in stitchery from a story or possibly an original graphic symbol.

- Give a "storytelling apron" to one of the students, with instructions in the pocket to interview another student, get a story from him or her, write the story out on a card, put the card in the pocket, and give the apron to the storyteller. The process continues, and the person who has the apron just before the next group storytelling session brings the apron to the session. The teacher judges the stories on the cards and an award is given for the best story.

- Develop a simple string figure, chalk-talk, or overhead story. (See Pellowski 1984, pp. 3-46 and 47-76.)

- Have the students create a mural for a story. Chalk or paint might be used as the medium.

- Give the students one square each of white muslin, and have them, using either fabric paint or needle and thread, illustrate one scene each from a story. The squares can then be sewed together and quilted to form a decorative wall hanging and storytelling device.

- Have the students create original music and dance movements to accompany a story.

- Have the students illustrate stories with computer graphics, using the software program Logo.

- Have the students carve story characters or objects from bars of Ivory soap.

- Have the students create three-dimensional or soft-sculpture characters and scenes from a story and organize them into a mobile.

- Have the students make larger soft-sculpture characters and settings and arrange them in a tableau.

- Have the students use papier-mâché or plaster of Paris to create a large-as-life storyteller. (One elementary-school principal served as the model for a plaster cast of a decorated and clothed [with the principal's clothes] storyteller, seated in a rocking chair and displayed in the library/media center.)

- Have the students investigate the history of your school and the community and then create a soft-sculpture character for each decade to represent the clothing and cultural changes. Arrange these figures in a grouping. Tape the students' stories about and for each one of them. (Students at one Denver school [celebrating its hundredth birthday] gathered stories from retired teachers and former students and turned them into an immensely successful oral history community project. The historical figures are on display in the main entry to the school.)

- Videotape or photograph (for a slide/tape show) the final elaborate expressive arts project with a narration for future sharing.

- Select a story ballad for the students to illustrate. The artwork could then be photographed, using either a super-8 movie or 35-mm slide format (or both). Develop a taped audio track to accompany it and have your own illustrated multimedia presentation for special events. (One third-grade teacher involved his students in an integrated curriculum experience while making their ballad film. They used mathematics to determine the number of frames needed for each scene, as well as reading comprehension, sequencing, and oral interpretation skills. His students and their school now shoot one animated film each year along with additional slide/tape programs.)

- Extend the activity described in the Social Studies section of this chapter, in which students developed a Japanese version of the Norwegian folktale "Why the Sea Is Salt," by having them work in pairs and practice telling the story to each other. Can they add more details and embellish the events of the story?

  Following these tellings, have the students develop a story board of events of the story (see fig. 7.1, page 362). In preparing this story board they need to determine important events, sequence them, and then decide who will illustrate each event. The students need to decide what the characters should look like and dress like so the story board will be consistent.

  After all the scenes have been artistically depicted, have the students use these pictures to make either slides or possibly an animated film (8-mm or video). Then a student can tape a telling of the story and synchronize it with the slide advance or film. This media production could be shared with other classes and featured at back-to-school night.

This coordinated activity involves many types of learning and draws upon many skills, among them creativity, listening, speaking, thinking, reading, writing, and math.

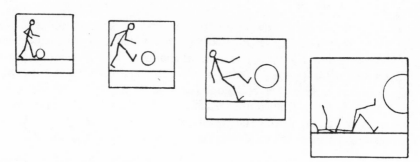

Fig. 7.1. A simple story board.

School Storytelling Clubs

Many teachers have successfully organized after-school storytelling clubs. Such clubs are usually much more successful when students volunteer for them than when they are drafted. The club established by one middle-school principal included the following activities, incentives, and rewards for members:

- Everyone who attends regularly gets a membership button.

- Everyone designs his or her own nametag button at one of the meetings. Just as C.B. radio users adopt handles, so can storytellers. The buttons are kept in the storytelling room and are passed out at each meeting for the students to wear.

- Bars or ribbons are attached to the buttons each time a student successfully tells a story to the group. Success is measured by the use of such storytelling skills as eye contact, effective dialogue, adequate volume, sound effects, voice expressiveness, body expressiveness, and use of props. Audience reaction should also be considered.

- Traveling club members who tell stories to other groups in their own and other schools receive a button bearing the club logo for each story told.

- Storytellers who travel to tell stories to groups of adults earn a gigantic blue ribbon rosette.

- Everyone who participates in the all-day storytelling jamboree held at the end of the year earns a T-shirt with the club logo silkscreened by the art department on it.

- Students may choose to make themselves illustrated storytelling vests, skirts, shirts, or hats; each time they tell a story they add a character from the story to it.

- Certificates of achievement with amusing sketches are awarded at an "academy awards of storytelling" ceremony.

REFERENCES

Bettelheim, Bruno. 1976. *The Uses of Enchantment*. New York: Knopf.

Brand, Oscar. 1974. *When I First Came to This Land*. New York: Putnam.

Brunvand, Jan Harold. 1981. *The Vanishing Hitchhiker*. New York: Norton.

Chase, Richard. 1943. *The Jack Tales*. Boston: Houghton Mifflin.

Courlander, Harold, and Albert Kofi Prempeh. 1957. "The Liar's Contest." In *The Hat-Shaking Dance and Other Ashanti Tales from Ghana*. New York: Harcourt, Brace and World.

Frasconi, Antonio. 1958. *The House That Jack Built*. New York: Harcourt, Brace and World.

Gag, Wanda. 1928. *Hundreds of Cats*. New York: Coward, McCann and Geoghegan.

Graber, Rebecca. January 1984. *New England Storytelling Center Newsletter*. Cambridge, Mass.: Lesley College.

Hoffmann, Hilde. 1968. *The Green Grass Grows All Around*. New York: Macmillan.

Jacobs, Joseph. 1892. "The Old Woman and Her Pig." In *English Fairy Tales*. New York: Putnam.

Kent, Jack. 1971. *The Fat Cat*. New York: Scholastic Books.

Krauss, Ruth. 1945. *Carrot Seed*. New York: Scholastic Books.

Lang, Andrew. 1965. "Why the Sea Is Salt." In *The Blue Fairy Book*. New York: Dover Publications.

National Council of Teachers of English. October 1982. *Essentials of English*. Urbana, Ill.: National Council of Teachers of English.

O'Callahan, Jay. "The Magic Mortar." (Available from Artana Records, 90 Old Mt. Skirgo Road, Marshfield, MA 02050.)

Pellowski, Anne. 1984. *The Story Vine*. New York: Macmillan.

Sakade, Florence, ed. 1959. *Urashima Taro and Other Japanese Children's Stories*. Rutland, Vt.: Charles E. Tuttle.

Seeger, Pete. 1964. "Abiyoyo." In *The Bells of Rhymney and Other Songs and Stories from the Singing of Pete Seeger*. New York: Oak Publications.

Wolkenstein, Diane. 1984. *The Visit*. New York: Knopf.

ADDITIONAL RESOURCES

Carlisle, Elizabeth, and Judithe Speidel. May 1979. "Local History As Stimulus for Writing." *English Journal*, 55-57.

Dundes, Allen. April 1969. "Folklore As a Mirror of Culture." *Elementary English*, 471-82.

Gardner, Howard. March 1982. "The Making of a Storyteller." *Psychology Today*, 49-53, 61-63.

Hogrogian, Nonny. 1971. *One Fine Day*. New York: Macmillan.

Jennings, Tim. April/May 1981. "Storytelling, a Nonliterate Approach to Teaching Reading." *Learning*, 49-52.

Jett-Simpson, Mary. March 1981. "Writing Stories Using Model Structures: The Circle Story." *Language Arts*, 293-300.

Kimmelman, Lois. April 1981. "Literary Ways toward Enjoyable Thinking." *Language Arts*, 441-47.

Laubach, David. May 1979. "Beyond Foxfire." *English Journal*, 52-54.

Lee, Hector. October 1970. "American Folklore in the Schools." *English Journal*, 994-99.

Livo, Norma J. September 1983. "Storytelling, an Art for All Ages." *Media and Methods*, 24-26.

Wiseman, Nell. May 1979. "Creative Writing and Storytelling: A Unit for Writing Children's Stories." *English Journal*, 47-49.

Zeitlin, Steven J., Amy J. Kotkin, and Holly Cutting Baker. 1982. *A Celebration of American Family Folklore*. New York: Pantheon Books.

8

Planning and Arranging Storytelling Events

Storytelling is theater of the mind.

(Norma J. Livo)

What are some considerations in choosing stories for a solo storytelling? A program with several tellers?

Should the storytellers mix music, poetry, and story in a program?

Are programs around a common theme feasible?

What are some hints for planning and developing contests, conferences, and programs?

This chapter will discuss preparation for a full program of telling, covering such topics as story selection and other materials for a variety of audiences. It will explore full programs of storytelling for schools, libraries, and other community groups. Finally, it will offer concrete suggestions for organizing and running conferences and camps.

DEVELOPING PROGRAMS

If several storytellers plan to present a program together, they need to confer on what stories they intend to tell, what techniques they will be using, and how long their stories will take to tell. The next step is to arrange the stories in a sequence that will provide a smoothly flowing program. They might not want to tell two heavy, long stories back to back, for example. They should aim to provide variety and complementary placement of their material.

Generally, the program should start with a bang. The first story will make or break the mood for the session. Observe musical groups and the programming of their selections. From symphony to rock group, they all recognize the value of emotional impact. After the strong start, humorous selections, musical pieces, short stories, dramatic ones, and soothing ones should be interspersed to provide the necessary change of pace. With careful planning and execution, storytellers can play on the participants' emotions and elicit a wide range of moods.

Developing a program around a common theme might have some special advantages. One group of storytellers shared a variety of stories and ballads around the theme "violins." There were poems about violins, fun stories, gypsy stories about the origin of the violin, and ballads. A fiddler performed several selections. The stories and music were distinctly different. Many members of the audience responded that they enjoyed the theme approach, and several commented that they had never realized there were so many possibilities for that particular topic. If the program is built around a common theme, the mood, length, and type of material should be varied. It is also necessary to plan if there will be tandem or cooperative collaboration among the storytellers. Such pieces add flexibility to the program. For instance, the song "There's a Hole in the Bucket" is a delightful chance for two people to take specific characters and play them off each other. Of course the end of the program should be considered. How will the last selection affect the listeners — will they leave the session reflective, excited, or amused?

The Folktellers, cousins Connie Regan and Barbara Freeman, are among the premier storytellers in our country. Their record "White Horses and Whippoorwills," which contains six selections appropriate for middle-schoolers through adults, is an excellent example of variety and complementary placement of material. The opening piece, "Two White Horses," told by Connie as a solo, is a dramatic, suspenseful story involving a mistaken burial. "Old Drye Frye," a solo piece by Barbara, is a humorous Appalachian story about a preacher who was notorious for his prowess in eating fried chicken. "Jazzy Three Bears" is a rhythmic children's classic. Barbara and Connie share its telling. "No News" is an old vaudeville selection told as a duet. Barbara tells a story/poem by Stephen Vincent Benet about the success of an underdog, "Mountain Whippoorwill." The final story—an intense one full of vivid imagery—is "Oliver Hyde's Dishcloth Concert," told by Connie.

The Folktellers caught the listeners right away, played with them a little bit, and ended with a memorable story—truly, a fine, well-balanced concert. This programming would be appropriate for middle school, junior high, and senior high students as well as any group of adults. A good mixture of story types, length, and solo and duet tellings gives the audience the chance to see both tellers with their strongest material as well as in some light cooperative moments.

Making a chart of a proposed program is a good planning technique that allows the teller to check for balance, length, etc. A chart of the Folktellers' concert might look like this:

Story	Type	Time	Teller
Two White Horses	Dramatic and powerful	10 min.	Connie
Old Drye Frye	Humorous	13 min.	Barbara
Jazzy Three Bears	Humorous and rhythmic	2 min.	duet
No News	Humorous	3 min.	duet
Mountain Whip-poorwill	Poem, fiddling contest	8 min.	Barbara
Oliver Hyde's Dishcloth Concert	Gentle and sensitive	15 min.	Connie
6 stories	3 humorous stories, 1 poem, and 2 longer dramatic stories	50 min.	4 solos and 2 duets

For younger audiences, kindergarten up to third grade, a sample program for two storytellers might consist of the following collection:

1. "Little Red Riding Hood" could be performed as a solo in a dramatic rendition.

2. A refrain about a foolish frog and his leap across a stream is repeated in the story/song "The Foolish Frog" (Seeger 1964). The two tellers could share the story and the sound effects of the children, chickens, cows, barn doors, stream, grass, wives, and summer people. The song about the frog could be taught to the children and they could all sing it at the end. This would also be a fitting solo presentation.

3. The cumulative story "The Old Woman and Her Pig" (Jacobs 1967) would fit well here. This story with its repeated characters and refrains could be used to involve the listeners in participating. The story could be told in tandem.

4. The poem "Mabel, Remarkable Mabel" (Prelutsky 1984) adds humor. (Youngsters could act it out following the telling.) A solo teller would be appropriate.

5. A final story might be "If You Say So, Claude" (Nixon 1980), which tells how Claude and Shirley travel across Texas in their covered wagon, looking for a peaceful place to settle down. This is a nice combination of folkloric style and humor and is perfect for a duet presentation.

Another story that would fit into this program is "The Stonecutter" (McDermott 1975). This Japanese folk story presents the theme that you do not always realize what you have until you lose it.

The combination of these stories, song, and poem would provide a mixture of action, participation, repetitious material, folklore, and drama. It could also be under an hour long, depending on how involved the tellers make it.

Much of the advice given above also holds true for the single performer. The placement of material in the program and the emotional impact to be striven for remain the same. Of course, as the program progresses, the story-teller should be aware of audience reactions and be guided by them. Some stories may be dropped and others substituted on the spot because of what the storyteller perceives to be happening with the group. This chance to adapt is one advantage of going it alone. There do not have to be rushed consultations to insert changes.

The disadvantage to going it alone, of course, is that the storyteller takes responsibility for the whole program. Also, there is no opportunity to take a break as someone else tells a story or to study the reactions of audience members while another storyteller is engaged with them.

As indicated earlier, there should be a mix of humor, drama, songs, stories of different lengths, audience-participation stories, stories involving props, and unadorned "straight" tellings in the program. Animal puppets might be used with the stories with animals in them. (The number of puppets used per story should be limited unless the storyteller is experienced in manipulating them.)

The following list outlines the general form of a program for a younger audience. The inclusion of a range of material such as songs, riddles, games, and stories varies the session.

1. Start

2. Song

3. Riddle

4. Long story

5. Activity game

6. Story

7. Song

8. Final remarks

9. End

Tashjian (1969) is an excellent source for ideas for games, chants, and activities.

The themes and subjects of the stories will vary from group to group. In a museum, for example, a storyteller might include stories and legends about animals, plants, rocks, and scientific information. A session might be built around a single subject or might include unrelated stories. The types of stories used should be varied also. Cumulative or repetitive stories can be mixed with fables, fairy tales, and "pourquoi" (how and why) stories.

The teller might also consider the efficacy of the program built around a single theme. Inspirational presentations to civic, community, political, or professional groups are an alternative to the traditional keynote or meal function speaker. When asked to present a program at these events, the story-teller can weave stories on a topic such as character building, imagination, love, death, or special gifts into an integrated, cohesive message. The message can be dramatized by using some props to involve the audience—a set of the Russian folk dolls that nest inside each other in graduated size, gift-wrapped boxes within boxes, or wooden eggs within eggs. All are empty except for slips of paper on which are written sayings relevant to the topic, which someone in the audience will receive and read. Chinese fortune cookies with new slips of paper inserted also work well. The following suggestions are based on the topic "The Imagination."

First, a general statement about the value of imagination might include the fact that folktales, myths, and legends in every culture have always addressed life's crucial questions and answered them through imagination.

The Swedish story "The Three Wishes" (de Spain 1979) is one illustration of this truth. In it, a poor woodcutter is granted three wishes by a tree nymph when he follows the nymph's request to save the tree, which is its home. Later that night, at home, eating a plain, poor meal with his wife, the woodcutter idly wishes for a sausage. When he instantly is rewarded with a fat, juicy sausage, he remembers what the nymph said. He tells his wife about the morning's happenings, and she immediately starts a long tirade about his waste of a valuable wish. When he can tolerate her abuse no longer, he angrily wishes the sausage would stick to her nose. They try several ways to remove it and finally have to resort to using the third wish. The story ends with the woodcutter telling his wife she cannot accuse him of wasting his third wish. All of the riches they might have dreamed of are gone.

This skeleton of a story, of which there are many variants, should be fleshed out with details by the storyteller. What was the forest like where the woodcutter was working? How hard did he work after the bargain with the tree nymph? How tired and hungry was he at home that night? What did the meal he and his wife were eating consist of? What conversations can you add to the story between the woodcutter and the nymph and later with his wife?

The telling of the story might be followed with a few remarks about the fact that it is really open ended. The outcome arose from choice, and there could have been many other choices.

The first message found in the first nesting item or fortune cookie is, "If your imagination is working well, you are able to do more interesting and valuable things." The storyteller might add the comment that if we are able to imagine our future optimistically, we will be free to develop and proceed in a positive manner.

The story "Cap of Rushes" from the Jacobs (1967) collection might be told next. When a proud king asks each of his three daughters how much they love him, the oldest one tells him, "As much as I love my life," the next says, "Better than all the world," and the third says, "As fresh meat loves salt." The king becomes angry and drives his third daughter away from his home for not loving him. She makes a hooded cloak out of rushes to cover her fancy clothes and finds lowly kitchen work in a neighboring wealthy home where a handsome, eligible young man lives. There are a series of three evening dances nearby. Cap of Rushes attends the dances in her fine clothes. The young man falls in love with the unknown beauty, who slips away each evening. He gives her a golden ring on the third evening. After failing to find her, he becomes lovesick and is dying. Cap of Rushes slips the ring he had given her into his bowl of porridge. When he finds it he of course discovers her and they plan to marry. Everyone, including her father the king, is invited to the grand wedding and she makes arrangements for the cook to use no salt at all in the wedding feast. The father discovers how much his third daughter really loved him, since each dish is quite tasteless. Naturally, there is a final happy reunion.

The saying in the second nesting item or fortune cookie reads, "Imagination helps to hope." Imagination can help us see our future with optimism and hope. Both Cap of Rushes and her suitor were optimistic about the future, and her imagination helped guarantee their happiness.

Next, imagination in its relationship to humor can be explored with the story "No News . . . Or What Killed the Dog," often related by the Folktellers (Regan and Freeman 1981). (The story was originally created by Nat M. Wills in the early 1900s.)

A fellow returns to his home in the mountains after having been away for three months. He is met at the train station by another fellow. When asked whether there is any news by the returning traveler, the second fellow replies, "No news . . . except that the dog died." The traveler's further questions elicit the information that the dog died because he ate some of the burned horse-flesh, after the ashes cooled off, after the barn burned down, killing all of the cows and horses, which had been set off by a spark from the burning house, which had been ignited by the candles, which were in the house around the coffin of the traveler's mother-in-law, who died because of the shock of hearing that the traveler's wife had run away with the chauffeur. Other than that, the fellow concludes, there is no news.

An audience member opens the third nesting item or fortune cookie and reads the saying, "Imagination helps us laugh and laughter is therapeutic."

Imagination also helps us solve problems. It takes an imaginative leap to see another person's point of view, put oneself in his or her position, and embrace a new idea. Medicine, world affairs, architecture, community planning, teaching, physics, law, or literally any area of endeavor needs a healthy dose of imagination.

The Chinese folktale retold by Wolkstein (1972) as "8,000 Stones" shows creative problem solving at its best. The small, clever P'ei, son of the Chinese ruler, outthinks the court advisers and courtiers. The emperor has received his yearly gift from the grand satrap of India. Since the Indian delegation does not know how much this gift, an elephant, weighs, the emperor decides he must impress the grand satrap with the information and show him the way to get the exact weight of this wondrous beast. P'ei comes up with the solution that others had failed to do.

The fourth slip of paper reads, "The habit of observation is only one part of solving problems. It takes imagination to think about familiar things in an unaccustomed way."

The storyteller might then reiterate the following points:

1. If your imagination is working well, you are able to do more interesting and valuable things.

2. Imagination helps to hope.

3. Imagination helps us laugh and laughter is therapeutic.

4. The habit of observation is only one part of problem solving. It takes imagination to think about familiar things in an unaccustomed way.

A member of the audience may then be chosen to open the final nesting item or fortune cookie, with a final slip of paper that reads, "Gifts are given to everyone who is willing to have the imagination to accept them." In the final item could be a tiny flower, sparkling crystal, or some other attractive surprise.

This whole suggested program on imagination is outlined in the following list. The approximate time involved is 52 minutes.

1. Initial introduction to the topic "Imagination" and the story "The Three Wishes" (3 minutes)

2. "The Three Wishes" (10 minutes)

3. Prop and statement 1 (2 minutes)

4. Introduction (3 minutes)

5. "Cap of Rushes" (10 minutes)

6. Prop and statement 2 (2 minutes)

7. Introduction (3 minutes)

8. "No News" (5 minutes)

9. Prop and statement 3 (2 minutes)

10. Introduction (3 minutes)

11. "8,000 Stones" (10 minutes)

12. Prop and statement 4 (2 minutes)

13. Concluding statement (3 minutes)

14. Final prop (1 minute)

A question-and-answer session might complete the program if there is time. The length of the program is easy to adjust after the stories have been developed and timed. This sample presentation is, of course, adaptable to many groups and levels of sophistication. The theme approach is equally appropriate for mixed-age groups. We all hear and understand the same stories with different levels of understanding.

As we have seen, there are many instances in which props can add to the story, song, poem, or program. This has also been true historically. Scientific investigators have identified what may be one of the oldest (8,500 years old) storytelling devices (Marshack 1972)—the uniquely carved Ishango bones, discovered in central equatorial Africa. The bones quite likely served as a notation system that "contained some storied meaning" (p. 26). Members of a

Mesolithic civilization possibly used these bones as a record and as memory aids for sharing important events in the history of the Ishango people.

The more recent traditional storytelling customs of India and Japan also included props. In India, the kalamkari and pabuji pat (large hand-painted tapestries) had the life story of the god Ganesh painted on them. These tapestries hanging in the village square served as an announcement that there would be storytelling as well as serving as a memory device for the storyteller. In this way these traveling tellers passed on a religious history in story and visually in art. The Japanese kamishibai, large picture cards, were used until recently. For a small amount of money you could hear the kamishibai card story and eat dried seaweed provided by the storyteller.

Scrolls from Egypt demonstrate another interesting way of sharing stories. In the Balinese shadow play, or wayang, the ritual story of Ramayana is presented using dramatic shadow puppets. In the Jewish tradition, a storyteller might travel with a carved staff on which were depicted the characters and objects important to the story. The storyteller could feel the story with his hand as he told it. All of these artifacts served as traditional ways to alert the audience to the upcoming storytelling experience as well as to add to the artistic sharing of the story.

Props are found today in some unique, creative adaptations. For instance, Jewell Wolk of Cut Bank, Montana, has combined quilting with storytelling. Her first storytelling quilt documented in stitchery the passing of sheep ranching in the sweet-grass area of Montana.

Her second quilt depicted lunchtime at a rural one-room schoolhouse in the early 1900s. She has included dozens of individual stories in this one quilt. To collect the stories, Wolk would take her in-progress quilt to community gatherings, and as people asked her what she was doing they would invariably add a few stories of their own to her growing collection.

For Wolk's third quilt, she interviewed elderly Blackfoot Native American women who lived on a reservation near her home. Their stories led to a wide-ranging collection of information about the lives of Plains Indian women at the turn of the century. Innocent questions such as "What did you use for diapers?" led to interesting discoveries that were then recorded in stitches.

Storytellers should be aware, however, that inappropriate use of props can be distracting. They must be carefully selected, tested in a storytelling situation, and modified or discarded as required. Ultimately, props must add to rather than detract from the storytelling experience.

HINTS FOR ARRANGING STORYTELLING EVENTS

Obviously the first, main requirement for a storytelling conference is outstanding storytellers. For the first year of the conference you may have to depend on personal and professional favors from friends (be prepared to tell a lot of stories yourself in return), the generosity of a publisher, or maybe the death of an unknown millionaire relative to finance the conference. But it is worth it. Make sure you invite a balanced mixture of "pure" storytellers and storytellers who use music, puppets, slides, quilts, real-life stories, theatrical touches, or scholarly aspects.

A two-day conference is just as easy to plan and pull off as a one-day conference. Give each speaker 45 minutes to an hour to present. The most important time slots are the first and last sessions. Probably the most difficult slot is after the lunch break. A lively storyteller or participatory activities are helpful here.

If possible, have several areas available so people can select between several storytellers presenting at the same time. The smaller groups provide for much more informal contact, but be sure there will not be interference or distractions, such as applause and sound effects from storytellers in several corners of one room.

Who will you invite to your conference? You could obtain names of people to contact from schools, libraries, and professional groups. You could also use newspaper and radio advertising to promote the conference. Advertising and other costs might be partially covered by grant money (contact your local library for information on humanities grants in your state). Establish a fee that will enable you to cover all of your costs: speakers' honoraria and transportation, hall rental, printing, postage, and any other expenses incurred. Be realistic as you estimate the number of people who will attend. You might also want to allow a little bit extra for seed money for next year.

A get-together of all of the presenters before the conference gives everyone the chance to meet, swap stories, and compare notes before they are swept up in the conference itself. If the conference starts in the morning, this gathering could take place the evening before.

Provide a form for written responses to the conference, including suggestions for next year. It is surprising how often you can get the name of a local storyteller you were not aware of, as well as practical suggestions to help make next year's conference better. If you are contemplating running a storytelling camp, include a question on the form asking about respondents' interest in such a camp (see p. 431). Make sure you ask for names and addresses—including ZIP code—and telephone numbers so you can contact interested people later.

Follow up the conference with thank-you notes to everyone who helped. Everyone needs to know his or her efforts have been appreciated.

Take a tip from Madison Avenue and develop a logo to be used with all the promotional materials going out about the conference. This helps build identification and creates awareness as people recognize the symbol.

If any of the presenters have books, records, or tapes out, provide copies of them for purchase and allow time and places for autographing them. These materials can be supplied by local book jobbers or bookstores.

Meet your speakers if they are arriving by public transportation and escort them to the conference. See them off properly, too. There is nothing more awkward for a speaker than to have finished and packed up and then look around to find him- or herself all alone.

Keep in touch with the speakers as conference time approaches, and make sure you provide any special equipment or materials they need. (Don't get surprised by a request for a wooden piano bench or floodlights at the absolute last minute.)

Keep a checklist, including time lines, of what needs to be done, when it needs to be done, and, if others are involved, who is to do what. You'll also want to keep a file folder on contacts (including names, addresses with ZIP code, and telephone numbers) for convenience.

Don't overload your speakers with additional requests such as, "Would you also tell some stories at my daughter's school?" unless you have already included that possibility in your original agreement.

Sometimes it is difficult to deal with teacher friends who tell you they cannot come to the whole conference but ask if they may bring their class to just part of it. If you have charged people money to attend, it is not fair to them to have unscheduled comings and goings unless you have established these options earlier.

Sometimes a representative of another group will contact your main speaker after hearing that he or she is going to be in town and will make arrangements for the speaker (for whom you have paid full transportation, room, and meals) to speak to that group one-half hour after he or she finishes at your conference. The other group's representative may become offended at the suggestion that the speaker's expenses be shared. This problem can be avoided if you establish in a contract with the speaker that there will be no local engagements one week before or one week after yours unless by mutual consent. After all, if you are counting on the speaker to attract people to the conference, it could mean a possible financial loss to have him or her speak somewhere else nearby and at a much lower fee.

If a speaker (such as a puppeteer) needs set-up time, schedule his or her slot in the program at a time when it is possible to get set up well before the session and gracefully speak to people who come up after the session and yet pack things up so the conference can continue smoothly.

If the response form for the conference has indicated sufficient interest in a storytelling camp, contact some local school district outdoor camps, YMCA camps, and commercial camps for rates, dates, and details. Select a date that seems to have a chance of drawing people. A weekend in August gives the working person a chance to attend, as well as vacationing drop-ins.

The reasons for attending a storytelling camp will differ for each person. These reasons might include the chance to swap stories, hear new stories, try a story out, just listen to stories, learn/teach/sing songs, and play/learn/teach some musical activities and games.

A featured storyteller should be scheduled at important times such as the evening campfire or the closing session. Others can be selected to head sessions to meet the varied needs of those attending.

One kind of storytelling session (ideally in the evening, following supper) that contributes to a lot of varied needs is the cric-crac session. This is based on the Haitian tradition of storytelling gatherings in which a person who wants to tell a story yells "Cric!" If the group wants to hear that person tell a story, they respond, loud and clear, "Crac!" In this way, after a featured storyteller starts the evening off, there is an opportunity for anyone who cares to tell a story to do so. It is sometimes surprising to discover unknown storytellers who feel comfortable about telling stories in this unstructured approach.

At one two-day storytelling camp, the evening cric-crac session was opened up to any local townspeople who cared to attend. They came with friends, relatives, and youngsters, and the session needed no formal explanation, just a couple of demonstrations. After that the session was wide open, and the visitors became unexpected storytellers.

Another valuable camp activity is a "not ready for prime time" session. The leader for this group must be sensitive and supportive. Members of the group have an opportunity to try a story out and get some immediate, helpful feedback as to what went well and what needs more work.

Although the emphasis above has been on adult opportunities to tell, hear, learn, and enjoy stories and storytelling, sessions by and for children can of course be included in conferences and camps. Good storytelling is good storytelling regardless of age.

As a natural outgrowth of conferences, camps, and other storytelling activities, people will want to hear more stories. Storytelling sessions can become a natural evening-out activity much the same as plays, movies, or musical concerts. The storytellers involved select a date, find an appropriate location, and advertise the concert through libraries, community newsletters, newspapers, radio, fliers, and local bulletin boards. A successful arrangement might include a concert for children in the afternoon and an adult concert in the evening. Charging an entry fee for the concerts will defray costs and provide an honorarium for each storyteller. Financial arrangements should be decided upon beforehand. The performers should of course have a set schedule of times and stories to tell. How often should concerts be scheduled? That depends on the response of the community and the skill of the storytellers involved. A once-a-month frequency would help to maintain continuity and also serve to provide exposure to more storytellers as well as challenge all storytellers to develop new stories.

Storytelling concerts can be held in a variety of places: libraries, museums, churches, art galleries, coffee shops, or other community gathering spots. The library is one of the most natural places for storytelling. Since the public library clientele spans a wide age range, many tie-ins are possible. Meeting space is usually no problem, and some library money may be available for special events. Storytelling featuring folklore and folk literature is a natural tie-in when the library spotlights a display of folkcraft.

Libraries sometimes work out cooperative projects with local high schools in which the students, as part of class projects, develop storytelling sessions for younger children. The authors have found several examples of successful projects of this type. The crucial link is coordination between the library and an interested teacher and group of students.

College or university students in children's literature classes, library-media programs, or drama programs could intern or present storytelling sessions in the library as part of their course requirements. Through this kind of cooperative effort, the college students would benefit greatly from a practical experience with real children. The professor of the class would be expected to work closely with the college students to ensure success through demonstrations and in-class opportunities for students to hear each other's stories and offer supportive, constructive criticism before the library presentation. Such storytelling sessions could also be expanded to nursing homes, museums, and zoos.

Storytelling in historical museums provides an ideal opportunity to add life to history. In the West, for example, "mountain men" in costume and with black-powder guns, telling stories of real mountain men, make human history come alive. "Miners" with gold pans can enrich an understanding of what it was to have been a gold miner during the rush of '49.

Museums of natural history are adding storytelling to their scientifically accurate displays. Legends, tall tales and stories based on real incidents add the human dimension to the dioramas.

Recently, the docents of an art museum were trained in techniques of storytelling for programs held in the Native American section of the museum. The storytellers researched stories related to symbols and designs. The docents then tried out stories with a partner and explored storytelling techniques first-hand. (See appendix C for an example of a telling held in conjunction with an event at an art museum.)

People in diverse disciplines such as psychology and religion are similarly honing storytelling skills to enhance their messages.

STORYTELLING CENTERS AND GROUPS

The American Storytelling Resource Center, Inc., 1471 Chanticleer Avenue, Santa Cruz, CA 95062. Telephone (408) 475-8939. Quarterly publication, conferences, and resources.

Connecticut Storytelling Center (Barbara Reed), Connecticut College, New London, CT 06320

Florida Storytellers Guild (Annette Bruce), P.O. Box 593, Eustis, FL 32726.

Great Lake Storytellers (Pamela van der Ploeg), 715 Washington, Grand Haven, MI 49417.

International Order of E.A.R.S. (Lee Pennington), 11905 Lilao Way, Louisville, KY 40243.

Montana Storytelling Guild (Dr. Sandra Rietz), Eastern Montana College, Billings, MT 59101. Telephone (406) 657-2167.

National Directory of Storytellers, provided through the National Association for the Preservation and Perpetuation of Storytelling, P.O. Box 112, Jonesborough, TN 37659. Telephone (615) 753-2171. NAPPS produces a monthly newsletter and a quarterly publication, *The National Storytelling Journal*, and has established a resource center.

The New England Storytelling Center (Lee Ellen Marvin), Lesley College Graduate School, 29 Everett St., Cambridge, MA 02238. Telephone (617) 868-9600,X449, or (617) 864-6445. This is a clearinghouse of information on storytelling in New England. The phone lines provide recorded listings of storytelling events in the Boston area that are updated weekly. A directory is available with a listing of more than sixty storytellers. Monthly gatherings of family groups and adults are held for the informal telling of stories. There is also a quarterly newsletter for members.

New York City Storytelling Center (Marcia Lane), 462 Amsterdam Ave., New York, NY 10024.

Northlands Storytelling Network, P.O. Box 758, Minneapolis, MN 55440.

Patchword Storytellers Guild (Robin Moore), 101 West Harvey St., Philadelphia, PA 19144.

Rocky Mountain Storyfolk (Dr. Norma J. Livo), University of Colorado at Denver, 1100 14th St., Denver, CO 80202. Telephone (303) 556-2717. Newsletter, resources, conferences; camps, concerts.

Seattle Storytellers Guild (Clare Cuddy), 4232 Corliss Avenue N., Seattle, WA 98103.

Southern Order of Storytellers (Loralee Cooley), 4163 Stonemont Dr., Lilburn, GA 30247.

Storyfest Productions, 4912 California St., San Francisco, CA 94118. Newsletter, resources, and international workshops.

Storytellers of San Diego (Harlynne Geisler), 4182-J Mt. Alifan Pl., San Diego, CA 92111.

Storytellers Unlimited, School of Library and Information Sciences, University of Pittsburgh, Pittsburgh, PA 15260.

Storytelling Center of Oneonta, P.O. Box 297, Oneonta, NY 13820.

REFERENCES

de Spain, Pleasant. 1979. *Pleasant Journeys*. Mercer Island, Wash.: The Writing Works.

Jacobs, Joseph. 1967. *English Fairy Tales*. New York: Dover.

McDermott, Gerald. 1975. *The Stonecutter*. New York: Viking Press.

Marshack, Alexander. 1972. *The Roots of Civilization*. New York: McGraw-Hill.

Nixon, Joan Lowery. 1980. *If You Say So, Claude*. New York: Frederick Warne.

Prelutsky, Jack. 1984. "Mabel, Remarkable Mabel." In *The New Kid on the Block*. New York: Greenwillow.

Regan, Connie, and Barbara Freeman. 1981. *White Horses and Whippoorwills* (audio recording). Asheville, N.C.: Mama-T Artists.

Seeger, Pete. 1964. "The Foolish Frog." In *The Bells of Rhymney*. New York: Oak Publications.

Tashjian, Virginia A. 1969. *Juba This and Juba That, Story Hour Sketches for Large and Small Groups*. Boston: Little, Brown.

Wolkstein, Diane. 1972. *8,000 Stones*. Garden City, N.Y.: Doubleday.

Appendices

A

Integrated Units
Built around Specific Topics

FROGS*

INTRODUCTION

"Everyone Needs at Least One Good Frog Story," said the well-known storyteller Jackie Torrence at a storytelling conference in March 1981. She then proceeded, in her warm, dramatic style, to tell a black tale from the Brazos Bottoms of Texas, "How Sandy Got His Meat" (B. A. Botkin, ed., "How Sandy Got His Meat: A Negro Tale from the Brazos Bottoms," in *A Treasury of American Folklore*, pp. 663-65, Garden City, N.Y.: Garden City Books, 1944, 1951). Torrence brought life and sound effects to the story and convinced her listeners that everyone needs at least one good frog story.

Frogs come in all varieties: factual, foolish, fairy, friendly, fable, ferocious, and fanciful. We find frog stories in Estonian folktales, Aesop's fables, Indian fables, Russian folktales, African folktales, Italian literature, Japanese folktales, Spanish collections, English songs, Hans Christian Andersen's stories, modern fables, and folklore collections. Frogs appear as characters on Japanese scrolls and in the stories of Mark Twain. They can be found in poems, picture books, advertisements, art, and cartoons. Frogs are definitely multimedia.

---

*See Norma J. Livo, "Variations on a Theme: Frogs," *Language Arts* (February 1976), 193-97.

FROGS WITH HUMAN QUALITIES

Frogs appear in stories as being foolish and wise, just like people. In the following collection of books and stories frogs have friends, enemies, problems, political aspirations, personal weaknesses like pride and boastfulness and strengths like heroism and resourcefulness.

Aardema, Verna. 1977. *Who's in Rabbit's House: A Masai Tale*. New York: Dial. Pp. 19-39.

Aesop. 1968. *Aesop's Fables*. Translated by V. S. Verson Jones. New York: Watts. P. 62.

_____. 1965. *Aesop's Fables*. Selected and adapted by Louis Untermeyer. New York: Golden. P. 42.

_____. 1964. *Aesop's Fables*. Retold by Anne Terry White. New York: Random House. Pp. 21-22.

_____. 1964. *Aesop; Five Centuries of Illustrated Fables*. Selected by John J. McKendry. New York: Metropolitan Museum of Art; Greenwich, Conn.: New York Graphic Society.

_____. 1950. *Fables of Aesop*. Selected by Joseph Jacobs. New York: Macmillan. Pp. 24-25.

_____. 1947. *Aesop's Fables*. New York: Grosset and Dunlap. Pp. 47-48.

_____. 1933. *Aesop's Fables*. Edited by Boris Artzybasheff. New York: Viking. Pp. 58-59.

Arbuthnot, May Hill. 1961. *Arbuthnot Anthology of Children's Literature*. Chicago: Scott, Foresman. Pp. 314-15.

Bang, Molly. 1973. *Man from the Village Deep in the Mountains and Other Japanese Folk Tales*. Translated by Garrett Bang. New York: Macmillan. Pp. 79-84.

Barlow, Genevieve. 1966. *Latin American Tales: From the Pampas to the Pyramids of Mexico*. Chicago: Rand McNally. Pp. 57-61.

Borski, Lucia Merecka. 1970. *Good Sense and Good Fortune and Other Polish Folk Tales*. New York: McKay. P. 60.

Bowman, James Cloyd, and Margery Bianco. 1936. *Tales from a Finnish Tupa*. Translated by Aili Kolehmainen. Chicago: Albert Whitman. P. 266.

Bryan, Ashley. 1980. *Beat the Story-Drum Pum-Pum*. New York: Atheneum. Pp. 3-13, 41-52.

_____. 1971. *The Ox of the Wonderful Horns and Other African Folktales*. New York: Atheneum. Pp. 11-14.

Carey, Bonnie. 1973. *Baba Yaga's Geese and Other Russian Stories*. Bloomington, Ind.: Indiana University Press. Pp. 58-60.

Carrick, Valery J. 1970. *Still More Russian Tales*. Translated by Nevill Forbes. New York: Dover. Pp. 88-94.

Cathon, Laura E., and Thusnelda Schmidt. 1962. *Perhaps and Perchance: Tales of Nature*. Nashville, Tenn.: Abingdon. Pp. 62-63.

Colwell, Eileen. 1976. *The Magic Umbrella and Other Stories for Telling*. New York: McKay. Pp. 107-10.

Courlander, Harold. 1962. *The King's Dream and Other African Stories*. New York: Harcourt, Brace and World. Pp. 58-59.

Credle, Ellis. 1957. *Tall Tales from the High Hills*. New York: Nelson. Pp. 89-95.

Evans, Katherine. 1962. *A Bundle of Sticks*. Chicago: Albert Whitman.

Fuja, Abayomi. 1971. *Fourteen Hundred Cowries, and Other African Tales*. New York: Lothrop, Lee, and Shepard. Pp. 214-36.

Ginsburg, Mirra. 1973. *The Lazies: Tales of the People of Russia*. New York: Macmillan. Pp. 26-27.

Gittins, Anne. 1977. *Tales from the South Pacific Islands*. Owings Mills, Md.: Stemmer House. Pp. 26-27.

Green, Margaret. 1965. *The Big Book of Animal Fables*. New York: Watts. P. 200.

Gruenberg, Sedonie M. 1948. *More Favorite Stories Old and New for Boys and Girls*. Garden City, N.Y.: Doubleday. Pp. 119-20.

Hardendorff, Jeanne B. 1969. *Just One More*. Philadelphia: Lippincott. Pp. 17-18.

Heady, Eleanor B. 1965. *Jambo Sungura: Tales from East Africa*. New York: Norton. Pp. 60-65.

Jacobs, Joseph. N.d. *More English Fairy Tales*. New York: Putnam. Pp. 184-85.

Jagendorf, Moritz A., and Ralph Steele Boggs. 1960. *The King of the Mountain: A Treasury of Latin American Folk Stories*. New York: Vanguard. Pp. 129-41.

Kaula, Edna Mason. 1968. *African Village Folktales*. New York: World. Pp. 122-25.

Lang, Andrew. 1901. *The Violet Fairy Book*. New York: Longmans, Green. Pp. 111-13.

Leach, Maria. 1961. *Noodles, Nitwits and Numskulls*. Cleveland: World. Pp. 26-27.

Lester, Julius. 1969. *Black Folktales*. New York: Richard W. Baron. Pp. 62-72.

Rice, Eve. 1979. *Once in a Wood: Ten Tales from Aesop*. New York: Greenwillow. Pp. 52-57.

Riordan, James. 1976. *Russian Tales, Volume I. Tales from Central Russia*. Harmondsworth, Middlesex: Kestrel Books. Pp. 241-42.

Rockwell, Anne. 1979. *The Old Woman and Her Pig and Ten Other Stories*. New York: Crowell. Pp. 79-81.

Ryder, Arthur. 1956. *The Panchatantra*. Chicago: University of Chicago Press. Pp. 388-94.

Shah, Idries. N.d. *The Incomparable Exploits of Nasreddin Mulla*. New York: Dutton. P. 31.

Siddiqui, Ashraf, and Marilyn Lerch. 1961. *Toontoony Pie and Other Tales from Pakistan*. Cleveland: World. Pp. 91-97.

Spellman, John. 1967. *The Beautiful Blue Jay and Other Tales of India*. Boston: Little, Brown. Pp. 56-58.

Tashjian, Virginia A. 1971. *Three Apples Fell from Heaven: Armenian Tales Retold*. Boston: Little, Brown. Pp. 40-41.

Turska, Krystyna. 1972. *The Woodcutter's Duck*. New York: Macmillan.

Van Woerkom, Dorothy O. 1975. *Sea Frog, City Frog*. New York: Macmillan.

Wiggin, Kate Douglas. 1936. *Tales of Wonder: A Fourth Fairy Book*. Garden City, N.Y.: Doubleday. Pp. 12-13.

The Frog Prince

There are quite a few versions of the old fairy tale "The Frog Prince." The tale collected by the Grimm brothers differs in a very important aspect from the popular modern version. In the Grimm version the beautiful youngest daughter of a king is aided by a frog who retrieves her golden ball from a well after she promises to love him and have him for her companion and play-fellow. Her father, the king, insists that she keep her promise after the frog follows her to her castle and requests the promised reward. She grudgingly eats with the frog, but in the privacy of her room she refuses to sleep with him. She picks the frog off her pillow and throws him with all her strength against the wall instead of bestowing a kiss on him to release him from his enchantment and return him to his handsome human form. In most versions, this happens after the frog has spent three nights with her. An original version is even more explicit: the princess must kiss the frog while he lies at her side in bed, and then it takes three weeks of sleeping together until the frog turns into a prince. Regardless of her method of releasing the prince from the spell, they get married and live happily ever after. The folktale has many sexual meanings as well as meanings related to maturing. For further information on these story messages, see Bruno Bettelheim's *The Uses of Enchantment: The Meaning and Importance of Fairy Tales* (New York: Knopf, 1976).

Which version is more meaningful—the folk version or the modern variants in which the princess sweetly gives the frog a kiss to wake him up? Have we "cleaned up" folk stories to the point that their powerful messages have been lost?

Sources for some of the versions of "The Frog Prince" follow.

Arbuthnot, May Hill. 1961. *Time for Fairy Tales Old and New*. Chicago: Scott Foresman. Pp. 43-45.

Dalgliesh, Alice. 1947. *The Enchanted Book*. New York: Scribner. Pp. 199-203.

Darrell, Margery, ed. 1972. *Once upon a Time: The Fairy Tale World of Arthur Rackham*. New York: Viking. Pp. 43-46.

Grimm, Jakob Ludwig Karl, and Wilhelm Karl Grimm. 1978. *The Brothers Grimm: Popular Folk Tales*. Translated by Brian Alderson. Garden City, N.Y.: Doubleday. Pp. 55-60.

_____. 1975. *The Frog Prince*. New York: McGraw-Hill.

_____. 1973. *The Juniper Tree and Other Tales from Grimm*. 2 volumes. Selected by Lore Segal, Maurice Sendak, and Randall Jarrell. Translated by Lore Segal. New York: Farrar, Straus, and Giroux. Vol. 2, pp. 169-79.

Grimm, Jakob Ludwig Karl, and Wilhelm Karl Grimm. 1968. *Grimm's Fairy Tales*. Edited by Frances Jenkins Olcott. Chicago: Follett. Pp. 82-88.

_____. 1954. "The Frog Prince." In *Grimm's Fairy Tales*. Garden City, N.Y.: Junior Deluxe Edition. P. 46.

_____. 1945. *Grimm's Fairy Tales*. Translated by Mrs. E. V. Lucas, Lucy Crane, and Marian Edwardes. New York: Grosset and Dunlap. Pp. 89-96.

_____. 1936. *Tales from Grimm*. Translated by Wanda Gag. New York: Coward-McCann. Pp. 179-88.

_____. 1886, 1966. *Household Stories*. Translated by Lucy Crane. New York: McGraw-Hill. Pp. 32-36.

Gruenberg, Sidonie M. 1942, 1955. *Favorite Stories Old and New*. Garden City, N.Y.: Doubleday. Pp. 295-98.

Haviland, Virginia. 1972. *The Fairy Tale Treasury*. New York: Coward, McCann and Geoghegan. Pp. 114-17.

_____. 1959. *Favorite Fairy Tales Told in Germany*. Boston: Little, Brown. Pp. 3-12.

Holme, Bryan, ed. 1977. *Tales from Times Past*. New York: Viking. Pp. 63-68.

Opie, Iona, and Peter Opie. 1974. *The Classic Fairy Tales*. New York: Oxford University Press. Pp. 183-87.

These versions could be further appreciated after reading Elinor Lander Horwitz's modern parody, *The Strange Story of the Frog Who Didn't Want to Be a Prince* (New York: Delacorte Press, 1971).

American children may find Richard M. Dorson's "The Frog and the Princess," the most accessible (*Buying the Wind*, Chicago: University of Chicago Press, 1964, pp. 257-58).

The Frog Bride

The story of three sons and their choice of brides is almost a universal one. Details vary, of course, from place to place, and the richness of the story varies as well. Some of the versions involve tests, magic, common sense, and the virtue of loyalty.

Bowman, James Cloyd, and Margery Bianco. 1970. "Mouse Bride." In *Tales from a Finnish Tupa*. Chicago: Albert Whitman. Pp. 25-33.

De La Mare, Walter. 1939. *Animal Stories*. New York: Scribner. Pp. 233-43.

Duvoisin, Roger. 1941. *The Three Sneezes and Other Swiss Tales*. New York: Knopf. Pp. 167-77.

Fillmore, Parker. 1921. *The Laughing Prince: A Book of Yugoslav Fairy Tales and Folk Tales*. New York: Harcourt, Brace and World. Pp. 163-70.

Finlay, Winifred. 1976. *Tattercoats and Other Folktales*. New York: Harvey House. Pp. 28-36.

Frost, Frances. 1943. *Legends of the United Nations*. New York: Whittlesey House. Pp. 240-44.

Grimm, Jakob Ludwig Karl, and Wilhelm Karl Grimm. 1973. *The Juniper Tree and Other Tales from Grimm*. 2 volumes. Selected by Lore Segal, Maurice Sendak, and Randall Jarrell. Translated by Lore Segal. New York: Farrar, Straus and Giroux. Vol. 1, pp. 3-10.

_____. 1971. *About Wise Men and Simpletons: Twelve Tales from Grimm*. Translated by Elizabeth Shub. New York: Macmillan. Pp. 58-61.

Lang, Andrew. 1948. *The Green Fairy Book*. New York: Longmans, Green. Pp. 207-13.

_____. 1901. *The Violet Fairy Book*. New York: Longmans, Green. Pp. 186-92.

Manning-Sanders, Ruth. 1970. *A Choice of Magic*. New York: Dutton. Pp. 26-38.

_____. 1969. *A Book of Princes and Princesses*. New York: Dutton. Pp. 84-96.

_____. 1965. *A Book of Magical Beasts*. Camden, N.J.: Nelson. Pp. 142-48.

Riordan, James. 1976. *Russian Tales, Volume I. Tales from Central Russia*. Harmondsworth, Middlesex: Kestrel. Pp. 129-37.

Sechrist, Elizabeth Hough. 1969. *Once in the First Times: Folk Tales from the Philippines*. Philadelphia: Macrae Smith. Pp. 150-56.

Toor, Frances. 1960. *The Golden Carnation, and other Stories Told in Italy*. New York: Lothrop. Pp. 25-27.

Whitney, Thomas. 1972. *In a Certain Kingdom: Twelve Russian Fairy Tales*. New York: Macmillan. Pp. 37-43.

Wiggins, Kate Douglas, and Nora Archibald Smith. 1967. *The Fairy Ring*. Garden City, N.Y.: Doubleday. Pp. 208-12.

FROGS AS FROGS

How-Why Stories

The next group of stories explains why frogs have spots, why they croak, how they communicate, how they lost their tails, how they lost their teeth, why you can see them on the moon, why their hands are flat, and why animals try to make frogs laugh.

Belting, Natalie. 1961. *The Long-Tailed Bear and Other Indian Legends.* Indianapolis: Bobbs-Merrill. Pp. 34-36.

Carpenter, Frances. 1959. *Wonder Tales of Seas and Ships.* Garden City, N.Y.: Doubleday. Pp. 29-36.

———. 1937. *Tales of a Chinese Grandmother.* Garden City, N.Y.: Doubleday. Pp. 190-97.

Converse, Harriet Maxwell. December 15, 1908. *Myths and Legends of the New York Iroquois.* New York State Museum, Albany, N.Y.: New York: *Museum Bulletin* 125.

Courlander, Harold. 1962. *The King's Drum and Other African Stories.* New York: Harcourt, Brace and World. Pp. 58-59.

———. 1957. *Terrapin's Pot of Sense.* New York: Holt. Pp. 91-92.

———. 1947. *The Cow-Tail Switch and Other West African Stories.* New York: Holt, Rinehart & Winston. Pp. 129-31.

———. 1942, 1964. *The Piece of Fire and Other Haitian Tales.* New York: Harcourt. Pp. 61-65.

Courlander, Harold, and Wolf Leslau. 1950. *The Fire on the Mountain and Other Ethiopian Stories.* New York: Holt. Pp. 111-12.

Courlander, Harold, and Albert Kofi Prempeh. 1957. *The Hat-Shaking Dance and Other Tales from the Gold Coast.* New York: Harcourt, Brace. Pp. 93-95.

Curry, Jane Louise. 1965. *Down from the Lonely Mountain. California Indian Tales.* New York: Harcourt, Brace and World. Pp. 68-69.

Duvoisin, Roger. 1941, 1957. *The Three Sneezes and Other Swiss Tales.* New York: Knopf. Pp. 234-45.

Fisher, Anne B. 1951. *Stories California Indians Told.* Berkeley, Calif.: Parnassus Press. Pp. 46-53.

Gaer, Joseph. 1955. *The Fables of India.* Boston: Little, Brown. Pp. 41-43.

Grimm, Jakob Ludwig Karl, and Wilhelm Karl Grimm. 1973. *Grimm's Fairy Tales: Twenty Stories.* New York: Viking. Pp. 29-31.

_____. 1947. *More Tales from Grimm.* Translated by Wanda Gag. New York: Coward-McCann. Pp. 89-94.

Hardendorff, Jeanne B. 1969. *Just One More.* Philadelphia: Lippincott. Pp. 73-77.

Harris, Joel Chandler. 1955. *The Complete Tales of Uncle Remus.* Compiled by Richard Chase. Boston: Houghton Mifflin. Pp. 45-48.

_____. 1920. *Uncle Remus, His Songs and His Sayings.* New York: Appleton. Pp. 69-72.

Jablow, Alta, and Carl Withers. 1969. *The Man in the Moon: Sky Tales from Many Lands.* New York: Holt, Rinehart & Winston. P. 24.

Jacobs, Joseph. 1916, 1967. *European Folk and Fairy Tales.* New York: Putnam. Pp. 66-71.

Kaula, Edna Mason. 1968. *African Village Folktales.* New York: World. Pp. 63-64.

Lang, Andrew. 1948. *The Rose Fairy Book.* New York: McKay. Pp. 64-71.

Leach, Maria. 1967. *How the People Sang the Mountains Up: How and Why Stories.* New York: Viking. P. 115.

Mullen-Guggenbuhl, Fritz. 1958. *Swiss Alpine Folk Tales.* Translated by Katherine Potts. New York: Walck. Pp. 177-80.

Robinson, Gail, and Douglas Hill. 1975. *Coyote the Trickster. Legends of the North American Indians.* New York: Crane Russak. Pp. 79-84.

Ryder, Arthur. 1956. *The Panchatantra.* Chicago: University of Chicago Press. Pp. 153-56.

Sechrist, Elizabeth Hough. 1969. *Once in the First Times: Folk Tales from the Philippines.* Philadelphia: Macrae Smith. Pp. 64-66.

Withers, Carl. 1965. *I Saw a Rocket Walk a Mile: Nonsense Tales, Chants and Songs of Many Lands.* New York: Holt. Pp. 131-32.

Leaping Frogs

Several stories involving leaping frogs could be suggested at this point. In Hans Christian Andersen's tale "The Leap Frog" (in *Andersen's Fairy Tales*, Garden City, N.Y.: Junior Deluxe Editions, 1956, pp. 121-24), three famous jumpers—a flea, a grasshopper, and a leap-frog— are involved in a jumping contest, with the king's daughter as the prize for the winner. The leap-frog wins the contest because of his intellectual performance.

The famous story by humorist Mark Twain, "The Notorious Jumping Frog of Calaveras County," is delightfully presented in a variety of sources.

Twain, Mark. 1971. *Jumping Frog*. New York: Dover Publications.

Twain, Mark. 1935. "The Jumping Frog" and "The Private History of the 'Jumping Frog' Story." In *The Family Mark Twain*. New York: Harper.

Professor Van Dyke of Princeton has pointed out that Twain's story was not an original one but dated back to the Greeks, a couple of thousand years earlier.

It was Twain's story that inspired the annual Jumping Frog Jubilee, held at the Calaveras County Fair (P.O. Box 96, Angels Camp, CA 95222) during the third weekend in May.

The jubilee offers a purse of $1,200 to the owner of a frog that sets a new world's record, $500 if it equals the record, and lesser amounts if it wins, places, or shows. The world's record was set in 1966 by a frog named "Ripple" with a distance of nineteen feet, three and one-eighth inches, according to the Jumping Frog Jubilee brochure. Another high-flying frog named "Hand-spring," which was entered by Governor Tom McCall of Oregon, leaped nineteen feet in the 1973 contest.

Another leaping frog is the bullfrog in Charles and Pete Seeger's story song "The Foolish Frog."

Seeger, Pete. 1972. *The Foolish Frog*. 16mm film. Weston Woods, Conn.: Weston Woods.

_____. 1964. "The Foolish Frog." In *The Bells of Rhymney*. New York: Oak Publications.

_____. "The Foolish Frog." *John Henry and Other Folk Favorites*. Columbia Records, HS 11337.

Seeger, Pete, and Charles Seeger. 1973. *The Foolish Frog*. New York: Macmillan.

Seeger's frog spends his time jumping across a stream from bank to bank and meets a very unfortunate end after he discovers everyone in the corner store is singing about him.

Factual Frogs

The *National Geographic* article by Paul A. Zahl, "In Quest of the World's Largest Frog" (vol. 132, no. 1, [July 1967], 146-52), provides interesting materials and pictures of frogs of a "world's largest" variety. Some of the following books will answer more questions than most people could think of concerning frogs.

Amos, William H. August 1970. "Teeming Life of a Pond." *National Geographic* 138, no. 2, 274-98.

Ballard, Lois. 1957. *My Easy-to-Read True Book of Reptiles*. New York: Grosset and Dunlap.

Darby, Gene. 1957. *What Is a Frog?* Chicago: Benefic Press.

Dickerson, Mary C. 1969. *The Frog Book*. New York: Dover.

Hawes, Judy. 1968. *Why Frogs Are Wet*. New York: Crowell.

Hogner, Dorothy Childs. 1956. *Frogs and Polliwogs*. New York: Crowell.

Langstaff, John. 1957. *Over in the Meadow*. New York: Harcourt, Brace and World.

Naden, Corinne J. 1972. *Let's Find Out about Frogs*. New York: Watts.

Simon, Seymour. 1969. *Discovering What Frogs Do*. New York: McGraw-Hill.

Zahl, Paul A. July 1973. "Nature's Living Jumping Jewels." *National Geographic* 144, no. 1, 130-46.

Zim, Herbert S. 1950. *Frogs and Toads*. New York: Morrow.

FROGS FROM DIFFERENT PLACES

Worldly Frogs

The following list includes stories of frogs from around the world.

Aesop. 1973. "The Two Frogs." In *Treasury of Aesop's Fables*, edited by Oliver Goldsmith. New York: Crown.

Garshin, Vsevolod. 1967. "The Frog Went A-Traveling." In *A Harvest of Russian Children's Literature*, edited by Miriam Morton. Berkeley, Calif.: University of California Press.

Maas, Selve. 1971. "The Northern Frog." In *The Moon Painters and Other Estonian Folk Tales*. New York: Viking.

Manning-Sanders, Ruth, editor. 1964. "Jack and His Golden Snuff-Box." In *The Red King and the Witch*. London: Oxford University Press.

Mistral, Gabriela. 1972. *Crickets and Frogs*. New York: Atheneum.

Sojo, Toba. 1954. *The Animal Frolic*. Text by Velma Varner. New York: Putnam.

In the collection of Estonian folktales (the location of Estonia might provide a topic for students to investigate), "The Northern Frog" tells of a unique creature. His body resembled a bull, but his legs were those of a huge frog, short in front and long behind; his tail was sixty feet long; his body was covered with scales; and he had piercing eyes that shone by day and night. (Children might enjoy drawing him.) Further, he was not a friendly fellow but a ferocious monster. Several motifs from other tales have been combined in this story: a quest for the powerful ring of King Solomon; a youth who could understand and communicate with birds; the magic of a drop of blood; a colossal iron horse on wheels; a hero chained to a rock; and a daughter given in marriage by the king. These motifs can be compared with other myths and tales.

American Folktales

A Connecticut folktale in which frogs play a very important part is "The Frogs of Windham Town," in which the old Puritan ethic against fun and frolic is clearly underscored. Richard Chase tells the tall tale "The Norther and the Frogs," in which certain Oklahoma frogs freeze in a pond and end up being shipped to Chicago for food.

The Texas story "How Sandy Got His Meat" tells of how Brer Rabbit outsmarts some frogs and provides a meal for Sandy the coon.

A favorite story for tellers is "The Wide-Mouthed Frog." The version listed below tells of the prideful resident of the Okefenokee Swamp, who conducts a survey of what every creature in the swamp dines on.

Botkin, B. A., editor. 1944. "How Sandy Got His Meat — A Negro Tale from the Brazos Bottoms." In *A Treasury of American Folklore*. Garden City, N.Y.: Garden City Books.

Chase, Richard. 1971. "The Norther and the Frogs." In *American Folk Tales and Songs*. New York: Dover.

Jagendorf, Moritz. 1948. "The Frogs of Windham Town." In *New England Bean Pot*. New York: Vanguard Press.

Schneider, Rex. 1980. *The Wide-Mouthed Frog*. Owings Mills, Md.: Stemmer House.

African Stories

Many of the African stories are quite complicated, but despite this, in "The Frog and Umdhlubu" several of the elements are recognizable to Western readers. For instance, the infant princess abandoned by a river is reminiscent of Moses left in the bullrushes. There is also the motif of the wicked step-mother (in this case, stepmothers).

An easier African folktale concerning a frog is "Ananse and the King's Cow." In this one, the frog gives the secret of the sweet fat he serves in meals to Ananse and thereby innocently seals the fate of his friend the cow along with modifying the king's future meals.

Aardema, Verna. 1969. "Ananse and the King's Cow." In *Tales from the Third Ear from Equatorial Africa*. New York: Dutton. Pp. 9-18.

"The Frog and Umdhlubu." 1966. *African Folktales and Sculpture*. New York: Pantheon. Pp. 106-07.

FROGS IN VARIOUS MEDIA

Picture Books

There are books of many varieties with frogs in them.

In the following collection of books there are Caldecott honor books, Newbery honor books and Notable Children's Books. The whimsical stories with frogs as the main characters are quite popular not only with the critical adult (who after all does the choosing for these awards) but also with the youngsters reading them.

Several of the books have no words. It is easy for children to follow the action and "tell" the story themselves using the pictures. For older children, these books could be studied as examples as to how to create their own word-less books. It is a challenge to develop a story and decide which scenes will depict the action intended to tell the story.

Abell, Kathleen. 1974. *King Orville and the Bullfrogs*. Boston: Little, Brown.

Cleveland, David. 1981. *The Frog on Robert's Head*. New York: Coward, McCann and Geoghegan.

Cooper, Marjorie. 1965. *Jeepers the Little Frog*. Eau Claire, Wis.: E. M. Hale.

Flack, Marjorie. 1934. *Tim Tadpole and the Great Bullfrog*. New York: Doubleday.

Freschet, Bernice. 1968. *The Old Bullfrog*. New York: Scribner.

Hodges, Elizabeth Jamison. 1969. *Free as a Frog*. Reading, Mass.: Addison-Wesley.

Kalan, Robert. 1981. *Jump, Frog, Jump!* New York: Greenwillow.

Lobel, Arnold. 1979. *Days with Frog and Toad*. New York: Harper and Row.

_____. 1976. *Frog and Toad All Year*. New York: Harper and Row.

_____. 1971. *Frog and Toad Together*. New York: Harper and Row.

_____. 1970. *Frog and Toad Are Friends*. New York: Harper and Row.

Mayer, Mercer. 1974. *Frog Goes to Dinner*. New York: Dial.

_____. 1973. *Frog on His Own*. New York: Dial.

_____. 1969. *Frog Where Are You?* New York: Dial.

Mayer, Mercer, and Marianna Mayer. 1975. *One Frog Too Many*. New York: Dial.

Rockwell, Anne, and Harlow Rockwell. 1970. *Olly's Polliwogs*. New York: Doubleday.

Roy, Ron. 1981. *The Great Frog Swap*. New York: Pantheon.

Tarrant, Graham. 1983. *Frogs*. Los Angeles: Intervisual Communications.

Terris, Susan. 1973. *Plague of Frogs*. New York: Doubleday.

Tresselt, Alvin. 1958. *The Frog in the Well*. New York: Lothrop, Lee and Shepard.

Welber, Robert. 1971. *Frog Frog Frog*. New York: Pantheon.

Songs

The old nursery song retold by John Langstaff in *Frog Went A-Courtin'*. (New York: Harcourt, Brace and World, 1955) is enjoyable because of the popular old ballad as well as the creative artwork. Historically, however, according to Evelyn Kendrick Wells in *The Ballad Tree* (New York: Ronald Press, 1950), this old folk song may have served as a safe way for the people during the reign of Queen Elizabeth I to indulge in satire without literally losing their heads. Wells suggests that the frog referred to the French ambassador, the duc d'Alençon, whose pending marriage to Queen Elizabeth was very unpopular with the English people. Another interesting use of the word might be pointed out here also. The queen referred to the duke as her frog, and this reference may be related to the slang term the English had for Frenchmen. (*Webster's New World Dictionary of the American Language* [New York: P. F. Collier and Son, 1952], however, attributes the usage to the fondness the French have for eating frogs' legs.)

Frog Went A-Courtin' could also be compared to the following picture books:

Caldecott, Randolph. N.d. *A Frog He Would A-Wooing Go.* New York: Warne.

Stevens, H. J. 1967. *A Frog He Would A-Wooing Go.* New York: Walker.

Caldecott's version has very different lyrics and meaning from the Langstaff retelling.

Other frog-oriented songs are

Kalb, Buddy. 1976. "Frog Kissin'." Nashville, Tenn.: Ahab Music Co.

Peter, Paul, and Mary. N.d. "I'm in Love with a Big Blue Frog." *Album 1700.* Burbank, Calif.: Warner Bros. Records. Cassette WS M5 1700.

Seeger, Pete. 1964. "The Foolish Frog." In *The Bells of Rhymney.* New York: Oak Publications.

Yolen, Jane. 1972. "The Frog in the Spring." In *Fireside Book of Birds and Beasts.* New York: Simon and Schuster. Pp. 118-19.

Shadow Puppet Plays

Children might also be interested in developing a shadow puppet play about frogs. This form of storytelling also thrived in the Indonesian countries. For further information on shadow puppet plays, see Joan Joseph's *Folk Toys around the World and How to Make Them* (New York: Parents Magazine Press, 1972).

Poetry

As was mentioned earlier, frogs are often the subjects for poetry. Students might create their own poems before or after reading or hearing existing ones. There are two anthologies of frog poems.

Donaldson, Gerald. 1980. *Frogs*. New York: Van Nostrand.

Shaw, Richard. 1972. *The Frog Book*. New York: Frederick Warne.

Frog poetry can also be found in the following sources:

Aiken, Conrad. 1970. "The Frog." In *Anthology of Children's Literature*, edited by Johnson, Sickels, and Sayers. Boston: Houghton Mifflin.

Bechtel, Louise Seaman. 1961. "Grandfather Frog." In *The Arbuthnot Anthology of Children's Literature*, edited by May Hill Arbuthnot. Chicago: Scott Foresman.

Belloc, Hilaire. "The Frog." In *Anthology of Children's Literature*, edited by Johnson, Sickels, and Sayers. Boston: Houghton Mifflin.

Cooper, George. 1940. "Frogs at School." In *Story and Verse for Children*, edited by Miriam Huber. New York: Macmillan.

Livingston, Myra Cohn, editor. 1973. *What a Wonderful Bird the Frog Are*. New York: Harcourt Brace and Jovanovich. P. 21.

Neruda, Pablo. 1965. *Bestiary*. New York: Harcourt, Brace and World.

Spilka, Arnold. 1972. *And the Frog Went Blah!* New York: Scribner.

ACTIVITIES

Movement

The youngsters might interpret the movements of frogs jumping, diving, and swimming and develop a physical understanding of how a frog moves. Treat Davidson's article "Bullfrog Ballet Filmed in Flight" (*National Geographic* 123, no. 6, [June 1963], 790-99) would serve as a good introduction to the movement of frogs. A picture book that introduces and illustrates familiar ballet steps, combining the technical with the humorous, is Donald Elliott's *Frogs and the Ballet* (Ipswich, Mass.: Gambit, 1979). The youngsters might also wish to create a dance to accompany a tape or record of frog sounds.

The background of the game of leapfrog tag and the directions for playing it are found in Iris Vinton's *The Folkways Omnibus of Children's Games* (Harrisburg, Pa.: The Stackpole Company, 1970).

Art

An endless variety of art experiences is available for individual or group projects. Some of them are listed below.

Make a frog wood or lino cut

Create a frog in stitchery

Design a frog rug or wall hanging

Paint a frog picture

Make a frog batik wall hanging

Create a frog mural

Sculpt a frog

Create a frog collage

Make a frog puzzle

Create a frog filmstrip

Make frog shadow puppets to use in a story

Make a frog puppet

Create an original frog cover to be used on a bound book

Some excellent examples of frogs in art are found in the following books:

Eisenstaedt, Alfred. 1971. *Witness to Nature*. New York: Viking.

Galdone, Paul. 1973. *Children's Book Week Frieze*. New York: Children's Book Council.

Hawley, W. M. 1971. *Chinese Folk Designs*. New York: Dover.

Neruda, Pablo. 1965. *Bestiary*. New York: Harcourt, Brace and World.

Williams, Geoffrey. 1971. *African Designs from Traditional Sources*. New York: Dover.

Advertising

Frogs have been characters in advertisements of a diverse variety. For instance, Honeywell recently used two frogs on a lily pad, which sounds typical—but typical it wasn't. The frogs were made of colored computer transistors and the advertisement was labeled "The Other Computer Company: Honeywell." To accompany this advertisement the youngsters could explore the meanings to the sayings, "He is a big frog in a little pond" and "He is a little frog in a big pond."

A recent classified advertisement showed several frogs with the traditional lily pads and it was labeled "The Great Pad!" which clearly indicates what was being promoted. Some individuals might want to investigate where the term *pad* comes from and discover what the term had to do with this particular advertisement.

Another use of frogs in advertisements is found on the outside of a beauty salon called "The Frog." There is a lovely pink frog decorating the front of the shop. The term "beauty is only skin deep" might be associated with this beauty shop. It also might mean that the beauticians can turn frogs into princesses.

After exploring why frogs were used in these particular promotions, the youngsters might want to create some of their own advertisements and selling slogans.

Language Arts

Youngsters could imitate the sounds illustrated in Mary Leister's *Silent Concert* (Indianapolis, Ind.: Bobbs-Merrill, 1970) and develop creative descriptive sounds of their own. Youngsters might want to investigate in story or fact the various terms used to interpret the sounds frogs make, such as *knee-deep*, *chug-a-rum*, and *rivet*, and go on to develop some of their own. Audio tapes of frogs could aid in this exploration.

A list of descriptive terms related to frogs could be devised. A large sheet of paper might be hung on the wall with a picture of a frog in the center of the paper. Anyone who can think of a word to describe the frog or the sound a frog makes may write the word on the paper with a marker.

Mention was made earlier of vocabulary study in conjunction with the song "Frog Went A-Courtin'," but the word *frog* has further possibilities for investigation. The dictionary lists several meanings for *frog* — the horny pad in the middle of the sole of a horse's foot, a corded or braided loop used as a fastener or decoration on clothing, and a device on railroad tracks for keeping cars on the proper rails at intersections or switches. There is also the frog used in flower arrangements. Children could develop their own creative reasons as to how these other objects got the name *frog* and then investigate the real reason behind the term. The terms frogman and *frog in the throat* might also be studied for literal and figurative interpretations.

Some suggested vocabulary activities for students follow.

Put some cutout pictures of frogs in an envelope and categorize them in a variety of different ways:
- largest frog
- smallest frog
- large frogs
- small frogs
- middle-size frogs
- frogs from smallest to largest

Can you think of any other ways to categorize them?

Write down as many words as you can that describe how frogs move.

Make a poster illustrating the different vocabulary meanings for the word *frog*.

Write down as many words as you can that rhyme with *frog*.

Use a record or tape of Twain's "The Celebrated Jumping Frog of Calaveras County." Listen and answer these questions:
- What regional dialect is used?
- What does the dialect tell you about the characters?
- What effect do you think the author was trying to create by using dialect?
- List the words you were not familiar with.

Read Claire Huchet Bishop and Kurt Wiese's *The Five Chinese Brothers* (New York: Coward-McCann, 1938) and Gerald McDermott's *Anansi the Spider* (New York: Holt, Rinehart & Winston, 1972). What is alike about them? What is different? Write a story about a group of frog brothers with special talents.

Read or listen to several different versions of the Frog Prince story. Compare and contrast them.

Collect advertisements with frogs in them. Develop your own advertisement incorporating frogs.

Read the story "The Letter" from the book *Frog and Toad Are Friends* by Arnold Lobel (New York: Harper and Row, 1970). What letter might you write to Frog or Toad?

Write a riddle about a frog.

Write a story about a backward frog named Gorf.

Write a different ending for one of the frog stories you have read or heard.

Use the technique of batik to make a frog creation. To accompany this, describe the steps involved in making it and tell something about it — do this on tagboard or paper.

Make and tell a flannelboard story about a frog.

Write an original frog story.

Write a haiku about a frog.

Write an original frog poem.

Make frog puppets and use them to tell a very froggy story.

Write and tell an original tall tale about a frog.

Write and tell a story about a day in the life of a frog.

Write and tell a story to explain how the frog got his spots.

Write and tell a story about the day all the frogs disappeared.

Use the words to "Frog Went A-Courtin' " and arrange it for a group experience in choral reading.

Teach a fingerplay about frogs which you have read or written to a small group of younger children.

Develop a play about frogs.

Act out one of the stories about frogs which you have read, heard, or written.

Write an original song about a frog.

Science and Mathematics

If frog eggs are available, keep a written and pictorial log of their development.

If, as in Twain's "Jumping Frog" story, a frog had ingested buckshot, how would you calculate how much the shot adversely affected the distance of the frog's jump?

Study frog population growth in a pond and graph your findings.

Investigate the folklore belief that the frog's back will predict if there will be a severe or a mild winter.

Describe how you would teach a frog to jump. Follow your directions and evaluate your success as a direction giver.

Why would the ability to jump be an asset for frogs?

Weigh frogs in various stages. Check their weight with the record frogs in *The Guinness Book of World Records* and compute their relative weights and sizes. Graph these.

Measure the average distance a frog jumps. Using this average, determine how many jumps it would take the frog to get across the room, from one end of the hall to another, across the schoolyard, or some other goal. If he hopped at a regular speed, how long would it take for him to accomplish this goal?

Investigate the myth that frogs and toads cause warts.

How do frogs drink?

Why do frogs have vocal sacs that expand?

Develop overlay transparencies illustrating the growth stages of frogs.

Investigate unique features about a frog's tongue.

Picture-taking Activities

Take pictures of frog activities in which you have participated.

Take pictures to illustrate a class scrapbook on frog activities.

Use pictures you have taken to make a bulletin board on "Fantastic Frogs."

Make a community newspaper concerning frogs. One copy using individual photographs can be made into a display for the people in school to read.

Use the camera to take pictures to make an original picture-story book. This could also be used for oral storytelling.

You are a frog—take pictures from that point of view illustrating what a frog would see.

Take several unrelated pictures and develop a story using these pictures.

Stage a frog race on the playground. Take action pictures, put them in sequence, and write a story about them.

Give the same picture to several children and have one write in first person, one in second person, one in third person, subjectively or objectively, about the picture. Then compare what was written.

How can you take pictures to give evidence of change in the frogs, their environment, etc.?

Take pictures during a field trip to a pond (or museum, etc.).

Take pictures of things in your community related to frogs.

Take pictures of different stages in the growth of frogs and write stories for the pictures.

General Activities

Buy used copies of the *National Geographic* and put the frog-related articles into a book.

Collect poems, haiku, fingerplays, and stories. Create your own classroom frog anthology. Copies of some of these could also be made
available for others.

Collect cartoons about frogs and develop your own frog cartoon book.

And so, here's to frogs!!

NOAH AND THE ARK AND THE RAINBOW

INTRODUCTION

The story of Noah and his ark and how the rainbow came to be is not
limited to a single religious dogma. The symbolism of the ark and the rainbow
has become part of general cultural awareness. We now find references to
Noah and the ark in greeting cards, wallpaper designs, cartoons, political
statements, state lottery promotions, advertisements, and also language usage
such as "Don't miss the boat."

The Bible story of Noah (in Genesis, chapters 6, 7, 8, and 9) culminates
(chapter 9, verses 13-15) with the significance of the rainbow:

I do set my bow in the cloud
and it shall be a token
of a covenant between me and the earth.

And it shall come to pass, when
I bring a cloud over the earth, that
the bow shall be seen in the cloud:

And I will remember my covenant,
which is between me and you and
every living creature of all flesh;
and the waters shall no more
become a flood to destroy all flesh.

Mythology concerning the rainbow can be found worldwide. People have
always felt the need to explain natural phenomena, and the rainbow, since it is
so closely related to rain, has a great variety of explanations. For instance:

African: The rainbow is a giant snake that comes out after rainfall to
graze.

African: The rainbow is a sign that never again will the gods hold the rain
and bring a drought that will kill the people.

Fon tribe, western Africa: Treasure can be found where the rainbow ends.

Estonian: The rainbow is the head of an ox, lowered to a river in drinking.

Ponca Indian: The rainbow is really petals from the flowers.

Shoshoni Indian: The rainbow is a giant serpent who rubs his back on a dome of ice.

Finnish: The rainbow is the sickle or bow of the Thunder God, whose arrow is the lightning.

North Asian: The rainbow is a camel with three people on its back. The first beats a drum (thunder), the second waves a scarf (lightning), and the third pulls the reins, causing water (rain) to run from the camel's mouth.

Germanic: The rainbow is the bowl God used at the time of the creation in tinting the birds.

Japanese: The rainbow is "the Floating Bridge of Heaven."

Buddhists: The colors of the rainbow were related to the seven planets and the seven regions of the earth.

Christians: The rainbow's colors are sometimes linked to the seven sacraments.

There are a wide variety of ways the topics of Noah, the ark, and rainbows can be used in all areas, at all levels of the curriculum. The following ideas are examples of curricular activities developed as an extension of telling a story (in this specific instance, a story about Noah's ark and the rainbow). The ideas listed here are by no means all-inclusive and can be adapted for use from kindergarten to high school.

ACTIVITIES

Language Arts

Listening

Give out slips of paper with animal names written on them. There should be two slips for each animal chosen. Have the students, all at the same time, make the sound of the animal whose name is written on their slip of paper. The object is for pairs of students to find each other, using only the animal sounds for identification. This activity could also be done using pantomimed actions for identification. When finished, have the students line up alphabetically using the animal names.

Suggestions for animals:

cat	fish	wolf
dog	chipmunk	sheep
monkey	horse	rattlesnake
donkey	elephant	cow
chicken	hyena	cuckoo
lion	seal	

Oral Sharing

- Select one of the versions of how rainbows came to be and develop it into a story to tell.

- Are there any stories about a time in your life when you saw a rainbow? Was it special? What do you remember? Tell about it. (Write about it.)

Writing

- Write and tell your own myth explaining how the rainbow came to be in the sky. (See Bibliography, pp. 411-16, for examples of stories.)

- What creatures did not get on the ark? As a group, brainstorm what those creaturs might have been. Make your creatures as off-beat as possible. Then write the story of why they "missed the boat" and illustrate it. Compare your creatures with *Roll Call: The Story of Noah's Ark and the World's First Losers* (Goldthwaite 1978).

- Have the students write new verses to sing to "One Wide River to Cross." What different animals and rhymes could they invent? (See Emberley 1966.)

- One story goes that the raccoons waited to get onto the ark until after the unicorns got there but that Noah's three sons, Shem, Ham, and Japheth slapped their hands over their eyes and dragged them on board, and that is why raccoons wear masks. Write your own version about why some of the animals today have the physical characteristics that they do.

- Keep a journal about all of the activities you have worked on related to Noah, the ark, and the rainbow. React to each of these activities. Some possible reactions to consider: Did you learn anything new? What did you enjoy? Why? Did you try something new? How did it feel when you did it? What do you see as possibilities for further study?

Discussion

- Ever since Marco Polo mentioned the existence of the ark in the thirteenth century, people worldwide have searched chasms, glaciated mountain passes, and subglacial lakes for evidence of a historical foundation for the story of Noah and the flood. Sporadic news releases on current explorations can be collected and shared.

- Develop class discussion questions for each of the newspaper articles. For example: What kind of person would seriously build an ark for another extended flood in an effort to be a modern-day Noah? A bomb shelter? What about modern survivalists? How are they like Noah? Different?

Advertising

- Look through catalogs, brochures, and novelty shops to discover how many different ways rainbows are being marketed. Create a rainbow product of your own, develop an advertising program for it (slogan, description, or sales pitch), and test the market with your friends and families. Do you think it would sell? Why?

Journalism

- Write a class newspaper called "Noah's News." What kinds of articles will be appropriate? Remember all of the different sections of the news-paper. For instance: Write an article about the appearance of the first rainbow as a news event or science fiction feature. Write an interview with Noah. Write ads to sell a used ark.

- Pretend you have just discovered the pot of gold at the end of the rainbow. Call a press conference and give your story to the reporters. Remember — it is important to have all the answers to the questions Who? What? When? Where? Why? How? Prepare an outline for your press release.

Vocabulary

- What is the difference between *arc* and *ark*? Use each word in a sentence.

- Read these sentences out loud. How are the sounds of the capitalized words alike or different?

Bow down to the queen and king.

The *Bow* and arrow belonged to Kim.

The biggest *Bough* of the tree was broken off.

Look the three words up in the dictionary and write the meaning or meanings for each one.

- Where do you think the expression "We missed the boat" came from? Investigate the origin of the phrase.

Reading

- Compare and contrast any two stories of how the rainbow was created.

- Use the lyrics of "Somewhere Over the Rainbow" (Harburg 1938) or "The Unicorn" (Silverstein n.d.) for choral reading. How will you establish the arrangement for this choral reading? How will the voices be used? What about emphasis? Speed? Tone? Pitch? Volume?

- Write a reader's theater script about what might have happened as Noah got instructions to build the ark, how he did it, how he got all the animals on board, what the trip was like, and what happened after it.

Poetry

- Collect poems related to the rainbow or Noah's ark. Make a class book of them.

- Write an original poem about the rainbow or Noah and the ark.

Book Reports

- Write a book report in code telling about one of the books listed in the bibliography. Develop your own code. Give your letter to a partner to see if he or she can decipher it.

- Write eight incomplete sentences about one of the books listed in the bibliography. See if someone else can complete your sentences.

- Investigate one of the authors or illustrators of books listed in the bibliography. What other works has he or she done? Which of these is your favorite? Why?

Science

- What colors are in a rainbow? Experiment: Place a pan of water in a beam of sunlight. Against one side of the pan, lean a small mirror. Move the mirror until you see the colors. Paint a rainbow using the colors you see.

- A rainbow in the morning
  Is the shepherd's warning;
  A rainbow at night
  Is the shepherd's delight.

  There are many folk rhymes and sayings regarding rainbows as weather forecasters. How many can you find?

- Observe rainbows and develop some generalizations about what you see. Where is the sun (even if it is hidden by clouds) in relation to the rainbow?

- Why do you only see an arc of the rainbow instead of a full circle?

- Invite a local TV weatherperson to come in and speak to the class about rainbows.

- Experiment with prisms. Create and write up an experiment and see if another student can follow your directions.

- Experiment with bubbles. How many different colors can you see in the soap film? Add food coloring to a soap solution. Does food color alter the colors on the surface of the bubble? Look at the bubble through colored cellophane. Do the colors in the bubble look different from before?

Cooking

- There is a recipe called "Rainbow in a Cloud" made of colored cubes of gelatin in a dish of whipped cream. Can you invent other rainbow ideas for eating? List all of the ingredients and directions for making your new dish. (Maybe the prize-winning recipe could be prepared and sampled by the class.)

Art

- Develop a bulletin board about Noah's ark (see fig. A.1, p. 410).

- Create a mural of Noah's ark.

- Create a stitchery collage of Noah's ark for a permanent school display.

Fig. A.1. Sample bulletin board.

- Construct a rainbow mobile and suspend figures of animals from it.
- Make puppets to use in telling the story or singing a song about Noah's ark.
- Develop a cartoon about Noah's ark.
- Make three-dimensional figures of animals that did not make it to the ark in time.

- Make a felt soft-sculpture ark with a pocket and figures of animals and Noah. The students can use these figures to tell or sing one of the stories they have read, heard, or written. (Or use a flannel board and flannel figures.)

- Study the art and media used in the picture books listed in the bibliography. For instance, how did Ed Emberley create the pictures for *One Wide River to Cross*? Antonio Frasconi in *How the Left-Behind Beasts Built Ararat*? Have the students experiment with woodcuts, linoleum cuts, and printmaking.

- Develop a class book in which students illustrate a myth about the rainbow or the ark. The book could be placed in the classroom or school library.

Music

- Listen to the recordings of rainbow songs (Harburg; Harburg and Lane; Silverstein; Williams). Create movement and dance to go with the mood and words of the songs.

- Make up a song about rainbows.

- Create movements to go with a rainstorm, rushing water, and a rainbow.

Bonus Activity

- Develop a trivia game for the story of Noah and the ark and the rainbow.

- With the help of the teacher, create an activity center, which might include games you develop, class books in various stages of development, records and tapes for listening, and a collection of art and science resources and books.

ANNOTATED BIBLIOGRAPHY

Anderson, Bernice G. 1979. "The Flowers' Forever Land." In *Trickster Tales from Prairie Lodges*. Nashville, Tenn.: Abingdon Press.

This is the Ponca Indian story about how the rainbow came to be.

Angel, Marie. 1973. *The Ark*. New York: Harper and Row.

The artist "crammed in as many animals as possible and looked for animals that were not the traditional inmates of the Ark." *The Ark* consists of fold-out pictures of animals boarding the ark.

Barlin, Paul, and Anne Barlin. 1964. *Dance a Story: Noah's Ark*. New York: Ginn and Co.

This book and the accompanying record present a story, lyrics, and illustrations to encourage creative dance movement and pantomime.

Bedford, Annie North. 1952. *Walt Disney's Ark*. New York: Simon and Schuster.

This story gives the point of view of the complainers, whiners, and sulkers on the ark.

Bolliger, Max. 1972. *Noah and the Rainbow*. Translated by Clyde Robert Bulla. New York: Thomas Y. Crowell Co.

This is a telling of the story of Noah, the ark, and the Rainbow accompanied by soft, gentle, warm art.

Brook, Judy. 1973. *Noah's Ark*. New York: Franklin Watts.

Noah's family has difficulties as they sail all over the world to collect the animals.

Burnford, Sheila. 1973. *Mr. Noah and the Second Flood*. New York: Praeger Publishers.

A cautionary fable about the descendants of the original Noah and the frightening prospects ahead for environmental survival for our earth.

Diamond, Jasper. 1983. *Noah's Ark*. New York: Prentice-Hall.

Everything, including the slip cover, gets converted into a model of the ark. There is a spiral-bound text for the story.

Duvoisin, Roger. 1952. *A for the Ark*. New York: Lothrop, Lee and Shepard.

Noah has the animals board in alphabetical order.

Elborn, Andrew. 1984. *Noah and the Ark and the Animals*. Natick, Mass.: Picture Book Studio.

A colt retells the story of Noah and the ark, providing the point of view of the animals. The watercolor pictures have a folk art quality full of softness and charm.

Emberley, Barbara. 1966. *One Wide River to Cross*. New York: Scholastic Book Services.

The words and music are provided to the folk song "One Wide River to Cross," and the verses are illustrated with powerful block prints.

Farber, Norma. 1978. *How the Left-Handed Beasts Built Ararat*. New York: Walker and Co.

Through verse we find out how Mt. Ararat came to be built and available for the ark to land on after its voyage of forty days and forty nights.

Farber, Norma. 1974. *Where's Gomer?* New York: E. P. Dutton.

The art in *Where's Gomer?* is quite whimsical.

Farber, Norma. 1967. *Did You Know It Was the Narwhale?* New York: Atheneum.

The unicorn was a great help to Noah in this tale told in verse about Noah and the flood. Did the unicorn really survive the trip?

Flanders, Michael. 1972. *Captain Noah and His Floating Zoo.* Indianapolis: Bobbs-Merrill.

Flanders' verse tells of those who came to mock Noah's boat building.

Freeman, Don. 1966. *A Rainbow of My Own.* New York: Viking Press.

A little boy longs to have a rainbow of his own in this picture book that combines reality and delightful fantasy.

Friedrich, Priscilla, and Otto Friedrich. 1961. *Noah Shark's Ark.* New York: A. S. Barnes.

This contemporary fable emphasizes the virtue of unselfishness.

Goffstein, M. B. 1978. *My Noah's Ark.* New York: Harper and Row.

An old woman tells about how her father built a toy ark for her when she was a little girl. The toy now holds ninety years of her life along with memories of her parents, husband, and children.

Goldthwaite, John. 1978. *Roll Call: The Story of Noah's Ark and the World's First Losers.* N.p.: Harlin Quist.

An amusing alphabet book of nonsense creatures that did not make it onto the ark.

Graham, F. Lanier, ed. 1979. *The Rainbow Book.* New York: Vintage Books (Random House).

A collection of essays and illustrations devoted to rainbows in particular and spectral sequences in general. Contains information on the arts and the rainbow, as well as the physics and metaphysics of the spectrum.

Graham, Lorenz. 1971. *God Wash the World and Start Again.* New York: Thomas Y. Crowell.

This narrative version of the Noah's ark story, based on a Liberian story, gives specifics of the building of the ark. God himself supervises the construction.

Haley, Gail E. 1971. *Noah's Ark.* New York: Atheneum.

Noah is an ecologist who sets out to save the animals from destruction by pollution in this futuristic depiction.

Harburg, E. Y. "Somewhere over the Rainbow." *The Wizard of Oz* (audio recording). Metro-Goldwyn-Mayer.

Harburg, E. Y., and Burton Lane. "Look to the Rainbow." *Finian's Rainbow*. Columbia CS 2080.

Haubensak-Tellenbach, Margrit. 1983. *The Story of Noah's Ark*. New York: Clarion Publishers.
A retelling of the story.

Hulpach, Vladimir. 1965. "The Rainbow Snake." In *American Indian Tales and Legends*. London: Paul Hamlyn.
This is an Indian explanation of how the shaman and the snake created the rainbow.

Jones, Harold, and Kathleen Lines. 1961. *Noah and the Ark*. New York: Franklin Watts.
A traditional story.

Lenski, Lois. 1948. *Mr. and Mrs. Noah*. New York: Thomas Y. Crowell.
A colorful, distinctive picture book with the story of the Noah family told in a humorous fashion.

Lorimer, Lawrence T. 1978. *Noah's Ark*. New York: Random House.
This is another retelling of the Bible story.

Lowrides, Rosemary, and Claude Kailer. 1983. *Make Your Own Noah's Ark*. Boston: Little, Brown.
A cut-out book for constructing your own ark.

Mee, Charles L., Jr. 1978. *Noah*. New York: Harper and Row.
As the animals are assembling, the Noah family checks them off on their checklists.

Mother Serena (Jolanda Colombini Monti). 1956. *Noah's Ark*. Milan: Piccoli.
The artist illustrates the population explosion that took place on board.

Parrinder, Geoffrey. 1967. *African Mythology*. London: Paul Hamlyn.
This resource gives a variety of African stories about the rainbow.

Piehl, Kathy. Summer 1982. "Noah as a Survivor: A Study of Picture Books." *Children's Literature in Education* 13, no. 2, 80-85.

Pitcher, Diana. 1981. "Rainbow." In *Tokoloshi*. Millbrae, Calif.: Celestial Arts, A Dawne-Leigh Book.
Gives the African drought story.

Pomerantz, Charlotte. 1981. *Noah and Namah's Ark*. New York: Holt, Rinehart & Winston.

Told in humorous verse and precise, detailed art, the story of Noah and the flood and the rainbow takes on an earthy humor as Noah's family begins begetting.

Rico, Ulde. 1978. *The Rainbow Goblins.* New York: Thames and Hudson.

Seven rainbow goblins (Red, Orange, Yellow, Green, Blue, Indigo, Violet) and their leader, Yellow, suck the colors out of the rainbows. The Goblins are tricked by the flowers so that after the Rainbow is reborn it lifts up the flowers and transforms them into glittering dragonflies, butterflies, and splendidly plumed birds. Magnificent oil-on-oak-panel paintings.

Robbins, Ruth. 1980. *How the First Rainbow Was Made.* Boston: Parnassus Press, Houghton Mifflin.

From Indian folklore, this is another explanation about how the rainbow came to be.

Rounds, Glen. 1985. *Washday on Noah's Ark.* New York: Holiday House.

After listening to weather reports, Noah builds an ark for his family and farm animals. Then the trouble starts with the rains. Wild animals force their way aboard. Some of the animals help Mrs. Noah with her enormous washday problem.

Schaaf, Fred. May-June 1983. "A Rendezvous with Rainbows." *Mother Earth News*, 70-72.

Silverstein, Shel. 1974. "The Unicorn." In *Where the Sidewalk Ends.* New York: Harper and Row. Pp. 76-77.

Silverstein, Shel. "The Unicorn." *The Unicorn.* Sung by the Irish Rovers. Decca DL 74951.

Simon, Hilda. 1981. *The Magic of Color.* New York: Lothrop, Lee and Shepard.

Just as a rainbow is "magic of color," there are many other magical uses of color. Demonstrations and explanations clarify some of these mysteries. Fascinating.

Singer, Isaac Bashevis. 1974. *Why Noah Chose the Dove.* Translated by Elizabeth Shub. New York: Farrar, Straus and Giroux.

Singer explains why Noah chose the dove to be his messenger and teaches the virtue of humility.

Spier, Peter. 1977. *Noah's Ark.* New York: Doubleday.

The Caldecott medal winner by Peter Spier presents a translation of a seventeenth-century Dutch poem followed by the story of the ark in wordless, detailed illustration format.

Weston, Martha. 1981. *Peony's Rainbow*. New York: Lothrop, Lee and Shepard.

What wonderful things could you do if you had your very own rainbow? Peony the pig captures one and experiences great joy, along with a few unexpected problems.

Wiesner, William. 1966. *Noah's Ark*. New York: E. P. Dutton.

The arching rainbow covers the survivors of the flood.

Wildsmith, Brian. 1980. *Professor Noah's Spaceship*. New York: Oxford University Press.

In the future, when the creatures of the world decide to leave for another place unspoiled by pollution, they may decide to use a spaceship. In this one, due to an error with the time guidance system, they travel backward through time. Brilliant artwork.

Williams, Paul. "The Rainbow Connection." *The Muppet Movie*. Atlantic SD 16001.

Wynants, Miche. 1965. *Noah's Ark*. New York: Harcourt Brace and World.

The traditional story.

Yolen, Jane. 1974. *Rainbow Rider*. New York: Thomas Y. Crowell.

An original, modern creation myth of the "time it all began," accompanied by luminous watercolor desert landscape illustrations.

B

Sample Real-Life Telling

Recently at a museum of art, a weeklong celebration of the cowboy and the West was held. The festivities included displays of cowboy art, country and western music, roping and branding demonstrations, chuckwagon lunches, hayrides, and storytelling. While four male storytellers told stories of brave and gallant male western heroes, the one female storyteller chose for her part to explore the lives of the women of the West as recorded in diaries, journals, books, and oral interviews. Her storytelling sessions were held near the quilting display. A huge cast-iron kettle was arranged beside her rocking chair, and she placed her props—a shawl, a patchwork apron, a wooden scrub board, and a McGuffey's reader—in it. As she told stories she used the appropriate prop. The following are the stories she told and the songs she sang.

WOMEN IN THE WEST

Carl Sandburg had this to say about the pioneers: "The cowards never started and the weak ones died by the way." Of course this had to be true for those intrepid adventurers who left home, family, and comfort to seek a new life in the West. Traveling out West involved not only months of hardship, discomfort, and danger, but also optimism. These pioneers had to be optimistic about the future, their abilities to succeed and hold to a dream of the future. All of these noble aspirations had to be dampened by the trek from the great Mississippi River and over the vast plains to the awe-inspiring sight of the Rocky Mountains looming ahead of them for weeks. Most European immigrants had nothing to compare this vastness to. How could they judge the oral reports of what existed out West based on their experiences with European geography? How could they comprehend a vastness that would require months to negotiate? The women who walked, rode, and cooked their way to the West had to be extraordinary women, did they not?

How extraordinary is extraordinary? The folk versions of the ballad "Sweet Betsy from Pike" give some insights into these women. They were not saints or ethereal beings—they had red blood and guts. In the first verse of "Sweet Betsy" the words of the ballad tell us that she crossed the wide mountains with her *lover* Ike. Is that a typical traveling arrangement? We usually think of devoted family units traveling together. Another verse tells of the night they camped on the prairie and broke out the whiskey. Our heroine got tight, sang, romped, and shouted, and "showed her bare bum to the whole wagon train." This is a rather earthy action and not at all stoic for our Sweet Betsy. Some things actually never change, just the history of them does. The ballad has some attempt at making an honest woman out of Betsy, as it tells of the marriage of Long Ike and Sweet Betsy. However, Ike got jealous, obtained a divorce, and our undaunted Betsy boasted with a smile, "I've six good men waitin' within half a mile." This of course was true. Women out West were not short of suitors. More about that later.

There were many diary and journal entries about the weather out West. Many sources maintain that there were two seasons: the winter and the Fourth of July. One oldtimer maintained that there was only a barbed wire fence between his town and the Arctic Pole and that two of the three strands were down most of the winter. To further compare the pioneers with our country's sense of hugeness, their stories were big as well. Tall tales were a natural form for a place where geysers spouted, mud pots boiled, and canyons were carved by rivers smaller than the larger rivers of the East. The people who reported on these sights were generally considered liars, so why not really stretch even the magnificent truth somewhat and create stories to match the country and the people who called it home?

One woman who had been left on the homestead while her husband was gone from home tells of the wonderful meal she provided for her family. She knew there were some grouse nearby, so she decided to get up before dawn, load her rifle, and get some of the birds for supper. She cautiously made her way in the dark down to the stream where the grass was tall and the alamosa (or cottonwood) trees grew. Just as the sun was glowing in the east, she saw four grouse land on a branch in a tree. She raised her gun slowly, took careful aim, squeezed the trigger, and prepared to gather up the prize. Instead, all four birds remained perched on the branch. Curious, she dashed to the tree to check things out. Her shot had shattered the branch, and the four birds were caught by their feet in the splintered wood. Her family ate well that night.

Or there was the time this same sharpshooting woman decided to get some ducks that were migrating in the spring. She had seen flocks of them settle in on the nearby pond. Again, she got up early to surprise the ducks before daylight. She steadied her rifle for the first shot and knew she would have not only food but some feathers for pillows before the morning was over. There was no way she could miss, because the pond was covered with ducks. She aimed at the biggest, fattest one and pulled the trigger. How can you explain her amazement as the whole duck population took off in flight, taking with them the whole pond? There had been a quick cold snap just as she shot, which froze the water and left her not only without succulent roast duck but also without a pond of water. There have been rumors that many respected people on the flight path of that pond lost their reputations that day. Would you believe anyone with a crazy story about a pond flying overhead powered by ducks?

These women and their families were dependent on their ingenuity and knowledge. It helped to know that if someone should get a gash in the leg it would help to apply a fresh chew of tobacco to the wound. Many pioneers used this home remedy. However, if no fresh chew of tobacco was available, cow manure could be used. People did not like to use this remedy if they could help it, not for the most obvious distasteful reaction, but because fresh cow manure left a white patch on the skin when it healed. A common folk cure for diarrhea was a healthy slug of blackberry wine, and many a settler indulged in preventative medicine.

The ways in which women could earn a living were rather limited in those days. One of the most obvious occupations was, of course, the oldest trade in the world. Some of the most notorious women of the West were camp followers, the madams and their ladies of the night. The nickname *chippie* was given to these female camp followers on the plains who were forced to gather buffalo chips for fires. Stories go that the elegantly dressed "ladies" never bothered to take their evening gloves off as they collected this fuel, and in fact they learned after a few outings to simply dust their gloves off before beginning to cook. One of the most famous madams of the West was Mattie Silks (1848-1929). There are two stories about how she got the name Silks. One of them has it that she got that name because she liked silk dresses so much, while the other story is that she married a man named Silks. Regardless, she started her business venture at the age of nineteen in Springfield, Illinois, where she ran a "boarding house for young ladies." The sign outside proclaimed, "Men Taken In and Done For." She was part of the legends of the West. (Remember that one definition of a legend is: a lie that has attained the dignity of age.) Mattie Silks was taught to shoot in Abilene by the city's trigger-happy sheriff, Wild Bill Hickok. Of course, this made her a contemporary of Annie Oakley in time as well as occupation.

The love of Mattie's life was a fair-haired Texas scoundrel, Cortez "Cort" Thomson. She placed a bet on him to win in a Chicago footrace and won him as well. Never mind that he was already married. She settled in Denver, Colorado, in 1876. Their lives made history, not romantically like Romeo and Juliet but in the style of the West. Another "lady," Kate Fulton, was involved with Cort, and Mattie challanged Kate to a duel with pistols. In the duel, Mattie's shot went wild, but somehow Cort ended up with a shot in the neck, probably from Kate. Kate left town quickly, and the two women made a place in the history books for the first duel between women.

Cort and Mattie's life together was never ordinary. For instance, there was the time a wealthy railroad magnate who was considering extending his railroad to Denver fell in love with Mattie. He asked her to go on a thirty-day tour of the West in his private railroad car, but she turned him down. A committee from the Chamber of Commerce appealed to her civic pride. She turned them down also, but Cort worked out a civic deal. He reminded Mattie that she had just borrowed $5,000 to expand her business, and $5,000 in those days was a considerable amount. Cort negotiated an agreement with the committee to write Mattie a check for $5,000 up front, so off she went to join high society. She consorted with millionaires, presidents, princes, princesses, and future kings. After sixty days the vacation ended, and Mattie returned to Cort and her business. "I showed those Newport society dames I was as good as any of them. But not a one of 'em could make the grade as a boarder in my parlor house," she boasted. Cort died in 1900 and was buried in an unmarked grave. Later Mattie was buried beside him under a headstone marked "Martha A. Ready."

Another class of women to inherit the West was the laundry women. There is a town in Colorado called Monument. In this town is a park called the Dirty Woman Park. It got its name because the Indians felt a very dirty woman must live in the log cabin there, since every time they passed through there were clothes hanging out to dry. Another laundry woman recorded heartbreak when a group of pesky children who had been playing in the stream found the sharp stones hurt their feet and took a quilt off her line and laid it out in the stream. Of course, the quilt suffered from the sharp rocks as much, if not more, than the youngsters' delicate feet. One eccentric laundry woman in a mining town in the mountains dreaded carrying her hard-earned money to town, so she carried it in her mouth to keep it safe. The store owner kept a glass of water on the counter for her to drop her money into. She later was charged with being insane, not because of her financial practices but because someone complained that she had kissed her cow. The laundry woman answered the charge in court with, "She is the only creature who loves me. Why not kiss her?"

Laundry women frequently washed clothes in muddy ponds or streams. In this day and age of new and improved washday wonders, we are so dependent on commercial products we would probably fail to get clothes sparkling clean under such conditions. These laundry women of the early West, however, learned that if they gathered pear cactus, split it carefully, and threw it into the muddy water, the cactus slime would attract every bit of dust and dirt and leave the water clear.

In the West, one of our most persistent oral legends is the story of La Llorona, or the Weeping Woman. Some of the versions have La Llorona as a laundress. The story goes that she was a young woman married to an old man and that they had three (or more) children. She was weary of her life of washing clothes in the stream while her man drank and slept. One day, in utter desperation, she drowned her children in the stream so she would be free to start a new life, which would be filled with dancing and enjoyment. Her punishment after death was to roam the waterways looking for her children throughout eternity. That is why if you are a youngster and do not obey your parents or are out after dark, you will hear the cries of La Llorona, and she will try to catch you. Many children today still believe the tales of the Weeping Woman and fear her moans and cries. A better explanation for the purpose of this tale would be one of keeping children away from the dangers of waterways. What a convenient bogey woman.

Another woman of the West was called the Wisdom Bringer: the teacher. In the one-room schoolhouses of the West, teachers were young, almost as young in some cases as their students. They generally did not remain teachers long, since there was not a shortage of eligible suitors. One oldtimer schoolboard member remembered, "I always favored hirin' the best-lookin' schoolmarms from the East that we could get. I always figured that the more we could fix it for cowboys to marry gals with sense and education to teach school, the better it was for the country. Not only that, but I owned a half-interest in an outfit that sold buggies and buckboards, and every time we fetched in a new schoolmarm, two or three lovesick cowboys was purt' near sure to buy them a new rig to take her ridin' in!" One schoolmarm remarked that she taught school in her residence. The younger and more stubborn pupils would hide under the bed and she would have to chase them out with a broom.

The following list of rules for teachers was allegedly posted in 1872 by a school principal:

1. Teachers each day will fill lamps, clean chimneys, and trim wicks.

2. Each teacher will bring in a bucket of water and scuttle of coal for the day's sessions.

3. Make your pens carefully; you may whittle nibs to individual tastes of pupils.

4. Men teachers may take one evening each week for courting purposes, or two evenings a week if they go to church regularly.

5. After ten hours in school, teachers shall spend the remaining time studying the Bible or other good books.

6. Women teachers who marry or engage in unseemly conduct will be dismissed.

7. Any teacher who smokes, uses liquor in any form, frequents pool or public halls, or gets shaved in a barber shop will give good reason to suspect his worth, intentions, integrity, and honesty.

8. Every teacher shall lay aside from each pay a goodly sum of his earnings for his benefit in his declining years so that he will not become a burden on society.

9. The teacher who performs his labors forth fully and without fault for five years will be given an increase of twenty-five cents per week, providing the Board of Education approves.

Students pulled tricks on their teachers regularly. One oldtimer tells of the time the pupils placed a mouse in the teacher's desk. They knew she was terrified of mice. When she opened her desk and the mouse jumped out, the teacher screamed bloody murder and jumped to the top of her desk. She hopped up and down there while the mouse, equally frightened, scurried around the classroom. The teacher then made a flying leap off the desk, tripped on a bench leg, fell, and broke her leg. Needless to say, she never came back to teach again.

Other ordinary women of the West told their stories in their journals. One young bride got a pair of new brogans for her wedding. She was sixteen years old and not used to wearing shoes. Shortly after the ceremony the bride was found wading in a stream to cool her swollen feet. These women knew poor times. One woman in a mining town asked her neighbor if she could borrow her yesterday's soup bone, only to be told that another neighbor had it that day. When a family was doing well it was said, "They are eating their white bread now."

One woman who missed the culture and comfort of the East could stand it no longer. She sold the family cow to get the money to buy an organ. After it arrived, there was only one problem — no one could play it. The first kerosene lamp in Boulder, Colorado, caused a panic. In 1859 no one had seen such a lamp. The family who brought the lamp to their home had wallpapered walls with space partitioned off with white cotton sheets. When the lamp was lit, a neighbor who saw it thought the Indians had set the house afire. He heard the husband calling his cows and mistook it for a cry for help. The neighbor then spread the alarm and all of the people in town fled to a place of safety.

In the gold mining towns of the West, the 49'ers would crowd around to pat and stare at what they called the "infant phenomenon." The appearance of a bonnet in the street was a signal for the entire population to rush to the door and gaze upon its wearer as at any other natural curiosity. A young mother traveling by stage saw a fellow passenger burst into tears at the mere sight of the baby in her arms. Do not infer that the menfolk became angels strictly because of the presence of a wife and children. In one Colorado mining town one of the miners had occasional "birthdays," which he celebrated in the local watering holes while wearing a high plug hat he kept in reserve for these events. He never brought the hat home with him after celebrating, but his wife knew about this habit. One day after celebrating, he staggered home with the hat on his head. His wife calmly sat him down to the table to eat supper and served him his food. He took the hat off and unsteadily placed it on the corner of the table. As he ate, his wife quietly took his high silk hat off the table, carried it to the knife holder, took out the butcher knife, and rammed it into the hat. She them hacked it up and crammed it into the stove, never saying a word. He opened his eyes wide but kept as quiet as she. It worked, because he never took part in any more "birthdays."

People may complain about the homes they live in, but the women of the West had homes that tried their souls. One woman told the story of the dugout house she lived in, which had a canvas roof. They were plagued by what she called mountain rats. There were seven people in the family living in two small rooms. Once in the middle of the night everyone was wakened by the screams of the baby. A mountain rat had bitten its hand. The next day while she was cooking at the stove, she saw the shape of the body of a mountain rat running across the canvas top. In fury, she stuck a fork into it and had to pay the price of knowing that she had speared him when the blood started dripping through. Another time a dirt roof caved in and kept a woman a prisoner for two days. A woman who had lived in a sod house wrote a variation on the tune of "The Cowboy's Lament." Her version told of the trials of trying to keep her home clean: "In March it is mud, it is slush in December, the midsummer breezes are loaded with dust. In fall the leaves litter, in muddy September the wallpaper rots and the candlesticks rust."

It was not unusual for women to have several husbands. Husbands did not seem to last long out West. When a miner was killed in a mine disaster in Colorado it was the custom for the mine company to give the widow $600 and for each of the miners working in the mine to give her a day's wages. One newly widowed woman with three children to raise took in laundry. During a diphtheria outbreak one of her children died. She did not have any money for a memorial for her daughter. The girl was buried in a pine box in a plot outside of town. The mother remembered a family with a wagon in the yard from the day she delivered the washing to their home. She stole the wagon in the middle of the night, went to the grocery store, and stole the white stone step from the entrance to the shop. She hauled it home, chipped out the name of her dead daughter on the stone with a nail, and hauled it to the grave for a headstone.

Yes, indeed, the pioneers were brave, strong people who survived the journey to the West, but the women of the West had to be extraordinary as they dealt with their everyday lives. Whenever you hear stories and ballads of the romantic West, the cowboys, miners, and brave men who were part of it, remember the amazing women of the West. They were extraordinary regardless of their occupation.

BIBLIOGRAPHY

Bird, Isabella L. 1960. *A Lady's Life in the Rocky Mountains*. Norman: University of Oklahoma Press.

Brown, Dee. 1981. *The Gentle Tamers*. Lincoln: University of Nebraska Press.

Cleaveland, Agnes Morley. 1977. *No Life for a Lady*. Lincoln: University of Nebraska Press.

Cooper, Patricia, and Norma Bradley Buferd. 1977. *The Quilters: Women and Domestic Art: An Oral History*. Garden City, N.Y.: Anchor Press/ Doubleday.

Ellis, Anne. 1980. *The Life of an Ordinary Woman*. Lincoln: University of Nebraska Press.

Hamil, Harold. 1976. *Colorado without Mountains, A High Plains Memoir*. Kansas City, Mo.: Lowell Press.

Hill, Alice Polk. 1976. *Tales of the Colorado Pioneers*. Glorieta, N. Mex.: Rio Grande Press.

Luchetti, Cathy, in collaboration with Carol Olwell. 1982. *Women of the West*. St. George, Utah: Antelope Island Press.

Magoffin, Susan Shelby. 1962. *Down the Santa Fe Trail and into Mexico (1846-47)*. Lincoln: University of Nebraska Press.

Myres, Sandra L. 1982. *Westering Women and the Frontier Experience 1800-1915*. Albuquerque: University of New Mexico Press.

Noren, Catherine. 1983. *The Way We Looked: The Meaning and Magic of Family Photographs*. New York: Lodestar Books/Dutton.

Schlissel, Lillian. 1982. *Women's Diaries of the Westward Journey*. New York: Schocken Books.

Steiner, Stan. 1980. *The Ranchers: A Book of Generations*. New York: Knopf.

Stewart, Elinore Pruitt. 1982. *Letters of a Woman Homesteader*. Boston: Houghton Mifflin.

Stratton, Joanna L. 1981. *Pioneer Women: Voices from the Kansas Frontier*. New York: Simon and Schuster.

Women as Tall as Our Mountain, Mini-biographies of Summit County Women. 1976. N.p., Climax Molybdenum Company.

C

Sample Conference Programs
and Publicity Flyers

The Second Pueblo Library District Storytelling Conference

A Storytelling Celebration
Saturday, April 14, 1984
8:00 a.m. – 5:00 p.m.

Registration 7:30 – 8:00 a.m.
Pueblo Library District Meeting Room

Norma Livo, coordinator of the popular University of Colorado at Denver
Storytelling Conference, has organized the program

STORYTELLING IS THEATER OF THE MIND

Experience the Magic of These Storytellers:

Joe Hayes	*The Day It Snowed Tortillas*
Norma Livo	*Women Of The West*
Bonnie Phipps	*Stories With Music*
John Stansfield	*Tall Tales*

Sponsored by Arkansas Valley Regional Library Service System
Friends of the Pueblo Library District
Pueblo Library District

- -

REGISTRATION

Name _____ Phone _____

Address _____

_____

☐ Registration (including rolls, coffee, and handouts) $15.00 if paid by April 1.
After April 1, registration is $17.00.
☐ Check here if you want information on Graduate Credit.
☐ Box Lunch $5.00 (please include with your registration payment)

425

Storytellers / in concert

The First Congregation Church
11 Garden Street
Cambridge

Admission $5
Students and Seniors $3.50

Explorations in contemporary and traditional stories for adults

Sunday 8 PM October 14	**GIOIA TIMPANELLI: AUTUMN STORIES** Gioia is a nationally known storyteller and performer of poetry. A sense of ritual and journey lives in all her tales. Join this magical story-teller for an evening of old stories from Italian folk tradition; new stories from her book *Italian Traveling*; and nature stories from her own life experiences.
Saturday 8 PM Wednesday 8 PM October 27 & 31	**THE DARK SIDE** Judith Black, Elizabeth Dunham, Doug Lipman, and Lee Ellen Marvin explore tales about ghosts; real and imagined, personal and mystic. These scary and mysterious stories will celebrate Halloweeen, when we begin the dark journey of the winter, and storytelling — the imaginative journey — is the main activity.
Saturday 8 PM November 10	**JACKSON GILLMAN: IN CHARACTER, TOO** Come witness Jackson's transformations into a Yiddish grandmother, a Maine Lobsterman, a Rudyard Kipling animal and assorted street people. This year Jackson returns with new stories and new personal-ities for his wonderful revue "In Character" which he brought to the *Storytellers in Concert* stage in 1982.
Saturday 8 PM November 24	**BROTHER BLUE: STREET SONG** Stories from the street for great musicians from early Blues to modern Jazz, told by Brother Blue. You've probably seen Brother Blue in the streets of Boston: dancing, singing, praying, and souling his stories out from, "the middle of the middle of Blue to the middle of the middle of you."
Saturday 8 PM December 8	**STORIES IN SIGN LANGUAGE** A complete visual world, told in American Sign Language, will spring before your eyes with Adrian Blue's visual stories. John Basinger com-plements with a vocal text; a total experience for all.
Saturday 8 PM December 22	**STORIES FROM THE SHTETL** Visit a little village in Eastern Poland and hear old friends and relatives share their memories — then follow them across the ocean to the new country and a new life. With Pamela Adelman, Judith Black, and Laura Pershin.

Come share your own stories at 7PM each evening. For Information and Reservations Call (617) 864-2121. Produced with the assistance of the New England Storytelling Center. To order tickets by mail, send checks to Storytellers in Concert: P.O. Box 994, Cambridge, MA 02238. Include a stamped self-addressed envelope. Wheelchair Accessible — Group Rates Available.

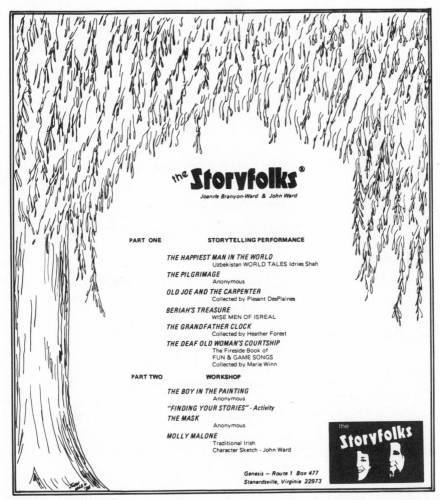

the **Storyfolks** ®

Joanne Branyon-Ward & John Ward

| PART ONE | STORYTELLING PERFORMANCE |

THE HAPPIEST MAN IN THE WORLD
Uzbekistan WORLD TALES Idries Shah

THE PILGRIMAGE
Anonymous

OLD JOE AND THE CARPENTER
Collected by Plesant DesPlaines

BERIAH'S TREASURE
WISE MEN OF ISREAL

THE GRANDFATHER CLOCK
Collected by Heather Forest

THE DEAF OLD WOMAN'S COURTSHIP
The Fireside Book of
FUN & GAME SONGS
Collected by Marie Winn

| PART TWO | WORKSHOP |

THE BOY IN THE PAINTING
Anonymous

"FINDING YOUR STORIES" - Activity

THE MASK
Anonymous

MOLLY MALONE
Traditional Irish
Character Sketch - John Ward

Genesis — Route 1 Box 477
Stanardsville, Virginia 22973

the **Storyfolks**

𝕾𝖚𝖒𝖒𝖊𝖗 𝖂𝖔𝖗𝖐𝖘𝖍𝖔𝖕 𝖋𝖔𝖗 𝖄𝖔𝖚𝖓𝖌 𝖂𝖗𝖎𝖙𝖊𝖗𝖘

𝟏𝟗𝟖𝟑

UNIVERSITY OF VIRGINIA
Charlottesville, Virginia

CONFERENCE ON CREATIVITY: STORYTELLING LIVES!

Friday, March 18, 1983

7:00–9:00   Registration

9:00–10:00   Joe Hayes – "Stories That Gives You A Dream"

10:00–10:45   Heather McQuarie – "Let Me Tell You A Story"

10:45–11:15   Break

11:15–12:15   Michael Hague – "Art As Storyteller"

12:25–1:30   Lunch – books and records autographing at the book store

1:30–2:30   Bonnie Phipps – "Pick Me A Story"

2:30–3:30   Lynn Rubright – "Discovering Heroes, Lore And Legends In Your Own Backyard"

3:30–4:00   Break

4:00–5:00   E.M. "Mel" McFarland – "Wildcats-Watertanks And Errant Locomotives"

5:00–7:00   Supper

7:00–9:00   Deborah Blanche – "Women Of The West"

Those of you have taken vows of friendship
    you are welcome.
Those of you have kept your vows of friendship
    you are welcome.
If you come from far away, you are welcome.
If you come from nearby, you are welcome.
Be careful my heart, the source of diamonds is in this room.
May you have no worries.
May you tell your stories forever.

                                        Laura Simms

"Storytellers make us remember what mankind would have been like, had not
fear, and the failing will and the laws of nature tripped up its heels."

                    William Butler Yeats

"Imagining and believing are the only forms of magic left in the world."

                    Michael Hague

SATURDAY, MARCH 19, 1983

9:00-10:00   JEWELL WOLK - "STORIES THROUGH STITCHERY"

10:00-11:00   SANDIE RIETZ - "SONGS, STORIES AND SURPRISES"

11:00-11:30   BREAK

11:30-12:30   BRENT WARREN - ALIAS "DOC MURDOCK", MASTER OF MILLIONS OF
              MAGNIFICENT MYSTERIES AND MAKER OF MONKEYS
              OUT OF MANY MINOR MANIPULATIONS FROM MICHIGAN
              TO MEXICO

12:30-1:00   WRAP-UP

1:00   CRIC-CRAC SESSION

"Once a story is absorbed into a book, it is divorced from its teller and
it becomes like the scenario of a film, a mere outline of the real thing,
neither bones nor flesh."

                    Lawrence Millman in Our Like Will
                    Not Be There Again

"It is only when our old songs and old tales are passing from one human
being to another, by word of mouth, that they can attain their full
fascination. No printed page can create this spell. It is the living
word -- the sung ballad and the told tale -- that holds our attention
and reaches our hearts."

                    Richard Chase

Irish saying:

"Put mouth to mouth,

but never put pen to paper."

Old Irish proverb:

"A good story fills a belly"

THE SCHOOL OF EDUCATION OF THE UNIVERSITY OF COLORADO AT DENVER
WOULD LIKE TO THANK THE FOLLOWING INDIVIDUALS AND GROUPS FOR
THEIR SUPPORT AND COOPERATION:

    MARY SCHAEFER CONROY, HEAD OF THE SPEAKER'S BUREAU
    BARBARA MILLMAN, OFFICE OF PUBLIC INFORMATION
    SUSAN STEUSSE, AURARIA BOOKSTORE
    LORRIE SPEARS, SCHOOL OF EDUCATION
    BETTY HOLMES, SCHOOL OF EDUCATION
    DEBRA BULLARD, SCHOOL OF EDUCATION
    MARILYN LAMBERT, SCHOOL OF EDUCATION

"Let us go forth, the tellers of tales, and seize whatever prey the
heart longs for, and have no fears. Everything exists, everything is true,
and the earth is only a little dust under our feet."

                    W.B. Yeats in The Celtic Twilight

D

Storytelling Camp Materials

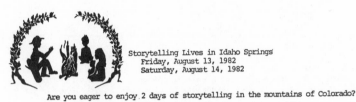

Storytelling Lives in Idaho Springs
Friday, August 13, 1982
Saturday, August 14, 1982

Are you eager to enjoy 2 days of storytelling in the mountains of Colorado?

_____ Come hear Rocky Mountain Storytellers from Montana
to New Mexico

_____ Hear stories of the mining days

_____ Swap stories with others

_____ Share in Idaho Springs Gold Rush Days

_____ Learn new stories and songs

When was the last time you shared spooky stories by firelight?

When did you last sing ballads in the moonlight?

From noon Friday, August 13th until evening Saturday, August 14th. We have
sleeping facilities for 100 at the Idaho Springs Outdoor Center as well as
2 meals on Friday and 2 on Saturday. The cost for overnight and meals will
be $30.00. If interested fill out the form below and mail to Dr. Norma
J. Livo, School of Education, University of Colorado at Denver, 1100 Fourteenth
Street, Denver, CO 80202.

- -

NAME _____

ADDRESS _____

_____
                                              (Zip Code)

PHONE: _____   _____
            (home)   (business)

I will have stories to share _____

What kinds of stories or songs _____

What suggestions would you have for these two days? _____

_____

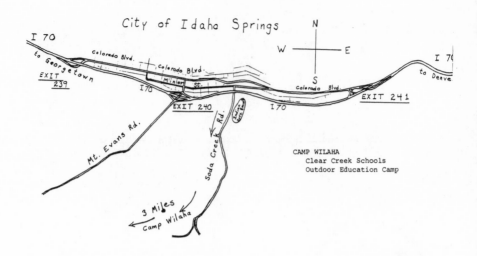

CAMP WILAHA
Clear Creek Schools
Outdoor Education Camp

Camp Wilaha has a lodge, dinning hall with fireplace and a gymnasium/auditorium. Each
cabin will house 18-24 people and most have a fireplace in the center. Toilets and
showers are within walking distance (translation: they are in separate facilities).

What to bring?

    Sleeping bag or linens and blankets
    Soap and towel
    Sturdy shoes or hiking boots (lots of hiking available)
    Personal items
    Flashlight
    Camera, binoculars, hand lenses
    Musical instruments
    Any literature you would like to make available to the weekend community
    Some good stories to swap
    A smile
    A heart to be warmed

From noon Friday, August 5 until evening Saturday, August 6. We have sleeping
facilities for 100 at the Idaho Springs Outdoor Center as well as 2 meals on Friday
and 2 on Saturday. The cost for overnight and meals will be $30.00. If interested
fill out the form below and mail to Dr. Norma Livo, School of Education, University
of Colorado at Denver, 1100 Fourteenth Street, Denver, CO 80202. Make checks payable
to: Dr. Norma J. Livo. (Prices will increase after July 1)
- -

Name _____

Address _____

       _____

Phone: _____   _____
         (home)   (business)

UNIVERSITY OF COLORADO AT DENVER

STORYTELLING LIVES IN IDAHO SPRINGS
FRIDAY, AUGUST 5, 1983
SATURDAY, AUGUST 6, 1983

Friday August 5

12:00	Registration
12:30-1:30	Lunch and "mill around" time
1:30-2:30	Introductions "Getting to Know You" "Describe Storytelling" What are your needs? Settling Schedule
2:30-3:30	
3:30-4:30	
4:30-5:30	
3:30-6:30	Chat Roam Settle in Whatever
6:30	Dinner
8:00	Hot chocolate and cider
8:30 until last song is sung and last story is told	Campfire -- Cric-crac sessions Songs and Stories

Saturday August 6

6:00	Morning hike for those who need it--meet at the upper lodge.
8:00	Breakfast
9:00	Group leaders will be available for general questions and answers in the upper lodge. Display of resources and materials
10:00-11:00	More story swaps and small group sessions
11:00-12:00	
12:30	Lunch Goodbyes Totally informal open P.M. (Visit Idaho Springs Gold Rush Days)

"Let us go forth, the teller of tales, and seize whatever prey the heart longs
for, and have no fear. Everything exists, everything is true, and the earth is
only a little dust under our feet"

W. B. Yeats in THE CELTIC TWILIGHT

EVALUATION

CONFERENCE ON CREATIVITY: STORYTELLING

1. What were the strengths of this conference:

2. What could be improved in this conference:

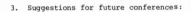

3. Suggestions for future conferences:

4. How did you learn about the conference:

UNIVERSITY OF COLORADO AT DENVER

STORYTELLING LIVES IN IDAHO SPRINGS
FRIDAY, AUGUST 5, 1983
SATURDAY, AUGUST 6, 1983

ROCKY MOUNTAIN REGION DIRECTORY OF STORYTELLERS

<u>Name</u>

<u>Address</u>

                              (Zip)

<u>Telephone</u>

<u>Storytelling specialties</u>

<u>Intended Audiences</u>

<u>Fees</u>

E

Course Syllabi

RCLEd 467 - Fall 1984
Intergroup Storytelling Syllabus

Thursday: 6:30-9:30

Course Summary

   RCLEd 467 deals specifically with authentic traditional literature
(folktales, fairy tales, myths, legends) of six U.S. racial minority groups
(African Americans, Alaska Natives, Asian Americans, Mexican Americans,
Native Americans, and Puerto Ricans) and one from each student's own ethnic
group. Each student will be responsible for knowing only eight stories
(seven self-researched stories and one from the instructor). Every student,
however, will receive several different stories (seven times the number of
students in the class; e.g., if there are 10 students in the class, each
student will receive 71 different stories). Concomitant with learning these
stories and how stories reflect culture, storytelling techniques will also
be learned. They are: feltboard, draw talk, puppetry, rhythmic, character
imagery, origami, shadow, pantomime, and traditional storytelling. Competence
in these storytelling techniques will be demonstrated to children, to your
peers in class and to the instructor on an individual basis. Representative
guest storytellers and storytelling experiences with children are integral
parts of RCLEd 467.

---

†Reprinted with the permission of Dr. Jane M. Madsen, Pennsylvania State University, University
Park, Pa.

Calendar

8/30: Basics/Film, *Anansi the Spider*, #10692, 10".

9/ 6: Guest Storyteller/Basics.

9/13: Guest Storyteller/Basics/Origami--bring a minimum of 10 pieces of
       onion skin paper (carbon copy kind of paper or tissue paper) cut in
       8 1/2 inch uncreased squares for origami work.

9/20: Guest Storyteller/Basics/Title of *personal ethnic story due. On
       a 3 x 5 card write the following information about your selection:
       your name, your ethnic group, title of traditional story and source
       (complete reference data). This story will be used for your puppetry
       demonstration and for your traditional storytelling demonstration.
       In addition, it will be used for your curriculum project.

9/27: Guest Storyceller/Basics.

10/ 4: Draw talk demonstrations; this story will be the first story you will
        prepare, according to a specified criteria, in a handout for every class
        member and the instructor.

10/11: Character imagery demonstrations; story handouts for class due.

10/18: Pantomime demonstrations; story handouts for class due.

10/25: Feltboard demonstrations; story handouts for class due.

11/ 1: Practicum with children--location to be determined.

11/ 8: Shadow demonstrations; story handouts for class due.

11/15: Rhythmic demonstrations; story handouts for class due.

11/22: Thanksgiving Holiday.

11/29: Practicum with children--location to be determined.

12/ 6: Puppetry demonstrations; story handouts for class due. This is your
        personal ethnic story. It will be used also to demonstrate your
        skill in traditional storytelling.

12/11: (NOTE: This is a Tuesday which is to follow the schedule for Thursday
        due to the Thanksgiving holiday.) Curriculum project due: Bring
        self-addressed, stamped envelope for return of these projects and your
        final grade; course evaluation.

     *Select a traditional literature story from your own personal ethnic
     background suitable to use with the puppetry storytelling technique.
     This story will also be the one you will use to demonstrate the
     traditional storytelling technique to your instructor at a time con-
     venient to both before November 22. At that time you will also
     demonstrate the origami storytelling technique using the same Puerto
     Rican legend of the coquí which was demonstrated in class on September
     13 by your instructor. Make a 30-minute appointment early in the
     semester--no later than November 22--to have your traditional and
     origami storytelling techniques evaluated.

Attendance Policy

     Due to the specialized content of this course and the fact that it meets
only once a week as opposed to the regular three times a week, even one
absence will be detrimental to your development. Therefore, attendance is
expected at all sessions. Please take note that the two practicum times will
be at another location on November 1 and November 29.

Course Needs

·Optional but strongly recommended:
   Modern Origami by James Minoru Sakoda. NY: Simon and Schuster
   (A Fireside Book), 1969.
·A minimum of 10 pieces of onion skin paper cut in 8 1/2 inch uncreased
   squares.
·1 smooth newsprint pad, 18 x 24 inches (PSU Campus Bookstore or Uncle
   Eli's).
·At least one wide felt tip pen or magic marker (color(s) to be determined).
·Pieces of felt (buy after instructor's approval).
·Simple puppet material (old socks and yarn are great).
·Cardboard, tag board, or old manilla folders.
·Wire coathangers and strong masking tape.
·7 manila folders.

Instruction Support System (ISS)

Your progress in RCLEd 467 will be reported to you on a weekly basis by
means of a computer print out. You will be receiving a packet of 17 computer
sheets with specific headings. In order for your progress and subsequent
evaluations to be recorded, the appropriate computer sheet must accompany each
assignment. Bring this packet of computer sheets with you at every class
meeting and the evaluation in the instructor's office. These ISS sheets will
be designated as follows:

		Weight	Grading
ST(TR)	Storytelling--Traditional	6% . . .	%
ST(OR)	Storytelling--Origami	6% . . .	%
ST(DT)	Storytelling--Draw Talk	5% . . .	%
ST(CI)	Storytelling--Character Imagery	5% . . .	%
ST(PA)	Storytelling--Pantomime	5% . . .	%
ST(FB)	Storytelling--Feltboard	5% . . .	%
ST(RH)	Storytelling--Rhythmic	5% . . .	%
ST(SH)	Storytelling--Shadow	5% . . .	%
ST(PU)	Storytelling--Puppetry	8% . . .	%
TL(AF)	Traditional Literature--African American	6% . . .	A-F
TL(AN)	Traditional Literature--Alaska Native	6% . . .	A-F
TL(AS)	Traditional Literature--Asian American	6% . . .	A-F
TL(ME)	Traditional Literature--Mexican American	6% . . .	A-F
TL(NA)	Traditional Literature--Native American	6% . . .	A-F
TL(PR)	Traditional Literature--Puerto Rican	6% . . .	A-F
TL(PE)	Traditional Literature--Personal Ethnic	6% . . .	A-F
TL(CP)	Traditional Literature--Curriculum Project	8% . . .	A-F

Grading Policy

Your final grade will be determined by a cumulative grade score on all
objectives. There are 17 required objectives which means that all objectives
must be attempted before a final grade will be given. There is no comprehensive final examination. The Curriculum Project, TL(CP), will serve in lieu
of a final examination. The final grade range is as follows: A = 90% - 100%;
B = 80% - 89%; C = 70% - 79%; D = 60% - 69%; F = < 60%.

Grades for the storytelling techniques will be reported by a minus point
factor and subsequently converted to a percentage value of the designated
weight for that particular objective. The traditional literature objectives
and the Curriculum Project will be evaluated by the letter grades of:
A = 100%; A- = 95%; B = 89%; B- = 84%; C = 79%; C- = 74%; D = 69%; D- = 64%;
F = 0%.

Note that specific objectives are due on specific dates. No stories will
be accepted after December 6. Late work will not be accepted in between classes.
A penalty of -10 points from your cumulative grade will be imposed for each late
assignment.

Group # Assignments

Be sure you know your group number. This is basic to your class assignments and significant to your final grade. You keep the same numbers all semester.

Technique	Date	Group #					
		1	2	3	4	5	6
Draw Talk	10/4	Na Am	Al Na	Af Am	As Am	PR	Me Am
Character Imagery	10/11	PR	Me Am	Al Na	Af Am	Na Am	As Am
Pantomime	10/18	Al Na	PR	As Am	Na Am	Me Am	Af Am
Feltboard	10/25	As Am	Af Am	Me Am	PR	Al Na	Na Am
Shadow	11/8	Me Am	As Am	Na Am	Al Na	Af Am	PR
Rhythmic	11/15	Af Am	Na Am	PR	Me Am	As Am	Al Na

Special Instructions

Storytelling Techniques

Review the Storytelling Evaluation handout for details of storytelling in general (page 1) and each technique in particular (page 2). Half of your evaluation for each storytelling demonstration will be on your cultural introduction and your ability to tie-in the cultural elements mentioned in your introduction to your actual storyline. The other half of your evaluation will be on your ability to use a particular storytelling technique.

For the feltboard storytelling demonstration, be aware that you have an actual working space of 26 inches in length and 16 1/2 inches in depth. The backdrop color is black. Having one of your own is strongly recommended but not required.

For the shadow storytelling demonstration, your actual working space is 23 1/2 inches in length but only 12 inches in depth. The remaining 5 1/2 inches in depth from a total of 17 1/2 inches conceals your hands while operating your silhouette figures. Having one of your own is strongly recommended but not required.

For your puppet presentation, be sure to demonstrate your story to the instructor at least once in order to clear up any problems. This should be done as early in the semester as possible. This is to be a lap story as opposed to a "behind the table" story.

Curriculum Project

Using your own personal ethnic story, show how your story might be used to teach any two skills in any curriculum discipline. Identify the mental age of the child with whom you might use the story. Write two behavioral objects making sure that each of the following parts is included in your objective:

1. Who is to perform the desired behavior (e.g., "the student" or "the learner").

2. The actual behavior to be employed in demonstrating mastery of the objective (e.g., "to write" or "to speak").

3. The result (i.e., the product or performance) of the behavior,
    which will be evaluated to determine whether the objective is
    mastered (e.g., "an essay" or "the speech").

4. The standard which will be used to evaluate the success of the
    product or performance (e.g., "90 percent correct," or "four
    out of five correct"). Remember that the material used in an
    exercise should not be used in the evaluation.

For each objective, give instructions on how to use the story to reach
the objective. For example, if there are particular interesting words in your
story (such as the names of Anansi's six sons in Anansi the Spider) which
would lend themselves to an exercise in syllabication, name the words, give
their syllabic breakdown and give in detail the procedures you would use to
teach the syllabic breakdown of these words. Be creative with your objectives
and procedures.

Attach a clear copy of the story (xeroxed from the source, if you wish)
to your project. It cannot be evaluated without it.

Practica

This course will have two practica. The details of these programs will
be discussed in class.

*Story Handouts to Class

(Typewritten preferred)

By whatever means of copy service you have available to you, you are
required to give to each member of the class (give 2 copies of each to your
instructor) only seven traditional literature stories, one from each of the
identified racial minority groups and one from your own ethnic group. You
will receive, in turn, by the end of the course, seven times, compounded by
the number of your peers, as many stories as you have given per class member.
Each story will be different in each ethnic group, if each class member takes
the responsibility for following the system.   While the typing of these
stories is not required, I am sure we all would appreciate having them in
that format.   In any case, professional writing skills are expected and the
instructor reserves the right to reduce grades accordingly for poor professional
writing skills which include legibility (each letter clearly identified) and
neatness.

---

*Be sure to touch base as a group so each member has a different story in the
designated ethnic group. It is suggested that you purchase seven manilla
folders--one for each of the ethnic groups and one for your own ethnic group.
Bring these to every class. You will be recording titles and using these
stories at nearly every class meeting.

Copy each underlined entry given below: Double-space between bracketed
sets but single space within each set. The books in the self-access area in
the Curriculum Materials Center are your best possible source for these stories.
As RCLEd 467 students, you may take any book from this area on a one week loan
(only). The staff must check your name on the class list before it can be
removed from the CMC. In as much as you do not have the enormous expense of
required textbooks in this course, it is suggested that you make a copy of your
story when you find it. Most of these stories are very short.

Ethnic Group: Edited by: YOUR NAME; Group #

Anthology Title: Author/Editor:

Legend Title: Publisher: Copyright:

Possible Theme: give a word or phrase such as "courage" or "how to make
                 friends."

Cultural Elements and Descriptions: give at least two in detail. You
                                     will need to research this information.

Main Characters: give names and physical descriptions, including sex. You
                  may need to research the physical descriptions and ethnic
                  garb.

Plot: give enough detail of the story so a person who has not read it from
       a text, as you have done, can also tell the story. The plot must
       reflect the theme and the above identified cultural elements. Do not
       copy it from the book but rewrite it in your own words, if necessary
       to include the cultural elements.

SYLLABUS 2†

EDU 402 Workshop in Education: Storytelling   1 Credit

Instructor: Dr. Karen Callas

Objectives:

This workshop is designed for students who wish to develop their own techniques and styles of storytelling with children and/or adult audiences.

The emphasis will be on the process of storytelling itself, and each student will be regularly involved in learning, and telling, stories. Time will be spent on improvisational storytelling, tandem and group storytelling, and the use of acoustical accompaniment. Storytelling as a form of oral history and its role in the transmission of culture will be considered, as well as its function within educational settings. It is expected that each student will necessarily improve her/his oral and nonverbal communication.

Recommended for teachers, education majors, English majors, and any individuals wishing to enhance their communication skills or expand their expertise in the creative arts.

Enrollment limited to ten students.

Methodology:

Demonstrations, individual and group storytelling sessions, film and discussion.

Evaluation:

1. Attendance
2. Learning, telling and refinement of at least three stories.
3. Completion of a minimum of four storytelling sessions with an outside group of children and/or adults. This can be done as an individual, or in tandem. Students are encouraged to explore different options for delivery.

Texts:

Sawyer, Ruth. The Way of the Storyteller. 1977, Revised ed. Paper, Penguin.

Clarkson and Cross. World Folktales: A Scribner Resource Collection. New York: Scribner, 1980.

††Reprinted with the permission of Dr. Karen Callas, University of Maine at Machias.

F

Survey of Storytelling Courses in Colleges and Universities

THE STATUS OF STORYTELLING IN INSTITUTIONS OF HIGHER EDUCATION

A survey was conducted in the fall of 1984 of 235 colleges and universities to get some indication of the status of storytelling in higher education. The schools surveyed were chosen from the 1983 edition of *The National Directory of Addresses and Telephone Numbers for Four-year Colleges and Universities.* A minimum of four colleges or universities was selected from each state, with the exception of Wyoming, which had only one institution listed. Additional schools were selected from states with a large number of institutions. Funds were limited, and this was not intended as a scientific study.

The questions on the survey were:

1. Are there storytelling courses being taught?

2. If so, where are they taught? (ex: English department, library science, media instruction, education, folklore, communication, or theater?)

3. How many courses are involved? Number of students yearly?

4. What research is being carried on related to storytelling?

5. Are there any results or suggestions as a result of this research?

Further, if storytelling was being taught, it was requested that the course syllabus be shared. Self-addressed, stamped envelopes were included.

445

One hundred and thirty-six professors responded to the survey—a 58 percent response. Thirty-six people replied that they teach courses or workshops in storytelling. The courses or workshops ranged from one to four courses at an institution. Class sizes varied from 10 to 450 individuals for a workshop. Where were these courses taught within the colleges and universities?

Library science	15
Instructional media	1
Education	17
Expressive therapy	1
Behavioral science	1
Speech	4
Theater	2
English	1
Comparative literature	1

Among the respondents who indicated there were no courses taught on storytelling, thirty replied that storytelling was incorporated into children's literature courses. Ten said it was included in language arts courses, two tied it in with adolescent literature, three stated it was part of library sciences courses, and one indicated that traditional storytelling was emphasized in a folklore course.

Storytelling might be considered the Rodney Dangerfield of higher education. A depressing number of reactions implied that it "gets no respect." Further, one respondent commented, "I do feel that the *art* of storytelling is lost. Videos, T.V., computers, etc., tell great stories in color and with terrific sound effects. Our technological and transit [sic] society negates the need for storytelling or a storyteller." Additionally, storytelling is misunderstood by academic scholars, as these responses illustrate: "Storytelling was dropped from the schedule to make room for more 'academic' subjects." "We teach only secondary courses. Therefore, of course, there is no storytelling."

Generally, the inclusion of storytelling in higher education courses seems to depend on the conviction and expertise of individual professors. In fact, in several instances, respondents suggested contacting people who formerly taught a storytelling course at their institution. They stated that after that particular person left, the course was no longer taught.

When storytelling is incorporated into education courses, it seems that generally it is included in children's literature and language arts courses, implying that it is restricted to elementary education. Only two respondents indicated they develop sessions on storytelling in adolescent literature courses.

Reported research efforts were scanty. One remark summarized the situation: "Needs more research and more emphasis. Now largely left to professional practititoners of the art." If storytelling is misunderstood and neglected by currently practicing academicians, then future researchers are probably not being introduced to it as a possibility for research. Many areas need to be studied besides story grammar and structure. The tender human element is being ignored. The need to quantify research results contributes to an avoidance of "messier" research, as one person called it. But then, the human element has always been delightfully messy. There must be a story in that.

Several miscellaneous facts emerged in the responses. One campus informed me that it had been closed by the state legislature. This symptom of what is happening in higher education was further reinforced by notes from three institutions indicating that their library science programs had closed down. Why do the library science programs seem to be taking the brunt of the existing financial situation? Why are they topping the list of academic expendables? Given this age of information storage and retrieval and the new programs being developed to accommodate it, why should these units of higher education be shrinking instead of growing?

Fourteen people included their course syllabi and indicated they would be interested in seeing what other people teach.

Many unanswered questions are evident in this survey. It will be interesting to follow this subject and observe its future role in higher education.

G

Permission to Use or Reproduce Oral Material

The permission form on p. 450 should be altered to fit the circumstances of the request and expanded to include stipulations regarding the time limit for use of material, possible expiration date of permission to use material, limitations as to the situation in which material may be used, and/or limitations on the nature of the audience or the exact forms of reproduction. Should a fee payment be a part of the agreement, an additional section should be included to stipulate the amount and nature of payment and an exacting description of the nature of the "purchase," such that the storyteller does not "sell" a story or the rights to a story when not intending to do so. The storyteller should investigate the nature of the request to determine that the user does not intend to "sell" the material in turn. ("Selling" can include take a fee for telling the borrowed story.) Should the user intend to "sell" the story, whether in recorded, printed, or oral performance form, the storyteller must determine and secure an appropriate fee. Copies of the agreement should be made available to both parties.

SOME POSSIBLE USES OF ORAL MATERIAL

1. Video or audio taped reproductions or recordings for sale, distribution, or demonstration
2. Retelling or replaying for public broadcast
3. Story publication as a transcribed work
4. Story illustration

5. Audio tapings of public broadcasts
6. Retelling for private/public audiences
7. Retelling for instructional/demonstration purposes
8. Use for curricular development
9. Teaching to other storytellers
10. Retelling to groups of other storytellers

SAMPLE PERMISSION FORM

I, _____[storyteller's name]_____, hereby permit _____[user's name]_____ to

utilize _____[name of story, song, game]_____, an

original work (or: a derived work taken, expanded, and developed from

_____[name of source]_____), in the form in which I deliver it, for the

purpose(s) of _____[specify use of material]_____. I expect

that appropriate credit will be given as follows when the named material is

used: _____[specify nature of credit]_____.

Any additional use of this material, or use of this material in a manner not here stipulated, is not allowed and will result in immediate cancellation of this agreement.

_____ Storyteller

_____ User of material

_____ Date

Index